The Poverty of the Ethnography of Poverty

The Poverty of the Ethnography of Poverty

Loïc Wacquant

OXFORD
UNIVERSITY PRESS

OXFORD
UNIVERSITY PRESS

Oxford University Press is a department of the University of Oxford.
It furthers the University's objective of excellence in research, scholarship,
and education by publishing worldwide. Oxford is a registered trade mark of
Oxford University Press in the UK and in certain other countries.

Published in the United States of America by Oxford University Press
198 Madison Avenue, New York, NY 10016, United States of America.

© Oxford University Press 2025
Originally published as *Misère de l'ethnographie de la misère*
© Éditions Raisons d'Agir, 2023

All rights reserved. No part of this publication may be reproduced, stored in a retrieval system, transmitted, used for text and data mining, or used for training artificial intelligence, in any form or by any means, without the prior permission in writing of Oxford University Press, or as expressly permitted by law, by license or under terms agreed with the appropriate reprographics rights organization. Inquiries concerning reproduction outside the scope of the above should be sent to the Rights Department, Oxford University Press, at the address above.

You must not circulate this work in any other form
and you must impose this same condition on any acquirer.

Library of Congress Cataloging-in-Publication Data
Names: Wacquant, Loïc, author.
Title: The poverty of the ethnography of poverty / Loïc Wacquant.
Other titles: Misère de l'ethnographie de la misère. French
Description: New York, NY : Oxford University Press, [2025] | Includes bibliographical references and index. | Summary: This book is inspired by Bachelard's philosophy of science. It draws an analytic tableau of one hundred years of US urban ethnography; detects its common methodological pitfalls and epistemological biases; and proposes remedies inspired by the theories of Pierre Bourdieu founding a rationalist approach characterized as "thick construction."—Provided by publisher.
Identifiers: LCCN 2024060783 (print) | LCCN 2024060784 (ebook) |
ISBN 9780197804018 (paperback) | ISBN 9780197804001 (hardback) |
ISBN 9780197804025 (epub) | ISBN 9780197804049 (ebook)
Subjects: LCSH: Urban poor—United States—Social conditions. | African American neighborhoods—United States—Social conditions. | Urban anthropology—Methodology. | Social surveys—United States.
Classification: LCC HV4045 .W3313 2025 (print) | LCC HV4045 (ebook) |
DDC 362.50973—dc23/eng/20250228
LC record available at https://lccn.loc.gov/2024060783
LC ebook record available at https://lccn.loc.gov/2024060784

DOI: 10.1093/oso/9780197804001.001.0001

Au Wisigoth

Contents

Prologue: In Praise of *"Thick Construction"*	1
1. Dissecting the Ethnographic Unconscious	**5**
Genesis of an academic controversy and the debate eluded	6
The three ages of American "urban ethnography"	13
Renaissance and the discovery of the state of misery	39
2. Poverty, Race, and Moralism in American Urban Ethnography	**51**
The saints of Greenwich Village: Duneier on homeless sidewalk vendors	54
The good, the bad, and the sociologist in black Philly: Anderson on the "moral life of the inner city"	72
Model citizens hidden at the heart of Harlem: Newman on fast-food workers	91
On some perennial pitfalls of urban ethnography	112
3. For a Political Epistemology of Fieldwork	**125**
Reflexivity and the social conditions of intellectual debate	126
Ethnographism, paralogisms, and "thick construction"	139
Bourdieu at *Mema's House*: The five missions of ethnography	168
Epilogue: Bachelard in the Ghetto	**191**
Acknowledgments	195
References	197
Index	219

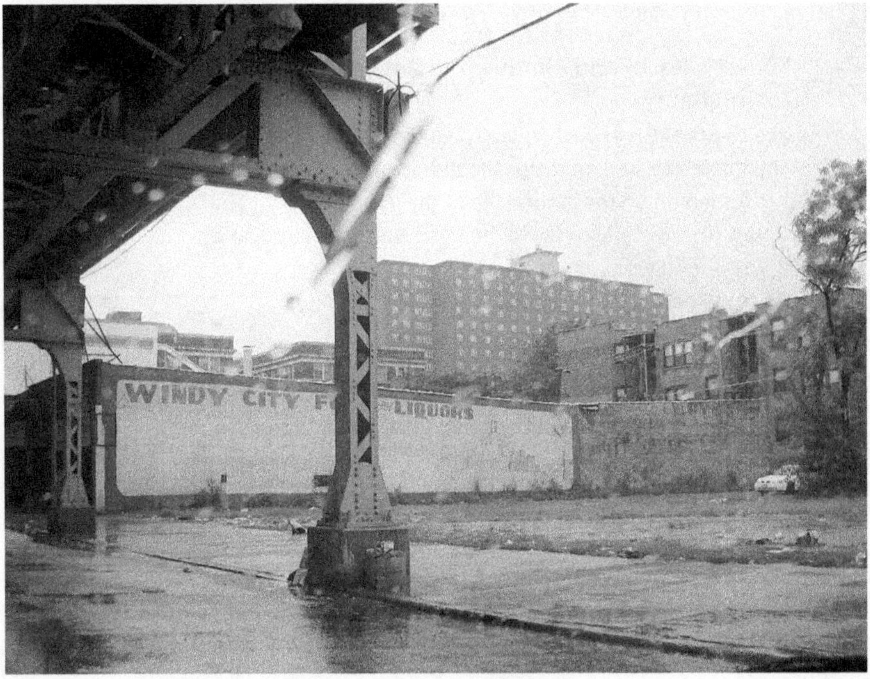
WINDY CITY F
LIQUORS

Prologue: In Praise of *"Thick Construction"*

> "When it comes to methods, moreover, we can only ever be provisional, because methods change as science advances."
>
> Émile Durkheim, *The Rules of Sociological Method*, 1895.

The present book is an exercise in scientific reflexivity, aimed not at weakening fieldwork, but at consolidating its epistemic underpinnings and, consequently, its practical rules. As the authors of *Le Métier de sociologue* suggest, *epistemology is an eminently political discipline*[1] : it always unfolds strategically, in line with the evolution of knowledge and techniques based on the relations of power and meaning constitutive of the scientific field, and thus in response to the shortcomings and dangers specific to an intellectual moment. At the start of this century, ethnography enjoys great popularity both inside and outside academic circles. Its ability to bring the reader into a foreign, even strange "social world,"[2] the intimate and vivid accounts it can provide of these worlds, and the civic lessons it suggests a a result of the cultural normalization it effects, make it, along with history, the "public face" of social science. Hence the internal and external pressure for *exoterism*, which, while guaranteeing success with a lay or expert public, can compromise the conceptual architecture, methodological rigor, and empirical validity of fieldwork.

It is this danger that I would like to point out and, as far as possible, exorcise in the course of a meticulous critique of what I shall call *moral empiricism*—or moralizing empiricism, for, as we shall see, the border between the two is dangerously porous—that guides American urban ethnography and,

---

[1] Pierre Bourdieu, Jean-Claude Chamboredon, and Jean-Claude Passeron, *Le Métier de sociologue. Préalables épistémologiques* (1968, 1973, 2022), pp. 96–100.

[2] This key concept was developed by Anselm Strauss, a major figure of symbolic interactionism and co-inventor, with Barney Glaser, of "grounded theory," based on the social psychology of George Herbert Mead. See Anselm Strauss, "A Social World Perspective" (1978).

singularly, the tradition of fieldwork descended from the Chicago School.[3] Moral empiricism may be defined as an epistemological position and a philosophical anthropology, that is, a conception of knowledge and being in the historical world, based on five principles: (1) the sensible given is directly accessible; everything is "on the surface" and "in plain sight"; (2) analytical concepts are in a relationship of logical and semantic continuity with folk concepts; (3) theory is a local systematization of facts carried out *post festum*; (4) social agents are above all moral beings situated in local "social worlds"; (5) life in society is primarily a matter of symbols and feelings.

As we will see throughout this book, what sinks and disappears without a trace with this approach are the notions of structure, hidden mechanism, epistemic discontinuity, material and symbolic interests and power relations, and struggle as the engine of history. For the symbolic interactionists who have long been the driving force behind urban ethnography in the United States, the central process in the fabrication of the social is *communication*, in direct line with John Dewey and George Herbert Mead. For the genetic sociology developed by Pierre Bourdieu and inspired on this point by Max Weber, which will guide my critique, it is *domination* that structures social relations and universes.[4] But above all, according to the empiricist approach to fieldwork prevailing in today's social sciences, the active role of theory as a reasoned instrument of fact-making is downplayed, if not denied outright, with data supposedly "collected" here and there—in the manner of mushrooms in a forest after the rain—before being organized by and for "analytic induction."[5]

Against this vision, which stipulates an epistemology specific to what is conveniently called "qualitative studies," it is necessary and sufficient to reaffirm that, like any scientific fact, the ethnographic fact is "conquered, constructed, constated" to free the horizon of sociological knowledge from the obstacles that certain romantic ideas of the human and society place in its path.[6] Against "*thick description*" as advocated by Clifford Geertz, the last anthropological refuge of empiricist renunciation,[7] I will defend "*thick construction*," derived

---

[3] On this "school," which is not really one, read Jean-Michel Chapoulie, *La Tradition sociologique de Chicago, 1892–1961* (2001), and Christian Topalov's enlightening article, "Écrire l'histoire des sociologues de Chicago" (2003). For an insider's view, see Andrew Abbott, *Department and Discipline: Chicago Sociology at One Hundred* (1999).

[4] For a contrast, read John Dewey, *Democracy and Education: An Introduction to the Philosophy of Education* (1916), for whom communication is "the highest of the arts of living," and Max Weber, *Domination* ([1920] 2014), for whom domination is "omnipresent" (which he expresses with the adjective *Herrschaftlich*).

[5] Jack Katz, "Analytic Induction" (2001).

[6] Bourdieu et al., *Le Métier de sociologue*, p. 24.

[7] Clifford Geertz, "Thick Description: Toward an Interpretive Theory of Culture" (1973).

from Pierre Bourdieu's reflexive sociology, a *construction squared* whose mission is to construct scientifically an ordinary social construction of reality, which must without fail and without ambiguity be anchored in the triple historicity of the agent, the world, and knowledge.

~ *~

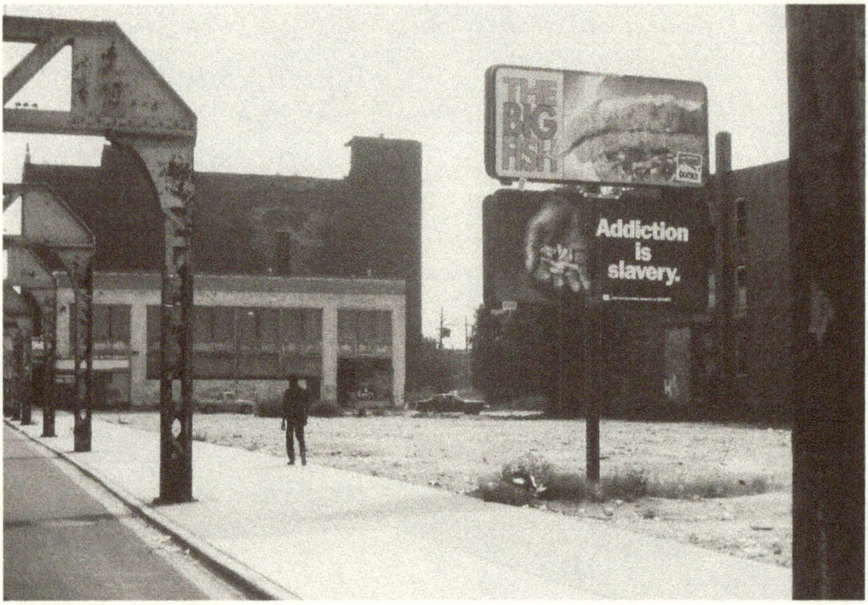
THE BIG FISH
Addiction is slavery.

1
Dissecting the Ethnographic Unconscious

> "If two men really want to understand one another, they must first contradict one another. Truth is the daughter of discussion, not the daughter of sympathy."
>
> Gaston Bachelard, *Le Matérialisme rationnel*, 1953.

This book intends to make a triple contribution to sociological debate and practice. First, through a methodical critique of three works immediately considered canonical on the subject, it is a contribution to the study of the relationship between race, class, and state in the American metropolis that sheds light not only on the transformations, real or imaginary, of the black American ghetto at the turn of the new millennium, but also, by ricochet, on investigations into the pairing of marginality and ethnicity in European cities in the neoliberal era.[1]

Next, it is a case study in the science of science that provokes, and then relates, a controversy that has entered the annals of American and international social science and, as such, can serve as a living analyzer of the roles of intellectual capital and bureaucratic capital in the functioning of a field of scholarly production. It points out the dangers of the inevitable interference of social factors in scientific polemics as the indispensable engine behind the progress of reason, an interference that scholars must collectively strive to minimize.[2]

Finally, *The Poverty of the Ethnography of Poverty* reflects on the construction of the ethnographic object, leading to practical recommendations aiming to forge closer and more solid links between theory, empirics, and the politics of knowledge in the conduct of fieldwork, particularly when the latter touches on objects that are tainted and overloaded with phantasms. So much to say

---

[1] For transposition, I refer the reader to the introduction to Loïc Wacquant, *Urban Outcasts: A Comparative Sociology of Advanced Marginality* (2008), pp. 10–12, and idem, "Marginality, Ethnicity and Penality int the Neo-liberal City: An Analytic Cartography" (2012).
[2] Pierre Bourdieu, Jean-Claude Chamboredon, and Jean-Claude Passeron, *Le Métier de sociologue. Préalables épistémologiques* (1968, 1973, 2021), pp. 14 and 102–106.

that, by dissecting the social unconscious of American sociology's diptych of race and poverty, I would like to warn European researchers against importing without epistemic "custom duties" the concepts, questions and themes from across the Atlantic.[3] To demonstrate the pressing need for reflexivity in the conduct of fieldwork, more so than in any other register of sociology,[4] it is necessary and sufficient to reveal the social presuppositions and scientific infirmities that these preconstructed problematics cart with them in their own province.

Genesis of an academic controversy and the debate eluded

The middle part of this book is my article "Scrutinizing the Street: Poverty, Morality, and the Pitfalls of Urban Ethnography," a long piece published in 2002 by the *American Journal of Sociology*, the discipline's leading journal in the United States.[5] The article is preceded by a historical and analytical tableau that provides the elements needed to understand it, and sheds light on the dispute it was to provoke, leading to rigid censorship and organized silence on the American side, and to an open and fruitful debate on other continents, a contrast I will use to draw out the social underpinnings of sociological debates. So as not to be suspected of rewriting history, I have retained the original text down to the last comma. The notes, on the other hand, have been enriched and updated to clarify the context and arguments, and some of them have been integrated into the text to make it easier to read.

This text is followed by an extended reflection on the political epistemology of fieldwork, in which I respond to the rejoinders to "Scrutinizing" and draw lessons for the sociology of the social sciences from this *Streit*, which we shall see is still relevant today, even if it takes on new forms. Indeed, twenty years later, at a time when fieldwork is enjoying a new golden age in the major American universities, the same shortcomings are marring American urban ethnography and threatening its status both inside and outside the academic cenacle, as illustrated by the political and scientific *furore* surrounding Alice

---

[3] A current example is the so-called "intersectionality" approach, about which read the devastating article by the feminist sociologist Kathy Davis, "Intersectionality as Buzzword: A Sociology of Science Perspective on What Makes a Feminist Theory Successful" (2008).

[4] On the difference between egological, textual, and epistemic reflexivity, see Pierre Bourdieu and Loïc Wacquant, *Invitation to Reflexive Sociology* (1992), pp. 36–47, and Pierre Bourdieu, *Retour sur la réflexivité* (2022), especially pp. 36–48.

[5] Loïc Wacquant, "Scrutinizing the Street: Poverty, Morality, and the Pitfalls of Urban Ethnography" (2002).

Goffman's sulphurous book, *On the Run*,[6] which was first widely praised and then just as widely discredited. The social demand for exciting books that take their readers into the "jungle" of the black ghetto—or what remains of it—continues to weigh on this sector of scholarly production and hinders the full integration of ethnography into the body of social science methods.[7] The same is true of the fierce protests of researchers, doctoral candidates, and commentators of all stripes against the fact that white field sociologists are studying the "problems" of "communities of color," reopening the question of the relationship between the ethnic identity of the ethnographer and that of her subjects, which had already contributed to the asthenia of fieldwork on race and class in the city in the 1970s and 1980s, as we shall see later.

Let us summarily set the scene and profile the protagonists. In the spring of 2001, the *American Journal of Sociology* invited me to write a review essay on three books on race and poverty in the American city. Immediately upon their release, Mitchell Duneier's *Sidewalk*, Elijah Anderson's *Code of the Street* and Katherine Newman's *No Shame in My Game* were unanimously acclaimed as touchstones of the genre.[8] I was well acquainted with the previous work of their authors, scholars recognized as authorities in their field, and I was myself engaged in ethnographic fieldwork on Chicago's South Side (leading to *Body and Soul* and *Urban Outcasts*),[9] so I was curious to take a close look at their latest production. I read and reread the three volumes and came, reluctantly and with regret, to the conclusion that, far from providing models to be imitated, they were problematic in several respects: a wobbly epistemology, conceptual prevarication, a propensity for moralism, a lack of reflexivity, and a surprising blindness to the great wealth of ethnographic material they marshalled. And yet they were highly praised, so why? What to do? Decline the invitation of the *American Journal of Sociology* (it is always more pleasant, and above all more profitable professionally, to publish

---

[6] Alice Goffman, *On the Run: Fugitive Life in an American City* (2014). For a penetrating analysis of this scientific scandal and its springs, read Ana Portilla, "On the Run. L'ethnographie en cavale?" (2016), as well as the box *infra*, pp. 134–139.

[7] A sustained and successful effort to foster that integration is Mario Luis Small and Jessica McCrory Calarco, *Qualitative Literacy: A Guide to Evaluating Ethnographic and Interview Research* (2022).

[8] Mitchell Duneier, *Sidewalk* (New York: Farrar, Straus & Giroux, 1999), 383 pp.; Elijah Anderson, *Code of the Street: Decency, Violence and the Moral Life of the Inner City* (New York: W.C. Norton, 1999), 352 pp.; and Katherine Newman, *No Shame in My Game: The Working Poor in the Inner City* (New York: Russell Sage Foundation and Knopf, 1999), 401 pp. It is worth noting that the journal could just as easily have entrusted this mission to a sociologist of labor, since all three books deal with informal work on the street (Duneier), the consequences for the ghetto of young black men's difficulty in entering the occupational world (Anderson), and the impact of fast-food restaurants on the lives of their employees in Harlem (Newman). But, between race and work, the ghetto and the firm, there is no contest: It is the first subject that wins hands down, crushing the class dimension of the social worlds examined.

[9] Loïc Wacquant, *Body and Soul: Notebooks of an Apprentice Boxer* (2004; expanded anniversary edition 2022); *Urban Outcasts: A Comparative Sociology of Advanced Marginality* (2008).

a rave review) and let the chorus of commendation resound, or express my reservations, at the risk of taking on the bad role of the ethnographic killjoy?

I resolved to fulfill my mission and spent several months patiently writing my critical note, in constant dialogue with Pierre Bourdieu, who reread its successive versions and urged me to take advantage of the opportunity to carry out a clarification of sociological epistemology in action: the *meticulous deconstruction of the wobbly construction of an object weighted down* with moral and political baggage revealing the social and racial unconscious of American sociology.[10] From the planned dozen pages, the text swelled to sixty-five printed pages. "Scrutinizing the Street" thus became not only the longest review essay in *AJS* history, but also "the most controversial ever published," *dixit* Michael Burawoy, president of the American Sociological Association at the time. Its publication was followed by three vitriolic responses from Mitchell Duneier, Elijah Anderson, and Katherine Newman who, to cut a long story short, over the course of sixty-seven pages, reduced my epistemological argumentation to a political conflict (and pamphlet) and questioned my professional competence,[11] after which Andrew Abbott, the head of the *AJS* editorial board, declined my request to respond to their replies.

In the months and years that followed, the three authors refused to cross sociological swords with me and tried to discredit me, in keeping with the saying, "if you don't like the message, kill the messenger." They sent me a registered letter on the letterhead of a law firm forbidding me to circulate their three responses to my article on copyright grounds, and set up an ad hoc website where they could be downloaded. They sent the text of their three replies (but not that of my article) to a long list of eminent colleagues. They publicly complained that I had supposedly "violated the code of ethics" of the American Sociological Association. They twice declined the offer to debate our scientific differences in public, in November 2003, at the invitation of William Julius Wilson, who wished to organize an in-person symposium on the paper symposium at Harvard University under the auspices of the departments of Sociology and African American Studies and the Kennedy School of Public Policy in order—he wrote me in an e-mail—"to engage the debate that did not take place in AJS"; then, in January 2004, at the invitation of Michael Burawoy, who offered to chair a plenary session on "The Politics and Ethics of

---

[10] Bourdieu wished to publish the review essay in book form as a follow-up to his Collège de France lecture course on *Science de la science et réflexivité* (2001). The text was translated into French at the time, but the publisher decided it would be wiser to let some time pass, so that academic minds could calm down and the epistemological argument could be fully heard.

[11] The titles of their answers suffice to indicate their chosen register: Elijah Anderson, "The Ideologically Driven Critique" (2002); Mitchell Duneier, "What Kind of Combat Sport Is Sociology?" (2002); Katherine Newman, "No Shame: The View from the Left Bank" (2002).

Ethnography" with the four protagonists at the annual meetings of the American Sociological Association, which he then presided. This refusal to publicly discuss the scientific arguments developed in "Scrutinizing" was all the more striking considering that, meanwhile, the article was widely debated outside the United States.

In October 2002, the Amsterdam School of Social Science organized a symposium on "After Scrutinizing the Street: Some Implications for Conducting Urban Ethnography" (with sociologists Abram de Swaan and Godfried Engbersen, anthropologist Peter van den Veer, and historian Don Kalb). In March 2003, a roundtable on "Scrutinizing" was convened at York University in Toronto (with Tim Diamond, Terra Milbright, Ronaldo Walcott and Fuyuki Kurasawa). In June 2003, the social science laboratory at the École normale supérieure in Paris held a seminar on "Heurs et malheurs de l'ethnographie urbaine américaine." The elided debate was discussed at the University of Porto in November 2004 under the title "Le paria, le savant, et le politique: questions d'ethnographie urbaine," and in September 2005 under the title "O que faz uma boa etnografia? A epistemologia e a política do trabalho de campo" at the Federal University of Rio de Janeiro. Finally, "Scrutinizing" was discussed under the title "Theory, Politics, and Reflexivity in Ethnography" at the Institute for Advanced Studies, University of Bristol, in June 2006.

In the United States, radio silence. Such is the *professional* lead blanket bearing on *intellectual* debate that several black sociologists of the up-and-coming generation wrote to tell me how "Scrutinizing" had "shaken" them and "done them good," but they could not risk saying so publicly. Yet many colleagues who taught urban sociology or ethnography had their students read the symposium in its entirety. It was not until May 2010 that the Spring Institute of the Society for Social Research, the association of doctoral students in sociology at the University of Chicago, dared to invite me to respond to a panel of the department's eminent ethnographers on "Scrutinizing."[12] The refusal to debate this text warped the reception of the English version of my ethnography of prizefighting as a bodily craft, *Body and Soul*. Thus, three representatives of symbolic interactionism were explicitly delegated by the journal *Symbolic Interaction* to "execute" the book and thus avenge the Chicago School in a symposium taking the form of an ambush.[13]

---

[12] They are Andreas Glaeser, author of *Divided in Unity: Identity, Germany, and the Berlin Police* (2000); Omar McRoberts, author of *Streets of Glory: Church and Community in a Black Urban Neighborhood* (2005); and Mario Small, author of *Villa Victoria: The Transformation of Social Capital in a Boston Barrio* (2004). It is significant that it was students, not professors, who initiated this roundtable, with the support of Mario Small, who defended his thesis at Harvard under Katherine Newman. The roundtable was preceded by two articles that sought to draw lessons from "Scrutinizing" for the practice of urban ethnography: William Julius Wilson and Anmol Chaddha, "The Role of Theory in Ethnographic Research" (2009); and Teresa Gowan, "New Hobos or Neo-Romantic Fantasy? Urban Ethnography beyond the Neoliberal Disconnect" (2009).

[13] I respond in "Shadowboxing with Ethnographic Ghosts: A Rejoinder" (2005). Curiously, a few months after the book's publication, a Chicago private detective tracked down and contacted my

As for Howard Becker, dean of the Chicago school and mentor to Anderson and Duneier, he spread vile untruths about "Scrutinizing" in every country he visited, including France.[14] It was on his initiative that the *Revue française de sociologie* published a critical note by Duneier on *Body and Soul* in 2006 (even though the journal had already reviewed the French original in 2001!), with the ostensible motive of contributing from France "to the debate" launched by "Scrutinizing," but to which the *RFS* conveniently forgot to invite me.

Who are the protagonists of this academic tragicomedy? Mitchell Duneier is a sociologist trained at the University of Chicago by the aging cacique of Parsonian theory Edward Shils, for whom every society is held together by the adherence of its members to charismatic values (a theme that would be revived by his protégé).[15] His first book, *Slim's Table* (1992), based on his doctoral thesis, received the Distinguished Scholarship Award in 1993, the most prestigious prize awarded by the American Sociological Association.[16] In it, Duneier describes in painstaking detail the face-to-face interactions between black working-class retirees whose daily lunch he shares in a Greek cafeteria located at the heart of Hyde Park—the upscale white neighborhood of the University of Chicago, but curiously the establishment is presented as typical of the South Side's black ghetto. Duneier celebrates the affirmation of a "respectable" African-American masculinity that attests to the moral capacity of blacks, and contrasts the working-class milieu with the disorganized and immoral world of the urban "underclass," which was dominating the political as well as sociological headlines at the time.[17]

Duneier's second ethnography, *Sidewalk*, published in 1999, immerses its readers in the social world of black homeless magazine vendors on the streets of Greenwich Village, New York's gentrified bohemian neighborhood. He intends to extend his demonstration that blacks are beings animated by morality and to raise high the banner of Chicago-style fieldwork. The book's popular success, beyond the academic world (where it won the C. Wright Mills Prize from the Association for the Study of Social Problems), opened the doors to Princeton University, where its author was offered a named chair shortly after the book's publication.

Woodlawn Boys Club ringmates with the avowed aim of unearthing some shameful fact with which to discredit *Body and Soul*. To no avail.

[14] Loïc Wacquant, "Lettre à propos de 'Scrutinizing the Street,'" *Liens sociaux* 4, April 2003.

[15] Edward Shils, "Charisma, Order, and Status" (1965).

[16] Mitchell Duneier, *Slim's Table: Race, Respectability, and Masculinity* (1992). In it, Duneier thanks Howard Becker for teaching him ethnography (p. 69).

[17] On this scarecrow category of urban sociology and the public debate of the time on race, class, and immorality, see Loïc Wacquant, *The Invention of the "Underclass": A Study in the Politics of Knowledge* (2022).

Elijah Anderson is the leading black sociologist in urban ethnography. The son of a working-class family from the industrial Midwest, he studied at the University of Chicago (where he earned a master's degree under Gerald Suttles) and then with Howard Becker at Northwestern University north of Chicago during the 1970s. His dissertation, reworked and published in 1978 as *A Place on the Corner*, draws on the Goffmanian analytical framework of *The Presentation of the Self in Everyday Life* to paint a fine-grained depiction of the microsociological construction of a local social order, one that links the "regulars," the "hoodlums," and the "winos" who frequent Jelly's liquor store on the corner of a decrepit street in Chicago's ghetto.[18]

As a young professor, Anderson became Erving Goffman's colleague at the University of Pennsylvania, where, a decade later, he published *Streetwise: Race, Class, and Change in an Urban Community* (1990), which won the Robert E. Park Award from the Community and Urban Sociology Section of the American Sociological Association (the prize is named in honor of the founder of the early Chicago School).[19] In it, Anderson deciphers the open conflict played out in public space between the black and white middle classes of an affluent Philadelphia neighborhood and the poor blacks of an adjacent ghetto ravaged by the drug trade. Or how the inhabitants of the polarized American metropolis acquire the "street wisdom" that enables them to negotiate the widening class and racial divide day to day, a divide that feeds the fear and urban fantasies incarnated by the "underclass." Each group struggles not only to protect its physical perimeter, but also to forge "a shared moral community," a theme dear to the Chicago School since the 1920s. A decade later, *Code of the Street* (1999) took up and refined this theme, applying it to the brewing conflict between "decent" and "street" families within the remnants of the black ghetto.

As for Katherine Newman, by the time she published *No Shame in My Game* (1999) on the tribulations of young fast-food workers in Harlem, she was already a renowned anthropologist who had left her original discipline for a distinguished position at Harvard University's Kennedy School of Government, which gave her a material platform, professional aura, and extra-academic audience far beyond those usually granted to anthropologists. In fact, for a decade, she had been the leading—and sole—anthropologist among the circles of specialists who dominate research on poverty, race, and public policy in the United States.

---

[18] Elijah Anderson, *A Place on the Corner* (1976); Erving Goffman, *The Presentation of Self in Everyday Life* (1959).
[19] Elijah Anderson, *Streetwise: Race, Class and Change in an Urban Community* (1990).

12   The Poverty of the Ethnography of Poverty

Newman obtained her doctorate in anthropology from the University of California, Berkeley, in 1979, under the supervision of Laura Nader, Ralph Nader's sister and a radical like him. She wrote a neo-Marxist-inspired dissertation on law in precapitalist societies, which earned her a position at that university's law school.[20] Two years later, she joined the Anthropology Department at Columbia University, where she wrote a remarkable and rightly acclaimed book on the lived experience of unemployment and downward social mobility among upper-class professionals, entitled *Falling From Grace*.[21] She was part of the stream in American anthropology which repatriated ethnographic practice and made its field site at home.[22] In point of fact, her investigations were based on in-depth interviews rather than *in situ* observation. Such is the case with *Declining Fortunes*, a work that delves into the theme of class betrayal that Newman places at the heart of the "American dream," no doubt in connection with her working-class background.[23] Thus, for *No Shame in My Game*, she shepherded a team of doctoral students funded by the Russell Sage Foundation who conducted field research whose materials she mined by linking them to demographic, economic, and statistical data as well as with her own field interviews with the owners of fast-food franchises.[24] With great success: the book sparked a wide-ranging public debate and went on to win the Robert F. Kennedy Book Award and the Sidney Hillman Prize (for investigative journalism).

The authors of the three books I will pass through an analytical sieve are all seasoned social scientists with impeccable academic pedigrees. The first two are disciples of Howard Becker and leaders of the rising generation of practitioners of microsociological empiricism à la Chicago (Anderson and Duneier later co-edited, with UCLA-based ethnographic theorist Jack Katz, the University of Chicago Press book series "Fieldwork Encounters and Discoveries," whose title aptly reflects its epistemological line). The third is an anthropologist well established in policy research circles. In other words, the author of these lines, then a professor at the University of California at Berkeley, the country's leading sociology department, was attacking the fortress of moral individualism that was—and still is—raging among symbolic interactionists and in schools of public policy. It was a crime of *lèse-majesté* against so-called "urban" ethnography, which was then experiencing the beginnings of a definite revival.

---

[20] Katherine S. Newman, *Law and Economic Organization: A Comparative Study of Preindustrial Societies* (1983).
[21] Katherine S. Newman, *Falling from Grace: Downward Mobility in the Age of Affluence* (1988).
[22] Mariza G.S. Peirano, "When Anthropology is at Home: The Different Contexts of a Single Discipline" (1998). Anthropologists who follow this approach include Philippe Bourgois, Arthur Kleinman, Sherry Ortner, Paul Rabinow, and many other tenors of the discipline who had earlier published one or more "exotic" books based on their doctoral thesis.
[23] Katherine S. Newman, *Declining Fortunes: The Withering of the American Dream* (1993).
[24] Katherine S. Newman, *No Shame in My Game: The Working Poor in the Inner City* (1999).

The three ages of American "urban ethnography"

To understand the deployment of what the national academic tradition calls "urban ethnography"—a designation which, as we shall soon see, is not as obvious and innocuous as it might seem—we need to take into account three factors deeply rooted in the social and academic history of the United States. The first is the centuries-old conception of the city as a place of social dissolution, moral perdition, and political disorder.[25] Since the country's origins as an agrarian colony of settlement, America's cultural elites have nurtured a virulent *anti-urbanism* that has had a lasting influence on urban sociology, prompting it now to strive to rehabilitate the city and its inhabitants, now to take up and amplify the trope of disorganization, the swing from one pole to the other concealing their common determination.[26]

Thus, following the wave of black uprisings in the 1960s in cities entering a phase of deindustrialization, the adjective *urban* became virtually synonymous with problem territories and populations, foremost among them the poor African Americans of the "*inner city*," a geographical euphemism commonly used to avoid referring to the ghetto and its historical vestiges as such.[27] This anti-urbanism goes hand in hand with anti-statism, such that the vituperation of the residents of deprived neighborhoods comes along with the denigration of the public assistance programs aimed at their residents, the close association between *blackness* and *welfare* scuppering the so-called "War on Poverty" launched in 1965 by President Johnson before fueling three decades of relentless legislative guerrilla warfare against public aid for the destitute.[28]

Secondly, the study of the city in the United States is backed up by the schemata of moral common sense, ordinary and political, that divide the poor into "deserving" categories, which arouse compassion and sometimes admiration (when they allegedly pull themselves "up by their own bootstraps"), and "undeserving" categories, whose work ethic and morality are in question, and who should therefore be stigmatized and disciplined.[29] Here

---

[25] Wacquant, *The Invention of the "Underclass,"* pp. 15–26. For a rich historiographic account, read Paul S. Boyer, *Urban Masses and Moral Order in America, 1820–1920* (1978).

[26] Steven Conn, *Americans Against the City: Anti-Urbanism in the Twentieth Century* (2014). This pendulum swing can be detected in the work of the early Chicago School: compare, for example, Harvey Zorbaugh, *The Gold Coast and the Slum* (1929), and Clifford R. Shaw and Henry D. McKay, *Juvenile Delinquency and Urban Areas* (1942).

[27] Thomas J. Sugrue, *The Origins of the Urban Crisis: Race and Inequality in Postwar Detroit* (1996).

[28] Jill Quadagno, *The Color of Welfare: How Racism Undermined the War on Poverty* (1994); Herbert J. Gans, *The War against the Poor: The Underclass and Antipoverty Policy* (1995).

[29] Michael B. Katz, *The Undeserving Poor: America's Enduring Confrontation with Poverty*, 2nd revised and updated edition (2013).

again, so-called "urban" ethnography throws its weight into the symbolic battle to exonerate categories deemed deviating from the idealized national norm by relating their reprobated practices to their specific social conditions and thereby "normalizing" them: thus Howard Becker's marijuana smokers, Elliott Liebow's idle black men in the ghetto, and the gay men who conspired to meet in public toilets during the era of prohibition of homosexuality.[30]

Thirdly and finally, ethnography is a methodological genre that occupies a technically subordinate and academically dominated position in the space of sociology in the United States. It did not establish itself as a specialty until late in the 1960s—that is, long after the consolidation of the orthodoxy of "instrumental positivism" that informed the dominant paradigm of structural functionalism for one half-century.[31] Indeed, it is impossible to understand the virulence of the controversy that "Scrutinizing the Street" was to provoke without placing this text in the long-term evolution of urban ethnography, from its burgeoning in the 1920s to its flowering in the 1960s, and then its fading for almost three decades.

The first of the three ages of American urban ethnography was launched by Chicago researchers working in the tow of Robert Park, a journalist who became a sociologist late in life and coined the term "*urban* sociology" in 1925, a conception he borrowed from the settlement movement and social work centered on deprived neighborhoods in a deliberate strategy of scholarly legitimation financed by the Rockefeller family.[32] The idea that the city is a distinctive milieu endowed with its own form, shaped by objective forces and made up of a "mosaic" of hermetic neighborhoods, and that to each "natural area" corresponds a "moral region," provided the bedrock for the first field studies of the American city recognized in the academic field.[33]

It is true that W.E.B. Du Bois's daring monograph, *The Philadelphia Negro: A Social Study* (1999), appeared twenty-six years earlier. In this thick tome based on direct observation among the 9,000 African Americans living in the city's Seventh Ward, a census of residents, surveys and extensive historical and statistical documentation, Du Bois paints a detailed portrait of the urban black community, complete with its demographic

---

[30] Howard S. Becker, *Outsiders: Studies in the Sociology of Deviance* (1963); Elliot Liebow, *Tally's Corner: A Study of Negro Streetcorner Men* (1967); Laud Humphreys, *Tearoom Trade: Impersonal Sex in Public Places* (1970).

[31] Bryant distinguishes three varieties of positivism: French positivism running from Comte to Durkheim, the logical positivism of the Vienna School, and "instrumental positivism" in the United States, characterized by the concern for methodological precision and sophistication embodied by the statistical apparatus. Christopher G.A. Bryant, *Positivism in Social Theory and Research* (1985).

[32] Christian Topalov, "Sociologie d'un étiquetage scientifique: *urban sociology*" (2008). On the transposition of journalistic techniques to sociology, see Rolf Lindner, *The Reportage of Urban Culture: Robert Park and the Chicago School* (1996).

[33] Robert E. Park and Ernest Burgess, *The City* (1925).

profile, its institutions, its most pressing problems (crime, pauperism, and alcoholism), its aspirations and its relationship with white society. He points out how color prejudice translates into a black social psychology stamped by "discouragement, bitterness, hypersensitivity and irresponsibility."[34] While this *field* study is not *ethnographic* in the contemporary sense of reconstructing the point of view of the inhabitants and the fine texture of everyday social and symbolic relationships, it is innovative in its holistic approach and impressive in its effort to link internal conditions and external forces, starting with the inflexible white domination that American social science would take for granted and make invisible for almost half a century.[35] It is without contest the first major *urban sociography* of the new century. However, Du Bois was carefully ostracized on account of his "race" by nascent academic sociology, and *The Philadelphia Negro* remained largely confidential until its republication nearly a century later, even though its author developed its principles and insights in his studies on "The Black North in 1901: New York" and in the Atlanta University Studies between 1897 and 1914.[36]

But back to Chicago. A bouquet of studies of urban life captured "from below" takes their readers into unknown social worlds located in the nether regions of social and physical space. In *The Hobo* (1923), Nels Anderson, who had himself been a hobo in his youth, depicts the daily lives of homeless seasonal workers who migrated from city to city by hopping on freight trains.[37] In Chicago, their capital and transit hub, they temporarily inserted themselves into a motley subproletariat with its own institutions: flophouses, dingy restaurants, pawnshops, religious outfits providing room and board in exchange for a simulacrum of conversion, and the barber school where one could get a free shave and haircut. Their zone of concentration, known as "the Jungle," was in one of those "interstitial spaces" of the city where the gangs studied by Frederick M. Thrasher in *The Gang* (1927) thrived.[38]

Thrasher's study is more impressionistic, but no less impressive for the variety of data it marshalls to describe the "ganging process" based on gender, age, class and ethnicity, but rooted above all in territory. What makes a group of young men a gang is precisely the *manu militari* defense of this territory against the intrusion of rival gangs from adjacent

---

[34] W.E.B. Du Bois, *The Philadelphia Negro: A Social Study* (1899, 1996), p. 325.

[35] W.E.B. Du Bois, *On Sociology and the Black Community* (1974), chapters 1, 2, and 7. For an excellent exegesis of Du Bois's contributions to what national sociologists call the doxic duo of "urban and community studies," see José Itzigsohn and Karida L. Brown, *The Sociology of W.E.B. Du Bois: Racialized Modernity and the Global Color Line* (2020), pp. 97–129. That is a long way from making Du Bois the inventor of urban ethnography in the broadest sense, for to do so would ignore the innovation of Friedrich Engels in *The Condition of the Working Class in England* a half-century earlier ([1845] 2009).

[36] On the deliberate ignorance of Du Bois by the emerging discipline of sociology, and singularly by Robert Park, co-founder of urban sociology, who nonetheless knew his work well, see Aldon D. Morris, *The Scholar Denied: W.E.B. Du Bois and the Birth of Modern Sociology* (2015).

[37] Nels Anderson, *The Hobo: The Sociology of the Homeless Man* (1923, 2014). For a related contemporary study, Douglas Harper, *Good Company: A Tramp Life* (1982).

[38] Frederic M. Thrasher, *The Gang: A Study of 1,313 Gangs in Chicago* (1927, 2013). An ethnographic reprise on this dynamic at the close of the century is Martín Sánchez-Jankowski, *Islands in the Street: Gangs in American Urban Society* (1990).

neighborhoods. Thrasher discloses the forms of sociability that the gang supports, the springs of its reputation and the diverse social types it harbors—the "funny boy," the "sissy," the "show-off," and the "goofy guys." He shows, unwittingly, that the gang as an organization is born in a space of so-called "disorganization."

Harvey Zorbaugh's *The Gold Coast and the Slum* (1929) reflects this interest in discerning the various social types corresponding to distinct places.[39] Zorbaugh contrasts the forms of social life prevalent in six "natural areas" sharing a motley Windy City neighborhood, ranging from the rooming-house zone and the slum to Little Sicily, the bohemian district, and the Gold Coast, the enclave harboring the city's "four hundred richest families." In the process, he provides an early empirical insight into the etiquette, institutions, and internal divisions of America's haute bourgeoisie and its world centered on self-care, leisure, travel to select locations, and charities.[40] A highly integrated milieu that stands in stark contrast with the rooming-house zone, in which Zorbaugh sees the very embodiment of urban disintegration in all its horror: "The rooming-house world is in no sense a social world, a set of group relationships through which the person's wishes are realized," due to the mobility, anonymity, and isolation of its population, which translate into "political indifference, of laxity of conventional standards, of personal and social disorganization."[41]

But the minor masterpiece of the period is Paul Cressey's *The Taxi-Dance Hall* (1932). In it, Cressey takes his reader into the city's disreputable dancings, usually run by Greek Americans, where single men, often of Asian descent, could "rent" a partner, frequently Polish, for ten cents a dance, payment of which she would keep half.[42] He draws the portrait and reconstructs the careers of the owners, the dancers, and their customers. He shows how the dancers, coming from unstable family backgrounds, are exploited on a downward slope in the combined order of gender, class, and ethnicity (an "intersectional" analysis ahead of its time) as their bodily capital deteriorates, sometimes ending up as prostitutes in the brothels of the black ghetto, the very bottom of the material and symbolic hierarchy. Caught up in the sociability of the dance hall, the dancers form "a moral milieu rather completely removed from the other more conventional forms of city life" which enables them to live a kind of double life for a time. The specificity of local culture rooted in a distinct corner or territory, a close-up and romantic vision, an interest in the moral forms of a group that diverges from the conventional norm: these are all themes that will be found again in contemporary urban ethnography, particularly in the books by Duneier, Anderson and Newman.

---

[39] Harvey Zorbaugh, *The Gold Coast and the Slum: A Sociological Study of Chicago's Near North Side* (1929, 1983).

[40] On this subject, read Edward Digby Baltzell's classic study, *The Protestant Establishment: Aristocracy and Caste in America* (1964, 1987).

[41] Zorbaugh, *The Gold Coast and the Slum*, p. 82.

[42] Paul Cressey, *The Taxi-Dance Hall: A Sociological Study in Commercialized Recreation and City Life* (1932, 1969).

Between 1930 and 1960, fieldwork in the city faded in the face of the spread of poverty due to the Great Depression—when "disorganization" struck all social milieus—and the irresistible rise of demographic, political, and quantitative sociology, animated at the theoretical level by the structural functionalism of Talcott Parsons and Robert Merton, when it was not proceeding from an unvarnished scientistic empiricism. It is the high tide of "urban ecology" and "social area analysis" carried out by synchronic statistical slices.[43] Social life at street level disappears from view.

One major exception: the master book by the black sociologists St. Clair Drake and Horace Cayton, *Black Metropolis* published in 1945, funded by the Works Public Administration and framed by the "caste and class" school led by the anthropologist W. Lloyd Warner, which paints an unforgettable portrait of the social structure and everyday culture of Bronzeville, Chicago's black ghetto then at its apogee.[44] Drake and Cayton scan the institutions of the "black city in the white": churches, the press, businesses, clubs and lodges, and places of public amusement. They paint a picture of social classes and lifestyles, stamped by the opposition between the respectable bourgeoisie and the dissolute lower class; and they reveal the unifying aspiration to racial equality, notwithstanding marked distinctions of color within the African American population itself.

A related ethnographic genre that flourished during the interwar years is what is conventionally called "community studies" carried out by teams of sociologists or anthropologists taking as their object a *small town* in its entirety—size is crucial here, as it defines a field of investigation that stands in stark contrast to the metropolis of urban ethnography *stricto sensu*.[45] These studies are tinged with nostalgia for a local world in the process of dissolution, made up of dense relations of mutual acquaintanceship anchored by a self-centered economy and nourishing a political and cultural life marked by parochialism and the domination of a closed clique of bourgeois families, a disappearance caused precisely by the growth and power of attraction of the big cities, the seats of industrial capitalism.

---

[43] Consider a typical article and book by two leaders of the genre: Donald J. Bogue, "Urbanism in the United States, 1950" (1955), and Leonard Reissman, *The Urban Process: Cities in Industrial Societies* (1964). On the erasure of history in urban sociology, read Bruce M. Stave, "A Conversation with Charles Tilly: Urban History and Urban Sociology" (1998). It was not until 1974 that the *Journal of Urban History* was founded.

[44] St. Clair Drake and Horace Cayton, *Black Metropolis: A Study of Negro Life in a Northern City* (1945, 1993). On the illuminating genesis of this historical tome, see Henri Peretz, "The Making of *Black Metropolis*" (2004), and Mitchell Duneier, *Ghetto: The Invention of a Place, the History of an Idea* (2016), chapter 2.

[45] Arthur J. Vidich and Joseph Bensman, *Small Town in Mass Society: Class, Power, and Religion in a Rural Community* (1958).

18 The Poverty of the Ethnography of Poverty

In the 1920s, sociologists Robert and Helen Lynd led a squadron of sociologists to Muncie, a white Indiana town of 30,000 residents, which they considered "typical" of small-town America. They give a holistic account of it in *Middletown: A Study in Modern American Culture* (1929), followed by *Middletown in Transition: A Study in Cultural Conflicts* (1937). The former emphasizes the social divide between the working class and local employers, the population's disdain for bookish culture despite rising levels of education, the supposed decline of public morality, the new role of the automobile as a status symbol and of radio in entertainment, and the rise of cynicism in politics despite fierce partisan affiliations. The Lynd couple insists on the rigidity of the class structure and dismantle the "myth" of social meritocracy. The second book maps out the impact of the Great Depression on the social structure and finds the latter to be surprisingly resilient. The core idea endures: "deep" America remains small-town America.[46] The Lynds' approach clearly diverges from the Chicago School in its insistence on power relations and the role of class division, and in its disinterest in the spatial and moral dimensions of urban life.

From 1930 to 1935, anthropologist W. Lloyd Warner and his collaborators explored the social structure, institutions, and symbolic practices of Newburyport, a coastal Massachusetts town of 17,000 residents. Inspired by Malinowskian ethnography, Durkheimian structural functionalism and the social psychology of George Herbert Mead, their fieldwork resulted in a spate of five volumes entitled *The Yankee City Series*, published between 1941 and 1959, exploring family and associative life, the class system (with its famous six-stratum division), ethnic stratification and integration, the factory world, and religious life. Warner's one-volume synthesis, published in 1963, testifies to America's attachment to its idealized "small town," which many ethnographers would subsequently strive to rediscover nestled in the heart of the metropolis.[47] This attachment is enduring: according to a 2001 Gallup poll, 35% of Americans wish to live in a rural area and 27% in a small town, while only 8% would prefer to reside in a metropolis.[48]

The second age of American ethnography opens at the turn of the 1960s with the blossoming of a new generation of sociologists trained in fieldwork by Everett C. Hughes, a Canadian expatriate in Chicago, where he became the mentor of Erving Goffman, Howard Becker, Anselm Strauss, Fred Davis, Elliot Friedson, and Joseph Gusfield.[49] To put it briefly, the proponents of

---

[46] Theodore Caplow and his research team carry out a first revisit of Muncie in *Middletown Families: Fifty Years of Change and Continuity* (1982), then a second in *The First Measured Century* (2000), a book accompanied by a documentary produced and broadcast by PBS. But, in a revealing change, the revisit is carried out by means of a quantitative survey rather than ethnographic study.

[47] W. Lloyd Warner, *Yankee City, the One-Volume Abridged Edition* (1963).

[48] Frank Newport, "Americans Big on Living in the Country" (2018).

[49] His most significant writings are collected in Everett C. Hughes, *The Sociological Eye: Selected Papers* (1970, 2017).

what is sometimes abusively referred to as the Second Chicago School are sociologists *in* the city, not sociologists *of* the city. For them, the city is merely the container for diverse, deviant, subaltern, and stigmatized categories, in particular the occupational milieus (jazz musicians, pool hustlers, cab drivers, janitors, teachers, etc.) that form the core target of their studies. With this generation, the connection between social relations and territory is coming unglued. Theoretical inspiration no longer comes from urban ecology, but from that current of social psychology descended from George Herbert Mead, whose roots go back to the pragmatism of William James and John Dewey, to which Herbert Blumer gave the name "symbolic interactionism" in an eponymous book published in 1966.[50] The fieldwork of these authors was often published in the journal with the telling title of *Urban Life*, which was renamed *Journal of Contemporary Ethnography* in 1972, proof of the loosening link with the city as sociospatial constellation.

No matter the defection of the Chicago boys; urban ethnography enjoyed a second golden age in the 1960s, stimulated by the "discovery" of poverty in an affluent society, the rise of delinquency, the sociodemographic upheavals in the metropolis linked to "urban renewal" programs, and the implosion of the black ghetto.[51] Field studies of working-class neighborhoods, where the city's stigmatized populations on both ethnic and class grounds are concentrated, flourished in the wake of the social movements shaking up American society and the "urban renewal" plans reshaping the face of many industrial cities with the twofold aim of arresting their economic decline and stanching the expansion of African-American neighborhoods.[52] These ethnographic studies aimed to rehabilitate the negative image of dominated groups and their spaces, an image reactivated by the sharp revival of anti-urban discourse triggered by the ghetto revolts.[53]

---

[50] Herbert Blumer, *Symbolic Interactionism: Perspective and Method* (1966). It should be noted that Goffman does not fit into this filiation, since his early work was inspired by an original combination of Émile Durkheim, Georg Simmel and Kenneth Burke.

[51] James T. Patterson, *America's Struggle against Poverty in the Twentieth Century* (2000); Kenneth J. Clark, *Dark Ghetto: Dilemmas of Social Power* (1965); Kerner Commission, *The Kerner Report: The 1968 Report of the National Advisory Commission on Civil Disorders* ([1968] 1989); Peter B. Levy, *The Great Uprising: Race Riots in Urban America during the 1960s* (2018).

[52] Arnold R. Hirsch, *Making the Second Ghetto: Race and Housing in Chicago 1940–1960* (1983, 2009). For a detailed analysis of urban renewal in the 1950s and 1990s, see Derek S. Hyra, "Conceptualizing the New Urban Renewal: Comparing the Past to the Present" (2012), and Samuel Zipp, "The Roots and Routes of Urban Renewal" (2013).

[53] The decade was marked by an explosion of catastrophist discourses on the "urban crisis," e.g., Edward C. Banfield, *The Unheavenly City: The Nature and Future of Our Urban Crisis* (1970). The black revolt in the cities created a profound collective racial trauma among whites, which would fuel the public demand for welfare restriction and prison expansion over the next half century, as I show in *Punishing the Poor: The Neoliberal Government of Social Insecurity* (2009).

Two authors mark this production on the side of white society: Herbert Gans at Columbia University and Gerald Suttles at the University of Chicago. An immigrant who arrived from Germany at the age of 13, Gans took the course in field methods taught by Hughes at Chicago before completing his doctorate in urban planning at the University of Pennsylvania. In *The Urban Villagers: Group and Class in the Life of Italian-Americans* (1965), he draws on eight months of participant observation to unravel the dense networks of peer sociability and document the institutional and family life of the Italian-American working-class district of Boston's West End, before it was razed to make way for luxury apartment towers, precisely on the pretext that it was an insalubrious neighborhood characterized by social disorder and the cultural ineptitude of its inhabitants.[54] Within the groups of young men, an opposition emerges between those who seek "routine" (and personal loyalty) and those who seek "action" (and the chance to break out of social shackles), analogues of which are to be found in studies of the ghetto. Contrary to the national tradition, Gans forcefully asserts the priority of class position over ethnicity as the key to the social practices and strategies of West End residents: "West Enders are not frustrated seekers of middle-class values. Their way of life constitutes a distinct and independent working-class subculture."[55]

A former naval officer with a doctorate in sociology from the University of Illinois at Urbana, Gerald Suttles joined the bastion of urban sociology when he became a professor at the University of Chicago in 1967. It was there that he synthesized the ecological and interactionist approaches in *The Social Order of the Slum: Ethnicity and Territory in the Inner City* (1968), a study of everyday interpersonal relations in a run-down public housing complex on Chicago's West Side, soon to be demolished, where he resided for three years in the guise of a social worker.[56] In this complex, blacks, Mexicans, Puerto Ricans and whites of Italian origin rub shoulders without ever mixing, sharing a territory where a "segmented order" reigns according to ethnic identity, which here takes precedence over class position. This order prevails not only in interpersonal relations, stamped by "face-to-face antagonisms," but also in religious congregations, neighborhood businesses,

---

[54] Herbert J. Gans, *The Urban Villagers: Group and Class in the Life of Italian-Americans* (1965, 1982). This is a textbook case where territorial stigmatization is used as a symbolic lever by the state to justify the destruction of a deprived neighborhood and its capture by the real estate circuits (Loïc Wacquant, *Bourdieu in the City: Challenging Urban Theory* (2023), pp. 166–167).

[55] Gans, *The Urban Villagers*, p. x. This theme of the strength of class culture resurfaces in Gans's ethnography of a model new subdivision in a prosperous suburb, Herbert J. Gans, *The Levittowners: How People Live and Politics in Suburbia* (1967, reprinted 2021).

[56] Gerald D. Suttles, *The Social Order of the Slum: Ethnicity and Territory in the Inner City* (1968).

and schools. Even language, gestures, and dress express this segmentation. But, above all, the Addams neighborhood on the West Side suffers from a "moral isolation" that Suttles argues is typical of "slums" as the very opposite of middle-class society. The fact remains that slum-dwellers display creativity as they invent their own moral order when the conventional order proves unworkable.[57]

Gans and Suttles thus update William Foote Whyte's thesis, in *Street-Corner Society: The Social Structure of an Italian Slum* (1948, 1955, 1992), that lower-class neighborhoods, far from being "disorganized," as Chicago orthodoxy would have it, are simply *organized differently* in response to the constraints and facilitations specific to their inhabitants due to their inferior position in the city's social and physical space. Released virtually on a self-publishing basis in 1948 (the University of Chicago Press insisted on the author subsidizing its production) to complete academic indifference, Whyte's monograph was rediscovered and republished in 1955, before being retroactively elevated to the rank of founding text of Chicago-style urban ethnography, not least because it contains a methodological appendix that, for the first time, codifies sociological fieldwork in the city.

This is a complete misinterpretation since Whyte was explicitly inspired by the anthropology of Eliot Chapple and Conrad Arensberg, and wrote in frontal opposition to the Chicago approach[58]—so much so that Louis Wirth rejected his thesis when it was first defended, and demanded that Whyte preface his dissertation with a review of the Chicago School's work on social disorganization, a study published in 1943 by Whyte in the form of an article with the vengeful title, "Social Organization in the Slums."[59] In point of fact, at the time of his fieldwork, Whyte was ignorant of the sociological literature on "slums" produced by Chicago researchers because he "saw [him]self as an anthropologist" and, when he did become familiar with it, he quickly grew convinced that "the bulk of that literature was useless and misleading."[60] The second point of divergence between Whyte and Chicago urban ethnography is that, contrary to symbolic interactionism, Whyte makes a point of *ignoring* the subjective meanings that Cornerville gang members give to their behavior, focusing instead exclusively on external behavioral indicators. A final point is the importance Whyte places on producing

---

[57] In the wake of this study, Suttles published *The Social Construction of Communities* (1972), a collection of articles that attempts—unsuccessfully—to formalize "the ways in which people use territory, residence, distance, space and movement" to create a moral order.
[58] William Foote Whyte, *Street-Corner Society: The Social Structure of an Italian Slum* (1948, 1955, 1992), pp. 286–287.
[59] William Foote Whyte, "Social Organization in the Slums" (1943).
[60] Whyte, *Street-Corner Society*, p. 356.

"a detailed report of actual behavior completely divorced from any moral judgment."[61]

These studies of white working-class neighborhoods were matched by a wave of field monographs on the black ghetto, which was then imploding under the combined effects of deindustrialization (which made African-American labor redundant), the exodus of millions of whites to the prosperous suburbs in reaction to the African-American influx (which undermined the cities' tax base), and black mobilization for civic equality leading to the emergence of Black Power activists (which provoked great fright not only among whites, but also among the black bourgeoisie). Three books stand out from the flood of publications that then closely explored the ferment of African-American culture, institutions and demands, attaining the status of classics of the genre. They are signed by Elliott Liebow, Ulf Hannerz, and Lee Rainwater.

In addition to these three authors, all three of whom are white, and in the same monographic vein of this prolific period, the following studies drawn from field dissertations can be read with profit: Patricia Cayo Sexton, *Spanish Harlem: An Anatomy of Poverty* (1965); Camille Jeffers, *Living Poor: A Participant Observer Study of Priorities and Choices* (1967); David Schulz, *Coming Up Black: Patterns of Ghetto Socialization* (1969); William Moore, Jr, *The Vertical Ghetto: Everyday Life in an Urban Project* (1969); and Joyce Ladner, *Tomorrow's Tomorrow: The Black Woman* (1971). It was the younger generation of sociologists and anthropologists who took up scientific arms in this sensitive field of burning urgency.

The book *Dark Ghetto: Dilemmas of Social Power* (1965), by the eminent black psychologist Kenneth Clark, is not strictly speaking an ethnography, but it is based on a field survey of delinquent teenagers in Harlem conducted by a charitable organization, and it caused quite a stir when it was published. (A major problem to which we will return (see *infra*, pp. 30–33), like the aforementioned studies, it confuses ghetto and hyperghetto, that is, what *remains* of the ghetto as an instrument of social ostracism *after* it has lost its function of economic extraction and, hence, the protective shield of its parallel institutions). Two novelized autobiographies about living and growing up in the dark ghetto also made their mark in this period, the one by the African-American writer Claude Brown with *Manchild in the Promised Land* (1965), and the other by the Puerto-Rican poet Piri Thomas with *Down These Mean Streets* (1967).

It is worth noting the significant contribution of American anthropologists on this front, which is generally overlooked in the panoramas drawn up by sociologists of the city—proof, if proof were needed, of the deep divide between these disciplines. It

---

[61] Whyte, *Street-Corner Society*, pp. 333–335, 287.

includes works by the folklorist Roger D. Abrahams, such *Deep Down in the Jungle: Negro Narrative Folklore from the Streets of Philadelphia* (1964), and by the ethnomusicologist Charles Keil, *Bluesmen* (1966); the collective book edited by Norman Whitten and John Szwed in response to the black uprising in the cities, *Afro-American Anthropology: Contemporary Perspectives* (1970), accompanied by John Zwed (ed.), *Black American* (1970); and, later, the participant observation conducted by black anthropologist Betty Lou Valentine, *Hustling and Other Hard Work: Lifestyles in the Ghetto* (1978), and the collection of life fragments by her colleague John Langston Gwaltney, *Drylongso: A Self-Portrait of Black America* (1980).

By the end of the 1960s, however, this vein was running out; anthropologists of black America reoriented themselves towards more "exotic" and less risky foreign field sites—thus Abrahams took his research to the Caribbean, Keil to West Africa, and Hannerz to the Cayman Islands and then Nigeria.[62] This is because white researchers were no longer welcome in the remnants of the ghetto, and the controversy over the "culture of poverty," intertwined with the explosive quarrel over the Moynihan Report (see *infra*, pp. 33–34), created a toxic intellectual atmosphere. This trend persisted until the mid-1990s: thus a comprehensive panorama of ethnographies on the United States by the country's anthropologists during the 1980s contains all of three publications on the black ghetto out of 245 references.[63] And when young anthropologists turned their attention back to the relationship between race and class in the city at the very close of the century, it is to the black middle class or to the "community" (a vague and warm term) on a neighborhood scale that they turned, as with Steven Gregory in *Black Corona: Race and the Politics of Place in an Urban Community* (1999), Roger Sanjek in *The Future of Us All: Race and Neighborhood Politics in New York City* (2000), and John L. Jackson in *Harlemworld: Doing Race and Class in Contemporary Black America* (2001).

In 1967, a young doctoral student in anthropology by the name of Elliott Liebow, who came from a line of Jewish immigrants who ran a family grocery store, published *Tally's Corner: A Study of Negro Streetcorner Men,* based on a year-long participant observation among a group of idle or intermittently working black men whose custom was to meet on a ghetto street corner at the heart of Washington, a stone's throw from the White House. The book was a huge success, both in the academic world and far beyond—it reportedly sold over a million copies—no doubt because it features engaging characters and teems with lively vignettes, giving pride of place to the views of its subjects expressed in their own words, and because in so doing it sheds light on a

---

[62] Ulf Hannerz, "Research in the Black Ghetto: A Review of the Sixties" (1974).
[63] Michael Moffatt, "Ethnographic Writing about American Culture" (1992). It is true that the journal *Urban Anthropology* was not launched until 1972, and *City and Society* (the journal representing the Society for Urban, National and Transnational/Global Anthropology) in 1987.

black society then in open rebellion in the city. Liebow "intend[s] to record and interpret the lower-class lives of ordinary people in their own terms" and in particular "to restore to the men and women [linked to his main informant Tally] dignity by indicating that they are complex, not simple, [beings]."[64]

Liebow documents how these men's denigration of work is not rooted in a "culture of poverty" (a notion popularized at about the same time by the anthropologist Oscar Lewis),[65] but stems from a coping strategy responding to chronic unemployment and menial jobs that are at once precarious, backbreaking, and degrading, and which, in addition, do not allow one to support a family: "The job is not a stepping stone to something better. It is a dead end. [...] Delivering little, and promising no more, the job is *'no big thing.'*"[66] What is more, unstable employment feeds self-doubt and fosters a temporal orientation focused on the immediate future, which in turn reinforces economic marginality.[67] (This dialectic of objective opportunities and subjective aspirations is echoed in Anderson's Philadelphia hyperghetto, *infra*, p. 88–89). It is the permanence of these external conditions that explains the persistence of African-American poverty across generations in the ghetto and not a process of normative learning.[68]

Similarly, it is the inability to fulfill the role of the breadwinner father that makes these men failed husbands and, consequently, childless fathers. "To soften his failure and to lessen the damage to his public- and self-esteem, he pushes the children away from him."[69] Hence, too, the quasi-institutionalized infidelity that is the last refuge of a humiliated and forbidden masculinity, recorded in the popular belief that "men are just dogs," reduced to the rank of animals by their sexual instinct.[70] The home being the place that constantly sends him back to the image and reality of his failure, the husband withdraws to the street corner in a movement of self-defense. "Here, where the measure

---

[64] Hylan Lewis, preface to Elliott Liebow, *Tally's Corner: A Study of Negro Streetcorner Men* (1967), p. xiii. The book was taught to generations of students and reissued in 2003 with a preface by William Julius Wilson. Liebow went on to an administrative career as Director of the Center for the Study of Work and Mental Health at the National Institute of Mental Health, and published only one other book, a third of a century later: Elliot Liebow, *Tell Them Who I Am: The Lives of Homeless Women* (1993).

[65] Oscar Lewis, "The Culture of Poverty" (1966), and, for a vigorous critique, Philippe Bourgois, "Culture of Poverty" (2001).

[66] Liebow, *Tally's Corner*, p. 63.

[67] This analysis echoes those of Marie Jahoda et al. in *Marienthal: The Sociography of an Unemployed Community* ([1933] 2017) during the Great Depression in Austria, and of Pierre Bourdieu, *Algérie 60. Structures économiques et structures temporelles* (1977), on Algerian subproletarians in the runup of urbanization during the war of national liberation.

[68] "Many of similarities between the lower-class Negro father and his son (or mother and daughter) do not result from 'cultural transmission' but by the fact that the son goes out and independently experiences the same failures, in the same areas, and for much the same reasons as his father" (Liebow, *Tally's Corner*, p. 223).

[69] Liebow, *Tally's Corner*, p. 86.

[70] Liebow, *Tally's Corner*, p. 78.

of man is considerably smaller, and where weaknesses are somehow turned upside down and almost magically transformed into strengths, he can be, once again, a man among men."[71] The exploitative relationship between husband and wife is echoed in the ambivalence of relations of friendship, which are at once fluid, ephemeral, and idealized, stamped once again by the seal of precariousness.

Thus, Tally and his buddies strive to live in accordance with what Liebow calls a "shadow system of values," an attenuated decal of conventional values "constructed out of public fictions" reminiscent of Du Bois's concept of "double consciousness."[72] As is characteristic of the genre, *Tally's Corner* "is not aimed directly aim at developing generalizations" but only to "to make sense of what was seen and heard." Liebow emphasizes his interviewees' aspiration for dignity: "The desire to be a person in his own right, to be noticed by the world he lives in, is shared by each of the men on the street corner."[73] This touch of epistemological false modesty and the theme of the quest for recognition would be echoed in the ethnographies of Duneier, Anderson and Newman half-a-century later.

In *Soulside: Inquiries into Ghetto Culture and Community* (1969), the Swedish anthropologist and son of a doctor Ulf Hannerz, whose doctoral fieldwork this is, paints a pointillist portrait of the space of lifestyles in the black neighborhood of Winston Street, also in Washington, D.C., where he moved in for two years at the time of the black uprisings of the 1960s.[74] Hannerz emphasizes the cultural heterogeneity of the ghetto and distinguishes four orientations: the "mainstreamers" live a conventional existence oriented towards the established order, work, conjugality, property; the "swingers" are hedonistic young adults with no family responsibilities, mobile in residence and employment, for whom life is a long series of parties (and some of whom will join the ranks of respectable families as they grow older); "street families" are improvised households with shifting contours, whose children are involved in street culture and gangs; and the unattached "streetcorner men" including beggars, drunks, and assorted criminals in constant search of "getting a taste" and "a piece of pussy," who find refuge in this negative confraternity on the edge of everything.

---

[71] Liebow, *Tally's Corner*, p. 136.
[72] Liebow, *Tally's* Corner, pp. 138–139; W.E.B. Du Bois, *The Souls of Black Folk* ([1903] 1982), p. 4.
[73] Liebow, *Tally's Corner*, pp. 16 and 38.
[74] Ulf Hannerz, *Soulside: Inquiries into Ghetto Culture and Community* (1969). The book was reissued with a new preface in 2004 by the University of Chicago Press, attesting to the continuing interest in the triad of race, class, and culture in the city. Hannerz went on to become a professor at Stockholm University and one of the most influential anthropologists of his generation, pioneering "multi-sited" ethnography and publishing a dozen books, including Ulf Hannerz, *Exploring the City* (1980), and *Foreign News: Exploring the World of Foreign Correspondents* (2004).

Folk categories, used by the people observed, or analytical categories, forged by the observer? A mixture of both, since Hannerz elaborates this rather vague typology on the basis of the dichotomy invoked by the inhabitants between the "respectables" of the middle class and the "undesirables" ("bums," "good-for-nothings," "trash") of the proletariat, a division that we will find again in Anderson's ethnography, *Code of the Street*, in the form of the opposition between "decent" families and "street" families. Hannerz insists that many individuals circulate from one style to another and sometimes even participate in several of them at once, in a process he calls "lifestyle drift."[75] The "mainstreamers" are tacitly perceived by the others as holding the upper hand, even if they are readily mocked for putting on airs and accused of servility toward whites. And the project of social mobility and moral respectability in black society is always paid for by the abandonment of loved ones and peers who remain trapped in the ghetto.

The Swedish anthropologist elaborates on the traits of what he calls "ghetto-specific masculinity," including the public valorization of sexual exploits, physical toughness and the ability to command respect, personal pageantry, alcohol consumption, and verbal dexterity.[76] He confirms the fragility of marriages and outlines the public image of women as pillars of the community through their personal strength and moral fervor—while men are seen as weak, obsessed with sex, and unreliable: it is well said that "men, they've got a lot of dog in them" and "men and liquor were made for each other."[77] The absence of the man in the matrifocal family, socialization by the peer group on the street, verbal jousting with improvised obscene poems (known as "playing the dozens")[78] are all manifestations of the social marginality of the black man in the world of the ghetto.

The richest chapter from *Soulside* is the one Hannerz devotes to the specific institutions that unite Winston Street's inhabitants in everyday life: the illegal liquor trade run by "bootleggers" (whom the neighborhood supports and protects), the informal street lottery called the "numbers game" (which plays a central role in the local economy),[79] and everything to do with *soul*, that constellation of expressions, values and feelings, that unspeakable carnal property that would unite all "authentic" blacks with each other, whatever

---

[75] Hannerz, *Soulside*, pp. 61–65.
[76] Hannerz, *Soulside*, pp. 79–88. On oral skills and expressive styles in the ghetto, see Thomas Kochman's fine anthology (ed.), *Rappin' and Stylin' Out: Communication in Urban Black America* (1972).
[77] Hannerz, *Soulside*, p. 99.
[78] A must-read on this subject is Roger D. Abrahams' little masterpiece, *Deep Down in the Jungle: Negro Narrative Folklore from the Streets of Philadelphia* (1964).
[79] Proof is provided by Ivan Light, "Numbers Gambling among Blacks: A Financial Institution" (1977).

their class position and trajectory.[80] "Soul" is rooted in the culture of the agrarian South and in the experience of poverty and racial oppression, but it also expresses for this reason the refusal to be crushed by suffering. It is disseminated by the three flagship institutions of church, radio, and entertainment businesses, which form the "specific cultural apparatus of the ghetto." Its three central themes are "the struggle for solidarity, a bittersweet mood and impiety towards society." It is this impulse "to affirm an emergent community morality,"[81] as much as grievances against the white shopkeepers who run the ghetto stores and against the brutal, contemptuous police, and the feeling of political impotence fostered by distance from black organizations run by a haughty bourgeoisie, that explains the riot that shook Winston Street in the summer of 1968.

But instead of raising the question of the political tenor of the black revolt, Hannerz timidly retreats to the cultural theme. In the end, black Americans turn out to be "bicultural": "They feel mainstream power impinging on their lives, they see the ghetto through a mainstream screen and the mainstream through a ghetto screen."[82] It is here that Hannerz falters for lack of conceptual clarity, notably through (1) the use of the catch-all, presociological notion of "mainstream"; (2) the analytical confusion between what belongs to culture and what to social structure, and the correlative hesitancy between culture and subculture;[83] (3) ignorance of the forces outside the ghetto, which are only mentioned incidentally, even though Hannerz seems to abandon his culturalist argument at the end of the book when he states that he cannot envisage "the ghetto variety of the culture of poverty [being a] lasting obstacle to change" demanded by the civil rights movement and driven by public policies rolled out under the label of "War on Poverty."[84]

It is the ambition to contribute to these changes in the social and racial order that motivates Lee Rainwater's book *Behind Ghetto Walls: Black Family Life in a Federal Slum* (1970). The son of a historian who taught at a university in Mississippi, Rainwater earned his master's degree in sociology and then his doctorate in human development at the University of Chicago in 1954, before working for thirteen years at Social Research, Inc. (a research and consulting firm founded by anthropologists W. Lloyd Warner and Burleigh

---

[80] On this notion, see Lee Rainwater (ed.), *Soul: Black Experience* (1970); Monique Guillory and Richard C. Green (eds.), *Soul: Black Power, Politics, and Pleasure* (1998).
[81] Hannerz, *Soulside*, pp. 156–157 and p. 174.
[82] Hannerz, *Soulside*, p. 156 and 191.
[83] For a stimulating reflection on the culture-structure dyad in the ghetto, see William Julius Wilson, *More than Just Race: Being Black and Poor in the Inner City* (2009), and Wilson, "Why Both Social Structure and Culture Matter in a Holistic Analysis of Inner-City Poverty" (2010).
[84] Hannerz, *Soulside*, p. 195.

Gardner, for whom Goffman conducted a study of gas station employees). He was a professor at Washington University in St. Louis, Missouri, when he wrote *Behind Ghetto Walls*, whose success led to his move to Harvard University.[85] The book presents the results of a three-year multimethod field study conducted by a team of a dozen researchers, including eight ethnographers, in the Pruitt-Igoe housing project, combining observation, repeated interviews and quantitative surveys. With a population of ten thousand, one hundred percent black, Pruitt-Igoe was the country's most notorious public housing project, sporting astronomical rates of crime, poverty, school failure, broken families, welfare receipt, and out-of-wedlock births—in short, what Kenneth Clark calls "the tangle of pathology" supposedly typical of the ghetto.[86]

Rainwater sets the tone from the outset: "White cupidity creates structural conditions highly inimical to basic social adaptation," which blacks cope with by developing strategies "which result in suffering directly inflicted by Negroes on themselves and on others."[87] Enclosure within the "ghetto slum" (an explosive coupling that hides the hyperghetto, as I will explain later, see *infra*, pp. 30–33) led to the creation of an autonomous physical and social space in which African Americans developed a "subculture" and "a range of institutions to give structure to the task of living a victimized life and to minimize the pain it inevitably produces":[88] social networks anchored by the family unit and street buddies; forms of entertainment (music, dance, oral culture; the church; and the black liberation movement. It is these internal social and cultural forms of the ghetto that Rainwater seeks to decipher by alternating chapters presenting the portrait of an informant, composed of very long interview excerpts, with chapters dissecting these raw materials. The result is a data-rich but largely descriptive book that deals with culture and social relations in the ghetto—everyday life, family and marital relations and disruptions, parent-child relations, socialization in the adolescent peer group—before concluding with an in-depth examination of lower-class black identity.

Rainwater opens his book with a thunderous denunciation of white domination but, surprisingly, closes it on income inequality. In his view, it is material deprivation that creates the abyss between the aspiration to the

---

[85] Lee Rainwater, *Behind Ghetto Walls: Black Family Life in a Federal Slum* (1970). Rainwater went on to conduct numerous quantitative studies focusing on class inequality through income analysis, such as *What Money Buys: Inequality and the Social Meanings of Income* (1974), and, with Timothy M. Smeeding, *Poor Kids in a Rich Country: America's Children in Comparative Perspective* (2003).

[86] The idea, if not the expression, of "tangle of pathology," was later taken up by other black intellectuals such as William Julius Wilson and Orlando Patterson.

[87] Rainwater, *Behind Ghetto Walls*, p. 4. The same syllogism informs Philippe Bourgois's book *In Search of Respect* thirty years later.

[88] Rainwater, *Behind Ghetto Walls*, pp. 4 and 6.

"good life," made up of dreamed-of family and marital stability, producing "a style of life hardly distiguishable from other working-class life, white or black,"[89] and "real life" in the housing estate, marked by personal defiance, cynicism towards institutions and contempt for the other, the "war between the sexes," mutual exploitation and manipulation, bodily deterioration and psychic depression, and the cultivation of a "dramatic self" as "an identity to be achieved within the expressive style of life."[90] While Rainwater notes that "the two primary forces that create and maintain the lower-class Negro community are economic marginality and racial oppression,"[91] he never confronts the latter, and all of his public policy recommendations, radical as they may be, center on income redistribution.

Because they limit themselves to the relations internal to the remains of the "black city within the white," the studies by Liebow, Hannerz and Rainwater take for granted the caste structure of which the latter is but the historical materialization in space. Paradoxically, *the "invisible man" of the hyperghetto*, to borrow Ralph Ellison's famous expression, is not the black man but *the white man*, as if African Americans had relationships only among themselves. Yet the employer, the landlord, the shopkeeper, the teacher, the social worker, and the policeman are so many agents of white power who are still present on the ground—this presence is the legacy of the communal phase of ghettoization that is coming to a brutal end during that decade. The virulent daily relations with the police, in particular, would have merited some elaboration, given that it was incidents with the forces of order that, again and again, triggered the spectacular riots that shook American cities from coast to coast during these years.[92]

This omission stems from a lack of theoretical and historical framing, as a result of which our three authors *confuse the unit of observation with the unit of analysis*, falling into the traps of interactionism, inductivism, and presentism to which I shall return in the third chapter (*infra*, pp. 143–145, 146–148 and 161–163). This age of urban ethnography thus crystallizes a conceptual confusion that sealed the baneful identification of the black ghetto with a space of danger and disintegration in the American social and scientific imaginary—what Elijah Anderson would later call "the iconic ghetto."[93] This

---

[89] Rainwater, *Behind Ghetto Walls*, p. 50.
[90] Rainwater, *Behind Ghetto Walls*, p. 380.
[91] Rainwater, *Behind Ghetto Walls*, p. 370.
[92] Levy, *The Great Uprising*; Janet L. Abu-Lughod, *Race, Space, and Riots in Chicago, New York, and Los Angeles* (2007); Simon Balto, *Occupied Territory: Policing Black Chicago from Red Summer to Black Power* (2019).
[93] Elijah Anderson, *Black in White Space: The Enduring Impact of Color in Everyday Life* (2022), chapter 2.

identification was then to have a lasting impact on both sociological analyses, particularly field studies, and state policies targeting racialized poverty in the urban core. Understanding the difference between the "communal ghetto" and the "hyperghetto" is essential to understanding the trajectory of the nexus of race, class and space in the post-industrial city and, consequently, the trajectory of American urban ethnography, which takes us to the debate sparked by "Scrutinizing the Street."[94]

From the ghetto of industrial Fordism to the postindustrial hyperghetto

Researchers immersed in segregated African-American neighborhoods during the 1960s use indifferently the vague terms *slum*, *inner city* and *ghetto* to refer to their site of observation, simply because these are the terms used in everyday life and in public debate at the time (1). And this "ghetto" has clearly become the receptacle for all the ills that have long been associated with the city in the country's anti-urban tradition. Thus, in his 1965 book *Dark Ghetto*, Kenneth Clark describes Harlem as "a tangle of social pathologies": "Low aspirations, poor education, family instability, illegitimacy [of children born out of wedlock], unemployment, crime, drug addiction and alcoholism, frequent illness and early death" (2). As irrefutable proof that the ghetto is a concentrate of pathologies, it is exploding in the face of the country in the form of a wave of black uprisings that are shaking cities big and small from coast to coast (3).

In reality, this is a category error that *confuses the ghetto with what remains of it after it has collapsed* due to losing its function of economic extraction and fulfilling only its function of social ostracization of a dishonored population. In its accomplished form, the ghetto is a sociospatial mechanism of ethnic closure—ethnoreligious for the Jews of Renaissance Europe, ethnoracial for blacks in Fordist America—that presents two faces (4). On the one hand, it makes it possible to exploit a stigmatized group in the city while keeping it at a distance so as to prevent mixing as a gateway to intimacy: this is the *vertical* face of domination and denigration. On the other hand, by granting this group its own space, ghettoization gives rise to a "parallel city" (Jewish in the Christian city, black in the white city), a breeding ground for communal institutions that act as a protective shield against subordination: this is the *horizontal* face of solidarity and dignity.

In point of fact, the ghettoization of black Americans between 1917 and 1968 translated into collective economic enrichment; the transformation of a insecure

---

[94] Loïc Wacquant, "A Janus-Faced Institution of Ethnoracial Closure: A Sociological Specification of the Ghetto" (2012), pp. 23–24.

peasantry into a comparatively stable working class; the consolidation of a black bourgeoisie; the accumulation of social capital (with the birth of the major civil rights organizations such as the National Association for the Advancement of Colored People, NAACP, and the Urban League); the flowering of African-American cultural forms (jazz, blues, literature, painting); and the formation of an identity affirming collective pride ("black is beautiful"), *non obstante* inflexible white domination. This is the antithesis of the ghetto as a place of misery, disorganization and, let us say the word, savagery. Despite persistent poverty and unflinching racial subordination, Chicago's "Bronzeville" as described by Drake and Cayton in 1945 is a vibrant world, full of life and animated by collective hope (5).

During the 1960s, three forces combined to bring about the implosion of the communal ghetto: (i) deindustrialization rendered black unskilled labor redundant and destabilized the class structure; (ii) the "Great Migration" of millions of whites to the prosperous suburbs, aimed at recreating physical distance from urban blacks, undermined the fiscal base of large cities and diminished their electoral clout; (iii) the political mobilization of African Americans against racial confinement put an end to legal segregation and opened the doors to civic equality. As a result, the ghetto imploded, to be replaced by a *dual spatial structure* composed, on the one hand, of *segregated black middle-class districts* located in areas left vacant by the white exodus and, on the other, of what I christen the *hyperghetto*, the remnants of the communal ghetto in which the precarious fractions of the black working class find themselves trapped, condemned to an endless social purgatory (6).

The hyperghetto of the postindustrial era is thus distinguished from the communal ghetto associated with industrial Fordism by four properties: (i) it no longer plays an economic role as a labor pool due to the decline and departure of factories, resulting in astronomical levels of unemployment and poverty; (ii) it is doubly segregated by race and class, instead of containing the full range of black classes, as the bourgeoisie managed to migrate outside its historical perimeter to found its own neighborhoods (7); (iii) it has consequently lost its network of ethnic institutions weaving the fabric of everyday existence and serving as a protective shield against white domination; it is now state institutions of social control, notably disciplinary welfare (for women and children) and the neutralizing penal apparatus (for their husbands, fathers, brothers and sons), that constitute the organizational framework of daily life; (iv) it is afflicted by a triple stigma, linked not only to race and class, but also to place. Despite white domination, the "Bronzeville" of the Fordist era was a space of hope and collective pride, as expressed through jazz, blues, and black poetry, whereas the constellation that succeeded it is a reviled and perilous space, to which rap lends its raucous and rhythmic voice. The ghetto was a magnetic territory that attracted and fascinated; the hyperghetto is a repulsive neighborhood that scandalizes and horrifies (8).

Why does this analytical distinction between ghetto and hyperghetto matter? It calls into question the catastrophist and demonizing discourse swirling around the black precariat at the heart of the city. It reestablishes the bidimensionality of the ghetto as (white) weapon and (black) shield and, in so doing, restores the historicity of ethnoracial domination by underlining its malleability—whereas racialization consists precisely in the naturalization and eternalization of subordination (9). It reveals that the "social pathologies" described by the field studies of the 1960s, starting with the economic marginality of black men, are the product of deindustrialization amplified by segregation, and not of ghettoization. At the apogee of the "black city within the white city," African-American adults enjoyed very high employment rates as their labor force was indispensable to the factories of the metropolis. Finally, the distinction between ghetto and hyperghetto underlines the lack of conceptual clarity that too often blurs the work of urban ethnographers, and it points to the growing role of the state in the production and reproduction of marginality, a theme to which I will return in my discussion of the third age of urban ethnography in America. In short, it is *the death of the ghetto*, not its advent, that is transforming the racialized core of the dual metropolis of postindustrial capitalism into a territory of misery, violence, and despair.

It should be noted in passing that specifying the structure and functions of the American black ghetto clearly refutes the thesis of the ghettoization of working-class neighborhoods on the urban periphery of France, and more broadly of Europe (10). Two properties suffice to separate them radically: the ghetto is ethnically homogeneous (only blacks live there) and socially heterogeneous (it contains all black classes); the districts of relegation in France are ethnically heterogeneous (they contain several dozen ethnicities) and socially homogeneous (their inhabitants leave them as soon as they climb the class ladder).

1. Robert E. Forman's valiant attempt at clarification in *Black Ghettos, White Ghettos, and Slums* (1971), only adds to the confusion.
2. Kenneth Clark, *Dark Ghetto: Dilemmas of Social Power* (1964), p. 27.
3. Peter H. Rossi (ed.), *Ghetto Revolts* (1970). According to Peter B. Levy, *Race Riots in Urban America during the 1960s* (2018), during the decade opened by the 1963 Birmingham uprising, over 525 cities were rocked by more than 750 black riots.
4. Loïc Wacquant, *The Two Faces of the Ghetto* (forthcoming).
5. St. Clair Drake and Horace R. Cayton, *Black Metropolis: A Study of Negro Life in a Northern City* (1945, 1993), chapters 14, 15, 19 and 23; Christopher Robert Reed, *The Rise of Chicago's Black Metropolis, 1920–1929* (2011); Davarian L. Baldwin, *Chicago's New Negroes: Modernity, the Great Migration, and Black Urban Life* (2007), on Chicago. See also Joe William Trotter, *Black Milwaukee: The Making of an Industrial Proletariat, 1915–45*

(1985); Peter Gottlieb, *Making their Own Way: Southern Blacks' Migration to Pittsburgh, 1916-30* (1997); Kimberley Louise Phillips, *AlabamaNorth: African-American Migrants, Community, and Working-Class Activism in Cleveland, 1915–45* (1999).
6. Loïc Wacquant, "Revisiting Territories of Relegation: Class, Ethnicity and State in the Making of Advanced Marginality" (2016).
7. See Mary Pattillo's rich ethnography of the black bourgeoisie of fin-de-siècle Chicago, *Black Picket Fences: Privilege and Peril among the Black Middle Class* (1999).
8. On the logic and specific effects of territorial stigmatization in the post-industrial city, see Loïc Wacquant, *Bourdieu in the City: Challenging Urban Theory* (2023), chapter 2; on the ghetto as magnet, David L. Lewis, *When Harlem was in Vogue* (1981), and as a foil, Clark, *Dark Ghetto*, and Chicago Tribune, *The American Millstone: An Examination of the Nation's Permanent Underclass* (1986).
9. Loïc Wacquant, "Resolving the Trouble With 'Race'" (2022), pp.78-79, and Wacquant, *Racial Domination* (2024), pp. 86-91.
10. Loïc Wacquant, *Urban Outcasts: A Comparative Sociology of Advanced Marginality* (2008), chapters 5-7.

This flowering of ghetto ethnographies in the tow of the black civil rights movement was followed by a long drought of three decades marked by a brutal social and racial backlash.[95] From Nixon to Clinton to Bush Junior, the political field kept sliding to the right, and with it the public policy debate on poverty, which, far from diminishing as expected when the "War on Poverty" was launched in 1965, only worsened in the large, declining urban centers of the country hit hard by deindustrialization and the retrenchment of the social state. At the close of the 1960s, scholars interested in the relationship between race and class in the American city were further intimidated, on the one hand, by the vitriolic controversy unleashed by the infamous 1965 "Moynihan Report" on the black family and by the regressive political implications of Oscar Lewis's notion of "culture of poverty" and, on the other, by the rising censorship coming from the African American intelligentsia.

On the right flank, Daniel Patrick Moynihan, political scientist and Secretary of Labor in the Johnson administration, penned an internal document entitled *The Negro Family: The Case for National Action* which, even though it had not yet been published, set off a vitriolic controversy by suggesting that the matriarchal form of the black family was the cause of the economic woes

---

[95] This reactionary dynamic is traced by Michael W. Flamm, *Law and Order: Street Crime, Civil Unrest, and the Crisis of Liberalism in the 1960s* (2005); Rick Perlstein, *Nixonland: The Rise of a President and the Fracturing of America* (2008); and Thomas B. Edsall and Mary D. Edsall, *Chain Reaction: The Impact of Race, Rights, and Taxes on American Politics* (1992).

of African Americans and threatened to ruin the country's racial advances. The suggested remedy: a battery of measures aimed at restoring patriarchy in the black community.[96] Elaborated by the anthropologist Oscar Lewis based on his field studies of Mexican and Puerto Rican (sub)proletarian families, the notion of "culture of poverty" refers to a set of behavioral and cognitive traits, including "feelings of hopelessness and despair," born of "the impossibility of achieving success" in "a class-stratified, highly individualized and capitalistic society," which, through their learning in the family, tend to perpetuate poverty from one generation to the next.[97] It was the subject of lively controversy among anthropologists, particularly as regards its degree of autonomy, its causal capacity and its political implications. It was in reference to this notion that psychologist William Ryan coined the famous expression, "blaming the victim," and that is the last thing that social scientists concerned about the fate of the black ghetto would want to do.[98]

On the left flank, black activists within the academic field challenged, even denied, the ability and right of white scholars to conduct research on and in the African-American community. The collective book edited by black sociologist Joyce Ladner under the shock title *The Death of White Sociology* posited the imperative need to break with "white sociology," deemed "racist" and "empirical," to assert the pressing necessity and epistemic primacy of a "black sociology" made by blacks and for blacks.[99] The journal *The Black Scholar*, launched in 1969, affirmed the specificity of African American knowledge, values and aspirations. The creation of departments of "Black Studies" within the university materialized this assertion in the academic field and demarcated a reserved precinct which was also a minefield, and which (white) sociologists were therefore reluctant to tread.[100]

A few rare studies did attempt to pierce through the wall of silence, the most punchy of which are the anthropologist Carol B. Stack's slim book, *All Our Kin: Strategies for Survival in a Black Community* (1974), which unspools—and celebrates—the networks of mutual aid among black women

---

[96] I dissect this controversy and its political-intellectual effects in *The Invention of the "Underclass,"* pp. 37–40. The report and its implications are still hotly debated half a century later: James T. Patterson, *Freedom Is Not Enough: The Moynihan Report and America's Struggle over Black Family Life—From LBJ to Obama* (2010).

[97] Oscar Lewis, "The Culture of Poverty" (1966), p. 21. The two books which develop the notion are *The Children of Sanchez: Autobiography of a Mexican Family* (1961), and *La Vida: A Puerto Rican family in the Culture of Poverty* (1966).

[98] Hyman Rodman, "Culture of Poverty: The Rise and Fall of a Concept" (1977).

[99] Joyce A. Ladner (ed.). *The Death of White Sociology: Essays on Race and Culture* (1973). The same argument, barely dusted off, can be found almost half-a-century later in the work of Tukufu Zuberi and Eduardo Bonilla-Silva (eds.), *White Logic, White Methods: Racism and Methodology* (2008).

[100] Fabio Rojas, *From Black Power to Black Studies: How a Radical Social Movement Became an Academic Discipline* (2010).

that keep the "ghetto" afloat, and Jay McLeod's rich comparative study of the social strategies and aspirations of black and white teenagers in the same low-income estate of a working-class suburb of Boston, *Ain't No Makin' It* (1987), which enjoyed exceptional success and longevity when its author augmented it with successive revisits of his research subjects over two decades.[101] Not to forget anthropologist Philippe Bourgois's epic monograph *In Search of Respect* (1995), on the crack trade in the Hispanic district of East Harlem, which brings to light the material and symbolic logics governing criminal careers in the street economy.[102] But it was not until the start of the new millennium that the third age of American urban ethnography dawned.

Before turning to the era of "Scrutinizing," let me draw some lessons from this analytical overview of the academic and intellectual trajectory of American urban ethnography in the twentieth century. Six of them stand out. Firstly, from the outset and ever since, this sociology has focused on "problem populations" in the city—in other words, groups prefabricated by common sense, salient in symbolic space, and targets of public and private poverty policy. As a result, it studies almost exclusively lowly categories and, in so doing, indirectly contributes to making invisible the city of the rich and powerful.[103] In this regard, it merely extends, rather than questions, the long anti-urban, miserabilist tradition of American social science from its origins. The very beginnings of sociology, even before the Chicago School, were closely linked to the project of establishing new forms of social control over urban categories considered dissolute. For Jane Adams, apostle of the "settlement movement," Edward Ross, and Charles Horton Cooley, it was urgent to improve working-class neighborhoods through schools, parks, the arts, and municipal ceremonies in order to combat vice and foster a new morality adapted to the conditions of the metropolis.[104]

Second, this research lineage is based on the presumption of a close link between territory and social relations, territory and culture, territory and morality, but it fails to specify the exact nature of this link: is it causal, functional, or symbiotic? What is more, it uses vague and spongy terms to designate the sociospatial constellations in which the populations studied are embedded. Proof of this is the repeated use, one half-century apart, of the

---

[101] Carol B. Stack, *All Our Kin: Strategies for Survival in a Black Community* (1974, 1983, 1997); Jay MacLeod, *Ain't No Makin' It: Aspirations and Attainment in a Low-Income Neighborhood* (1987, 1995, 2011, 2018).

[102] Philippe Bourgois, *In Search of Respect: Selling Crack in El Barrio* (1995, 2003).

[103] This is a bias of American urban sociology more generally, as I show in *Bourdieu in the City*, pp. 44–46. In his panorama of the studies of the early Chicago School, Hannerz notes that they focus on "the poor, foreigners and disreputable categories" (Ulf Hannerz, *Exploring the City* [1980], p. 45).

[104] Boyer, *Urban Masses and Moral Order in America, 1820–1920*, pp. 224–232.

term *slum*, a true-false concept that confuses not only inhabitant and habitat (it more or less covers the notions of low-income neighborhood, insalubrious district, and shantytown), but also the (white) *ethnic cluster*, the product of choice and cultural affinity, providing a "bridge" toward social and spatial integration in the city, and the (black) *ghetto*, resulting from coercion and racial hostility, a veritable "wall" that permanently locks African Americans into a world of their own.[105] We shall see that the euphemism *inner city* plays a similar role in turn-of-the-century works: it scrambles the nature of the linkages between race, class and space and, in so doing, evacuates the power relations and struggles in the city of which the formation, maturation, and implosion of the ghetto are the product.[106]

In the third place, with precious few exceptions, such as Carol Brooks' *Passing By* on sexual harassment in the street,[107] American monographs of urban ethnography tend to focus on the world of *men*, the world of *young men*, the *public* world of young men, to the detriment of the world of women, of established adults and of social and symbolic relations in the domestic universe and intimate sphere.[108] And, in the wake of the urban uprisings of the 1960s, on young *black* men in the street, where they are perceived as a latent or patent physical threat and, consequently, the object of a veritable "Orientalism" in which urban ethnography participates unwillingly (or willingly: the 900-page anthology edited by Duneier, Kasinitz, and Murphy, *The Urban Ethnography Reader*, includes no fewer than twenty-seven chapters out of fifty-two devoted to black men in the "inner city"![109] When black women appear on the scene, they are often divided between two stereotypical roles: the devoted, even heroic mother or grandmother who strives, against all odds, to keep her family afloat, and the teenage girl with a precocious and uncontrolled sexuality—two characters that we shall encounter later in Elijah Anderson's *Code of the Street*.[110]

---

[105] On the distinction between ghetto and ethnic cluster, see Loïc Wacquant, "Designing Urban Seclusion in the 21st Century: The 2009 Roth-Symonds Lecture" (2010). For a devastating critique of the notion of slum, see Alan Gilbert, "The Return of the Slum: Does Language Matter?" (2007).

[106] Wacquant, *Bourdieu in the City*, pp. 8–9, 67–69, 128–129, 150–151, 166–169.

[107] Carol Brooks Gardner, *Passing By: Gender and Public Harassment* (1995). In fact, there are several studies of black ghetto women from the 1960s, including monographs by Camille Jeffers (*Living Poor*, 1967) and Joyce Ladner (*Tomorrow's Tomorrow*, 1971), and, later, Carol Stack (*All Our Kin*, 1974) and Eleanor Miller (*Street Woman*, 1987). But they are generally overlooked in discussions of race and class in the inner city that are marked by a stubborn androcentric bias (my work included).

[108] In the ethnography of the United States, there is no book comparable to Olivier Schwartz's *Le Monde privé des ouvriers. Hommes et femmes du Nord* (1990).

[109] Mitchell Duneier, Philip Kasinitz, and Alexandra Murphy (eds.), *The Urban Ethnography Reader* (2014). Note also that this tome does not contain a single chapter on the spaces and institutions of the dominant class and a single chapter on a field site outside the United States.

[110] This second stereotype is dismantled by Mary Patrice Erdmans and Timothy Black, *On Becoming a Teen Mom: Life Before Pregnancy* (2015).

Fourth lesson: the ethnographies of these two ages of urban field research focus on the microsociological dynamics of local "scenes," in the double sense of trestles and parts in a theater play.[111] They describe interactional systems at ground level or contained within a singular institution, without making the effort to embed them in the macrostructural relationships that encompass and determine them. Particularly absent from their accounts are the role of capital through the market and the weight of the state in both the production and the management of poverty. Thus, in typical fashion, Hannerz describes the ghetto "community" as "a multitude of personal networks connecting relatives, peers and neighbors" within black Washington itself,[112] but he does not bother to situate these networks within the structural and functional machinery that constitutes the metropolis, of which the ghetto is (or was) just one cog. At no point does he refer to the ghetto's dual function of economic extraction and social ostracization, and to the loss of the former that determines the recent marginalization of black men. This *interactionist*, even *anti-structuralist bias* is a generic problem of urban ethnography, to which I shall return in my discussion of the fallacies of "ethnographism," the ruinous tendency to circumscribe the sociological object to the immediate perimeter of the site of observation (see *infra*, pp. 142ff).

A fifth lesson pertains to the weakness of the theoretical mooring. In its infancy, urban ethnography was openly empiricist and unencumbered by theoretical considerations, even though William Isaac Thomas, one of the Chicago masters, had proposed an original catalog of the social agent's "four wishes" in relation to psychoanalysis: the search for novelty, the desire for recognition, the concern for mastery, and the quest for security.[113] At this stage, the amorphous notions of "milieu" and "natural area" (each with its associated "moral region"), borrowed by Robert Park from the plant and animal ecology of his time, take the place of a concept of structure.[114]

During its second age, urban ethnography borrowed its conception of action primarily from the symbolic interactionism of George Herbert Mead and Herbert Blumer and, like this intellectual current, adopted a realist notion of structure as a system of directly observable social relations emerging from face-to-face relationships.[115] Field observation was thus coupled with

---

[111] On the notion of "scene" as a "configuration of well-known types of behavior by a group of actors," see John Irwin, "Surfing: The Natural History of an Urban Scene" (1973).
[112] Hannerz, *Soulside*, p. 34.
[113] Corey J. Colyer, "W.I. Thomas and the Forgotten Four Wishes: A Case Study in the Sociology of Ideas" (2015).
[114] Robert E. Park, "Sociology and the Social Sciences: The Social Organism and the Collective Mind" (1921).
[115] Blumer, *Symbolic Interaction*; David R. Maines, "Social Organization and Social Structure in Symbolic Interactionist Thought" (1977). And this notion of structure itself turns out to still be too "hard" and

a weakly formalized and articulated theory, close to the ordinary common sense of the national middle class, which is always "performing" on the stage of status struggles. The result is that, in the American sociological field as it organized itself across the decades of the last century, ethnography and theory are perceived as radically opposed poles, the one on the side of the "real," sensate, concrete, and fleeting, the other on the side of the "spiritual," textual and abstract. In the United States, if you "do" theory, you cannot "do" ethnography, and vice versa.[116] Otherwise you violate the epistemological unconscious of the discipline and openly insult the *decorum* of the profession.

Finally, and this is perhaps what distinguishes it most strongly from fieldwork carried out in Europe and Latin America, the American ethnography of the city is veritably obsessed with the question of the morality of the poor, and particularly the racialized poor, and with the relationship between their supposed "codes" and the standards of "mainstream" society—read, of the white middle-class.[117] This obsession is undoubtedly a heritage deeply rooted in the religious origins of American sociology and stamped by the influence of the militant Protestantism of its founders, who were convinced that "a positivist technocratic elite could improve society by helping to bring about a good life for the *deserving* while controlling the *undeserving*."[118] Mingled with Puritanism, this monomania is at the root of a drift from the *sociology of morality*—a subject that is not only legitimate but essential, as Durkheim suggested over a century ago[119]—to the *moralism of the sociologist*. Moralism, in this case, consists in making moral judgements about one's object of research instead of reporting that the subjects observed make moral judgements, and specifying which ones, and nourishes the ambition to invert the moral valence of the population studied in public perception by "rehabilitating" it.

This tendency towards moralism is accentuated, in the case of the study of the ghetto and its remnants—that is, the institution entrusted with containing a doubly marginalized and stigmatized population according to race and

---

reified for the taste of ethnomethodologists: Douglas W. Maynard and Steven E. Clayman, "The Diversity of Ethnomethodology" (1991).

[116] Yet this is exactly what ethnomethodologist David Sudnow attempts and succeeds in doing in his autoethnography of jazz piano improvization, *Ways of the Hand: The Organization of Improvised Conduct* (1978).

[117] Faith Deckard and Javier Auyero show that this concern is absent from the relevant Latin American field research on "Poor People's Survival Strategies: Two Decades of Research in the Americas" (2022).

[118] Cecil E. Greek, *The Religious Roots of American Sociology* (1992), p. 214. For a perceptive analysis of the origins and endurance of the "moral temptation" in social science, see Alan Hunt, "From Moral Science to Moral Regulation: Social Theory's Encounter with the Moral Domain" (2003).

[119] Émile Durkheim, *L'Éducation morale* (1925). For two rich sociological studies of morality in action, see Michèle Lamont, *The Dignity of Working Men: Morality and the Boundaries of Race, Class and Immigration* (2000), and Andrew Sayer, *The Moral Significance of Class* (2005).

class—by the fundamentally differentialist and exotic vision of African Americans that endured throughout the twentieth century, and which explains the incapacity of the national social science to anticipate, and thence understand, the upsurge of black revolts against caste domination, such as the civil rights movement yesterday and Black Lives Matter today.[120]

Renaissance and the discovery of the state of misery

The third age of American urban ethnography opens with the controversy surrounding "Scrutinizing the Street." Indeed, this timing partly explains the virulence of the reaction to this text, for the supporters of the Chicago School, led by Howard Becker, feared that the article would put a brake on their newfound momentum by denting its methodological foundation and professional status. For good reason: in the decade that followed, the most influential field monographs on the diptych of race and class in the city were not part of this stream.

These studies include Martín Sánchez-Jankowski' comparative ethnography of the key institutions in dispossessed and segregated urban districts, the corner grocery store, public housing project, barbershop, gang and the local high school, informed by rational action theory, *Cracks in the Pavement* (2008);[121] Timothy Black's long-term investigation, *When a Heart Turns Rock Solid* (2009), about the tribulations of three Puerto Rican brothers caught between the streets, the prison and precarious wage work, which draws on C.-Wright Mills;[122] Philippe Bourgois, and Jeffrey Schonberg's photoethnography of the daily survival strategies and social relations among white and black homeless heroin addicts on the streets of San Francisco, *Righteous Dopefiend* (2009), which mobilizes Bourdieu and Foucault;[123] Mary Pattillo's chronicle of the battle between bourgeoisie and precariat in an African-American neighborhood of Chicago in the midst of "black gentrification" in *Black on the Block* (2010), which leans on the works of Max Weber, E. Franklin Frazier and William Julius Wilson;[124] and the deep dive into the world of Dominican brigands in the declining crack economy of the Bronx alongside Randol Contreras in *The Stickup Kids* (2012), which finds its

---

[120] James B. McKee, *Sociology and the Race Problem: The Failure of a Perspective* (1993); Keeanga-Yamahtta Taylor, *From #BlackLivesMatter to Black Liberation* (2021).
[121] Martín Sánchez-Jankowski, *Cracks in the Pavement: Social Change and Resilience in Poor Neighborhoods* (2008).
[122] Timothy Black, *When a Heart Turns Rock Solid: The Lives of Three Puerto Rican Brothers on and off the Streets* (2009).
[123] Philippe Bourgois and Jeffrey Schonberg, *Righteous Dopefiend* (2009).
[124] Mary Pattillo, *Black on the Block: The Politics of Race and Class in the City* (2010).

conceptual instruments in Robert Merton, Jack Katz, and Randall Collins.[125] What characterizes these five studies, aside from their empirical intrepidity and their deep social and temporal embeddedness, is their implacable refusal of moralism and their tenacious desire to fuse theory and field data.

By emancipating itself from the tutelage of moral empiricism à la Chicago, urban ethnography in the twenty-first century has given itself new ways of constructing the nexus of race and class in the city, and the means to focus on the role of an institution that is decisive in determining the life chances of the poor, in the United States no less than in European countries, namely, public authority—I use this evocative word on purpose.[126] That institution was conspicuous by its absence in the studies of the first two eras of urban ethnography and, as we shall see, it is still invisible in the three monographs dissected in chapter 2. In recent years, three domains have been the subject of remarkable ethnographies that converge to highlight *the multifaceted role of the state in the production and reproduction of urban marginality*: welfare, housing, and the crime-and-punishment duo.

The first domain covers the implementation of the *disciplinary social policy* initiated at the close of the century, which hit hardest at the women of color from the precariat and their children living in the hyperghetto. In *Flat Broke with Children* (2003), Sharon Hays draws on three years of observation in two public aid offices to trace the bureaucratic obstacle course that recipients of new-formula welfare must complete in an attempt to restore wage work and the nuclear family.[127] She shows how these two imperatives of the new assistancial legislation collide in practice, as deskilled and insecure jobs make any marital plans unlikely. Hays rejects both the miserabilist and the populist visions of public aid recipients and she breaks out of the interactional perimeter to point to the social function of welfare reform: to render poverty invisible and to elevate precarious employment to the rank of obligation of citizenship for the most dispossessed. Black misery in America—both literally and figuratively—is first and foremost a matter of state.

Celeste Watkins-Hayes takes us to the other side of the welfare counter in *The New Welfare Bureaucrats* (2009), a study of the frontline employees responsible for the day-to-day implementation of workfare policy.[128] The latter adopt three competing identities: social worker (personally invested in their "clients"), efficiency engineer (focused on the mechanical processing of

---

[125] Randol Contreras, *The Stickup Kids: Race, Drugs, Violence, and the American Dream* (2013).
[126] Loïc Wacquant, *Urban Outcasts: A Comparative Sociology of Urban Marginality* (2008), pp. 267–70 and 274–279.
[127] Sharon Hays, *Flat Broke with Children: Women in the Age of Welfare Reform* (2003).
[128] Celeste Watkins-Hayes, *The New Welfare Bureaucrats: Entanglements of Race, Class, and Policy Reform* (2009).

files), or survivalist (seeking only to stay afloat amidst the new occupational obligations), depending on their ethnic identity, gender, and childhood experiences. The ethnoracial divide runs through the bureaucratic field at ground level, placing black and Hispanic female employees in an ambiguous, even painful predicament: most of them come from poor families and so they know from experience the weight of discrimination suffered by racialized recipients; but they believe in the goals of the new-style welfare system, and so they take on the mission of "placing" recipients from their own group in degraded jobs out of ethnic solidarity.

In *Trapped in a Maze* (2022), Leslie Paik refocuses the sociology of the state management of poverty by adopting the point of view of families relying on public services and aid for the poor. Based on a six-year study of sixty-three New York households of color, she unravels the tangle of contradictory rules and obligations imposed by the dozen institutions that, at any given time, jointly govern the lives of the urban precariat: the school, the hospital and psychiatric services, medical aid and welfare, public housing, drug rehabilitation programs, the justice system, child protective services, immigration services, and so on. She discovers that the "multi-institutional maze" in which impoverished families are caught has neither a clear entrance nor a marked exit route, and that the dictates and whims of these agencies combine to impose exorbitant social, financial, emotional, and temporal costs. What emerges from this bureaucratic cacophony is that "despite attempts at reform to streamline services or increase surveillance of the poor in order to punish them, families move in and out of the maze in ways that no one can predict or control."[129] The lack of formal rationality is compounded by a lack of substantive rationality: far from supporting the poor, the maze keeps them in a state of instability and dependency.

The second theme of the new urban ethnography concerns *precarious housing* as a fundamental dimension of social insecurity, a subject long neglected or left solely to students of homeless populations.[130] In *Evicted*, Matthew Desmond follows three white families in a trailer park then five black families and their children in Milwaukee for twenty months, to uncover the economic mechanisms, legal means, and social consequences of evictions.[131] Backed by a quantitative survey revealing that eviction in that city strikes one in eight

---

[129] Leslie Paik, *Trapped in a Maze: How Social Control Institutions Drive Family Poverty and Inequality* (2022), p. 18.
[130] Rigorous monographs on this issue include David A. Snow and Leon Anderson, *Down on their Luck: A Study of Homeless Street People* (1993); Teresa Gowan, *Hobos, Hustlers, and Backsliders: Homeless in San Francisco* (2010); and Forrest Stuart, *Down, Out, and Under Arrest: Policing and Everyday Life in Skid Row* (2016).
[131] Matthew Desmond, *Evicted: Poverty and Profit in the American City* (2016).

renter households every two years and one in five black women during their lifetime, and that the latter pay up to 80% of their monthly income in rent, Desmond meticulously reconstructs the residential trajectories of his interviewees. He discloses how, by periodically losing their housing, they lose their meager possessions, their access to welfare benefits, their jobs when they have one, their children's schools and even custody over their children, their brittle social ties, their sense of orientation in society and even their mental health. What is more, a single eviction can be enough to bar them from all accommodation, as housing court keeps a register of evictees, which landlords consult before renting out.

Residential tenancy being an economic and legal relationship, Desmond follows two "slum" landlords to understand how they navigate strained relationships with their tenants and activate various extraction mechanisms with the support of the court.[132] But, in doing so, he acknowledges the setbacks and risks faced by small inner-city landlords, often black, who must manage bounced checks and vandalized apartments, tenants addicted to alcohol and drugs, violence, neighborhood disturbances, unauthorized occupants, and the cost of legal proceedings. Two strong theses emerge: housing is a site of exploitation in the hyperghetto and eviction is not only a consequence but also a cause of persistent poverty. Worse still, "mass eviction" is to poor black women what "mass incarceration" is to their men: the institution that keeps them in intense, dead-end urban marginality as the state refuses to regulate the bottom end of the housing market, let alone make housing a public good.

In *Exiled in America*, Christopher Dum takes the reader into the heart of one of those cheap motels where the "social refugees" of the American city languish in rooms rented by the week. He spent a year at the Boardwalk Motel, studying the residents' forms of sociability, survival strategies, and stigma-management tactics. Prisoners on parole; ex-sex offenders banned from residing elsewhere in the city; drug addicts and fragile families placed there by social services; homeless, crippled or mentally afflicted people brought there by the police; and the working poor: such is the clientele of these dilapidated, ill-famed establishments, which serve to "clean up urban public space by sweeping off the streets categories deemed unsightly and undesirable."[133] Having thus compacted the social refuse of market society,

---

[132] This research design is in line with the principle of "relational ethnography" which invites the researcher to explore the social relationship under study from both of its ends: Matthew Desmond, "Relational Ethnography" (2014).

[133] Christopher P. Dum, *Exiled in America: Life on the Margins in a Residential Motel* (2016), p. 10.

the state leaves a gaping organizational void that is filled by the fragile networks of mutual aid developed by residents despite the taint that envelops them.[134] Far from embellishing the "community" they form, Dum pays as much attention to moments of solidarity and compassion as to the conflicts and exploitative relationships between residents.

Housing insecurity in America is not an accident, but the product of the meeting between a public policy of radical commodification of housing for the destitute and a predatory real estate industry that thrives on their misery. Nothing reveals this better than the "trailer parks," mobile housing developments where residents own their homes but rent their location, from which they can be evicted at any moment.[135] This state-sanctioned legal arrangement means that they live permanently under the "spectre of deportation," either individual or collective, when the park closes to reclaim the land for more profitable uses.

This is demonstrated by Esther Sullivan in *Manufactured Insecurity*, an ethnography of mobile home parks in Florida and Texas based on two years of fieldwork in two of these parks before and during their eviction.[136] It finds that residents are proud of their homes, which they have improved over the years, and attached to their park and their neighbors, despite the stigma they bear.[137] The collective trauma felt during evictions is all the greater, not to mention the fact that residents then discover that, contrary to their expectations, their homes are not transportable and that by migrating they lose their only tangible asset. The steady decline in the low-cost housing stock of the country has made mobile home parks a lucrative sector of the real estate industry, enriching the financial investors who own them and the local governments who regulate them. So much to say that one cannot understand the poverty of housing for the destitute without taking into account the struggles at the intersection of the economic, bureaucratic, and juridical fields.

---

[134] City inspectors charged with enforcing the "housing code" could easily close these establishments for multiple violations. But, perversely, it is in the city's interest to keep them running, otherwise it would not know where to rehouse their residents. On the ambiguous role of these agents at the interface of landlords, tenants, and the local state, see Robin Bartram's ethnography, *Stacked Decks: Building Inspectors and the Reproduction of Urban Inequality* (2022).

[135] The other public policy that artificially supports the most degraded sector of the housing market is the federal housing "voucher" scheme, which gives the poorest households access to private-sector rentals. Far from reducing poverty, this scheme concentrates it spatially, as shown by Eva Rosen's ethnography *The Voucher Promise: "Section 8" and the Fate of an American Neighborhood* (2020).

[136] Esther Sullivan, *Manufactured Insecurity: Mobile Home Parks and Americans' Tenuous Right to Place* (2018). With 18 million residents nationwide, these parks are the leading private housing sector for low-income families.

[137] A particularly biting class slur, "trailer trash," refers to the residents of these parks, generally perceived as white people stricken with social and moral indigence ("white trash").

44 The Poverty of the Ethnography of Poverty

Finally, excellent recent fieldwork explores the interface between *race, class, and the penal state*, from everyday police surveillance, violence, and control; to the socially and ethnically differentiated and differentiating workings of the courts; to incarceration and its long-term consequences.[138] The exponential growth of incarceration over the past half-century—it ballooned from 380,000 in 1973 to over 2.3 million inmates in 2008—has revealed that the jail and prison are urban institutions par excellence, focused as they are on the punitive management of precarious and stigmatized populations, the one nestled in the heart of the city and the other functioning in the manner of a satellite for the containment of the city's rabble.[139]

A former gang member who miraculously escaped the fate of his peers—addiction, prison or early death—Victor Rios shadowed a group of black and Latino teenagers from East Oakland, his childhood neighborhood, for three years, to sketch the contours of their abrasive contacts and conflictual relationships with penal institutions.[140] According to his book *Punished*, the "hyper-criminalization" of teenagers of color in the vestiges of the ghetto translates into the deep penetration of family, school, stores, and street by police and probation officers. In reaction to the suffocating omnipresence of agents of the penal state, these adolescents adopt oppositional identities and develop an aggressive form of "hypermasculinity" that puts them askew on the job market, fuels domestic violence, and sinks them deeper into crime as a paradoxical vehicle for local dignity and agency.[141] As for the youths who take the "legit" path, they face a double indictment: on the one hand, they are reviled by their peers for wanting to "act white" and suspected in the neighborhood of being "snitches"; on the other, they are treated as criminals by the police and the justice system, even when they are not involved in delinquency. All in all, Rios shows that, far from "abandoning the poor," the state has become deeply embedded in their neighborhoods and lives through its penal arm, with profoundly noxious human and civic consequences.[142]

---

[138] For a comprehensive overview of this work, read Victor M. Rios, Nikita Carney, and Jasmine Kelekay, "Ethnographies of Race, Crime, and Justice: Toward a Sociological Double-Consciousness" (2017).

[139] Wacquant, "The Jail as Core Urban Institution," in *Bourdieu in the City*, pp. 137–143.

[140] Victor M. Rios, *Punished: Policing the Lives of Black and Latino Boys* (2011). The unlikely trajectory of its author is retraced in Victor M. Rios, *Street Life: Poverty, Gangs, and a Ph.D* (2011).

[141] On the fusion between the racialized identities of the street and the penitentiary, see Patrick Lopez-Aguado, *Stick Together and Come Back Home: Racial Sorting and the Spillover of Carceral Identity* (2018); on the long-term social fallout of prison time, read Reuben Miller's subtle *Halfway Home: The Afterlives of Mass Incarceration* (2021).

[142] Another ethnography demonstrates the harmfulness of so-called "therapeutic" policing of the homeless in Los Angeles is Forrest Stuart, *Down, Out, and Under Arrest*. See also Stuart's *Ballad of the Bullet: Gangs, Drill Music, and the Power of Online Infamy* (2020), which depicts the counterinteruitive ways in which gang members deepen their embroilment with police and prosecutors.

In *Misdemeanorland* (2018), the sociologist, legal scholar and criminal lawyer Issa Kohler-Hausmann deconstructs the workings of New York's misdemeanor criminal court based on three years of participant observation and case-flow analysis.[143] To float the uncontrollable flood of defendants generated by zero-tolerance policing, the court has abandoned the "adjudicative model," which aims to determine guilt as basis for sentencing, in favor of a "managerial model." The latter puts defendants under administrative surveillance for months on end and subjects them to three operations: "marking" (via publicly accessible judicial databases), "procedural hassle" (multiplying hearings and stretching judicial processing), and "performance," (the imposition of steps attesting to individual responsibility and "governability"), even though more than half the cases will result in a dismissal. Misdemeanor justice therefore does not lead to incarceration or even community sanctions; it merely imposes bureaucratic guardianship and the associated costs to defendants (in terms of time, money and dignity).[144] It follows that the study of the penal state must be refocused from the prison to the courtroom.

Similarly, over the course of a year, the overwhelming majority of people deprived of their liberty in America, 80% of whom are indigent, are not put in prison after conviction but locked up in jails, either awaiting the adjudication of their cases or serving jail sentences of less than a year for minor offenses.[145] Such is the case of African American sociologist Michael Walker, whose *Indefinite* (2022) is an astonishing "organic ethnography" of the jail, based on a six-month stint spent serving a sentence for repeat traffic violations while he was a doctoral student.[146] Walker recollects in painstaking detail the stages of induction into the carceral microcosm and its rules of operation: the system of classification and stratification of the population by the correctional administration and the sharing of authority between guards and "shot-callers," inmates who are informal "representatives" of the various sectors of the establishment; the racial division into three categories (blacks, Latinos and whites) that permeates all activities, regulates communication, divides space and both stirs up and channels violence; and the dynamic interface between the jail and the court.

---

[143] Issa Kohler-Hausmann, *Misdemeanorland: Criminal Courts and Social Control in an Age of Broken Windows Policing* (2018).

[144] In this regard, *Misdemeanorland* updates Malcolm Feeley's classic study, *The Process is the Punishment: Handling Cases in a Lower Criminal Court* (1979), for the age of hyperincarceration. For a complementary approach from the defendants' side, read Matthew Clair, *Privilege and Punishment: How Race and Class Matter in Criminal Court* (2020).

[145] Every year, some 800,000 people enter prison in the United States to serve an average sentence of 2.4 years, compared with 10 million in prison for an average of 26 days.

[146] Michael L. Walker, *Indefinite: Doing Time in Jail* (2022). Walker complements and updates John Irwin's model ethnography, *The Jail: Managing the Underclass* (1980).

Walker unpacks what the detainees call "*jailing*," "the set of strategies used to manage the psychic, biological and emotional realities of incarceration"[147] and the phenomenology of time wasted, forced and endured, which erodes all identities other than that of criminal and isolates each inmate despite all efforts to create collective timetables. In the end, daily life is dominated by hunger, cold, boredom, cruel sleep deprivation, and the constant chaos that contrasts with the stable regimentation of the penitentiary—a defendant compares doing time in prison to "working as a civil servant" and in the jail to "working at McDonald's." We can see here how the penal state perpetuates the individual disorganization and social suffering it claims to curb.

These three faces of state urban poverty—disciplinary welfare, precarious housing and penal intrusion, but also economic abandonment, urban disengagement, and the dereliction of child welfare—are interwoven in Patricia Fernández-Kelly's powerful book, *The Hero's Fight*, a decade-long historical ethnography of life trajectories in Baltimore's hyperghetto conducted over a decade among sixty families totaling 263 members, including five children for whom the author became a "godmother."[148] Pointing to the extraordinary density and overlap of public institutions charged with managing problem populations, Fernández-Kelly places the state at the heart of her analytical and empirical framework. She develops the concept of "distorted engagement" to characterize the relationship between the Leviathan and the racialized poor in the postindustrial city. This relationship is "characterized by suspicion, surveillance, containment and penalization."[149]

Through meticulous, poignant and edifying sociological biographies, we discover how public bureaucracies treat the inhabitants of West Baltimore, not as citizens or consumers, but as burdens and parasites, "deceitful and undeserving," requiring panoptic and coercive actions aimed at modifying their behavior, even their dispositions.[150] These actions take the form of "palliative measures" (for market failures), "intensive regulation" (which erodes individual autonomy and provokes confrontation and subversion), and the use of official violence (the most brutal expression of which is

---

[147] Walker, *Indefinite*, p. 147.
[148] Patricia Fernández-Kelly, *The Hero's Fight: African Americans in West Baltimore and the Shadow of the State* (2014), pp. 6–10 and 357–359.
[149] Fernández-Kelly, *The Hero's Fight*, p. 2. In a similar vein on another continent, read Javier Auyero, *Patients of the State: The Politics of Waiting in Argentina* (2012).
[150] On the emergence of a similar logic in France with the implementation of neoliberal measures to combat "*assistanat*," see Vincent Dubois, *Contrôler les assistés. Genèses et usages d'un mot d'ordre* (2021).

incarceration).[151] By marrying sociological theory and social history, conceptual rigor and empirical richness, biography and observation, narrative and analysis, *The Hero's Fight* points the way to a *structural and historicized ethnography,* for which I will advocate in the third chapter of the book.

Today, fortunately, sociological urban ethnography in the United States has been "provincialized" by a triple development: (1) the flowering of field research in many other topical domains; (2) the deployment of participant observation across disciplines; (3) the internationalization of ethnographic practice. Domains: the city and its problem populations are no longer a privileged object of research, which now targets the most diverse themes: organizations and science, finance and the police, elites and the global South, work and immigration, schools and the economy, politics and social movements, law and sexuality, health and the digital world, and so on.

Disciplines: fieldwork is practised by all the social sciences and beyond, including geography, ethnic and gender studies, public policy, management, communication, design, architecture, medicine, and so on. Even a discipline as dominated by rational choice theory and quantitative modelling as American political science has made room for ethnographic practice and analysis, and its prestigious journals have recently opened up to work of this kind.[152] Similarly, business schools have become welcoming to organizational ethnography, whose works regularly appear in top-ranked journals such as *Administrative Science Quarterly, Academy of Management Journal* and *Organization Studies*—indeed, these articles top the hit-parade of most-read texts. Ethnographers in this field even launched the *Journal of Organizational Ethnography* in 2012.

Internationally: fieldwork has developed in many European countries (see, for example, the Italian journal *Etnografia e ricerca qualitativa* and work on immigration, crime, and penality in Scandinavian countries) and in Latin America.[153] The transdisciplinary journal *Ethnography*, which I founded with Paul Willis and Mats Trondman back in 2000 with the aim of building a bridge between sociological and anthropological fieldworkers, has been based in the Netherlands for the past decade. The international anthropology outlet *HAU:*

---

[151] Fernández-Kelly, *The Hero's Fight*, pp. 116 and 118–128.
[152] Lisa Wedeen, "Reflections on Ethnographic Work in Political Science" (2010); Edward Schatz (ed.), *Political Ethnography: What Immersion Contributes to the Study of Power* (2013); John Boswell and Jack Corbett, "Who are we Trying to Impress? Reflections on Navigating Political Science, Ethnography and Interpretation" (2015); Timothy Pachirat, *Among Wolves: Ethnography and the Immersive Study of Power* (2017); Erica S. Simmons and Nicholas Rush Smith, "The Case for Comparative Ethnography" (2019); and Matthew Longo and Bernardo Zacka, "Political Theory in an Ethnographic Key" (2019).
[153] Deckard and Auyero, "Poor People's Survival Strategies: Two Decades of Research in the Americas" (2023).

Journal of Ethnographic Theory, launched in 2011 with the mission of restoring "ethnography as anthropology's principal heuristic and bringing it back to the forefront of the discipline's conceptual developments,"[154] is anchored in London.

Another indicator of the growing interest in ethnography is the success of the Ethnographic Café (ethnographiccafe.org), a virtual debate site with 138 members from a dozen nations and a subscriber list of over 800. Finally, on the editorial front, the "Ethnographic encounters and discoveries" book series at University of Chicago Press (edited by Stefan Timmermans) has been joined by the series "Global ethnography" at Oxford University Press (Javier Auyero), "Ethnography of Political Violence" at University of Pennsylvania Press (Adriana Petryna), and "Atelier: Ethnographic Inquiry in the Twenty-First Century" at University of California Press (Kevin Lewis O'Neill). In France, the book series "L'envers des faits" edited by Paul Pasquali and Fabien Truong at La Découverte prominently features books based on fieldwork.

As for fieldwork in sociology in the United State, it is flourishing: all the country's major departments now have their own "in-house ethnographer(s)" (Berkeley has six), and their best students in turn find positions with this profile at top universities. Dedicated research centers have multiplied: among them, Berkeley's Center for Urban Ethnography (directed by Martín Sánchez-Jankowski since 1998), the Yale Urban Ethnography Project (Elijah Anderson, 2007), the Ethnography Lab at the University of Texas at Austin (founded by Javier Auyero in 2012) and at Stanford (Forrest Stuart, 2019), and the Ethnographic Incubator at the University of Chicago (Kimberley Hoang, 2017). In short, despite the brouhaha accompanying the Alice Goffman scandal (on which more later, see *infra*, pp. 134–139), ethnographic production is booming and genre boundaries have become more porous, so that the parameters of fieldwork on race and class relations in the Chicago mold are largely relativized. It is at the dawn of this third age of urban ethnography that we come upon "Scrutinizing," the controversial text that forms the next chapter.

~ * ~

---

[154] Giovanni Da Col and David Graeber, "Foreword: The Return of Ethnographic Theory" (2011).

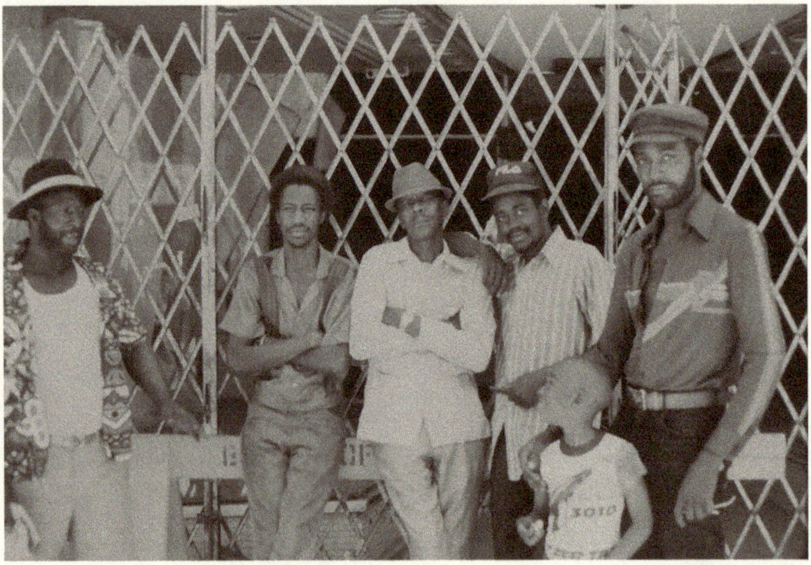

2
Poverty, Race, and Moralism in American Urban Ethnography

> "In the course of a scientific investigation we say all kinds of things; we make many utterances whose role in the investigation we do not understand. For it isn't as though everything we say has a conscious purpose; our tongues just keep going. Our thoughts run in established routines, we pass automatically from one thought to another according to the techniques we have learned. And now comes the time for us to survey what we have said."
>
> **Ludwig Wittgenstein,** *Vermischte Bemerkungen,* **1947.**

After a long decade during which researchers, following journalists and policy pundits, focused on the alleged rise, (mis)conduct, and threat of an "underclass" characterized by its presumed social isolation and antisocial behaviors,[1] students of race and poverty in the US metropolis have recently turned to issues of work, family, morality, and individual responsibility, in keeping with the newfound political concern for, and media interest in, those topics fostered by "welfare reform" and the bipartisan rightward turn of social policy.[2] Three ethnographically based books offer a composite portrait of the dark figure of "the street" seen from different yet converging angles in just this light: Mitchell Duneier's *Sidewalk* tracks the trials and tribulations of black homeless book vendors and magazine scavengers who ply their trade in a touristy section of Lower Manhattan; Elijah Anderson's *Code of the Street* chronicles the raging battle between "street" and "decent" families in the ghetto of Philadelphia; and Katherine Newman's *No Shame in My Game* depicts the

---

[1] Christopher Jencks and Paul Peterson (eds.), *The Urban Underclass* (1991). I dissect this notion historically and conceptually in Loïc Wacquant, *The Invention of the "Underclass": A Study in the Politics of Knowledge* (2022).

[2] In 1996, President Clinton signed a bill concocted by the Republicans which replaced the right to social assistance for single women with children ("welfare") with the obligation to engage in precarious employment as a condition of receiving drastically reduced and time-limited assistance ("workfare"). See R. Kent Weaver, *Ending Welfare as we Know It* (2000). For an overview of the relevant research at the century's turn, see Mario Luis Small and Katherine Newman, "Urban Poverty after *The Truly Disadvantaged*: The Rediscovery of the Family, the Neighborhood, and Culture" (2001).

gallant struggles of the "working poor" of Harlem to uphold the hallowed values of thrift, family, and community in the bowels of the deregulated service economy.[3]

These books assemble a mass of rich and nuanced empirical data variously drawn from firsthand observation, in-depth interviews, life stories, and institutional reports, gathered over years of fieldwork conducted individually or in teams. They would have greatly advanced our knowledge and understanding of the ground-level social dynamics and lived experience of urban marginality and racial division in the United States at century's end, were it not for their eager embrace of the clichés of public debate (albeit in inverted form), the pronounced discordance between interpretation and the evidence they offer, and the thick coat of moralism in which their analyses are wrapped, which together severely limit the questions they raise and the answers they give. Thus *Sidewalk* proffers a sprawling stockpile of data without any theory to organize it and strives, by default, to bring these data to bear on a crime-and-policing issue which these data are ill-suited to address; *Code of the Street* is animated by a thesis, that proximate mentoring makes a difference in the fate of ghetto residents, that is glaringly disconnected from, even invalidated by, its own findings; and *No Shame in My Game* subordinates both observation and theorization to public policy considerations, such as the ideological dispute over "family values," that are so constricting that it ends up slighting its own discoveries and reading like a business tract in praise of low-wage work.

Most significantly, all three authors put forth truncated and distorted accounts of their objects due to their abiding wish to articulate and even celebrate the fundamental goodness—honesty, decency, frugality—of America's urban poor. To do this, Duneier *sanitizes* the actions and neighborhood impact of sidewalk bookselling by systematically downplaying or suppressing information that would taint the saintly image of the vendors he wishes to project; Anderson *dichotomizes* ghetto residents into good and bad, "decent" and "street," and makes himself the spokesman and advocate of the former; and Newman *glamorizes* the skills and deeds of her low-wage workers, extolling their submission to servile labor as evidence of their inner devotion to the country's ordained "work ethic." All three authors make the urban poor, and to be more exact the *black* subproletariat of the city, into *paragons of morality* because they remain locked within the *prefabricated problematic*

---

[3] Mitchell Duneier, *Sidewalk* (1999); Elijah Anderson, *Code of the Street: Decency, Violence, and the Moral Life of the Inner City* (1999); and Katherine S. Newman, *No Shame in my Game: The Working Poor in the Inner City* (1999). Note that all three books, totalling 1,136 pages, are published by prestigious New York–based commercial presses rather than academic publishers: *Sidewalk* by Farrar, Straus & Giroux; *Code of the Street* by W.W. Norton; and *No Shame in My Game* by Knopf (in association with the Russell Sage Foundation, which funded the research on which the book is based).

of public stereotypes and policy punditry, for which it is the only guise under which this subproletariat is deemed "presentable."

In a 1946 talk on "Principle and Rationalization in Race Relations," Everett C. Hughes noted that a major obstacle to the rigorous study of ethnoracial inequality is the impulse to "counter the exaggerated statements of our opponents with exaggerations in another direction," leading one to portray subordinate groups as "paragons of virtue, delightful in their manners—better, in fact, than is common for human creatures to be."[4] A half-century later, that remark applies in full to the black poor who stand at the epicenter of America's "urban Orientalism." I read it as confirmation that the "opportunism of logic" which Hughes diagnosed as a "fault common enough in American social science" is a deep seated and long standing problem.

The earnest labors, good intentions, and personal generosity of these scholars are beyond dispute. But moral munificence is no guarantee for rigorous social analysis, and even less so a substitute for it. And the task of social science, ethnography included, is not to exonerate the character of dishonored social figures and dispossessed groups by "documenting" their everyday world in an effort to attract sympathy for their plight. It is to dissect the social mechanisms and meanings that govern their practices, ground their morality (if such be the question), and explain their strategies and trajectories, as one would do for any social category, high or low, noble or ignoble. Appealing to popular pieties about the downtrodden would not be so serious a problem if the evidence presented in these books supported the appeal. But, taken singly or collectively, *Sidewalk*, *Code of the Street*, and *No Shame in My Game* do not bring about "the street" the message that their authors wish them to convey. Their blindness to issues of class power and their stubborn disregard for the deep and multisided involvement (or, to use their own language, "responsibility") of the state in producing the social dereliction and human wretchedness they sensibly portray condemn Duneier, Anderson, and Newman to elaborating variants of the classical fallacy of *argumentum ad populum*, in which a thesis is asserted, even acclaimed, because it resonates with the moral schemata and expectations of its audience, but at the cost of a dangerous suspension of analytic and political judgment.

After presenting and evaluating their core arguments in turn, I will suggest that the proximate causes of the common limitations and liabilities of these three tomes—their uncontrolled skid from morality to moralism, their naïve acceptance of ordinary categories of perception as categories of analysis, their

---

[4] Everett C. Hughes, "Principle and Rationalization in Race Relations" (1971), p. 216.

utter subservience to policy prescriptions and propaganda—can be found in the parochialism of the US tradition of poverty research, the unwarranted empiricist disjunction of ethnography from theory, and the changing economics of social science publishing. Their collective failure to go beyond a homiletic vision of "the street" also points to a broader quandary faced by ethnographic researchers today, as the craft enjoys renewed popularity but also faces unprecedented threats to its autonomy and integrity. And it spotlights a watershed moment in the politics of urban sociology in the United States: just as the *romantic* ethnographies of the cool, the marginal, and the lowly produced during the progressive 1960s in the style of the second Chicago school were organically tied to the *liberal* politics of America's semi-welfare state and its then-expanding "social-problems complex,"[5] the *neo-romantic* tales spun by Duneier, Anderson, and Newman at the close of the regressive 1990s suggest that US sociology is now tied and party to the ongoing construction of the *neoliberal* state and its "carceral-assistential complex" for the punitive management of the poor, on and off the street.[6]

The saints of Greenwich Village: Duneier on homeless sidewalk vendors

During his stint as a law school student at New York University, Mitchell Duneier became intrigued by, and acquainted with, street sellers of "black books" occupying a busy three-block area at the crossroads of Eighth Street and Sixth Avenue, at the heart of Greenwich Village, the gentrified bohemian quarter of New York City.[7] Through his friendship with one of these vendors (who eventually co-taught a course with him at the University of California, Santa Barbara, on "The Life of the Street in Black America"), he gained access to the site and returned to work there as a "general assistant" and "magazine vendor and scavenger" for about one year (stretched over three summers and one fall season plus a spring from 1996 to 1999). *Sidewalk* (hereafter cited as SW) draws a detailed portrait of the social organization of this informal street trade plied by homeless African American men with checkered journeys at the margins of society, complete with pages upon pages of transcripts

---

[5] Alvin Gouldner, "The Sociologist as Partisan: Sociology and the Welfare State" (1973).

[6] Loïc Wacquant, *Prisons of Poverty* ([1999] 2009), pp. 83–94. See also Wacquant, "Crafting the Neoliberal State: Workfare, Prisonfare, and Social Insecurity," (2010).

[7] "Black books" are works that deal with the history and culture of African Americans. They range from novels and militant pamphlets to poetry, religion, and biographies celebrating sports champions (Arthur Ashe, Mohammed Ali, Michael Jordan), artists (James Brown, Maya Angelou, Michael Jackson), and political leaders (foremost among them Martin Luther King, Malcolm X, and Barack Obama) who are the pride of the group.

of running conversations and some seventy-two pictures by *Chicago Tribune* photographer Ovie Carter. It documents patterns of cooperation and competition among sellers, their contrasted interactions with black and white patrons, and their exchanges with neighbors, business organizations, and city authorities as represented by local Business Improvement Districts (BIDs) and the police.[8]

Duneier's aim is to "offer a framework for understanding the changes that have taken place on the sidewalk over the past four decades" (SW, p. 8), since Jane Jacobs's sentimental account of the role of "public characters" in the production of urban civility in *The Death and Life of Great American Cities*.[9] Two questions anchor his inquiry: how do vendors of written matter and assorted secondhand goods in the Village "have the ingenuity" to "live in a moral order" in "the face of exclusion and stigmatization on the basis of race and class?" and "How do their acts intersect with a city's mechanisms to regulate its public spaces?" (SW, p. 9). Duneier finds that his subjects lead "moral lives" and even act as "mentors" for one another and their clients, notwithstanding their offensive appearance and behavior. He also contends that, far from being a criminogenic factor, they enhance the safety and welfare of the neighborhood, thus challenging the "zero-tolerance" policing campaign launched by Mayor Rudolph Giuliani in an effort to cleanse the city streets of its rabble.[10]

Duneier uses these findings to make a plea for amending the so-called broken windows theory of public (dis)order and spare from its application the moral strivers among the urban outcasts. As we shall see, Duneier's central claims are either unexceptional (that sidewalk vendors live in a moral world: who does not?) or unsupported (that they improve neighborhood safety and social cohesion: his own data are either inapposite or indicative of the contrary). And the corresponding plea for a kinder, gentler street policing is profoundly misguided as well as unconvincing: "zero tolerance" is not, contrary to what Duneier asserts, responsible for the drop in urban crime, and tweaking its implementation to allow for more sidewalk entrepreneurship would hardly affect the life chances of the urban poor.

---

[8] These districts are areas where the city authorizes large local corporations to levy a tax that finances services that the city provides only imperfectly to their liking: investment in buildings and infrastructure, road cleaning, park maintenance, and surveillance by private police.

[9] Jane Jacobs, *The Death and Life of Great American Cities* (1961).

[10] The "zero tolerance" policy, launched with much fanfare by New York City's Republican mayor Rudolph Giuliani in 1992, involved diligently cracking down on minor offenses in order to improve the "quality of life," in line with the "broken window theory" that punishing incivilities would halt the mechanical escalation to violent crime. See Wacquant, *Prisons of Poverty*, pp. 25–29.

Sidewalk commerce in this section of Greenwich Village involves three interlinked and loosely hierarchized roles: book vendors, scavengers of magazines and secondhand goods, and the panhandlers who assist them in various capacities. The vendors specialize by type of books (art volumes, dictionaries, best-sellers, "black books," out-of-print tomes, comics, etc.) and take in $50 to $200 daily from a mix of passers-by and neighbors who patronize their half-dozen tables. By selling printed matter on the street, Duneier proposes, these homeless men not only exercise a worthy and complex occupation;[11] they also "serve an important function in the lives of their customers," offering them an attentive ear, the "expectation of continued discussion," and "a symbol of those values necessary to live in accordance to ideals of self-worth" (SW, pp. 19, 38, 34). Duneier speaks effusively of the relationships that Hakim Hasan, his main informant, develops "with many young black men" from the poor boroughs of New York City who stop by, likening Hasan's role to the function of the ghetto "old head" of yesteryear but one "located squarely in the new economy,"[12] whose "presence emphasizes that gang leaders and drug dealers are not the only alternatives" (SW, pp. 37, 33, 40).

Like the book vendors, magazine scavengers are African-American men in their mid-30s to mid-50s, all but one former or current drug addicts, half of whom have been to jail (or prison: one cannot tell as Duneier's account conflates these two very different institutions).[13] Nearly all claim that they "made a choice to live on the streets" (SW, pp. 23, 49, 54), where they work a few days a week, combining their sales with welfare payments and veteran pensions to eke out a living. They would have succumbed to a retreatist "'fuck it!' mentality," entailing the loss of one's sense of shame and embarrassment, were it not for what Duneier calls the "rehabilitative forces of the sidewalk": street entrepreneurship has enabled them to "take control and earn respect within a limited domain," and thereby escape the downward cycle of economic

---

[11] "There is substantive complexity to this work: finding the magazines, taking them in and out of storage, setting them up, knowing what kind of magazines to carry, how to price them, and what to charge" (SW, p. 68). By that definition, it is hard to think of a trade that is not complex. Indeed, we shall see that Newman finds also that fast-food employees hold highly skilled jobs. Anderson, by contrast, recognizes the lousy jobs that his informants have for what they are: lousy.

[12] The *"hold head" is* an "elder" of the neighborhood, a mature or old man endowed with authority by his history and social position, who serves as an informal mentor to the men of succeeding generations. Anderson gives him a central place in his analysis of the ghetto's transformation, see *infra*, pp. 81–83.

[13] Jails hold people who have been arrested by the police and are awaiting criminal adjudication and are therefore presumed innocent, or serving sentences of less than a year for misdemeanors, while prisons hold people sentenced to more than a year of imprisonment for felonies. In jail, stays are very short (a few days for the majority of defendants) and population turnover very high; the exact opposite obtains in prisons.

redundancy, social disaffiliation, and escalating entanglement with the criminal justice apparatus (SW, p. 79).[14]

The crack-addicted panhandlers who hold the door and beg for money at the vestibules of automated-teller machines partake of this sidewalk economy in that they supplement their income by working as assistants to the book vendors, holding their place at night, watching their tables when they need to take a break, "laying shit out," and moving merchandise to and from the nearby parking garages and storage lockers where it is stowed after dark. Again, Duneier's main argument is that the panhandlers are moral beings who "derive self-respect from the way they conduct themselves" and "have chosen to engage in a worthy enterprise" which, despite the mutual scorn that the two subgroups have for each other, offers panhandlers an opportunity to move up to the position of street vendor and eventually benefit from the morally uplifting and socially integrative pull of this informal street business (SW, pp. 84, 85, 83).[15] Echoing compassionate conservatism, compassionate sociology intimates that deep-seated problems of urban poverty and inequality can be effaced by an infusion of personal "responsibility" and one-on-one mentoring: no matter how economically desperate and socially marginal, a sidewalk tradesman can be a "sponsor" for other wayward souls "in a way that no government or social-service agency, religious institution, or charity can. The task of the sponsor is to encourage responsible behavior" out of his own goodwill. And Duneier to wax: "I am thinking about the sidewalk. Thank goodness for the sidewalk" (SW, p. 80).

Now Duneier concedes that the sidewalk system of "informal social control" anchored by inner morality and mutual respect is hardly perfect. It cannot entirely contain untoward behavior, such as sleeping out, urinating in public, and aggressively "coming on" to women passing by on the street. But, according to him, even these violations of common standards of propriety are motivated not so much by brute constraints (such as the "access problem to the bathroom resource itself," discovered during a firsthand visit to the public latrines of Washington Park and verified by the testimony of a golfer friend)[16] as by a sense of decency and "respect for society." Thus homeless vendors innovate the technique of urinating into a cup held under

---

[14] "They have used the opportunity provided by the sidewalk to become innovators—earning a living, striving for self-respect, establishing good relations with fellow citizens, providing support for each other" (SW, p. 79).

[15] It is not clear why panhandlers would want to become written-matter sellers since, according to Duneier's data, they earn much more than the lower end of book vendors ($75 a day, nearly twice the minimum wage) and they do not have to scavenge, keep a spot, lay out and store away merchandise, or maintain a clientele.

[16] "I have also heard from Adam Winkler, a friend who plays golf at the Hillcrest Country Club, that it is not uncommon to see men urinate on the golf course, despite the restrooms scattered throughout the

an untucked shirt while pretending to hail a cab out of concern "about the feelings of [their] fellow citizens" in restaurants and other commercial establishments who might be offended by their appearance, drunkenness, or body odor if they came in. Invoking ecological theory, Duneier claims that vendors sleep out on the block because of "the complementarity of the various habitat elements," namely cheap food, readily available shelter, the opportunity to make money, and the presence of friends who help make them feel safe and comfortable. Students of homelessness—and, even more so, advocates for the rights of the homeless—will be surprised to learn that being "unhoused" (a curious neologism used throughout the book by Duneier) is a voluntary phenomenon: vendors and scavengers "choose" to sleep on the streets either because of the brute habituation of their body to "sleeping on hard surfaces" or as an expression of their abiding commitment to entrepreneurialism.

For the incredulous reader, the former explanation must be cited in full: "Mudrick's [a magazine scavenger] 'Once you're homeless, you're always homeless' seems to be linked to his body's response to the social and physical experience of sleeping on a hard surface. His body seems to have grown to prefer a particular experience . . . For some of these men, sleeping in a bed no longer feels natural. Although most Americans take sleeping in a bed as basic to decency, the conventional bed is not a physical necessity but a cultural artefact; many people of the world regard a bed as less healthy for sleeping than a hard surface" (SW, p. 168).

This learned preference of the body for "hard surfaces" fails to explain why Mudrick does not opt to snooze on the floor of an apartment or hotel room rather than risk his life sleeping out on the streets. Nor does the commitment to entrepreneurialism explain (somewhat redundantly) why Mudrick "chooses to sleep on the block": millions of Americans define their personal identity by their job, yet they do not for that feel the need to bed down at their workplace.

"Talking to women" on the sidewalk can also "create a 'quality of life' problem in the minds of residents,"[17] especially when the homeless black vendors attempt to draw upper-class white women who pass by their tables into sexually laden conversations. Deploying the analytic techniques of "a kind of policy-oriented applied conversation analysis" enables Duneier to "con-

---

tract. In all socioeconomic classes, the male act of urinating in public seems to be common, though those who work on the streets seem to have fewer options as to where to go" (SW. p. 186).

[17] The term "quality of life" refers to a category of infractions that New York's innovative zero-tolerance policing was designed to curb. See Bernard E. Harcourt, *Illusions of Order: The False Promise of Broken Windows Policing* (2001).

sistently discover" that "rudeness" is indeed what "makes some residents of the Village feel annoyance and even anguish" at the street peddlers and scavengers. And that "for the women, the men's 'eyes upon the street' do not bring about a sense of security among strangers but a feeling of deep distrust" (SW, pp. 199, 216).[18]

Duneier concedes that a "few men who commit 'interactional vandalism' give a bad name to others," but he reassures us that, while such breaches of "conversational ethics"—also commonly known as gender harassment—do "create tension," they "rarely harm" and should not reflect badly on the vendors since "at other times . . . each of these men would be seen as acting in 'positive' and straightforward ways toward others, including the women in their lives" (SW, pp. 190, 210, 314). As for the accusation by local bookstore owners that the sidewalk vendors steal books and sell them at cut-rate prices, Duneier rebuts it with a long exegesis on the organization of publishing suggesting that the "sale of written matter is always a corrupt enterprise" (SW, p. 221) and that theft is rampant in the business of bookselling. Presumably, the fact that store owners and customers filch books provides a warrant for vendors to do so also.

Duneier is to be commended for his persistence, sensitivity, and assiduity in the field. Unlike his previous book, *Slim's Table*, in which he conjectured rashly about social structure and culture in the ghetto of Chicago's South Side without having set foot in it,[19] *Sidewalk* is firmly grounded in direct observation (supplemented with twenty interviews paid at $50 apiece) and extensive personal engagement with the street scene. But Duneier's admirable patience and boundless empathy, verging on devotion, for his subjects blinds him to evidence and processes that do not fit his portrait. The irenic vision of a fragile community of dispossessed, street-living men triply burdened with racial stigma, criminal records, and drug addiction who nonetheless resolve conflicts peacefully and do not commit illegal acts in their gallant struggle for independent living "on the legit side"; who, better yet, enhance social cohesion and public order in the city, is a heartwarming tale—complete with the "Kodak moments" of happy times spent with a loving grandchild or visiting

---

[18] This would seem to be a textbook case of methodological overkill: does one need to track "adjacency pairs," spot "disaffiliative responses," measure the delay between question and answer with a stopwatch in tenths of a second, and resort to the intricate transcription techniques of Conversation Analysis to "discover" that women use "distracted facial gestures," hurried moves, and curt replies to ward off unwanted invites to face-to-face exchange by male strangers in public spaces?

[19] *Slim's Table* (Duneier 1993) is based on the sayings and conduct of a few elderly black patrons and one white customer inside a white-owned ethnic restaurant located on 53rd Street, at the heart of the white, affluent neighborhood of Hyde Park, the stronghold of the University of Chicago and safest neighborhood in the city.

a sick elderly aunt (SW, pp. 76–78, 108–111)—but it is simply not believable on the face of it.[20]

1

Duneier presents no evidence that Hakim and his colleagues actually have any influence over young men from the ghetto who take advice and purchase books from them, unless one counts as evidence the incidental statement to that effect of *one* youth during a quick interview on the fly. Given that the streets of lower Manhattan are also filled with black service workers, black clerks, black executives, and black professionals who provide plenty of conventional "role models,"[21] it is hard to see why homeless vendors would acquire the symbolic visibility and sociomoral efficacy that *Sidewalk* attributes to them.

Duneier also speculates that the vendor's table is "a site for interaction that weakens the social barriers between persons otherwise separated by vast social and economic inequalities" (SW, p. 71) but he presents no data and suggests no mechanism whereby such fleeting and superficial contacts would produce this weakening. Customers of department stores interact daily with cashiers and corporate executives frequently run into the black and Latino janitors who clean their offices nightly without *eo ipso* reducing class differences and bridging ethnoracial divides. Duneier asserts that the ethnic variety of buyers "gives a good sense of the wide-ranging impact a book vendor *can* have on the lives of many people on the street" (SW, p. 25, emphasis added) but, again, there is no evidence that they *do* have an impact on any of them.

Thus the moral salience and cultural sponsorship thesis of the book is unsubstantiated and rests entirely on a continual confusion between sociability and solidarity, cordiality and cohesion (as when Duneier asserts that "sidewalk life still provides strangers with a source of solidarity"; SW, p. 293). As for the notion that "there is no substitute for the power of the informal social relations that constitute a wholesome sidewalk" (SW, p. 42), it is simply

---

[20] In this, *Sidewalk* is an ironic vindication of Duneier's warning that a major obstacle to adhering rigorously to the rules of the ethnographic method is the "strong attachments one develops with one's subjects, which can lead to emotions that make the idea of social science less than realistic" (SW, p. 79).

[21] The sociological concept of the role model was coined by Robert Merton in the 1940s as part of the theory of "roles" and "reference groups." Adopted by psychologists, publicists and journalists, it has become part of the everyday vocabulary of American society. In particular, it suggests that an individual will raise her aspirations and police her behavior if she comes into direct contact with social agents higher up the "status hierarchy" than herself. See Robert K. Merton, *Social Theory and Social Structure* (1968), chapter 11.

fanciful: cities and neighborhoods without sidewalk vendors have not for that reason plunged into moral strife and social chaos.

2

The saintliness of vendors in Duneier's portrait is the cumulative effect of three strategies of selective data collection, interpretation, and presentation: disconnecting, censoring, and skewing. First, Duneier *disconnects the legal from the illegal economy* and excludes by fiat the latter from his purview, on grounds that the topic was "addressed in detail by other scholars" (SW, p. 159). This is surprising, first, because the Village is renowned as one the region's prime open-air markets for narcotics, a variety of which can be openly purchased on the streets, in Washington Park, and around the nearby basketball courts. It is also unwarranted since previous research of the subsistence strategies of the homeless in New York City by Waterston (1993) and Dordick (1997) as well as studies of the city's informal economy (by Bourgois [1995], Freidenberg 1995, and Sharff 1998)[22]—which Duneier studiously ignores—have consistently shown that there is no separation between the licit and illicit sectors of street commerce: drug-addicted homeless and poor people routinely combine intermittent wage labor, odd jobs, pilfering, scavenging, drug peddling, and prostitution—whatever is at hand to stay afloat.

When Duneier maintains that even panhandling "makes the sidewalk safer by providing an outlet for [derelict men] to earn money to support their drug habits by means *other than* stealing or themselves selling drugs" (SW, p. 85; emphasis added), he does not explain why panhandlers could not at the same time beg for money, work for book vendors, *and* engage in a variety of less commendable activities to satisfy their addiction and other needs as the occasions arise. His postulate that there exists a patent incompatibility between worthy street entrepreneurship and unlawful pursuits is untenable and begs the very question to be investigated.

It may well be that sidewalk vendors do take up the trade as an "alternative to stealing" but there is no way of knowing since Duneier also systematically

---

[22] See Alisse Waterston, *Street Addicts in the Political Economy* (1993), and Gwendolyn Dordick, *Something Left to Lose: Personal Relations and Survival among New York's Homeless* (1997), as well as studies of the city's informal economy by Philippe Bourgois, *In Search of Respect: Selling Crack in El Barrio* (1995); John Freidenberg (ed.), *The Anthropology of Lower Income Urban Enclaves: The Case of East Harlem* (1995); Jagna Wojcicka Sharff, *King Kong on 4th Street: Families and the Violence of Poverty on the Lower East Side* (1998).

censors unflattering and deviant behavior that would contradict his contention that they are engaged in a wholesome enterprise of moral uplift of self and other. He repeats time and again that street selling has a civilizing effect on all involved and that "on most occasions the vendors are self-regulating," but then he had a policy of exiting from the scene whenever vendors became drunk and aggressive (SW, pp. 95, 47) and he supplies ample incidental evidence that directly belies this notion. Thus many scavengers are chronic cocaine and alcohol abusers who cannot be relied upon to man their own table because they will run off to appease their habit as soon as they get enough cash. One of their motivations for sleeping out, rather than in a cheap hotel, is to score crack and "keep bingeing all night long—smoking or drinking" until they pass out, hardly behavior that bolsters conventional social norms (SW, pp. 92, 160, 165).[23]

Some vendors also frighten tourists into giving them money in exchange for directions, while fierce competition for valuable spots on the street is regulated by intimidation and likely by force. Yet there is scarcely any account of physical commotion and confrontation in the book and no trace of weapons (outside of one cursory mention; SW, p. 244), even for self-defense, which leaves unexplained how homeless men who carry hundreds of dollars in cash on them manage to fend off violent street predators after dark (but then Duneier did not follow them at night). Might the routine use of violence have something to do with the fact, also left unexamined, that sidewalk vending is an exclusively masculine endeavor (with the exception of one Filipina seller), when the activities that compose it seem tailor-made for poor women? That Duneier did *not* grant his informants cover of anonymity, contrary to the norm in ethnographic research, strongly reinforces the bent to exclude illegal and immoral activities from their accounts.[24]

Even the treatment of sidewalk sellers by the forces of order is interpreted not as the product of relations of power and authority but as "crises of personal respect between police and those who do not comply" during which the "officer's anguish over the prospect that the vendors see him as unprofessional" goads the vendor to act as "confidant and even therapist" [?] for the officer (SW, pp. 256, 284). The fixation on respect

---

[23] "If [vendors] were using drugs," writes Duneier, "we might reasonably conclude that they had given up on the struggle to live in accordance with society's standards" (SW, p. 170). This is a curious proposition since (i) Duneier provides profuse indications that sidewalk vendors are using drugs and (ii) millions of Americans of all classes and ethnic groups use illegal drugs regularly without for that matter having forsaken "society's standards."

[24] This sanitizing thrust is further solidified by Duneier's uncritical acceptance of his informants' self-portraits ("I have *never* doubted *any* of the things Hakim told me about his life"; SW, p. 360, emphasis added) and express desire to not make them look bad: "I believe I should never publish something about an identifiable person which I cannot look him or her in the eye and read" (SW, p. 352).

applies to the sociologist's own endeavor and interactions with his informants: "Would I be safe on the streets? Would the toughest and most violent men [?] on Sixth Avenue accept what I was doing as worthy of respect? . . . To this day, I cannot say how much 'acceptance', or 'rapport' or 'respect' I have on the sidewalk, or how much 'respect' I have shown these men in our personal relations" (SW, pp. 334, 357).

A third technique for beautifying street commerce consists in *skewing the display and interpretation of data* so as to showcase the virtuousness of the booksellers. Thus the brunt of conversation transcripts deal with being good, doing good, mending one's ways and supporting others, and seeking and expressing respect; there are precious few moments of anger, jealousy, dissension, and conflict, let alone villainy, among the vendors. The tritest and most inconsequential aspect of their trade, such as scavenging monthlies rather than weekly magazines, are transmuted into tokens of ingenuity and marks of achievement (SW, pp. 153). Whenever a "cultural" explanation spotlighting the morality of the street peddlers and material considerations of expediency and power suggest themselves to account for a pattern of behavior, Duneier systematically latches onto the former without examining the latter.

For example, Duneier maintains that vendors do not display pornography during the day, not because they might run into trouble with adult buyers or attract the attention of the police, but "out of respect, they say, for passing children." The cut on his sales that a vendor gives to the watcher of his table is presented, not as payment for services, but as a token of "respect and trust" between them and as proof of "a certain creativity" on the watcher's part. Mudrick's reconversion from a thug who "robbed deliverymen and sold drugs to support his needs" to sidewalk seller is attributed to his newfound "commitment to society" without checking whether aging and increased violence and police repression on the street might help account for it. When magazine scavengers take pains to "leav[e] the trash they sort through neat and orderly," it is not because they want to avoid being caught and charged with a class E misdemeanor but out of occupational pride (SW, pp. 77, 108, 88, 87, 150).[25] The point here is not to deny that sidewalk vendors develop mutual social ties, pursue moral ideals, and achieve a sense of individual and collective worth. They do. It is that Duneier gives us a one-sided, truncated picture of their world that makes it seems like this is all that is going on, when in reality, as in any social universe, the pursuit of morality is neither the sole spring nor the exclusive design of their actions.

[25] Duneier is so intent on casting the trade in all-around positive light that he reports this bracing fact: "I discovered that magazines tend to be very clean. Storing stacks of them in my apartment never led to any problem with roaches" (SW, p. 69).

3

Sidewalk connects neither with research on homelessness and addiction on the street, which demonstrates that legal and illegal activities are not separable, nor with the existing literature on street vendors, which would have enabled its author to locate his booksellers and magazine scavengers in the broader galaxy of informal city trades. The result is that, even as a "social world" study of an occupation in the mold of the second Chicago school,[26] *Sidewalk* presents serious lacunae. How do vendors deal with uncertainty in supply, demand, and income flow?[27] How do variations in their activity relate to changes and cycles in other economic circuits and sector?[28] Are there no differences between subproletarian sidewalk peddlers who engage in the trade as a "stop-gap" means of survival and college-educated bibliophiles and beatniks who take it up as an avocation, for the love of books and of the people they meet? What accounts for the rigid racial partitioning of the occupation, with black vendors monopolizing the spot near Sixth Avenue while white booksellers congregate only a few blocks away on West Fourth Street, as Jason Rosette (2000) reveals in *The Book Wars*, his award-winning documentary film on the craft?

It is surprising, given Duneier's express interest in race, that he does not mention them and the conflictual relationship they apparently entertain with some of his vendors, for a comparison of the practices and relations of black and white vendors with their customers and with the Manhattan police would have shed considerable light on how race, class, and state effectively intersect on the sidewalk. Much more so than Duneier's mysterious invocations of a "black collective consciousness" and bizarre speculations about a "hypothetical conventional black family from Vermont selling Christmas trees on Jane Street" which he (sort of) compares to the white Vermonters who actually come every winter season to sell Douglas firs and Canadian balsams to the locals (SW, pp. 239, 304–306). Surprisingly, Duneier also does not make anything of the fact that his main informant Hakim Hasan (and possibly other vendors) come from the Virgin Islands, even though the social dispositions and pathways of West Indian blacks in New York City are quite different from those of native-born blacks.[29]

---

[26] Everett C. Hughes, *The Sociological Eye: Selected Papers* (1970), chapters 28, 34, 43.
[27] Alfonso Morales, "Uncertainty and the Organization of Street Vending Businesses" (1997).
[28] Yvonne V. Jones, "Street Peddlers as Entrepreneurs: Economic Adaptation to an Urban Area" (1988); John Gaber, "Manhattan's 14th Street Vendors' Market: Informal Street Peddlers' Complementary Relationship with New York City's Economy" (1994).
[29] Milton Vickerman, *Crosscurrents: West Indian Immigrants and Race* (1999); Mary C. Waters, *Black Identities: West Indian Immigrant Dreams and American Realities* (1999).

How do African Americans maintain a lock on the area despite the crunch on vending space and the wide diffusion of immigrant vendors from Africa in other neighborhoods of Manhattan?[30] And how do they survive periods of forced inactivity, such as rainy weeks and the long months of winter when the arctic cold empties the street of potential customers? Surely Hakim and his colleagues must have other income-generating activities then. Duneier's silence on this is likely a consequence of having conducted fieldwork essentially in the summertime. This prevents him from examining how seasonal shifts in subsistence strategies affect the social morphology of book vendors and, through that mediation, the moral physiology of the community they form (as Mauss and Beuchat [1904] did in their classic study, "Seasonal Variations among the Eskimos").[31] None of these issues are addressed in *Sidewalk*.

Duneier does not discuss the structural forces—the desocialization of labor, the erosion of the patriarchal household, the retrenchment of the welfare state, the criminalization of the urban poor, the conflation of blackness and dangerousness in public space—that directly bound and shape the material and symbolic space within which vendors operate. As a result, he never returns to the question, posed at the beginning of the book, of "the changes that have taken place on the sidewalk over the past four decades." He offers a profusion of dispersed notations, vignettes, and slices but not the kind of systematic life histories needed to connect the local world of the vendors to the major institutions that coprocess them, the deregulated labor market, the criminal justice system, health and welfare bureaucracies, charitable organizations, and personal networks beyond the street scene.[32] Such biographical-*cum*-institutional data would reveal the pathways in and out of that world and allow the reader to see whether and under what conditions sidewalk commerce exercises its alleged salvaging virtues on homeless vendors, rather than sustaining their addictions, entrenching their marginality, and perpetuating their misery.[33] Instead of linking the trajectories of vendors to the transformation of extant social structures, Duneier insists that it

---

[30] Paul Stoller, "Spaces, Places, and Fields: The Politics of West African Trading in New York City's Informal Economy" (1996).

[31] Marcel Mauss and Henri Beuchat, "Essai sur les variations saisonnières des sociétés Eskimos. Étude de morphologie sociale" ([1904] 1950).

[32] A model study of these institutions, captured through *in situ* observations and life stories of homeless heroin addicts in San Francisco, is Philippe Bourgois and Jeffrey Schonberg, *Righteous Dopefiend* (2009).

[33] *Sidewalk* closes on an unresolved conundrum in this regard: Given its manifold social benefits and redeeming moral virtues, why does Hakim Hasan abruptly announce in his afterword that he has chosen to leave the sidewalk (especially now that the book has made him something of a celebrity in the Village, which cannot but help his sales)?

is "difficult to rigorously project individual cases onto the template of social processes" so that all we can do is "speculate with caution" (SW, p. 51). This speculation proceeds essentially by embracing the folk theories of their own lives that the vendors produce, as when Jamaane explains that he "believe[s] highly in role models and trying to set examples" (SW, p. 58).

4

The obsessive focus on respect and "ideals of self-worth" within an interactional microcosm severed from its institutional moorings and seemingly devoid of material determinism and power vectors expresses a deeper theoretical flaw of *Sidewalk*: Throughout the book, Duneier takes the statements of his informants at face value and conflates "vocabularies of motives" with social mechanisms, the reasons invoked by vendors to make sense of their actions with the causes that actually govern them.[34] Why does Duneier swallow whole the sing-song claim of his subjects that they "made a conscious decision to 'respect' society by scavenging trash or panhandling (instead of breaking into cars or selling drugs)" (SW, p. 159)? Because it resonates with the Victorian trope that informs public stereotypes of the urban (black) poor—even as it inverts its valence, turning a negative into a positive—as well as with his own conception of the social world as a stage for the affirmation of individual moral valor. The narrative of "men motivating one another to try to live 'better' lives" is one he could readily hear and record in the field, because he brought it there with him.

Instead of selecting a site to answer a sociological question, the twenty-nine-page methodological appendix that closes *Sidewalk* makes it clear that Duneier happened onto a site that, for whatever reasons, attracted him and in which he developed rich and rare contacts. So he went about "fishing" for questions to which these informants might have answers. But his problematic did not emerge inductively, as in the epistemological fairy tale of "grounded theory" or "diagnostic ethnography";[35] it resulted from the projection, onto the sidewalk, of Duneier's personal interest in morality and "respectability"

---

[34] "Checking Stuff" (SW, pp. 345–347) to establish the *factual veracity* of statements made by informants is commendable (as well as routinely expected of any fieldworker). But it is not the same as establishing the *sociological pertinence and analytic adequacy* of the statements for explaining the social practices of these same agents.

[35] Barney Glaser and Anselm Strauss, *The Discovery of Grounded Theory: Strategies for Qualitative Research* (1967). "Diagnostic ethnography" is the label coined by Duneier's University of Wisconsin colleague Erik Wright to characterize this inductivist, "I-began-to-get-ideas-from-the-things-I-was-seeing-and-hearing-on-the-street" approach to field-based inquiry (SW, p. 341). The name is catchy and the

(already evident in *Slim's Table*). Duneier must be given credit for the candor with which he acknowledges it:

> I hadn't formulated a precise research question. I had no theories that I wanted to test or reconstruct, and I didn't have a particular scholarly literature to which I knew I wanted to contribute... I sought mainly to diagnose the processes at work in this setting and to explain the observed patterns of interactions of people. I also have a general theme that guides me in collecting data *in all of my work: whether and how the people I am with are or are not struggling to live in accordance with standards of "moral" worth*. (SW, pp. 340–341; emphasis added)

The inquiry then became a matter of pursuing and spotlighting those strands of everyday life on the sidewalk that fit and filled out that righteous interactionist vision, which Duneier did with impressive zeal,[36] but to the exclusion of all other issues, and especially material constraint and symbolic violence, that would risk muddying it. Still the sidewalk would acquire its full significance as a miniature of and template for urban civility (embedded in a Shilsian conception of society as a web of concentric circles of deference and charisma)[37] only if street book vending could be linked to broader controversies about public order. This is where the thesis about crime and policing comes in.

5

Jumping from the sidewalk to the public policy arena, Duneier alleges that the presence of homeless vendors, scavengers, and panhandlers does not feed crime on the streets of Greenwich Village but on the contrary *reduces* it. What crime, committed when and where, we are not told exactly, but it must be the offenses vendors would commit were they not engaged in "innocent entrepreneurial activity" as well as those they deter by watching

---

analogy attractive but it is invalid: a therapist who "gains an appreciation of the 'symptoms' that characterize a 'patient'" does not extract a medical theory out of clinical data; she anchors her observations in a nosography and a nosology backed up by an aetiology. And her primary task is to sift through information to select a *recipe* so as to cure a condition, not discover the hidden *mechanisms* that produce it (indeed, the therapist typically knows that mechanism well, thanks to the science of medical biology).

[36] At one point, Duneier asks a vendor who was occupying a disputed spot on the sidewalk: "Did you feel while you were waiting that if you did set up here you were being *some kind of bad person*?" Then he notes: "My presence became an occasion for the men to discuss what constituted suitable behavior" (SW, p. 248; emphasis added).

[37] Edward Shils, "Charisma, Order, and Status" (1965).

over the street. It follows, Duneier pleads, that "a new social-control strategy is needed" that would retain as its "core the unrelenting demands for responsible behavior," which subtends "quality-of-life" policing, but would imbue it with "greater tolerance and respect for people working the sidewalk" (SW, p. 313). This is the boldest claim advanced in *Sidewalk*; it is also the weakest.

It must be noted first that Greenwich Village is an odd place to assess the workings of any law-enforcement strategy, since it is a diverse yet wealthy area (the median household income is $70,000 per year)[38] with a mix of functions and an unusually large proportion of university affiliates, tourists, artists, gays and lesbians, and a public ethos of cultural tolerance—in short, a one-of-a-kind locale on the American urban landscape. The problems of public-order maintenance that arise in it are different from those faced by homogenous residential or commercial neighborhoods and even more so the ghettoized communities that bear the brunt of "quality-of-life" policing.[39]

Be that as it may, Duneier supplies not a single piece of hard evidence that sidewalk commerce deflects the incidence of crime there. Instead of presenting data on police complaints or arrests (available in geocoded sets from the city's Police Department) or narrating specific incidents of crime prevention, he is content with affirming that he has personally "rarely seen any crime spring from this environment" (SW, p. 79)—which suggests that he does not know that the purchase and possession of crack, for instance, is a felony punishable by multiple years of prison in the state of New York. Yet we do not know that street vending was *not* accompanied by criminal activity on the side; and it is unclear how the "eyes upon the street" of a dozen sidewalk sellers would make a tangible difference at a busy crossroads that is dotted with tens of shops and that harbors regular pedestrian traffic from residents and tourists alike at all hours of the day.

Duneier's discussion of the "broken windows theory" is especially feeble, as it eschews the relevant criminological and legal literature and misdiagnoses its nature, means, and uses. It confounds sixties-style "community policing" (as studied famously by Egon Bittner) with nineties-style "zero tolerance"

---

[38] This corresponds to $110,000 in 2023 currency.
[39] Duneier acknowledges that Greenwich Village is "unique in a multitude of ways" but he refrains from discussing how its peculiarities impact the validity and generalizability of his claims: "I must leave it to the readers to test my observations against their own, and hope that the concepts I have developed to make sense of this neighborhood will prove useful in other venues" (SW, p. 11). It would have been more helpful to sketch even a summary comparison with the lively sidewalk vending scene on Fourteenth Street (studied by John Gaber, "Manhattan's 14th Street Vendors' Market" [1994]), or the open-air market on 125th Street in Harlem (described in detail in Paul Stoller, "Spaces, Places, and Fields" [1994]).

(SW, p. 375),[40] which purports to reclaim public space by systematically arresting, fining, and jailing those accused of minor offenses such as littering, panhandling, prostitution, drinking, urinating in public, and vandalism. The center-piece of "zero tolerance" is not the strict enforcement of municipal codes, which Duneier describes and complains about in the case of his vendors and scavengers, but "stop-and-frisk" patrols targeted at tens of thousands of young men in ghetto and barrio neighborhoods and resulting in their mass dispatch to Rikers Island. The city, goaded by the Village Alliance (a local business association) and vigorously assisted by New York University, tried to remove the vendors from their spot and failed precisely because the latter operate in full legality, owing to the peculiar manner in which the municipal council chose to implement the constitutional right to free speech (SW, pp. 132–136).

The fact that Duneier never had a single occasion to bail a member of his sidewalk group out of jail or go fetch him at night court over the length of four years would seem to indicate that street sellers of printed matter are largely spared the harshest side of the campaign for "quality of life." The loathsome "squeegee men," and not sidewalk vendors, are its iconic target.[41] Even if they were, the New York City police made 376,316 arrests in 1998 (over 227,500 of them for misdemeanors), a figure superior by about 50,000 to the total number of crimes recorded by the authorities that year and resulting in 130,000 admissions to Rikers Island jail. It is difficult to discern what exempting a dozen or even a few hundred street peddlers of printed matter would change in that picture.

Duneier presents as fact the propaganda of the Mayor's office and neoconservative ideologues of the "war on crime," according to which "zero tolerance" has lowered crime in New York City (SW, pp. 287, 313) in spite of solid research findings to the contrary.[42] It is well established that (1) violent

---

[40] Egon Bittner, "Police Discretion in Emergency Apprehension of Mentally Ill Persons" (1967); Ralph B. Taylor, *Breaking Away from Broken Windows: Baltimore Neighborhoods and the Nationwide Fight Against Crime, Grime, Fear, and Decline* (2001); Harcourt, *Illusions of Order*.

[41] The "squeegee man" is a homeless person who, without always asking for permission, hurriedly washes the windshields of motorists stopped at a traffic light, then demands payment in small change. He was a central figure in the public perception of the encroaching urban fringe in the 1990s, and Mayor Rudolph Giuliani made him the prime target of the "quality of life" police, publicly calling them "vermin." Alex S. Vitale, *City of Disorder: How the Quality of Life Campaign Transformed New York Politics* (2008). In the United States, city police forces are the responsibility of the municipality, which creates, pays, and runs them independently. There are some 18,000 independent police departments in the country.

[42] "We grant that the 'broken windows' has viability and that it has been used to lower crime rates" (SW, p. 313). I mention here only works available while Duneier was still in the field. Among the other problems in Duneier's discussion of policing, he cites as support for the "broken windows" theory an "excellent study" by Wesley Skogan (1990), *Disorder and Decline*, whose results in fact indicate that poverty and segregation, not disorder, are the best predictors of crime, and whose statistical findings on the disorder–crime nexus have been invalidated by Bernard Harcourt's painstaking reanalysis of the same data ("Reflecting on

crime started dropping years before Giuliani launched that policy; (2) other large cities that have applied police tactics divergent with "zero tolerance" sport equally large drops in criminal offenses;[43] and (3) that "quality-of-life" enforcement was *not* based on the so-called broken windows theory of George Kelling and James Q. Wilson but on the common lore of beat cops, who encapsulated it by the less elegant name of "Breaking Balls" theory.[44] Duneier's minor emendation of that theory, consisting in "defining disorder with greater accuracy" while endorsing its "viability" (SW, p. 298), reads timid if not silly in light of Bernard Harcourt's thorough dismantling of its basic postulates and categories, including its muddled conception of disorder.[45] Finally, the notion that challenging the conceptual logic of order-maintenance policing will lead to altering its implementation (SW, pp. 287–288) is whimsical at best: like other law-enforcement strategies, it was never adopted on "intellectual grounds" but for political, bureaucratic, and symbolic reasons.

Finally, one must ask: Why should homeless sidewalk vendors have to *reduce* crime rather than simply *abstain* from it in order to be allowed to exercise their trade? Why should one require of them a *higher contribution to civility* than is demanded of regular commercial operators and other users of public space? To show that they are not a blight to the neighborhood, Duneier feels that he must find them to be a boon, and in seeking to meet this uneven burden of proof he enshrines the double standard by which the urban poor are judged in American society. And one cannot but wonder, too: what if Duneier, having cast his ethnographic net a bit wider, had found that book vendors do *not* enhance neighborhood safety, would he then be calling for their removal?

---

the Subject: A Critique of the Social Influence Conception of Deterrence, the Broken Windows Theory, and Order-Maintenance Policing New-York Style" [1998], esp. pp. 309–329). Duneier refers to a 1988 piece by Robert Sampson and Jacqueline Cohen that concludes that empirical support for that theory is lacking (SW, p. 370), and he overlooks more recent publications by the same author explicitly refuting it (Robert Sampson and Stephen Raudenbausch, "Systematic Social Observation of Public Spaces: A New Look at Disorder in Urban Neighborhoods" [1998]). Duneier also claims to introduce a distinction between physical and social order that is epicentral to Skogan's earlier work (SW, p. 288). Finally, he presents George Kelling and Catherine Coles's *Fixing Broken Windows* as a scholarly tome when it is an ideological tract bankrolled by the Manhattan Institute as part of its campaign to legitimize the rolling out of the police state to manage poverty (SW, p. 374).

[43] Jeffrey Fagan et al., "Declining Homicide in New York City: A Tale of Two Trends" (1998); Judith A. Greene, "Zero Tolerance: A Case Study of Police Policies and Practices in New York City" (1999); Ana Joanes, "Does the New York City Police Department Deserve Credit for the Decline in New York City's Homicide Rates? A Cross-City Comparison of Policing Strategies and Homicide Rates" (1999); Benjamin Bowling, "The Rise and Fall of New York Murder: Zero Tolerance or Crack's Decline?" (1999).

[44] Jack Maple and Chris Mitchell, *The Crime Fighter: How You Can Make your Community Crime-Free* (1999).

[45] Harcourt, *Illusions of Order*, esp. pp. 343–377, and "Reflecting on the Subject."

6

The upshot of Duneier's arguments is that there exists two categories of street people: those who, being moral and entrepreneurial, enhance social order and should be supported as well as "honored" (SW, p. 317), and those who do not and must presumably be cleaned out and away. Under the appearance of a critique of "zero-tolerance" policing, *Sidewalk* supplies a blueprint for a refocused, more efficient, class-cleansing of the street[46] that would stringently enforce the norm of "personal responsibility" but accord the worthy poor the room necessary to administer for themselves a sort of workfare program or "moral bootcamp" composed of begging, scrounging, and recycling second-hand merchandise:

> We can observe the following process. A man comes out of prison and goes to Sixth Avenue to panhandle. He watches another man's vending table and in time learns how to scavenge and find magazines that citizens will buy. Through his positive relations with customers and the self-direction that comes from being his own boss, he begins to feel the self-respect that also comes from knowing that he is earning an "honest living." After a time ... he makes his way off the streets to an apartment ... If residents come to see his behavior as a positive contribution, they treat him with a respect that he isn't used to. At the same time, other men who come out of jail or who know no other way of self-support than robbery will see models of positive behavior and begin to imitate them. "Fixed windows" and "broken windows" can work together. (SW, p. 311)

This Pollyannaish tale, premised on an artificial disjunction between sidewalk entrepreneurship and illegal activities, might in the best-case scenario apply to a handful of duly (self-)selected men, but it is evidently not replicable by the 60,000 ex-convicts who flood out of state prisons *every year* in New York State, three-fourths of whom come from and return to the seven poorest neighborhoods in New York City.[47] How many of them can realistically hope to find a place to peddle used magazines when vending spots are already overloaded, and how many can expect to earn enough that way to pay rent and move off the street when even full-time workers at low-wage

---

[46] "The 'broken windows' theory as applied to street life seems to have worked so well because it has been used so broadly that it can hardly fail. In effect, with an unsystematic definition of disorder, it has been applied unscientifically, with a large margin of error that is usually unobserved ... A better approach would be to define disorder with greater accuracy. In particular, I would like to see 'broken windows'-style regulation work without disrespecting people who are engaging in innocent entrepreneurial activity" (SW, p. 289). Just as respect rules the life of sidewalk vendors, it must guide the punitive action of the authorities.
[47] Loïc Wacquant, "Deadly Symbiosis: When Ghetto and Prison Meet and Mesh" (2001), pp. 114–115.

jobs cannot? Yet, in Duneier's view, what urban subproletarians need is a few "positive and inspiring models" to clue them in on how to make "an honest living" and a hearty serving of mutual and self-respect, and they will be just fine. Left to fend for themselves and each other on the sidewalk, they will learn self-direction, discover morality and, as a bonus, increase civility and "social solidarity" in the city.

One could hardly formulate a better brief for continuing the state policies of urban abandonment, social disinvestment, workfare, and "prisonfare" that have spawned the mounting social refuse strewn on the streets of the US metropolis. Indeed, Duneier endorses the *institutionalization of economic dispossession and social marginality as queer antipoverty policy* when he proposes that "we will improve our well-being by making provisions for more persons, not fewer, to engage in informal entrepreneurial activity," and that city government stay out of the way and accept such activity not only as "inevitable" but as downright "admirable" (SW, p. 315). Admirable indeed, is the ingenuity with which American society—and social science—keeps devising novels ways of making its poor shoulder the weight of their own predicament.

The good, the bad, and the sociologist in black Philly: Anderson on the "moral life of the inner city"

Whereas Duneier cleanses the street vendors of Manhattan's bohemian district by censoring and deflating those aspects of their activities that would render them less appealing to conventional society, Elijah Anderson does not shy away from unpalatable characters and facts. In *Code of the Street* (hereafter COS), he gives the reader a close-up view of the good, the bad, and the ugly on the rough streets of black Philadelphia with a frankness that places his study squarely in the genre exemplified by William Julius Wilson's 1987 book, *The Truly Disadvantaged*, with its unvarnished account of "social pathologies" in the urban core.[48] Anderson's book is striking for the candor and aplomb with which its author confronts realities that most observers either *cannot* see, because they remain safely remote from the scene, or *do*

---

[48] William Julius Wilson, *The Truly Disadvantaged: The Inner City, the Underclass, and Public Policy* (1987). *Code of the Street* can be read as the cultural elaboration and micro-sociological specification of the thesis advanced by Wilson (who praises the book on the inside dust jacket) that attributes the ills of the contemporary ghetto to the combination of unemployment caused by deindustrialization and social isolation fueled by family dissolution and the exodus of middle-class "role models" backed by persistent racial segregation. The back cover notes that Anderson's work "provides a new understanding of the lives of the *truly disadvantaged*," echoing the language of Wilson's book.

not want to see because it would ruffle their cherished preconceptions of the poor.

The culmination of years of difficult fieldwork and deep scholarly as well as personal engagement with the topic, *Code of the Street* seeks to explain "why is it that so many inner-city young people are inclined to commit aggression and violence toward one another" (COS, p. 9). The answer resides in the rise and spread of a "code of the street"— that is, an oppositional culture of masculine defiance and interpersonal brutality fueled, on the inside, by the declining availability and authority of wholesome "role models" and, on the outside, by economic dispossession (caused by deindustrialization) and by racial exclusion, variously manifested in white prejudice, discrimination, and segregation. To arrive at this answer, the Pennsylvania sociologist patiently exposes the overlapping cultural divisions, social tensions, and internecine struggles that rend the *fin-de-siècle* ghetto asunder and contribute to its collective quandary from within. But his analysis of these struggles is marred by (1) the reification of cultural orientations into groups; (2) conceptual equivocation about the notion of "code"; and (3) a persistent disconnect between data and theory that make it an unfinished work which ultimately raises more questions than it settles. In particular, Anderson's argument about the centrality of moral mentors is wedded to a theory of action, "role modeling," that is conceptually defective and continually contradicted by the evidence in the book. As for the narrative of deindustrialization and racial exclusion, it is artificially overlayed onto field descriptions that nowhere display how such external macrostructural forces come to impact life inside the ghetto.

Code of the Street reads like two separate books. The first, composed of the first four chapters, on the contest between conventional and street values, on the quest for manly respect in public encounters, on drugs and violence, and on the sexual mores of ghetto youth, revisits, revises, and generally repeats the themes and theses propounded in Anderson's (1990) previous book, *Streetwise*.[49] The second, also comprising four chapters, brings fresh materials on the two social types that Anderson considers the "moral pillars" of the ghetto, the "decent daddy" and the "inner-city grandmother," and on the travails of two young men who battle to tear themselves from the clutches of the street, the first unsuccessfully, the second with more sanguine results.

Both parts turn on the central opposition between "decency" and "the street," which Anderson introduces by taking the reader on a ride down

---

[49] Elijah Anderson, *Streetwise: Race, Class and Change in an Urban Community* (1990). *Code of the Street*'s chapter on "The Mating Game" is even an identical reprint of the chapter entitled "Sexual Codes and Family Life among Northton Youth" contained in *Streetwise*.

Germantown Avenue, a major artery of Philadelphia that runs from the white, affluent district of Chestnut Hill through Mount Airy, a mixed, middle-class area, to Germantown, a dilapidated black neighborhood where the "code of street" overwhelms the "code of civility." There, amidst a desolate urban landscape, young men "profile" and "represent" in and around "staging areas" that are so many proving grounds for a virulent and aggressive form of masculinity; public decency is openly flouted, crime and drug dealing are endemic, and fracas commonplace; streets, schools, stores, and homes are suffused with sociability but also with danger, dread, and destitution due to the dearth of jobs, the deficiencies of public services, racial stigma, and the profound sense of alienation and despair they feed (COS, pp. 20–30). Yet, far from being homogenous, like the city itself, this segment of the ghetto is differentiated along "two poles of value orientation, two contrasting conceptual categories" of "street and decent" which "organize the community socially" and determine the tenor of life in the neighborhood by "the way they coexist and interact" (COS, pp. 35, 33).

1

Anderson insists at the outset that these paired terms are "evaluative judgments that confer status upon local residents," "labels" that people use "to characterize themselves and one another." He wisely warns against reifying them by stressing that "individuals of either orientation may coexist in the same extended family" and that "there is also a great deal of 'code-switching,'" such that the same person "may at different times exhibit both decent and street orientation, depending on the circumstances" (COS, pp. 35–36). But he immediately casts aside his own warning and proceeds to treat these flexible cultural orientations as fixed repertoires—codes, cultures, or value systems—and even as sets of households arrayed against one another.

This is not a mere terminological problem. Despite his early insistence that "street" and "decent" are labels and not individuals or populations, Anderson handles them as such throughout the book. Thus chapter 1 is entitled "Decent and Street Families" and its main sections—"Decent Families," "The Single Decent Mother," and "The Street Family"—present individuals who are embodiments of two tangible social types. In the last chapter alone, Anderson insists that "most of the residents are decent," yet that "decent people seldom form anything like a critical mass." He estimates, based on visits in "numerous inner-city high schools," that "about a fifth of the students are invested in the code of the street" and that, by the fourth grade, three quarters have "bought into the code." He reports that "employers sometimes discriminate against entire census tracts or zip codes because they cannot or will not distinguish the decent people from these neighborhoods." And he refers to a decrease in "the ratio of decent to street-oriented people" as one moves deeper toward the heart of the ghetto or what he somewhat cryptically calls "ground zero" (COS: 309, 311, 317, 319, 324).

This classic case of *Zustandreduktion*, the "reduction of process to static conditions," to use Norbert Elias's idiom,[50] has three unfortunate consequences. First, transmuting folk notions that residents use to make sense of their everyday world into mutually exclusive populations prevents Anderson from analyzing the dynamic contest of categorization out of which the distinction between "street" and "decent" arises and how this contest affects individual conduct and group formation.[51] For it leaves unexamined the social mechanisms and paths whereby different persons drift toward this or that end of the spectrum, and what facilitates or hinders their sliding alongside it.[52]

Next, by taking his cue from the folk concepts of the residents without anchoring their points of view firmly in the social order, Anderson presumes precisely that which needs to be demonstrated: that these two sets of families are properly differentiated by their moral values rather than by the distinct *structural locations* they occupy in local social space and the objective life chances and liabilities associated with these locations. Anderson is fully aware that "the inner-city community is actually quite diverse economically," and he points in passing to variations in assets, occupation, income, and education (COS, p. 53). But he does not construct the system of places that these variations compose, so that practices that may be effects of social-structural position are *by default* automatically attributed to "culture" under the guise of "the code." Instead, he draws a dichotomous portrait of "decent families" and "street families" that leaves no middle ground, little overlap, and faint symbolic interplay between them.

Decent families display all the hallowed virtues of the stereotypical American family of dominant ideology: They are "working hard, saving money for material things, and raising children to try to make something out of themselves" in accordance with "mainstream values" (COS, p. 38). They hold on

---

[50] Elias, Norbert, *What is Sociology?* ([1968] 1970), p. 112.
[51] On the notion of "classification struggles," see Pierre Bourdieu, *Langage et pouvoir symbolique* (2000), pp. 206–211 and pp. 281–285; Bourdieu, *La Distinction.Critique sociale du jugement* (1979), pp. 559–564; Bourdieu, *Sociologie générale*, vol. 1, *Cours au Collège de France 1981–1983* (2015), pp. 84–87, 126–130.
[52] There are places where Anderson hints at this question, as when he notes that "the kind of home a child comes from influences but does not always determine" whether a child goes "decent" or "street," or when he writes that the inability of street-oriented kids to code-switch is "largely a function of persistent poverty and local neighborhood effects, but is also strongly related to family background, available peers, and role models" (COS, p. 93). But this listing of factors stops the inquiry right where it should begin.

to their jobs even when these are insecure and underpaid, ally themselves with "outside" institutions such as churches and schools, and keep faith in the future. Their deep religious commitment allows them to maintain "intact nuclear families" in which "the role of the 'man in the house'" predominates and instills in all a sense of personal responsibility. Street families are their mirror opposite: they "often show a lack of consideration for other people and have a rather superficial sense of family and community"; being deprived of good-paying jobs, their resources are limited and frequently misused, their lives "marked by disorganization" and filled with frustration. They are derelict in their parental duties, inconsiderate towards neighbors, and have periodic run-ins with the police; by example, they teach their children "to be loud, boisterous, proudly crude, and uncouth—in short, street" (COS, pp. 45–47). The question looms, *unanswered*: Are these families destitute because they are morally dissolute or the other way around? Is their cultural orientation the spring or the spin-off of their lower position in social space and of the different relation to the future that comes with it?

Note that Anderson's characterization of the "street family" is wholly negative: it is defined by deficiency, deficit, and lack; the street family's orientation and actions are grasped from the standpoint of "decent" families who strive to distance themselves from "uncouth" neighbors. By thus adopting the folk concepts of the residents as his analytic tools, Anderson runs into a third problem: like the "decent folks," he attributes all the ills of the "community" to the street people, in effect *taking sides* in the battle that these two factions (or class fractions) of the ghetto population wage against one another, instead of analyzing how their opposition operates practically to frame, curtail, or amplify objective differences in social position and strategies in the neighborhood. Anderson's candor about the unsavory aspects of ghetto life is thus accommodated by compartmentalizing behaviors and assigning flattering and offensive patterns to two distinct populations defined precisely by their contrasted moralities. Throughout the book, he is openly committed to documenting (and lamenting) the predicament and vindicating the point of view of the "decent" people. This personal commitment to "decency"—spotlighted by the term's presence in the subtitle of the book—limits Anderson's observations, colors his analyses, and truncates his ability to make sense of street values other than as the desecration of decent ones even as they are fostered, as we shall see below, by "adaptation" to material hardship and blocked opportunities.

The only negative property that Anderson reports about "decent families" is that their efforts at upward social mobility can be perceived as an expression of "disrespect" for their neighbors and is liable to trigger a "policing effort" designed to keep them from "'selling out' or 'acting white,'" which means adopting middle-class manners and moving out of the neighborhood. This is in sharp contrast to Anderson's earlier work, particularly *A Place on the Corner* (1978), a masterful study of the interactional construction of the ghetto social order, in which the points of view of the "regulars," the "winos," and the "hoodlums" are treated on a plane of full epistemic equality.

2

The centerpiece of Anderson's book is its grounded description of the workings of the "code of the street," this "set of prescriptions and proscriptions, or informal rules, of behavior organized around a desperate search for respect that governs public relations" in the ghetto (COS, p. 10). For the young men who embrace it, life is a perpetual "campaign for respect" waged by conveying through appearance, deportment, and demeanor, speech, and act that they are prepared to defy and dish out violence without fear of consequence so as to get their share of "juice," as manly regard is called on the streets. The diffusion of this bellicose mindset from the street into homes, schools, parks, and commercial establishments such as taverns and movie theaters infects all face-to-face relations. It feeds predatory crime and the drug trade, exacerbates interpersonal violence, and even warps practices of courtship, mating, and intimacy between the sexes.[53]

Here Anderson extends and enriches the previous abbreviated analysis by Richard Majors and Janet Billson of "the cool pose," that "ritualized form of masculinity" through which marginalized African Americans affirm "pride, strength and control" in the public theater of everyday life.[54] Majors and Billson saw the "cool pose" as a symptom of oppression manifested in disastrous education, rampant unemployment, high poverty, uncontrolled fertility, and hypermorbidity; they portrayed it as a product of "underlying structural violence that jeopardizes the equal opportunity of blacks" and "breeds violence

---

[53] On these topics, *Code of the Street* does not add much to the existing literature because it presents mostly stylized facts based on what Anderson himself calls "impressionistic materials from various social settings around the city" (COS, p. 10) that leave key processes underspecified. One finds thicker descriptions and deeper dissections of the crack trade in Philippe Bourgois, *In Search of Respect: Selling Crack in El Barrio* (1995, 2003); of the dynamics and dilemmas of stickup work in Richard Wright and Scott Decker, *Armed Robbers in Action: Stickups and Street Culture* (1997); of the sensual and moral construction of male honor through violent confrontation in Jack Katz, *Seductions of Crime: On the Moral and Sensual Attractions of Doing Evil* (1989); and of the plight and hopes of inner-city adolescent girls in Elaine Bell Kaplan, *Not Our Kind of Girl: Unraveling the Myths of Black Teenage Motherhood* (1997).

[54] Richard Majors and Janet Billson, *Cool Pose: The Dilemmas of Black Manhood in America* (1992), p. 23.

in its enraged victim." Anderson likewise presents the "code of the street" as "a complex cultural response to the lack of jobs that pay a living wage, to the stigma of race, to rampant drug use, to alienation and lack of hope" (Anderson's flapcover text).

But what exactly is a code, where does the "code of the street" come from, and how does it actually generate particular behaviors? One would expect that Anderson's book would elucidate these issues, but the more one reads the more muddled they seem to become. First, the code is variously described as a set of "informal rules," an "etiquette," a "value orientation," an "oppositional culture" and the objective regularities of conduct they prescribe, but also as a "script," a set of roles and their patterned expectations, a personal identity, a "milieu," and even as the "fabric of everyday life" *in toto*.[55] This loose and overexpansive definition creates problems, for if the code is both a cultural template that molds behavior and that behavior itself, the argument becomes circular. Next, there is considerable confusion as to the origins and vectors of the "code of the street." The notion is first introduced as a contemporary, group-specific, normative constellation spawned in the ghetto by the unique confluence of racial domination, economic devastation, and distrust of the criminal justice system. But a few pages later we learn that it is only the latest avatar of an ancient conception of masculine honor that reaches back to the dawn of civilization and is shared by a multiplicity of older and newer immigrant groups in American society.

> On the one side, Anderson writes that "the code is a complex cultural response to the lack of jobs that pay a living wage, to the stigma of race, to rampant drug use, to alienation and lack of hope." On the other, he maintains that "this code is not new. It is as old as the world, going back to Roman times or the world of the Shogun warriors or the early American Old South. And it can be observed in working-class Scott-Irish or Italian or Hispanic communities." (COS, flapcover text and p. 84)

For clarification, Anderson refers the reader to the "plausible description tracing the tradition and evolution of this code" supplied in two books by journalists, Fox Butterfield's *All God's Children* and Nicolas Lemann's *The Promised Land* (COS, p. 328). This does not clarify much, not only because neither book meets the usual standards of historical scholarship, but because they flat out gainsay Anderson's thesis of an aggressive conception of honor

---

[55] "The code of the street is not the goal or product of any individual's actions but is the fabric of everyday life, a vivid and pressing milieu within which all local residents must shape their personal routines, income strategies, and orientations to schooling, as well as their mating, parenting, and neighbor relations" (COS, p. 366).

spawned by a combination of deep poverty and racial exclusion leading to virulent alienation in the US metropolis after the 1970s. Lemann's (1986) book claims that the culture of the postindustrial ghetto is an import from the agrarian South brought there by the Great Migration of the interwar decades;[56] for him, the "code of the street" is a Southern complex rooted in sharecropping and thus operative also in rural regions. As for Butterfield, rampant violence in the inner city "has little to do with race or class, with poverty or education, with television or the fractured family"; it is neither recent nor peculiarly urban since it "grew out of a proud culture" of honor among whites in the antebellum South, which itself had its "roots in the blood feud between clans and families dating to the Middle Ages."[57]

Contradictory recountings of its origins and carrying group means that the "code of the street" can be variously interpreted as a conception of *masculinity* (shared by all classes), as a *lower-class* cultural model (shared by all ethnic groups), as an *ethnic* or regional cultural form (but specific to one gender), or yet as a sociomental construct spawned by a particular *place* of extreme destitution and alienation (the street, the jobless inner city, or the hyperghetto) perhaps with influences from the criminal or convict culture. Some clarification is in order here to better locate the "code of the street" somewhere between a timeless masculine propensity to aggression and the peculiar expression of ethnoracial, regional, or class atavism.

3

Tracing the genesis of the "code of the street" as historically sedimented and class-ethnically inflected masculine ways of thinking, feeling, and acting in urban public space would not only help specify its tenets and chart its transformation, showing how the "cool pose" of the 1970s mutated into the "hard case" of the 1990s for black men entrapped in the nether regions of US social space. It would also clear up another ambiguity in Anderson's account: the street code is said, at times, to organize and curtail violence by supplying "a kind of policing mechanism, encouraging people to trust others with a certain respect," while, at other times, it is found responsible for sowing distrust,

[56] Nicolas Lemann, *The Promised Land: The Great Black Migration and How it Changed America* (1986). What American social science calls "the Great Migration" refers to the exodus of millions of Black peasants, sharecroppers, farm workers, and domestic servants from the agrarian South to the industrial cities of the North in the years 1914–1930 and 1940–1965. See Loïc Wacquant, "De la 'terre promise' au ghetto. La 'Grande Migration' noire américaine, 1916–1930" (1993), and Stewart E. Tolnay, "The African American 'Great Migration' and Beyond" (2003).

[57] Fox Butterfield, *All God's Children: The Bosket Family and the American Tradition of Violence* (1995), pp. xviii, 11.

destabilizing relations, and diffusing aggression so that even "decent and law-abiding people become victims of random violence" (COS, pp. 105, 108).

This suggests that the "code" cannot explain a particular pattern of conduct *except in conjunction with other social forces* and factors that act as "switchboards" turning its (dis)organizing power on or off. Among these factors that beg for a more sustained discussion than Anderson offers are the wide availability of handguns and the growing symbiosis between the street and the prison culture due to the astronomical rates of incarceration of young African Americans from urban centers. This, in turn, implies that rising internecine violence in the ghetto is the unanticipated product of public policies of tolerance of private weapons (ownership and commerce) and of penal management of poverty in the metropolis via the "prisonization" of the street habitus, which points less to the local culture of masculinity than to to the state.[58]

For Fagan and Wilkinson, it is not the informal rules of masculine honor but the *implements and purposes of violence* that have changed in the ghetto over the past two decades.[59] In the early 1990s, the mass circulation of guns and their rampant use by street gangs to conquer and regulate expanding street-level drug markets caused a sudden upsurge and epidemic-like spread of violence (and account also in part for its recent decline). Then "guns became symbols of respect, power, identity and manhood to a generation of youth, in addition to having strategic value for survival" in an environment of dispossession and an "ecology of danger."[60]

Specifying how the code of the street produces more or less violent behavior on the ground would likely disclose its dubious conceptual status. As a *depictive* device designed to capture the everyday perspective of ghetto residents, it is useful and illuminating; as an *analytical* tool aimed at explaining social conduct, it suffers from severe shortcomings. Code is a concept that comes from cybernetics and information theory via structural linguistics and anthropology. But, as numerous critiques of structuralism have shown—the most thorough being Bourdieu's (1972, trans. 1977) well-known dissection of Lévi-Strauss in *Outline of a Theory Practice*[61]—such an approach reduces individuals or groups to the status of passive supports of a "code" that works

---

[58] Wacquant, "Deadly Symbiosis: When Ghetto and Prison Meet and Mesh."
[59] Jeffrey Fagan and Deanna L. Wilkinson, "Guns, Youth Violence, and Social Identity in Inner Cities" (1998).
[60] Ibid, p. 105. Bernard E. Harcourt explores the symbolic and emotional significance of gun use among adolescent criminals in *Language of the Gun: Youth, Crime, and Public Policy* (2006).
[61] Pierre Bourdieu, *Esquisse d'une théorie de la pratique, précédé de trois études d'ethnologie kabyle* (1972), pp. 169–174, and, for a stimulating reinterpretation, Antoine Lentacker, *La Science des institutions impures. Bourdieu critique de Lévi-Strauss* (2010).

out its independent semiotic logic "behind their backs"; it cannot grasp practice other than as the mere *execution* of a timeless cultural model that negates the inventive capacities of agents and the openendedness of situations, thereby freezing dynamic relations into eternal replicas of a single blueprint.

In many passages of Anderson's book, the code does appear as a *deus ex machina* that moves people about in the manner of puppets and dictates behavior irrespective of material and other factors. The "code of the street" is even invoked in instances where it is clearly superfluous: for example, one hardly needs to "acquire the street knowledge of the etiquette" of the stickup to figure that it is better to cooperate with an assailant who sticks a gun to your head and defer to his demands—which Anderson overinterprets as acknowledging "the authority, the worth, the status, even the respectability of the assailant" (COS, p. 128). It is a simple matter of trying to avoid injury or death, which any properly socialized urban denizen understands no matter her "code."

4

What a wayward youth caught by the street "needs is a serious helping hand: a caring old head can make a real difference" (COS, p. 136). With this pronouncement, Anderson sets the stage for the second part of *Code of the Street*, in which he seeks to demonstrate that wholesome "role models" such as the "decent daddy" and the "inner-city grandmother" have an impact on social life in the ghetto. The trouble here is that, as with Duneier's depiction of sidewalk vendors, upon close reading his own data continually rebut this thesis.

"The decent daddy is a certain kind of man," a "highly principled and moral" man with "certain responsibilities and privileges: to work, to support his family, to rule his household, to protect his daughters, and to raise his son to be like him," as well as "to carry the weight of the race on his shoulder" (COS, p. 180).[62] His authority rests on his embrace of the work ethic, his abiding commitment to propriety and property, support from the church and access to economic resources, chief among them jobs. But "today the decent daddy's role of sponsorship is being challenged by deindustrialization" and his "moral aura" is waning. Having lost his economic footing, his ranks are

---

[62] To "carry the weight of race" here means not to suffer the burden of prejudice and discrimination, but to prove oneself worthy of one's ethnic community and to advance its honor and interests. For an illuminating discussion of the social type of the "race man" and the "race hero," see St Clair Drake and Horace C. Cayton, *Black Metropolis: A Study of Negro Life in a Northern City* ([1945] 1993), pp. 390–395.

dwindling, he is becoming less visible, and many young men "play the role poorly" because they know only "the outlines of the model" for lack of having been exposed to it firsthand in its full splendor (COS, p. 185). They are thus liable to become defensive, hypersensitive, and short-tempered, and they sometimes take out their frustration on their women when the latter dare "challenge their image as the man in control" (COS, p. 187).

For proof that the "decent daddy" remains "important for the moral integrity of the community," Anderson adduces a string of loosely assembled observations, anecdotes, and interview excerpts, including eleven pages of a rambling and highly repetitive account, by one such "decent daddy," of an incident twenty-five years ago in which his beloved, model son was killed in a banal if horrific confrontation with gang members (COS, pp. 194–204). This father is understandably distressed and bitter that life should be so unfair to someone who has steadfastly honored precepts of "decency." But voicing such pain and tracing out the ripples of emotional damage through the family does little to specify the social conditions and mechanisms whereby the morality he aspires to and embodies can or cannot become socially effective. Indeed, this "decent daddy" and his compatriots emerge as anachronistically yearning for a bygone world of stable factory employment and retrograde gender arrangements in which the man is the provider and the woman keeps to "her place, which is taking care of the house and preparing food to his satisfaction" while being watchful "not [to] speak out of turn or talk too much and make him look small" (COS, p. 183).

Anderson's own nostalgia for this age of Fordist patriarchy blinds him to the fact that, far from being content with domestic subservience, African American women have long assumed a major role in the affairs of their community and that the waning of the influence of the "decent daddy" is due not simply to the declining economic position of black men and their inability to deliver tangible rewards ("Their moral authority is weakened when being nice doesn't lead to material benefits: a good job for a young man, a good household for a young woman"; COS, pp. 204–205). It results from a sea change in the shape and dynamics of family, gender, and age relations sweeping over a profound and long-standing rift between black men and women that is especially pronounced at the bottom of the class structure but affects all classes.[63] No amount of bemoaning the rise of the "'bad heads' (like certain

---

[63] For a description contrary to the indigenous masculinist vision of "decent daddies," documenting the less visible but no less decisive role of women as "makers of the race," see Evelyn Brooks Higginbotham, "African-American Women's History and the Metalanguage of Race" (1992), and Higginbotham, *Righteous Discontent: The Women's Movement in the Black Baptist Church, 1880–1920* (1994); Deborah Gray White, *Too Heavy a Load: Black Women in Defense of Themselves, 1894–1994* (1998); Darlene Clark and Kathleen

rap artists),'" who now allegedly supplant the "decent daddy" as beacon of achievement, will restore the conditions that made the latter a salient social type and bring back "'the old days [when] the black man was strong'" so that "'even the white man would take note,'" as of Anderson's informants put it (COS, pp. 205 and 194).

Much as the role of the "decent daddy" is fast eroding, "the network of grandmothers continues to form a communal safety net" of sorts but "that net is weakened and imperiled" (COS, p. 207). Because of economic retrenchment, the spread of drugs, and the attendant crystallization of the oppositional culture of the street, the "black grandmother is once again being called upon to assume her traditional role" as "selfless savior of the community," valiantly taking care of unwanted children, compensating for "the inability—or unwillingness in many cases—of young men to fulfill their parental obligations and responsibilities," and wielding moral authority at large (COS, pp. 208, 211). Though there exists, not surprisingly, two types of grandmothers, the respectable and the street-oriented, the traditional grandmother is basically the older female counterpart to the "decent daddy": financially secure, God-fearing, ethically conservative, dependable, and insistent on authority and accountability. But if it is true that she has become "a conceptual touchstone [?] of the value system into which many young girls are initiated and actively grow" (COS, p. 214), then why do so many of these same girls behave so recklessly?

Instead of subjecting his informants' romanticized vision of the past to a methodical critique informed by the social and oral history of the ghetto, Anderson lionizes it, leaving unresolved two contradictions at the heart of his account. First, the two major roles of the "decent daddy" and the "heroic grandmother" cannot have blossomed together since their functional importance is inversely related: who needs the valiant grandmother to take care of the babies of a wayward daughter if the decent father has successfully "modeled" proper morality and raised his children, and especially his sons, the right way? Indeed, neither social type plays a major part in historical depictions of the midcentury ghetto and in contemporary life story accounts.[64] Second, the "traditional grandmother" succeeds as *grandmother* only because,

---

Thompson, *A Shining Thread of Hope: The History of Black Women in America* (1998). For a methodical treatment of the profound "crisis of just about every aspect of gender relations in all classes of African Americans," see Orlando Patterson's stimulating and disturbing essay, "Broken Bloodlines" (1998).

[64] For example, Drake and Cayton, *Black Metropolis*; Cheryl Lynn Greenberg, *Or Does It Explode? Black Harlem During the Great Depression* (1991); Joe W. Trotter, *Black Milwaukee: The Making of an Industrial Proletariat, 1915–45* (1985), and Trotter, "African Americans in the City: The Industrial Era, 1900–1950" (1995); Kimberley Louise Phillips, *AlabamaNorth: African-American Migrants, Community, and Working-Class Activism in Cleveland, 1915–45* (1999); and, for the contemporary period, Bettylou

in Anderson's own terms, she has failed as *mother*: despite her "enormous moral authority and spiritual strength," she was unable to rein in her adolescent daughters and prevent their untimely pregnancy. And now she has to pick up the pieces as best as she can in the context of public indifference such that she can rely on no one but herself and her close female kin.

As evidence for the ethical prowess of the "inner-city grandmother," Anderson supplies the fifteen-page-long, underedited transcript from "a tape-recorded conversation" with Betty (COS, pp. 219–233), one such grandmother. To the degree that one can trust an account that is uncorroborated by observational data, this transcript suggests not that Betty embraced a glorious moral calling on behalf of the "community," but that she was forced to take over the care of her teenage daughter's babies owing to the criminal ineptitude of the city's child, health, and social services. The latter did next to nothing to protect a twelve-year-old girl who reportedly was pulling knives on her own mother, ran away repeatedly, was raped on the streets, and infected with syphilis and herpes, as well as addicted to crack (which the hospital staff where she delivered a two-pound baby failed to detect; COS, p. 224–225). Brute necessity and the tragic bankruptcy of public institutions rule the day in the ghetto. Betty is understandably exhausted and exasperated: she wishes that her daughter and her babies would "just go and stay away" and that doctors would forcibly sterilize her.

Anderson titles the closing section of the transcript "The Final Reality: Betty Accepts Her Heroic Role," but there is little heroism in such *kinship servitude* thrust upon (sub)proletarian women by the faltering of the social welfare wing of the state. The state's contribution to this calamity is even greater yet, as Betty had to give up her job as a nurse's aide to be allowed to receive welfare for her daughter's babies. Anderson unwittingly concedes that material push, and not normative pull, is what trapped her in this predicament: "The lack of affordable day care in conjunction with the rules of welfare eligibility left Betty with only one responsible course of action: to leave her job in the private sector in order, in effect, to become employed by the state to raise her grandchildren" (COS, p. 233).

In no other Western society would a grandmother have to pay such a high price for the combined errant conduct of her daughter and the gross dereliction of the state. Indeed, Anderson admits in the closing lines of the chapter that, "although generally loved and respected even when disobeyed," the grandmothers "are losing clout" and "may come to seem irrelevant" (COS,

---

Valentine, *Hustling and other Hard Work: Life Styles in the Ghetto* (1978); John Langston Gwaltney, *Drylongso: A Self-Portrait of Black America* (1980); Sylvester Monroe and Peter Goldman, *Brothers: Black and Poor-A True Story of Courage and Survival* (1988); and Alex Kotlowitz, *There Are No Children Here* (1991).

p. 236), an admission that contradicts the thrust of his analysis hitherto. All in all, Anderson presents a moving portrait of the "decent daddy" and the "inner-city grandmother" as the backbone of the urban black community; however this portrait suggests, not that they operate as viable moral anchors and social mentors, but that they are overloaded and out of touch with current gender, family, and state relations.

Anderson does not consider the possibility that, just as she can serve as a moral anchor, a grandmother may act as a malevolent force, drawing her children and grandchildren into a web of drug addiction and trafficking, theft, prostitution, and other criminal activities, in response to abject poverty and rampant violence affecting the lineage she heads. Yet that is precisely the case of America's most famous "inner-city grandmother," whose "harrowing true story" is recounted by Pulitzer Prize-winning journalist Leon Dash in *Rosa Lee* (1997) and was chronicled in a widely watched PBS documentary.[65]

5

The final two chapters of *Code of the Street* recount the travails of two young men struggling to gain a footing in the legal economy and achieve a measure of material stability and social standing. Here, Anderson offers a rare window onto the perilous obstacle course that African American men face as they seek to trump their preordained fate at the bottom of the class and caste order. The book finally comes alive with stirring and eventful materials that richly repay a close reading and allow Anderson to display his deft touch for ethnographic probing. We get a close-up view of how John and Robert attempt to juggle the conflicting demands of employers and kin, sort out loyalty to the proximate peer group and commitment to established society, and conciliate the defiant masculine ethos of the street with resignation to the dull life of the low-wage laborer. The problem is, not only is the ratio of analysis to narrative and interview transcripts quite low (some eight pages out of fifty-two in the first case examined), but the latter hardly support the theory of mentoring and deindustrialization-*cum*-racism that Anderson intends them to illustrate. "John Turner's Story" (chap. 7) is emblematic of this stubborn disconnect between data and interpretation.

John Turner is a twenty-one-year-old high-school graduate and father of six children from four different women, with extensive ties to gangs and repeated collisions with the law, whom Anderson first encounters in a carry-out

[65] Leon Dash, *Rosa Lee: A Mother and her Family in Urban America* (1996).

restaurant where John toils as a busboy for $400 a month. The "college professor" helps him gain a respite from the court, then finds him a solid job working as a janitor at a hospital where, despite a rough start and the declared reticence of the union steward, John promptly posts a stellar record. But, a few weeks later, he is thrown back in jail for failing to pay his monthly court fine of $100, even though his hourly wages have jumped from $3.50 to $8.50—John maintains he has other, more pressing, needs to meet, such as saving for his children's future college education. After he returns to work, the young man confronts the open disdain and ostracism of the older janitors, who feel threatened by his presence and devalued by his demeanor. As a result, John abruptly quits his job and resumes dealing drugs, burning his way through mounds of "easy money" in a spree of personal dissipation, conspicuous consumption, and gifts to kin.

A year later, the streets have turned out too wild and treacherous for his own taste and John wants to "cool out." So he returns to begging for money, a suit, and a job from Anderson who, after unsuccessfully trying to enroll him in the military (John's criminal record makes him ineligible) eventually lands the young man yet another entry-level position in a restaurant kitchen, making him "the happiest man on earth" simply for having a job this time. When John later insists that he needs money to help his children, Anderson gives him $150 as a means to sever their relationship.[66] Later, we learn that John got shot in the gut in a drug deal gone sour in Baltimore and finds himself a cripple for life at age twenty-seven.

As in previous chapters, Anderson asserts that "the system of legitimate employment is closed off to young men like John Turner: by prejudice, by lack of preparation, or by the absence of real job opportunities. But they observe others—usually whites—enjoy the fruits of the system, and through this experience they become deeply alienated. They develop contempt for a society they perceive as having contempt for them. The reality of racism looms large in their minds" (COS, p. 286). The trouble is, this explanation does not fit John Turner's story at all: thanks to Anderson's personal assist, the employment system was opened to him (as well as by his own mother, who earlier got him a job as a technician in the pharmaceutical company where she works), and he did gain access to a secure, well-paid position with full benefits. Moreover, there were no whites on the scene to exclude or

---

[66] Anderson is brutally honest about the motives and conditions of their parting: "I had continued to help John even after it had become apparent that he was using me, because I wanted to see how he responded to various situations. At this point, however, I felt I had developed a rather complete picture of him; furthermore, I was beginning to feel uneasy about our association" (COS, p. 285). No such negatively charged intercourse is reported with "decent families."

block him, as it was *black* janitors who "dogged" and harassed him out of the hospital: the shop steward who was supposed to sponsor him nicknamed him "the half-way man,"[67] put his "shit out on the street" (revealing to others John's paternity and family situation), and routinely "dissed" him by making derogatory remarks about his sexual habits ("Keep that thing in your damn pants!"). Likewise, in recounting Robert's story, Anderson claims that "people associated with the criminal element . . . justify their criminal behavior by reference to racism, which they and their friends face daily" (COS, p. 317). Yet one striking feature of Robert's trajectory is precisely that he never encounters a single white person; even when he runs into trouble with city officials, it is a black city inspector who gives him grief over his license as a street vendor.

So neither deindustrialization nor racism provides a straightforward explanation for John Turner's backslide to the demimonde of the street, i.e., for why he could not *hang on* to a firm spot in the legal economy after he had been given a royal chance to ensconce himself in it. This is not to say that labor market restructuring and racial domination are not at play here, for clearly they are: the virulent *class* prejudice *among* African American workers that detonates John's relapse into the informal economy is overdetermined by their collective vulnerability in the age of desocialized wage labor and made potent by the embeddedness of black employees in a structure of authority governed and surveilled by whites. But it is equally clear that a number of crucial mediations are missing here if we are to link the macrostructures of class and caste inequality to the micro-setting in which John Turner's actions acquire their logic and meaning. Nor is the "lack of an effective role model" responsible for John Turner's undoing (COS, p. 237). For surely, if a mentor as powerful as Anderson, with his extensive connections, impeccable cultural credentials, and multifaceted interventions (he gets John a top-flight attorney, contacts his parole officer, intercedes time and again to get him jobs, and supplies a supportive ear, stopgap money and sage advice throughout) could not extricate John from his troubles, what chance would a dispossessed and isolated "old head" from the neighborhood stand to have an impact?

The lesson Anderson draws from this biographical case study is that there exists "a basic tension between the street and the decent, more conventional world of legitimate jobs and stable families" and that, at the end of the day, "the draw of the street is too powerful, and [John] was overcome by its force" (COS, p. 285). But this merely *re-describes* the phenomenon at hand; it does

---

[67] The expression is derived from the term *halfway house*, meaning a transitional residence ran by the Department of Corrections between prison and final release. In other words, it is a mocking reference to John's legal troubles.

nothing to explain it. Anthropomorphizing the street, as folk wisdom does, cannot reveal whence its power comes and how it operates. To unlock that enigma, one must recognize that John's conduct is neither the blind execution of a normative model ("the code") nor the rational pursuit of opportunities effectively offered to him at a given time, but the product of a discordant dialectic between the *social structures* he faces and the *mental structures* through which he perceives and evaluates them, which are themselves issued out of the chaotic world of the street and therefore tend to reproduce its patterns even when faced with a different environment.[68] What ultimately foils John Turner's escape from the subproletariat is not a generic opposition between the "culture of decency" and the "code of the street" but the specific *disjuncture between* the social *position* opened to him and the *dispositions* he imports into it: John's strategies continue to be driven by a street habitus even as his objective possibilities momentarily expand beyond those usually afforded by the ghetto.

Adopting the static theory of "role enactment" and its correlate, Robert Merton's notion of "anomie," not only forces Anderson to regress to an *ad hoc* psychological explanation, as when he proposes that John Turner could not escape the street because "he never seemed fully committed to improving himself" (COS, p. 274).[69] It also prevents him from inquiring into the social constitution and workings of what is a *broken habitus*, made up of contradictory cognitive and conative schemata, disjointedly assembled via durable immersion in an entropic universe of extreme economic marginality and social instability, which continually generates irregular and contradictory lines of action that make its bearer ill-suited to the requirements of the formally rational sector of the economy.[70] The built-in limitations of role theory block Anderson from capturing the evolving dialectic between social position and disposition that governs the *double-sided production of urban marginality* and explains, in cases of disjuncture such as this one, how the

---

[68] For a detailed analysis of this dialectic in the case of Algerian subproletarians, see Pierre Bourdieu, *Algérie 1960. Structures économiques et structures temporelles* (1977).

[69] This argument also suffers from circularity, as the evidence for John's alleged lack of commitment to "decency" is the very behavior that the lack of decency is supposed to explain. Had John secured a foothold in the legal economy, one could argue *a contrario* that this proves that he is indeed devoted to conventional values. Nothing would be demonstrated in either case.

[70] For an empirical illustration of how a fractured habitus functions to produce unstable and volatile strategies in the hyperghetto economy, which reinforce the objective irregularities of its collective organization, see Loïc Wacquant, "Inside the Zone: The Craft of the Hustler in the Black American Ghetto" ([1992] 1998). For a fuller discussion of this dialectic of objective structures and subjective apirations among deproletarianized African American men, read Alford A. Young, *The Minds of Marginalized Black Men: Making Sense of Mobility, Opportunity, and Future Life Chances* (2004), and, for a telling contrast with John Turner's failure, see Fernández-Kelly's recapitulation of "Towanda's Triumph: Social and Cultural Capital in the Transition to Adulthood in the Urban Ghetto" (1994).

latter may paradoxically be perpetuated by the very people upon whom it is imposed.[71]

6

Because he starts from an overly monolithic vision of the ghetto and conflates folk with analytic concepts, Anderson cannot relate the *moral distinctions* he discovers in it to its internal *social stratification*. He thus boxes himself into a culturalist position with deeply disturbing political implications insofar as they render ghetto residents responsible for their own plight through their deviant values or role ineptness. To preempt this, Anderson must superimpose the trope of deindustrialization and racism onto his "role-model" theory, even though little in his field observations points to these factors. Had he started from a systematic map of social differentiation inside the ghetto, he would have found that what he depicts as the "coexistence" of two "codes" that seem to float up above the social structure is in fact a low-grade cultural war and social antagonism, centered over the appropriation of public space, *between two fractions of the black urban proletariat*, the one situated at the cusp of the formal wage economy and tenuously oriented toward the official structures of white-dominated society (the school, the law, marriage), the other deproletarianized and demoralized to such an extent that it is turning inward to the informal society and economy of the street.

The distinction between these two categories is not a hard and fast one but, on the contrary, labile and porous, produced and marked by microdifferences imperceptible to the "distant gaze" of outsiders. But these small positional differences are associated with homological differences in dispositions that tend to reinforce them and, through a cumulative dialectic of social and moral distanciation, determine divergent fates among people who seem to have started out from about the same place (especially if they are observed from afar and from above, as in survey research).

Much as a battle rages inside the ghetto between the "street" and "decent" orientations, that is, between two relations to the future anchored in adjacent but distinct social positions and trajectories, an unresolved clash runs through the pages of *Code of the Street* between two Elijah Andersons and two theories of the involution of the ghetto, "role-model deficit" and "deindustrialization-*cum*-racism," which express the different political facets of the work and carry with them divergent policy prescriptions.

---

[71] This paradox is a central theme of Philippe Bourgois's book *In Search of Respect*.

Anderson-the-conservative, propounding a *normative* theory of social action and a *moral* theory of social order, keeps asserting the importance of (masculine) values and commitment to (patriarchal) decency. Anderson-the-liberal, wedded to a *rational choice* model of conduct and a *materialist* conception of social structure, counters that lack of jobs caused by deindustrialization and persistent racial exclusion doom inner-city residents anyway. Anderson-the-moralist recommends the rebuilding of "the social infrastructure" of the ghetto, which requires that "the old heads of the community [be] empowered and activated,"—that is, a conservative return to a past that never was. Anderson-the-materialist calls in mantric fashion for the "opening up [of] the world of work" via "a comprehensive plan that will allow no one to fall through the cracks," (COS, p. 316)—that is, leap into a liberal future that will never be.

In the first version, ghetto residents are *agents* of their own moral and cultural dereliction, but only insofar they are utter "cultural dopes" deceived by a "code" gone awry.[72] In the second, they are hapless *victims* of structural changes in the economy and continued domination by whites. The stitching together of these contradictory theses is effected by making the "code" an "adaptation" to circumstances, and cultural alterity a by-product of structural blockage (a similar resolution of this antinomy is found in William Julius Wilson's *When Work Disappears*).[73] But this move guts out the symbolic dimension of social life in the ghetto: it robs culture of any autonomy, it strips agents of all "agency," and it takes us back to a mechanical model wherein behavior is deduced from a cultural code that is itself directly derived from an objective structure wholly external to the ghetto. And this, in turn, negates the important lesson of Anderson's book: that there exists significant if fine-grained cultural and moral distinctions inside the ghetto, inscribed in both institutions and minds, that help explain the diversity of strategies and trajectories followed by their residents that only long-term ethnography can detect and dissect.

Another paradoxical consequence of this mechanical reversion to economic determination-in-the-last-instance is that it leads Anderson to dismiss the very cultural and moral distinctions that he has spent the entire book elaborating when he concludes: "The condition of these communities was produced *not by moral turpitude but by economic forces* that have undermined black, urban, working-class life and a

---

[72] This is Harold Garfinkel's term for the structural-functionalist theory of action, according to which the agent mechanically obeys norms, as opposed to a conscious, reflective, and skillful agent in the conduct of everyday affairs. Harold Garfinkel, *Studies in Ethnomethodology* (1967), p. 68.

[73] William Julius Wilson, *When Work Disappears: The World of the New Urban Poor* (1996).

neglect of their consequences on the part of the public ... The focus should be on the *socioeconomic structure*, because it was structural change that caused jobs to decline and joblessness to increase ... But the focus also belongs on the *public policy* that has radically threatened the well-being of many citizens" (COS, p. 315; emphasis added). Why, then, devote 350 pages to anatomizing the "moral life of the inner city" if it is but an epiphenomenon of industrial restructuring and state neglect? And why does the book not contain a single statistic on the evolving economic and employment makeup of Philadelphia nor a single line on the changing public policies pursued at the municipal, local, and federal levels?

Model citizens hidden at the heart of Harlem: Newman on fast-food workers

Newman's team study of "the working poor in the inner city" was sparked by a banal street scene: en route from New York's Upper West Side to the airport one morning to attend a conference on *The Truly Disadvantaged*,[74] she was struck by the sight of Harlem bus shelters packed with "lines of men and women dressed for work, holding the hands of their children on their way to day care and the local schools ... This place was a far cry from the jobless ghettos described by the literature on the 'urban underclass.'"[75] Stuck in traffic, from her car window, Newman "saw the working poor people who were still in the community, *soldiering on*" and wondered: "Should we not learn something from these people, whose *strength* we might be able to build on, before we consign our whole poverty policy to the ups and downs of the welfare system? ... By the time I reached La Guardia Airport, the outlines of this book had formed in my head" (NSMG, pp. x–xi; emphasis added).

To demonstrate that the ghetto is "teeming" with unseen solid citizens, devoted to "family values" and steeped in the "work ethic," Newman hired a large "multiethnic research team" of graduate students whom she directed to interview and collect the life stories of two hundred young workers at four Harlem fast-food outlets and to follow a dozen such laborers, who also turned in personal diaries, for about a year. While her "research team donned the crew uniform to work behind the counters of the restaurants for four months," she "spent time alone with the owners and managers of the

---

[74] This theme of "jobless ghettos" is developed in particular by William Julius Wilson in his book *When Work Disappears: The World of the New Urban Poor* (1996).
[75] The scene takes place near the Columbia University campus where Newman teaches, a campus that partly abuts the Harlem ghetto, or what is left of it.

same restaurant, . . . absorbing the admirable blend of profit motives and missionary zeal that led them to establish their firms" in Harlem and learning about the secret virtues of working at disparaged "McJobs" (NSMG, p. 36).

This initial revelation and the research strategy adopted to authenticate it contain *in nuce* the categories and concerns that organize *No Shame in My Game*, the ingredients for its contribution as well as the fount of its biases, shortcomings, and gaps. On the positive side, Newman launches a frontal attack on the reigning public image of ghetto residents as slothful and immoral freeloaders who burden the societal body, showing that "the nation's working poor do not need their values reengineered" but rather employment that would enable them to achieve a modicum of material stability and social dignity (NSMG, p. 298). By tracking at ground level the daily battles of Harlem fast-food workers to find, retain, and subsist on the famine-wage, part-time jobs that are the norm of that service sector, she shines a bright light on the plight of one salient segment of the 7 million Americans (7% of the country's labor force, one black man and one white woman in four, two thirds of them adults) who toil in the underbelly of the urban economy yet cannot escape the yoke of crushing poverty. By making visible "the invisible poor" who drudge under Third-World conditions at the heart of the First World city just as "welfare reform" denies them vital social services and combines with immigration to put downward pressure on wages by flodding an already overcrowded unskilled labor market, she demonstrates, after others, how profoundly miscast the US debate and policy on poverty, welfare, and race has been.[76]

The problem is that Newman fights the prevalent stereotype of the inner-city social parasite by turning it squarely on its head and replacing it by *its mirror opposite*, the media-*cum*-political stereotype of the "working family,"[77] which makes ghetto residents over into virtual clones of worthy middle-class suburbanites, indistinguishable from "mainstream Americans" save by the color of their skin, their unattractive residence, and their hapless circumstances.

---

[76] Newman confirms and extends recent studies on welfare and work: Wilson, *When Work Disappears*; Joel F. Handler and Yeheskel Hasenfeld, *We the Poor: Work, Poverty and Welfare* (1997); Kathryn Edin and Laura Lein, *Making Ends Meet: How Single Mothers Survive Welfare and Low-Wage Jobs* (1997); on race and welfare: Jill Quadagno, *The Color of Welfare: How Racism Undermined the War on Poverty* (1994); Michael Brown, *Race, Money, and the American Welfare State* (1999); Martin Gilens, *Why Americans Hate Welfare: Race, Media, and the Politics of Anti-Poverty Policy* (1999); and on low-wage and part-time work in the US: Harry Holzer, *What Employers Want: Job Prospects for Less-Educated Workers* (1996); Chris Tilly, *Half a Job: Bad and Good Part-Time Jobs in a Changing Labor Market* (1996).

[77] Vague by design, the term "working family" emerged in political discourse in the 1980s and was taken up by some sociologists to refer to middle-class (white) families destabilized by the fact that both parents had to work to maintain their class status. See Arlie Hochschild with Anne Machung, *The Second Shift: Working Families and the Revolution at Home* (1989).

Newman writes: "One of their greatest assets is the commitment they share with more affluent Americans to the importance of the work ethlc. These arc not people whose values need reengineering. They work hard at jobs the rest of us would not want because they believe in the dignity of work. In many instances they are not only not better off, they are actually worse off from a financial perspective for having eschewed welfare and stayed on the job. But it also benefits them, as it benefits their middle-class counterparts, because working keeps them on the right side of American culture. Nonetheless they are poor, and because of this unhappy truth, they are subjected to many of the same forces that the nonworking poor must contend with: decaying housing, poor diet, lack of medical attention, lousy schools, and persistent insecurity." (NSMG, p. xv)

In so doing, Newman entrenches several misconceptions central to the very conventional wisdom she wishes to displace including (i) the presociological notion that social conduct is a direct, instantaneous precipitate of "culture" understood as a simple linear hierarchy of values (crowned by the national calling for work) consensually adhered to and untainted by power and interests; (ii) the dualistic division between "people ... who [are] outside of the labor market, sitting on the welfare sidelines" and "the others, the hardworking people of communities like Harlem struggling to get to work on time" (NSMG, p. xi), which her own evidence reveals to be both artificial and misleading; (iii) the national obsession with moral valiancy and "family values" that purportedly enable the working poor to "summon the personal strength to blast past the stigma" of substandard wage employment (NSMG, p. xiv) in the deregulated service economy, even though sheer material necessity is more than sufficient to account for their practices; (iv) a remarkably benevolent view of business—she hails Harlem fast-food operators as "unsung heroes"—which blinds her to the brutal class relations and malign state policies that undergird and underwrite the despotic labor regimes she extensively documents; (v) the persistent confusion between issues of *mobility* (or "opportunity"), which concern the allocation and movement of persons across positions, and issues of structured *inequality*, which has to do with the objective gap between places along the "occupational pyramid" and their associated rewards, risks, and penalties. This last confusion leads her to formulate policy recommendations guaranteed to perpetuate the very problems she diagnoses by further expanding desocialized wage labor and the life insecurity it entails.

Newman's depiction of the working sections of the ghetto population as run-of-the-mill middle-class Americans in poor people's disguise—"hardworking tax-paying citizens [who] are also poor" (NSMG, p. 36) and who, like the author, sacralize work even as it fails to sustain them—results from the methodical *inversion of material compulsion into moral impulsion* which gives *No Shame in My Game* a distinctive schizophrenic feel and skews its analyses from start to finish. One passage among many is paradigmatic of its continual conversion of economic necessity into cultural virtue. Early in the book, Newman notes that structural changes in the country's economy, welfare, and public services retrenchment, and the renewed influx of migrants "have pulled the rug out from under the low-wage labor market." But this "bad news" is counterbalanced by "the good news":

> [D]espite all of these difficulties [!], the nation's working poor continue to seek their *salvation* in the labor market. That such a *commitment* persists when the economic rewards are so minimal is testimony to the *durability of the work ethic*, to the powerful reach of mainstream American *culture*, which has always placed work at the center of our collective *moral existence*. (NSMG, p. 61; emphasis added)

"Commitment," "ethic," "culture," "moral existence": these are the central categories that Newman deploys to describe and explain the life and labor of Harlem youth employed at fast-food outlets. As with Duneier, this spiritual language automatically suppresses coarse material matters of class, struggle, exploitation, and domination. But, here again, the major advantage of *a moral idiom to analyze the functioning of an economy* is that it is spontaneously adjusted to the cognitive and evaluative lens of "mainstream American" readers, and especially of policymakers who appear to be the book's primary target audience.

This conceptual muzzling is redoubled by the design of the study, which effectively selects on the dependent variable: by focusing on the "working poor," who by definition participate in the low-wage sector of the economy, Newman is bound to find that ghetto residents do cling to the margins of the labor market. Indeed, where else could they "seek salvation" when the state is, on the one side, rolling back its social safety net and forcing the poor into inferior jobs via workfare and, on the other, widening and tightening its penal dragnet to sweep away those who would seek escape from servile wage labor in the illegal sectors of the street economy?[78] Together, the research design and the moral(istic) reasoning of its author make the main conclusions of *No Shame in My Game* a matter of *petitio principii*.

---

[78] Loïc Wacquant, *Punishing the Poor: The Neoliberal Government of Social Insecurity* (2009), pp. 1–8, 11–16, 29–32.

1

In keeping with its purpose to raise the standing of minority low-wage employees in the symbolic hierarchy of the country, the book opens with a series of moral tales of family hardship and individual courage against formidable odds. These stories are intended to show that the "values" of the "working poor" of Harlem "place work and family at the center of their own culture in a form that would be embraced even by conservative forces in American society" (NSMG, p. 201). But, while these stories paint a grisly portrait of overwhelming material constraint and crushing socioeconomic adversity, Newman's gloss consistently stresses cultural valor and personal purpose—as if the analyst and the people she depicts somehow obeyed different laws of causality.

The book's core chapters narrate how young, uneducated Harlemites search for and find jobs in their borough, and how they cope with the practical hardships and social disrepute attached to these jobs in order to cling to the world of work. We learn that ghetto youths pursue paid employment in clothing outlets, pharmacies, bodegas, cosmetics, and sporting goods stores, as well as security firms and fast-food establishments, first and foremost to gain protection from the pressures of the street and to escape trouble at home and in the neighborhood. They are also anxious to relieve the financial burden they represent for their families, which explains why they start laboring in their early teens, bagging groceries and doing odd chores off the books in local stores, or at publicly funded summer jobs, to bring cash into their home and cover the cost of their clothing, food, and schooling. For young mothers, low-wage employment offers an insurance policy of sorts against dependency on unreliable and often violent men, while having and gaining new friends at work is a major attraction for all.

Throughout the book, we encounter Harlemites who engaged in state-tolerated and even state-sponsored child labor reminiscent of the 19th century, such as Tamara, who toiled selling newspapers at 11 and Tiffany, who bagged groceries at age 10 and worked as a clerk for a public agency providing assistance to victims of domestic violence before her thirteenth birthday (NSMG, pp. 71, 78, 95). None of this disturbs Newman in the least. In all other major OECD countries (except South Africa and Turkey), such preteen labor is considered child abuse and liable to criminal prosecution.

It would thus seem that an array of *material factors and social forces* explain why poor black and Latino teenagers seek and hold on to substandard employment slots even as they gain little from them financially (often no more than a few dollar a day). Not so, insists Newman, who points time and again to the "dignity of work" and the inner desire of ghetto youths to honor the nation's most sacred value. Will power, character, resolve, and responsibility: not sociological concepts, but the everyday moral categories of the American middle class serve to depict and decipher their conduct.

In nearly every case presented, individual willpower seems to be the decisive factor. Thus Jamal "started drinking and taking the occasional hit of cocaine" one summer but soon "pulled himself out of it by *sheer force of character*" because he "is different" from those who would give in to such pressure: "He takes his *responsibilities* seriously... Most notable about Jamal is his *commitment to work*, to the importance of trying to *make it on his own*" (NSMG, p. 12, emphasis added). Kyesha "is *strong-willed* ... The *choice* she made, to terminate the pregnancies, resulted directly from the *desire* she had to hold on to the one part of her life that really worked: her job ... There is little hope that Kyesha and Juan will ever marry, settle down, and give their son a home of his own," given the famine wages they are earning (five dollars an hour each after years of hard labor), but "still, they are *responsible* parents who work for a living" and wish to avoid becoming "one more statistic in the long litany of problems in the welfare system." (NSMG, p. 26, 30, emphasis added)

This rhetoric of choice is so suffusive that it overlays even constraint, which enters into the analysis as the product of previous choices made by individuals: "Values are only part of the story. Social structure tells the rest. Some people are positioned to act on their ambitions and others are trapped," not by an objective structure of relations made up of the confluence of socioracial inequality and superexploitative job chains anchored by a given configuration of firm and state, but "*trapped by choices* they have made in the past" (NSMG, p. 159). Even the fact that fast-food workers flee their jobs in droves at the first chance because the drudgery is so dreary and unrewarding is presented as a positive effect of the "culture of work" and the aspirations it breeds in those who have the seed of the work ethic in them: "There is a collective culture behind the counter that sends hamburger flippers down to the civil service exam whenever they are held. Everyone wants to do better than minimum-wage [sic]" (NSMG, p. 35).

Fast-food work is widely reviled not only because it is precarious, dull, soiling, and pays a pittance, but also because those who hold such jobs must display subservience to management and servility toward customers even when the latter are rude, scornful, and aggressive. One Harlem youth poignantly recounts how he hid his Burger Barn uniform in a bag, made up fake jobs, and walked to his place of work through roundabout routes so that his friends would not find out that he flipped hamburgers and subject him to razzing and ridicule. To "develop the backbone it takes to stay the course" in such tarnished and tarnishing jobs, ghetto residents again are said to "call upon widely accepted American values that honor working people, values that 'float' in the culture at large," chief among them the notion that "self-respect comes from being on the right side of the chasm that separates the deserving (read 'working') and the undeserving (read 'nonworking')" (NSMG, p. 100).

But to fully overcome the stigma of quasi-servitude in the deregulated service economy, "something stronger is required: a workplace culture that actively functions to overcome the negatives by reinforcing the value of the work ethic." Here veteran employees and managers play the lead role by creating "a cocoonlike atmosphere in the back of the restaurant where they counsel new workers distressed by bad-mouthing." Assisted by their supervisors, fast-food workers thus "take the process of carving an honored identity one step further: they argue that their jobs have hidden virtues" (NSMG, p. 102, 103) and that any job, even the most abject, is inherently worthy. And so does Katherine Newman after them. This self-mystifying motif of the sanctity of work and its corollary, the unseen blessings of superexploitative wage labor, is drilled throughout her examination of the relationship between schooling, skills, and (im)mobility in low-wage employment, a relation she finds to be positive at every step and turn.

2

Precocious participation in the world of substandard work, Newman contends, not only supplies ghetto youngsters with the "financial aid" they desperately need to pay for their (formally free) high school education and minimal postsecondary instruction.[79] The "culture of work" instills in them discipline, a sense of temporal organization, and the forbearance to set goals and meet challenges that inept inner-city schools are incapable of nurturing. Fast-food employers are "caring adults" who shoulder the role of surrogate teachers: they kindheartedly support their employees in their educational endeavors and steer their personal growth. They also improve the human capital of their staff by giving them ample "opportunities for learning, for

[79] The majority of young Americans with a postsecondary education do so not at a four-year university, but at "community colleges," which offer a two-year diploma that is widely devalued on the job market. Steven G. Brint and Jerome Karabel, *The Diverted Dream: Community Colleges and the Promise of Educational Opportunity in America, 1900–1985* (1989).

developing skills that should make a difference in occupational mobility" (NSMG, p. 139).

By flipping hamburgers, handling the cash register, cleaning oil vats, and mopping floors, ghetto adolescents get to formulate and monitor information, develop their memory and their money-counting abilities, hone their "people skills," engage in multitasking, and cope with the stress generated by a frantic work pace, authoritarian supervision, and offensive customers. While their middle- and upper-class counterparts attend academies to study classical music and sojourn overseas to imbibe foreign languages, Harlem teenagers join in the modern "ballet [of] the multiple stations behind the counter" at their local Burger Barn, where they meet others like them "from a multitude of countries" who "come together and learn bits and snatches of each other's languages" so that "they can communicate at a very rudimentary level in several dialects." This pragmatic syncretism entices them "to reach across the walls of competition and cultural difference" and makes the fast-food outlet "a living laboratory of diversity, the ultimate melting pot for the working poor" (NSMG, pp. 144, 145). Even the menial, repetitive, and repellent nature of work in a fast-food joint turns out to be an invaluable motivational asset in the pursuit of education: "There is nothing quite like slaving over a hot, greasy deep fryer for eight hours to teach people that they need to put some effort into making sure they have the credentials to qualify for something better in the future" (NSMG, p. 133).

It does not occur to Newman that the horrid working conditions, demeaning dress codes, high tension, insecure tenure, and starvation wages of such "slave jobs"—as they are commonly called in the ghetto—are powerful incentives for young men in particular to shun the formal labor market altogether and join in the "booty capitalism" of the street where, by entering into gangs and the commerce of drugs, they can at least salvage a sense of masculine honor, maintain self-respect, and even entertain hopes of economic advancement.[80] The will to "make it," which she celebrates among the "working poor" struggling to gain a foothold in the legal economy, is also the driving engine behind the careers of criminal entrepreneurs and their employees.[81]

---

[80] See Bourgois, *In Search of Respect*, and William M. Adler, *Land of Opportunity: One Family's Quest for the American Dream in the Age of Crack* (1991); also, Martín Sánchez-Jankowski, *Islands in the Street: Gangs in Urban American Society* (1991); Terry Williams, *Crackhouse: Notes from the End of the Line* (1992); Felix M. Padilla, *The Gang as an American Enterprise* (1992); John M. Hagedorn, "Gang Violence in the Postindustrial Era" (1998).

[81] Reviewing statistical and ethnographic studies, Richard Freeman (1995) finds strong support for a causal link between the rapid deterioration of the low-wage labor market in the 1980s and the sharp increase in the propensity to criminal activity among the noninstitutionalized population.

Newman expresses just as little concern for the fact that school and degraded wage work compete for scarce time, limited attention, and finite energy, despite her own evidence that Harlem teenage wage earners routinely cut back on their sleep, drastically compress their social life, and forfeit all pastimes to accommodate their overburdened schedule.[82] And that sheer material constraint is the reason why they find themselves at work so young: "I don't want to work—I fear that if I work I might be setting myself up to fail in school," laments Ianna, "but then again, I don't have any other money" (NSMG, p. 137). The bankruptcy of public schools is presented as a *datum brutum* of life in the ghetto that can be mitigated only by coupling what passes for education with low-wage servitude. "The best thing we could do to encourage school performance among those who are at the highest risk for dropping out" is not to mobilize to improve their schools so as to give them conditions of learning, academic achievement, and self-realization remotely approaching those enjoyed by their white, higher-class mates in charter schools, private establishments, or in the suburbs, but "to saturate their neighborhoods with part-time jobs and permit the structured environment of the workplace to work its magic on the other, often less orderly, parts of the day" (NSMG, p. 124).

3

Newman takes the structure of class and caste inequality in the metropolis as a given and, in the name of realism, urges ghetto residents to adapt to it by seeking low-wage work as the best stopgap remedy to just about every problem at hand. "While working may not be the ideal choice for them, it is probably the best choice under real-world circumstances, one that provides structure, sources of discipline, caring adults who watch over them, and a better shot at a future" (NSMG, p. 132). One is reminded of the arguments put forth by apologists of slavery in the 18th century and by advocates of child labor in the early era of industrial capitalism who highlighted, the former, the "civilizing virtues" of bondage for the inferior races, and the latter, the "moralizing" effect of factory work on the offspring of the dissolute working class. The more enlightened of them fully recognized that slavery and wage labor

---

[82] The student-worker literature is much less cheerful than Newman about lower-class teens who combine school with employment. Greenberger and Steinberg (1986), for instance, found that when such work is routine and repetitive, devoid of initiative and problem solving, and offers no training and learning opportunities, as is typical of restaurant labor, it tends to diminish school performance, to increase involvement in delinquency, and to stimulate drug and alcohol consumption.

have many drawbacks but maintained that, on balance, "under real-world circumstances," these institutions of labor extraction were a blessing for those upon whom they were enforced.

To make this nostrum more attractive, Newman systematically *inflates the job qualifications of fast-food workers and exaggerates their chances for occupational mobility* within the firm and industry. In an effort to "enskill" restaurant labor, she portrays the ability to handle overloads, speed-ups, and the crush of multiple tasks created by deliberate understaffing as qualifications that deserve recognition and reward. But the fact that "fast food jobs provide the worker with experience and knowledge that ought to be useful as a platform for advancement in the work world" does not make them so (NSMG, p. 147).[83] For the recognition and reward of skills depends less on the intrinsic properties of an employment slot than on the relative scarcity of people to fill it and the power relations between employers and employees.[84] And the brute reality here is that, what with all their kitchen-floor know-how and counter dexterity, fast-food employees are eminently disposable and instantly replaceable. This is not because of "the popular impression that the jobs they hold now are devoid of value," as Newman would have us believe, but because the tasks that compose these jobs have been methodically subdivided, impoverished, and routinized to make it "economically feasible to use a kid for one day and replace him with another kid the next day."[85] It is remarkable that fast-food outlets in Harlem have "never, in the entire history of their restaurants, advertised for employees" owing to the "steady flow of willing applicants coming in the door" (NSMG, p. 62) who have ample qualifications for jobs that require virtually none.

Newman is particularly sanguine about the promotion prospects of fast-food employees. Over and against their public image as occupational dead ends, she wishes to prove that "McJobs" offer real opportunities for movement into the managerial ranks because "fortunately, the industry is committed enough to its workforce to open those opportunities to promising internal candidates" (NSMG, p. 175). Her oratory to that effect is relentless, but the evidence she adduces is less than compelling: her data indicate that at most 5% of those who stay on the job and exhibit both subservience and diligence

---

[83] The notion that routinized jobs require more skill and initiative than their official descriptions allow, and that low-level employees skirt rules, use shortcuts, and develop shopfloor knowledges and strategies for "making out" that exceed official definitions of qualifications, is a staple of the anthropology of work (Burawoy 1979), a research literature curiously absent from Newman's copious endnotes, perhaps because it could not be squared with her assertion that fast-food managers and workers share "a craft ethic" and have joint problems and common interests in the organization of labor.
[84] William Form, "On the Degradation of Skills" (1987).
[85] Barbara Garson, *The Electronic Sweatshop: How Computers are Transforming the Office of the Future into the Factory of the Past* (1988), p. 21.

in enforcing the order of the franchise have a chance to rise up to "swing manager," a position that is managerial in name only since it entails little decision-making capacity and pays barely above minimum wage—Kyesha is promoted to "swing manager" at a wage of *$6 an hour with no "benefits" after nine years of diligent services*, a meager dollar more than a rank-and-file employee at that time; no wonder she "shows no great hunger for advancement on the job" and toils at a second job cleaning the grounds of her housing project in the mornings (NSMG, p. 299).

Fast-food workers themselves evaluate these prospects bluntly by "voting with their feet," resulting in an average tenure of under six months, translating into a yearly turnover rate pushing 300% for the industry. They flee their industry en masse, dream of getting a public service job instead, and actively look for alternatives in clothing stores, drugstores, and grocery chains, which they regard as offering better employment because, even though they also pay poorly, at least in them one does not have to suffer grease, heat, stress, and behave like a menial with customers. Try as she may, there is no getting around the fact that, as Newman belatedly concedes in a conclusion that confutes her entire chapter on the topic, "the typical Burger Barn worker can expect to come and go from the firm without seeing much advancement at all," because fast-food jobs "are built for churning, a pattern that is acceptable for teenagers looking for summer jobs, but distressingly limited for adults who are trying to make a real go of it in the private labor market" (NSMG, p. 185).[86] Indeed, Harlem fast-food employees have a far less enchanted vision of their condition than does Newman, and their quotes evince a fair degree of penetration of the reality of class superexploitation. As one of them put it:

> You're working, man, but you're still struggling. You're not laid back. You're still humble . . . What makes it difficult is when you're smart. [Burger Barn] is not for anybody who has any type of brains. . . . *You're being overworked and underpaid. You're making somebody else rich*. So. . . you really got to *brainwash yourself* to say, "Well okay, I'm going to make this guy rich and I'm just happy to be making this little five dollars an hour." (NSMG, p. 116; emphasis added)

Newman's sermonizing about the hidden virtues of fast-food work is also directly gainsaid by the short chapter devoted to interviews with one hundred job applicants who were turned away from hamburger outlets in Harlem.

---

[86] Even that acknowledgement is problematic, as it perpetuates the "unquestioned age-based prejudice against youth (teenage) workers in America" which, together with state tolerance and deregulation, continually replenishes a "low-wage, low-status, stopgap pool of youth labor" (Stuart Tannock, *Youth at Work: The Unionized Fast-Food and Grocery Workplace* [2001], pp. 1, 11) that is a central component of the national economy and a major medium for the reproduction of class and ethnoracial inequality.

Despite having long histories of intermittent employment and very modest expectations (their "reservation wage" stood below the legal minimum and their best job ever averaged $6.77 an hour), and although they had searched hard all over the city, three-fourths of them were still unemployed a year later, due mainly to increased competition from older workers pushed down into "youth jobs." Patterns of rejection further disclose that low-level credentials are of no value and confirm the marked preference of employers for immigrant over native labor, for Latinos over African Americans, and for applicants commuting from distant areas over area residents, whom employers perceive to be more prone to crime—findings that contradict Newman's image of a ghetto "community in control," her insistence that "education matters, skills matter," and her pet belief that fast-food operators are motivated by ideals of community service (NSMG, pp. 167, 242–245). All of this converges to indicate that fast-food managers are bent on recruiting the most vulnerable and docile workforce in the context of massive labor surplus at the bottom of the occupational tier fed by the collective downward slide of the working class.

4

To hold on to their jobs, fast-food employees must streamline their social activities, shrink or forsake their interpersonal ties, and compress their schedules so as to suit the needs and whims of their employer. Newman approves of this astringent reorganization of life around precarious and underpaid work for the "hidden benefits" that it brings:

> The more workers withdraw from nonworking friends and neighbors, the more the influence of the workplace—its mores, customs, networks, and expectations—shape them. . . . What recedes from view is the more irregular, episodic culture of the neighborhood and the streets. Working people gradually leave those less ordered worlds for the more predictable, more demanding, and in the long run more rewarding life of a wage earner. (NSMG, pp. 106, 109)

In this schema, *the more despotic the work regime and the more desperate the worker is to retain subpar employment, the better off* she turns out to be: "The further Burger Barn workers sink into their jobs, the more they pull away from the negative elements in their environment" and separate themselves "in every respect from the friends and acquaintances who have taken a wrong turn in life" (NSMG, p. 109) and gone on to be hustlers, drug dealers, and welfare recipients, whom fast-food employees are keen to vituperate in their interviews with Newman's research team. There are at least four problems with this argument.

The first is that it rests on series of *false dichotomies between workers and nonworkers*, the neighborhood and the firm, the world of the street—equated with disorder and immorality—and the world of the wage labor—presented as the serene temple of order and virtue.[87] For the strength of Newman's field data lies precisely in documenting that social life in Harlem is *not* organized according to these dualities borrowed from policy discourse (and enshrined in the standard variables of census and survey research); rather, it incessantly intermingles formal and informal activities, legal and illegal pursuits in a mishmash of market, state, criminal, and kinship-based forms of support. The life stories presented in *No Shame in My Game* amply indicate that most Harlem youngsters cycle in and out of jobs that hardly provide a shield against daily insecurity anyway; their family trees reveal that licit and illicit money-making endeavors accrete in the same households, and that lineages commonly cumulate wage earners, artisans, workers of the street economy, and recipients of public aid who pool resources and services in a "never-ending swap system" (NSMG, pp. 189, 190–191). Low-wage employees thus remain embedded in the social webs of both the neighborhood and the workplace, and they draw on these two cultures simultaneously to construct their life strategies and *Lebenswelt*.

Second, in language evocative of nineteenth-century ideologues of ascending industrial capitalism (and contemporary neoconservatives), Newman presents most ghetto youths as "free to choose"[88] between drug dealing and legitimate employment, between welfare check and paycheck, and between the shame of state "dependency" and the honor of servile wage work.

Among numerous passages: "*Everyone on the block had to choose* which means to glory was worthy of admiration. Tamara's own hard work tipped her in the direction of the working man [sic]. . . . Juan, Kyesha's ex, has had to make the same kinds *of choices*. Once he secured his Burger Barn job, he had to *decide what to do* with his friends and acquaintances who operate on the wrong side of the law. . . . Many a young woman *opts* for the work world and sacrifices some of her standard of living in order to live by the mainstream credo. . . . Patty has been on both sides of the fence. Her experience on the

---

[87] On several occasions, Newman (NSMG, p. xiv) notes that "the working poor are perpetually at risk for becoming the poor of the other kind: they are one paycheck away from what is left of welfare, one sick child away from getting fired, one missed rent payment short of eviction." Yet, instead of forsaking the untenable opposition between two "kinds" of poor, she makes it the pivot of all her analyses.

[88] The expression "free to choose" evokes the title of the best-selling book by Milton Friedman, Nobel Prize winner in economics and pope of libertarian capitalism: Milton Friedman and Rose D. Friedman, *Free to Choose: A Personal Statement* (1980).

job convinced her that the honor gained has been worth the cost. But she has had to *make the conscious choice* to pull back from welfare. . . . Young people in Harlem are constantly *faced with choices*, presented with drastically *different models* of adulthood and asked to *decide* between them." (NSMG, pp. 110–111; emphasis added)

Couching these alternative paths in (and out of) the local socioeconomic structure in terms of individual volition and discretion thwarts the analysis of the mechanisms and conditions under which differently positioned youth follow this or that circuit and with what consequences. And it does nothing to elucidate the predicament of those Newman acknowledges are not "among the lucky ones who did find work" and had "no real choice, no matter how much they had internalized the work ethic" (NSMG, p. 109, 111).

Third, the idea of a radical opposition between the hell of the ghetto and the haven of the workplace founders on the fact that fast-food jobs display many of the salient properties of the world of the street: they are irregular, episodic, and insecure; social relations on the kitchen floor are riven with distrust and brutality; and the pay they provide is so meager as to make it impossible to attain minimal financial stability, garner savings, and project oneself beyond tomorrow. By taking up employ in hamburger joints, then, Harlem teenagers join a segment of the service economy that looks like a first cousin of the street economy and keeps them close to the street, rather rather than isolates them from its pull. They also walk into the horns of an insuperable value dilemma.

5

Newman writes approvingly that American "culture confers honor on those who hold down jobs of any kind over those who are outside of the labor force. Independence, self-sufficiency—these are the virtues that have no equal in this society" (NSMG, p. 119). But therein lies the rub for fast-food employees and the fourth flaw in Newman's model: by complying with the holy commandment of work in that deregulated service sector, they bind themselves to capricious employers for famine wages and thereby desecrate the value of independence; by submitting to degrading mistreatment at the hands of managers and customers (company policy strictly forbids responding to their insults), they daily violate the ideals of autonomy and dignity that are also core American values. And thus they are disparaged and *devalued* in the very movement whereby they "seek salvation" through work.

To say that hamburger flippers "shift their identities from kid in the neighborhood to worker, albeit a worker with a complex identity: part admired, part scorned" (NSMG, p. 116) only displaces the contradiction; it does not and indeed *cannot* resolve it, for that contradiction resides in reality, in the antipodean makeup of desocialized wage labor that is the normal horizon of subsistence for the unskilled proletariat in the age of neoliberalism.

Newman cannot grasp this value conflict at the core of the existence of the low-wage worker in post-Fordist America because of the *built-in limitations of her normative concept of culture as a monolith* constituted of a single paramount value that trumps all others as well as overwhelms competing springs of action (such as interest, tradition, and affect, to recall Max Weber's typology).[89] Where Elijah Anderson diagnoses the cancer-like growth of an "institutionalized oppositional culture" in reaction to the confluence of economic dispossession and racial relegation in the ghetto (COS, p. 323), Newman maintains that the "mainstream culture" of work and abstemious individualism reigns supreme there as everywhere, so that all social, economic, and moral distinctions in American society are erased "in favor of a simpler dichotomy: the worthy and the unworthy, the working stiff and the lazy sloth ... Here in America, there is *no other metric* that matters as much as the kind of job you hold" (NSMG, p. 87; emphasis added).[90]

One need not be a fervent apostle of multiculturalism to recognize that there exist salient cultural differences between the ghetto and the so-called mainstream—a vague designation that fosters, and then papers over, the conflation of class, caste, and symbolic power—as well as within the ghetto; that values are diverse, contested, and not always congruent; and that they constitute not only guides for action, but also weapons and stakes in group struggles over work and worth. But Newman's constrictive conception of culture, seemingly issued straight from a structural-functionalist textbook from the 1950s, cannot accommodate such a dynamic relationship among values, social structure, practice and, even less, power.

No Shame in My Game offers the paradox of an anthropological analysis that pursues the cultural dimension of social and economic life in the ghetto *in order to obliterate it* through a series of nested reductions, first of practices to the simple "acting out" of a cultural model; second, of this cultural model to values; and third, of values, plural, to the sole supreme value of (wage) work. All noncultural sources of action are elided or given short shrift; all non-normative dimensions of culture are omitted; the "polytheism of values" and

---

[89] Max Weber, *Economy and Society* ([1918–1920] 1978), pp. 307ff.

[90] Note the subtle but consequential difference between "equating moral value with employment" and measuring worth by "the kind of job" one holds (NSMG, p. 87): In the first formulation, all jobs, bar none, are a source of honor and employment anchors a categorical hierarchy (in/out, worthy/unworthy); the second suggests a gradational scale (more/less) in which honor is relative and leaves open the possibility that some jobs might be dishonorable and those who hold them unworthy.

the "deadly, unremitting struggle between them"—to speak like Weber[91]—are replaced by cultural monotheism and static consensus. Thus, even as Newman denies Anderson's thesis that the ghetto is now dominated by a "code of the street" antithetical to the "work ethic," she joins him in depicting the social conduct of its residents as the mechanical execution of a cultural script over which they have no say or reach.

6

Much as she overlooks the contested nature of "values" and their dynamic shaping in and through (inter)action, Newman is blind to the relations of material and symbolic power that traverse the workplace and make it a site of struggle between collectives endowed with vastly different powers and interests, as opposed to a mere locus of production and sociability. She presents a stunningly benign portrait of the fast-food industry in which owners, managers, and employees are a "community" united by a common "culture of work" and mutual care, "trust and affection" (NSMG, p. 300). She endorses the business fiction that wages, tenure, and employment conditions in that sector are the natural product of "competitive pressure" rather than employers' ability to dictate contractual terms and successful efforts to deskill and disorganize the workforce in the context of state laissez faire. She politely avoids any mention of the long record of vigorous and vicious antiunion activism by its leading firms, both in the United States and in the foreign countries where they have expanded.[92] Yet studies of the historical development, national deployment, and international diffusion of US fast-food franchises have shown that they have coupled new-age computerization with old-style Taylorism not *because* labor was unqualified and unstable but *in order to* make it so and to employ disposable workers needing no more than fifteen minutes of training to be operational.

Inverting cause and consequence, Newman borrows from the rhetoric of the National Restaurant Association to assert that, "in order for the industry to keep functioning with such an unstable labor force, the jobs themselves must be broken down so that each step can be learned... in a very short time. A vicious cycle develops in which low wages attached to low skills are encouraging high departure rates" (NSMG, p. 96). Then, for good measure, she adds: "Fast food employers run businesses in highly competitive markets.

---

[91] Max Weber, *From Max Weber: Essays in Sociology* (1948), pp. 123, 147–149.
[92] Robin Leidner, *Food Food, Fast Talk: Service Work and the Routinization of Everyday Life* (1993); Tony Royle and Brian Towers (eds.), *Labour Relations in the Global Fast Food Industry* (2002).

Constant pressure on price and profit discourage them from paying wages high enough to keep a steady workforce" (NSMG, p. 287).

According to the chief of labor relations at McDonald's through the 1970s, "unions are inimical to what we stand for and how we operate," and not a single one of the four hundred serious drives for union organizing at McDonald's outlets during the early part of that decade succeeded due to tireless company opposition. In the 1990s, McDonald's strove to thwart or destroy unions not only in the United States but in countries across the world where it has exported its consumer products and marketing techniques as well as its flexible labor policies calling for the mass use of part-time, nonunion, student, and dependent workers paid below prevailing wage rates.[93]

When speaking of minority fast-food owners and managers, Newman resorts to the exalted language of the religious apostolate: these are people with "a special spark" who "often possess a missionary impulse" that took them to the heart of the ghetto "because it is important to them to bring job opportunities to depressed neighborhoods, to lift their own people up through the most mainstream of mechanisms: a steady job." But, aside from the bothersome fact that fast-food jobs are decidedly *not* steady, the observations of her research team consistently rebut this cheerful vision of Harlem hamburger franchises as "civic-minded" concerns whose endeavors are "more like social work" than conventional money making (NSMG, p. 127, 183).

First, fast-food owners locate their establishments along commercial strips at the edges of the ghetto and not at its core, where poverty is deepest. Next, they systematically discriminate against local residents and, like every other low-wage employer,[94] hire in priority non-blacks and non-residents (barely half of Burger Barn employees *inside Harlem* are African American). They also manipulate the ethnic mix of their staff to the detriment of the local population so as to increase profits by extending their customer base, even as this generates serious ethnic tension and resentment among African-American employees (NSMG, p. 178). And, last but not least, they almost never reside or reinvest in the neighborhood that Newman claims they wish to serve.

Why, then, do Harlem restaurateurs "monitor the report cards of their charges, pay for books, and sponsor tutoring programs for their workers," or help them get prescription glasses and open bank accounts, when they also steadfastly refuse to supply regular hours, pay decent wages, and extend

[93] Rick Fantasia, "Fast Food in France" (1995).
[94] Holzer, *What Employers Want*.

minimal health care?[95] Because such firm-level personal favors are part of a *paternalistic power arrangement* that allows fast-food managers to retain and better control a transient workforce, much like, until the 1950s, Southern planters provided their black laborers with rudimentary social benefits to bind them to the farm at the same time as they opposed any national-level welfare program that would interfere with this highly profitable relation of asymmetric dependency.[96] As for the ostentatious sponsoring of education, which Newman makes much of, it is an industry-wide policy imposed on all fast-food franchisees as part of a national public relations campaign to counter the negative image of "McJobs" as instruments of exploitation of young workers (as she herself reveals, NSMG, p. 127).

7

All told, Newman's picture of unskilled work in the fast-food industry is one of a benevolent and enlightened wage-labor dictatorship that offers mostly benefits for those upon whom it is wielded, thanks to the ethnic compassion of inner-city business owners and the country's reverent stress on work as a cultural obligation of citizenship. It is no surprise, then, if she concludes that "we need millions more of these entrepreneurs to help solve the employment problems of urban ghettos" (NSMG, p. xvii) and if her policy recommendations consist of measures designed to further expand irregular and underpaid labor for those consigned at the bottom of the class and caste order—so much so that some readers may find that the book crosses from social research over into outright business propaganda.[97]

Newman endorses "enterprise zones," wage subsidies, and tax breaks for firms that hire the urban poor, on the one side, and programs to help prepare and shuffle the latter into those precarious jobs, on the other. For instance, she supports refurbishing the curriculum and pedagogical organization of ghetto schools to turn them into direct feeders of pliable labor for the city's low-wage employers. She singles out for special commendation

---

[95] Employees in the United States have no nationally regulated Social Security coverage. So-called "benefits" attached to employment (medical coverage, sick and maternity leave, paid vacations, retirement) depend on the employer's goodwill. The overwhelming majority of low-wage employees have no coverage at all and millions are forced to rely on welfare and Medicaid programs for the indigent even while working.

[96] Lee J. Alston and Joseph P. Ferrie, *Southern Paternalism and the American Welfare State* (1999).

[97] In an interview published by the newsletter of the Russell Sage Foundation (RSF) to promote her book, Newman confesses that, in carrying out this research project, she "became enamored with what the inner-city business people [are] trying to do and the limitations they face in providing good employment... They are here to make a profit but they are also a social resource that makes a difference in the inner city" (*RSF News*, 4 [1999]: 3).

("a hands-down winner") the National Youth Apprenticeship Program developed by McDonald's, the Hyatt Hotel chain, and Walgreen's (NSMG, p. 279), three of the nation's most notorious suppliers of substandard jobs who consume disproportionate quantities of disposable immigrant, youth, and elderly labor.

Newman's prescriptions are definitely *not* a variation on the usual "liberal" agenda of "big government" intervention to fight poverty by shoring up the perennial failings of the market. Quite the contrary: They assign to the state the minimalist mission of bolstering market discipline by better outfitting the poor for it and giving low-wage enterprise incentives and room to prosper and proliferate. And this reduced social and economic role of the state comes complete with a reaffirmation of its charge to enforce law and order: "Employment training and opportunities need to go hand in hand with expanded programs of community policing" (NSMG, p. 296). But Newman diverges from Duneier, who recommends that the state leave the poor to their own devices to fabricate a street economy out of the scraps of the regular economy, in that she urges business, churches, philanthropic foundations, and other private operators to roll up their sleeves and join in the battle against urban poverty.

Newman is so wedded to a business-first and "small government" vision that she does not so much as consider such obvious possible measures as increasing the minimum wage, mandating medical insurance and other "benefits" that are an integral part of the labor contract in every other advanced society, lowering the legal work week in order to share employment, and creating public-sector jobs, to say nothing of increasing the social wage, extending the state safety net, and bolstering the collective bargaining capacity of service workers. Arguing that "we should be pragmatic and accept political realities for the moment, focusing policy energy on improving access to better-paid jobs in the private sector," she devotes all of *nineteen lines* to vague generalities on unions, only to stress their lack of traction on low-wage employees (NSMG, pp.276, 274–275),[98] a fact that is profoundly anomalous for her theory: if it is true that "the acquisition of a mainstream identity as a working stiff" (NSMG, p. 105) is a primary motivation of low-wage employees and that inner-city employers are dedicated to realizing the welfare of their personnel and community, how is it that that such prideful bonding

---

[98] American unions are financed by dues deducted from their members' wages, which mechanically creates an insurmountable economic barrier to unionization in low-wage industries. To create them requires a majority vote in the firm, which employers oppose by every possible means (advertising, smear campaigns, employment blackmail, recourse to law firms specializing in union-busting, etc.).

"within the organization and across the nation of fellow workers" fails to lead to the formation of strong unions?

In concert with business organizations, Newman explains that "the low-wage labor market is notoriously difficult to organize" by the inherent characteristics of those jobs and the surfeit of labor, without even a passing reference to employer opposition to and retaliation against unions. The fact that three-fourths of nonunion workers in the country believe that employees who seek union representation will lose their jobs is safely tucked away in a distant endnote (NSMG, p. 370) to avoid the distasteful topic of the balance of class power between low-wage employees and business and the even less savory question of the state's role in upholding it.

Newman repeatedly invokes the language of class consciousness and solidarity to depict the desperate attachment of subproletarians to their marginal jobs, but hers is the negation of the class analysis needed to unlock the *mysterium* of "working poverty" in the wealthiest society on earth[99]—a society, furthermore, in which workers toil ever-longer hours when every other advanced nation has reduced labor time.

The policies advocated by Newman, then, are not liberal but distinctly *neo*liberal. Accepting the unfettered rule of the market as their premise, they aim at enlarging the sphere of desocialized wage labor and "moving people into jobs"[100] via business consortia that will tap into the national "culture of work" and "personal responsibility," whose vibrancy she celebrates in every chapter.[101] But these prescriptions are at loggerheads with the central findings of *No Shame in My Game*, which conclusively shows that *low-wage work in the United States, far from being a cure, is a root cause* of material destitution and life insecurity in the urban core. More precisely, they demonstrate that the quandary of America's "working poor" in and out of the ghetto is not that they stay too long in substandard jobs; it is that these jobs, pegged at Third-World standards, are allowed to exist and flourish due to the gross power imbalance between employers and unskilled laborers and to state policies that actively

---

[99] In this regard, the new discourse on the "working poor" is in full continuity with the scholarly myth of the "underclass," which, while using the suffix "class," has impeded a class analysis of the transformation of the urban (sub)proletariat in the post-Fordist city with its diverting focus on antisocial behaviors, cultural deviance, and "neighborhood effects" (Wacquant, *The Invention of the "Underclass,"* pp. 118–121).

[100] One of the slogans of the 1996 welfare reform was "moving people from welfare to work."

[101] "The best recipe for ending a lifetime of working poverty lies not in government subsidies, but in imaginative reconfigurations of the matching and promotion process that harvests those who have proven themselves" (NSMG, p. 292). But what if the private sector does not generate enough above-poverty jobs for all those deserving of promotion? And what is to be done with those who, for whatever reason, do not "prove themselves" in the workplace? Should they be left to their own devices, at the mercy of their families, or institutionalized in asylums, hospitals and prisons?

foster commodification through a mix of welfare, workfare, police, and penal programs.

They confirm that "the problem" of poverty and work in America is composed of two distinct yet closely linked and mutually reinforcing quandaries: *exclusion* from employment (deproletarianization) and *inclusion* into precarious wage labor (casualization) that maintains employees in a state of deprivation, dependency, and dishonor that is only marginally preferable to joblessness and "welfare dependency" and breeds many of the same secondary problems. This is something that black leaders discerned well on the morrow of abolition, as historian Jacqueline Jones reminds us: Frederick Douglass "understood that irregular and poorly paid employment could render even free men and women dependent, 'at the mercy of the oppressor to become his debased slaves'" and that "the terms and conditions" under which a people works is the crucial determinant of "their place and their possibilities within American society."[102] The struggle for *decent* jobs, not just *any* job, has always been at the center of the life of American labor, black and white.

A "reinvigorated escalator" that would lift a select subgroup of low-wage workers into more stable and better-paid position on grounds of "merit" (NSMG, p. 289) does nothing to alter the flawed design of a social edifice in which the vast distances between floors condemns the residents of its lower tier to a life of material misery and social indignity by leaving them and their families at the permanent mercy of the whim of unreliable employers, the vagaries of business cycles, and the hazards of the life course. Facilitating mobility up the occupational ladder does nothing to remedy the fact that (1) the minimum wage puts a full-time, year-round employee well below the official poverty line; (2) American workers in the bottom decile of the employment distribution earn a paltry 38% of the national median, as against 68% for European workers and 61% for their Japanese counterparts; and that (3) the vast majority of them toil without health care, without a retirement plan, and increasingly without unemployment coverage as well.[103] Moreover, given the clear preference of low-wage employers for hiring recent immigrants, expanding the number of contingent jobs will benefit primarily pliant foreign laborers and, absent a frontal attack on persistent segregation and ethnic queueing, can only "harden and institutionalize processes of labor segmentation" and intensify the "double marginalization" of African Americans.[104]

---

[102] Jacqueline Jones, *American Work: Four Centuries of Black and White Labor* (1998), p. 13.
[103] Richard Freeman, *The New Inequality: Creating Solutions for Poor America* (1999).
[104] Jamie Peck and Nik Theodore, "Contingent Chicago: Restructuring the Spaces of Temporary Labor" (2001), p. 492; Alejandro Portes and Alex Stepick, *City on the Edge: The Transformation of Miami* (1993);

In short, the "employment problems of urban ghettos" are due not to a penury but to a surfeit of slave-like jobs. They pertain not to the hoary and ideologically consensual issue of *opportunity* but to the broader, and politically as well as intellectually more troublesome, question of the new *inequality* spawned by an "apartheid economy"[105] in which the state has allowed the bottom rungs of the workforce to collapse by both omission and commission. The remedy for precipitous inequality redoubled by the foundering of labor is not—and has never been—to "open up the opportunity structure"; it is to *alter that very structure* so as to raise its lower tier and thwart the spread of work insecurity and "flexibility" that now threatens not only the livelihood of the working class as a whole but growing segments of the middle class as well.[106]

To tackle extreme inequality and the social devastation wrought by the conflux of joblessness and servile jobs in the nether regions of social space requires one to think outside the narrow ambit of the market. This is precisely what Newman fails to do. Just as cotton was king in the slave economy of the antebellum South, in the United States of the early twenty-first century the deregulated market reigns supreme over the urban economy of low-wage services. *No Shame in My Game* fêtes its crowning and gives it the unction of official social science.

On some perennial pitfalls of urban ethnography

To counter common sense and to fight social stereotypes are well-established tasks of social science, and especially ethnography, for which it supplies one traditional "warrant."[107] But this task is hardly fulfilled by replacing those stereotypes with inverted cardboard cutouts issued out of the same symbolic frame, as our three authors do. For Duneier, sidewalk vendors turn out to be not crime vectors but crime busters; according to Anderson, the majority of ghetto residents are or wish to be "decent," despite street appearances to the contrary; and in Newman's eyes, willing low-wage laborers, far from being extinct, overflow the inner city and need only more servile work to

---

Roger Waldinger, *Still the Promised City? African-Americans and New Immigrants in Postindustrial New York* (1996). Newman acknowledges the permanence of rigid racial segregation but sees it merely as "a discouraging backdrop" to "job-seekers from poor communities" (NSMG, p. 284) rather than as a powerful force actively contributing to the splintering of the labor market and to the collective weakening of low-wage workers in the face of business dictates.

[105] Freeman, *The New Inequality*.
[106] Manuel Castells, *The Rise of the Network Society* (1996), pp. 201–272; Teresa A. Sullivan, Elizabeth Warren, and Jay Lawrence Westbrook, *The Fragile Middle Class: Americans in Debt* (2000).
[107] On the notion of "warrant" and its varieties, see Jack Katz, "Ethnography's Warrants" (1997).

snap the bridles of stigma and poverty. In all three studies, the inquiry substitutes a *positive version of the same mishappen social figure* it professes to knock down, even as it illumines a range of social relations, mechanisms, and meanings that cannot be subsumed under either variant, devilish or saintly. But to counter the "official disparagement of 'street people'" (COS, p. 255) with their Byronic heroization by transmuting them into champions of middle-class virtues and founts of decency under duress only replaces one stereotype with another.

Newman states in the preface to No Shame in My Game that she wishes to avoid "painting a saintly portrait of struggling heroes" but does just that throughout the book, and by the epilogue she cannot refrain from gushing about Jamal, one fast-food worker: "He seemed to me something of a hero" (NSMG, pp. xv, 303). Anderson hails the "inner-city grandmother," the "old heads" and the "other 'decent' people" in the ghetto as "the heroes of this story" (COS, p. 324). And Duneier concludes his tome on these hearty and heartening words: "The people we see working on Sixth Avenue are persevering. They are trying not to give up hope. We should honor that in them." (SW, p. 317)

This inversion does nothing to get us out of the binary logic of *categorization* (in the etymological sense of "public accusation") and its twin tropes of prosecution and defense, incrimination and apology, which, however much they may satisfy our political urges and ethical yearnings, remain antithetical to the sociological devoir of "analytically ordering empirical reality" through interpretation and explanation, as Max Weber counseled long ago.[108]

The failure to construct a properly sociological problematic independent of the common sense of agents (Duneier), of mainstream poverty scholarship (Anderson), or of journalists and policymakers (Newman), leaves an embarrassing residue that cannot but resuscitate the original stereotypes—for there are plenty of homeless men who do not engage in "honest" street peddling, ghetto residents committed to the "street code," and youths who seek subsistence and success in the illicit economy rather than submit to the ignominy of substandard wage labor. This residue mandates the crafting of *bifurcated ethnographies of sameness*, in which the poor are first cleaved into two subgroups, the good and the bad, before the good ones are revealed to be just like you and me: homeless sidewalk vendors, regular folks, and low-wage workers in the ghetto have the same moral thirst for "self-worth," the same attachment to "decency," and the same "work ethic" as the middle-class reader; only their "opportunities" differ. This is what makes Duneier's, Anderson's,

---

[108] Max Weber, "Objectivity in Social Science and Social Policy" ([1904] 1946), p. 58.

and Newman's accounts *neoromantic* tales, distinct from the straightforward romantic narratives of the liberal generation of the 1960s and 1970s which, in the main, labored to produce *unitary* tales of *difference*, encapsulated by the categories of "lifestyle" and "subculture"—then central and now forsaken.[109] This also leads to policy prescriptions that leave untouched the plinth of material destitution and racial exclusion in the American metropolis or, worse, are doomed to perpetuate urban marginality even as they purport to attack it.

In every advanced society, the fate of workers, the jobless, and the poor hinges on the capacity of progressive political forces to harness the agency of the state to reduce economic inequality, bridge glaring social gaps, and protect the most vulnerable members of the civic community from the unfettered rule of capital and the blind discipline of the market.[110] Not so in the United States, according to the three books reviewed here, which advise that street-level self-help, local moral engineering, and business altruism be entrusted with that formidable task.

For Duneier the sidewalk, with its combination of entrepreneurial opportunity and morally uplifting sociability, offers a ready remedy to the predicament of the homeless. In Anderson's scenario, the return and reinforcement of the "old heads" will help turn the ghetto around, though not without the concurrent return of steady jobs—which he does emphasize but without giving any hint of how it might come about. According to Newman, low-wage firms will save the nation from the scourge of urban poverty once they are provided sufficient leeway and assistance to tap the willing labor and the unexplored profit reserves of the inner city. By leaving social movements, politics, and the state out of the picture and by acquiescing to extreme levels of class inequality, urban ethnography spontaneously accords with and even endorses the ambiant neoliberalism. And its recommendations, anchored in the presumption of individual responsibility, the centrality of "values," and the sacralization of work, help legitimate the *new division of labor of domestication of the poor*, distributed among a dictatorial business class, a disciplining welfare-workfare state, and a hyperactive police and penal state, leaving a cosmetic philanthropic and private foundation sector to mop up the rest.

---

[109] For example, Howard S. Becker (ed.), *The Other Side: Perspectives on Deviance* (1964); Gerald D. Suttles, *The Social Order of the Slum: Ethnicity and Territory in the Inner City* (1968); Ulf Hannerz, *Soulside: Inquiries into Ghetto Culture and Community* (1969); William McCord, *Life Styles in the Black Ghetto* (1969); James P. Spradley, *You Owe Yourself a Drunk: An Ethnography of Urban Nomads* (1970); Lee Rainwater, *Behind Ghetto Walls: Black Families in a Federal Slum* (1970); Arlie Russell Hochschild, *The Unexpected Community: Portrait of an Old-Age Culture* (1973); Bettylou Valentine, *Hustling and other Hard Work: Life Styles in the Ghetto* (1978).

[110] Gösta Esping-Andersen, *Social Foundations of Postindustrial Economies* (1999); Duncan Gallie and Serge Paugam (eds.), *Welfare Regimes and the Experience of Unemployment in Europe* (2000).

Three reasons suggest themselves to account for the common limitations of these books. The first is that, in keeping with the established norm in that sector of research, Duneier, Anderson, and Newman write in blissful ignorance of field inquiries conducted in other countries on the topics that exercise them. This unthinking *parochialism* fosters the false universalization of uniquely American patterns and preoccupations, in particular the national bias toward moral issues and away from class, power, and the state. Ethnographies of homelessness, street trades, urban violence, low-wage work, and everyday life in neighborhoods of relegation in Europe and Latin America are not similarly cramped by moralism.[111]

This is because (1) other intellectual and political fields do not censor work alert to the class basis and political import of urban marginality; (2) these works are not written against the backdrop of an antiurban culture that casts the metropolis as a place of dissolution and disorder, constitutively injurious to morality; (3) liberal individualism is not the sole idiom in which the analysis and critique of inequality can be couched; (4) researchers are not under the compulsion to validate the public dignity of the poor—as these are not *presumed* to be "unworthy"—and therefore they are less inclined to limit their agenda to the debunking of negative stereotypes of marginal groups. Taking a broader, international, or better yet comparative, view of "the street" would help inject a much-needed dose of critical reflexivity into US studies of urban dispossession and assist in identifying the theoretic and political limitations inscribed in its tacit premises, accepted categories, and conventional questions.

The other privileged instrument of reflexivity is the historicization of problematics. There exits a distinguished and productive current of historical research on the discourse, policy, and politics of poverty in the United States that has questioned (and overturned) virtually every major tenet of the contemporary debate—the propensity to categorize the poor, the belief that urbanism and welfare undermine their morality, the association of single motherhood with social decay, the racial skewing of images and treatment

---

[111] Read, among other notable monographs, Séan Damer, *From Moorepark to "Wine Alley": The Rise and Fall of a Glasgow Housing Scheme* (1989), and Jean-François Laé and Numa Murard, *L'argent des pauvres. La vie quotidienne en cité de transit* (1985), on social life in the stigmatized neighborhoods of, respectively, Glasgow in Scotland and Rouen in France; David Lepoutre, *Coeur de banlieue. Codes, rites et langages* (1997), on young people in a declining HLM housing estate in the Paris suburbs and Catherine Lanzarini, *Survivre dans le monde sous-prolétaire* (2000), on the survival tactics of the homeless in French cities; Mercedes Gonzáles de la Rocha, *The Resources of Poverty: Women and Survival in a Mexican City* (1994), on daily subsistence strategies among Guadalajará's working class; Vera Malaguti Batista, *Difíceis ganhos fáceis. Drogas e juventude pobre no Rio de Janeiro* (1998), on young drug dealers in the favelas of Rio de Janeiro; Javier Auyero, *Poor People's Politics: Peronist Survival Networks and the Legacy of Evita* (2000), on violence and the informal economy in a Buenos Aires *villa miseria*; and Patrícia Marquez, *The Street is My Home: Youth and Violence in Caracas* (2000) on the same subjects in Caracas.

of the destitute and dangerous, the novelty of an "underclass."[112] But, curiously, it runs parallel to official poverty research without the latter ever paying attention to or being affected by it, almost as if they dealt with different countries.

Adopting a comparative and historical point of view, however briefly, would reveal also the extent to which the insatiable hunger of American social science for *heroic characters*—indomitable individuals who overcome formidable odds and buck massive social-structural forces—bespeaks its continued attachment to the hackneyed belief in "American exceptionalism" and in the national ideology of "opportunity," even in the face of overwhelming empirical evidence of its bankruptcy at the bottom of urban social space.[113]

A second reason is the deeply problematic relationship between theory and observation in *Sidewalk*, *Code of the Street*, and *No Shame in My Game*. Together these three books illustrate well the perennial pitfalls of ethnography as embedded social research when it is carried out under the banner of raw empiricism.[114] It can get so *close* to its subjects that it ends up parroting their point of view without linking it to the broader system of material and symbolic relations that give it meaning and significance, reducing sociological analysis to the collection and assembly of folk notions and vocabularies of motives (Duneier). It can stand too *far* and force observations into the procrustean bed of a preconceived causal schema that does not do justice to the complexities detected on the ground (Anderson's deindustrialization-plus-racism thesis). Or it can push theory ostensibly *aside* and stay marshed in the doxic formulations of current public discussion even as it brings forth materials that directly challenge the latter's categories and parameters (as with Newman and the incoherent notion of "working poor"). The remedy here is to recognize that there is no such thing as ethnography that is not guided by theory (albeit vague and lay) and to draw the implications, that is, to work self-consciously to integrate them actively *at every step in the construction of*

---

[112] For example, Paul S. Boyer, *Urban Masses and Moral Order in America, 1820–1920* (1978); Linda Gordon, *Pitied but Not Entitled: Single Mothers and the History of Welfare 1890–1935* (1994); Michael B. Katz, *In the Shadow of the Poorhouse: A Social History of Welfare in America* ([1986] 1996), and Katz (ed.), *The "Underclass" Debate: Views from History* (1993); Daryl Michael Scott, *Contempt and Pity: Social Policy and the Image of the Damaged Black Psyche, 1880–1996* (1997); Alice O'Connor, *Poverty Knowledge: Social Science, Social Policy, and the Poor in Twentieth-Century U.S. History* (2001).

[113] On this theme, see the articles collected in the two special issues of *Actes de la recherche en sciences sociales* on "L'Exception américaine" (vols. 138 and 139, June and September 2001), and Dorothy Ross, *The Origins of American Social Science* (1991), for a homegrown historical view on the umbilical relationship between American social science and American exceptionalism.

[114] This is a problem that afflicts not simply these three books but ethnographic inquiry in the United States generally, owing to the sharp methodological cleavages, the hegemonic hold of instrumental positivism, and the bifurcation of research and "theorizing" that characterize American sociology.

the object, rather than pretend to discover theory "grounded" in the field,[115] import it wholesale *post bellum*, or borrow it ready-made in the form of clichés from policy debates.

A conventional counter to the critique of the theoretical flaws in field-based studies is that such works are more "modest" than the critic implies, that their only ambition is to "dig out" fresh empirical materials to accurately "document" the inner workings of a local social world, and that it is therefore unfair to take them to task for their lack of conceptual clarity and muddled causal claims beyond their insular site. This defense is based on the assumption, instilled by professional training and sustained by the organization of careers in US academe, that doing serious fieldwork somehow gives one *licence to theoretical absent-mindedness*—that, just as "social theorists" should not muddy their hands in empirical research, lest they no longer be taken seriously as theorists, ethnographers need not concern themselves with the theoretical underpinnings, architecture, and implications of their work.

This assumption is both unwarranted and deeply detrimental. For there is, *pace* Geertz,[116] no such thing as a description, thick or thin, that does not engage a theory, understood as a principle of pertinence and proto-model of the phenomenon at hand adumbrating its nature, constituents, and articulations. Every microcosm presupposes a macrocosm that assigns it its place and boundaries and implies a dense web of social relations beyond the local site; every synchronic slice of reality observed has built into it a double "sedimentation" of historical forces in the form of institutions and embodied agents endowed with particular capacities, desires, and dispositions; every property selected for depiction is predicated on hunches or unstated hypotheses, which orient the cutting up of discrete data out of the infinity of the empirical manifold.

To fail to exercise theoretical control at every step in the design and implementation of an ethnographic study—as with every other method of social observation and analysis—is to open the door to *theoretical simple-mindedness* whereby ordinary notions issued out of common sense fill in the gap and steer crucial decisions on how to characterize, parse, and depict the object at hand (e.g., in Duneier's case, the ordinary American view of morality as a medium for the construction of a worthy self). So much to say that far from being antithetical, vivid ethnography and powerful theory

---

[115] Barney G. Glaser and Anselm L. Strauss, *The Discovery of Grounded Theory: Strategies for Qualitative Research* (1967). I return to this inductivist bias of "ethnographism" in chapter 3, *infra*, pp. 146–148.
[116] Clifford Geertz, "Thick Description: Toward an Interpretive Theory of Culture" (1973).

are complementary and that the best strategy to strengthen the former is to bolster the latter.[117]

A third factor contributing to the shared shortcomings of *Sidewalk*, *Code of the Street*, and *No Shame in My Game* is the sea change that has swept through publishing in America over the past decade. University presses have turned into clones of trade presses, while trade houses, having been absorbed by huge media conglomerates, strive relentlessly to hike up their profit margin. The result is a mad scramble for accessible books on "sexy" topics and controversial issues liable to catch the fancy of a broad, educated audience and thereby generate high sales and quick commercial success.[118] This creates intense pressure on academics who investigate such topics to tailor their work to the popular expectations of the "generalized market" rather than to the scientific norms of the "restricted market" of their discipline, in accordance with the well-established opposition that structures every field of cultural production.[119]

The politics of publishing in America today makes any volume mixing black men, criminal violence, and poverty enormously appetizing, while the economics of book-selling virtually prescribe that such work, to "cross over," take the form of a set of *depoliticized moral tales*, thick with vignettes of individual trials and personal challenge, spontaneously fitted to the categories of judgment of the educated middle class. Award-winning journalist Leon Dash (1996, p. 279) reports that his editor "had a favorite expression when cutting entire sections of [his] prose: 'Too academic,' he'd say." It is an open secret among sociologists that "too much sociology" is also a favorite refrain of trade press editors who balk at manuscripts that they deem conceptually too demanding for a lay readership.

Newman's book is unabashedly aimed at policymakers, as indicated by Herbert Gans's back-cover endorsement: "[A] story-filled and surprisingly hopeful book . . . Written for the general reader and social scientist alike . . . [It] should be required reading in every corporate and governmental executive suite." Anderson confessed at the "Author Meets the Critics" session of the American Sociological Association devoted to *Code of the Street* that he wrote the book at the behest of W.W. Norton who saw it as a means to capitalize on the success of Anderson's 1996 *Atlantic Monthly* article by the same title. It

---

[117] To stay on the topic of homelessness, youth and crime, see John Hagan and Bill McCarthy's work, *Mean Streets: Youth Crime and Homelessness* (1999), which is rooted in criminological theory. See also the monographs cited *infra*, pp. 183, n. 145.

[118] André Schiffrin, *The Business of Books: How the International Conglomerates Took Over Publishing and Changed the Way We Read* (2000).

[119] Pierre Bourdieu, *The Field of Cultural Production* (1994), especially chapter 3.

is clear also that Duneier's monograph would not muster quite the same appeal if it dealt with white book vendors in a mid-sized Midwestern city.

Now, there is nothing wrong—quite the contrary—in reaching beyond the narrrow confines of one's academic discipline, in tackling salient social issues, and even in having literary agents negotiate lucrative contracts to publish with a prestigious trade press. So long, that is, as one does not for that unduly constrict one's questioning, curtail conceptual complexity, and streamline one's writings, in short, compromise scientific standards in the quest for readability, topicality, and congeniality. In the case at hand, there are abundant marks of *intellectual heteronomy* that raise the worrisome question of the analytic sacrifices consented to produce books friendly to journalists and accessible to neophytes.

To mention but three: the absence of discussion of design and data and the striking paucity of references to scholarly works in *The Code of the Street* (which leads, for instance, to featuring child advocate Marian Wright Edelman as an authority on the black family); the dragging transcripts of tedious and vacuous conversations (such as the eleven-page section devoted to choosing a Christmas tree; SW, pp. 295–303) that needlessly lengthen *Sidewalk*, and the absurd reduction of the ethnographic method to a variant of investigative journalism in its methodological appendix; the uncritical embrace by Newman of the ideological notion of "family values" (even after it has been exposed and exploded by feminist sociologists and historians such as Kristin Luker, Judith Stacey, Linda Gordon, and Stephanie Coontz), and her correlative neglect to provide the slightest justification for ressuscitating a normative concept of culture long ago discarded by anthropology and other cultural disciplines in favor of cognitive, semiotic, dispositional, and discursivist conceptions that organically tie it to power and difference.[120]

Sociologist or journalist?

Sidewalk's methodological appendix makes it clear that, for Duneier, there is no epistemological divide separating ethnography from journalism: these are kindred

---

[120] Craig Calhoun, *Critical Social Theory: Culture, History, and the Challenge of Difference* (1996); Hans Joas, *The Creativity of Action* (1996); E. Valentine Daniel and Jeffrey M. Peck (eds.), *Culture/Contexture: Explorations in Anthropology and Literary Studies* (1996); Nicholas B. Dirks (ed.), *Near Ruins: Cultural Theory at the End of the Century* (1997); Victoria E. Bonnell and Lynn Hunt (eds.), *Beyond the Cultural Turn: New Directions in the Study of Society and Culture* (1999); Sherry Ortner (ed.), *After Culture: Geertz and Beyond* (1999).

practices that employ the same techniques and obey similar canons, except that journalists are apparently more honest and more rigorous.

"To use the tape recorder effectively, the sociologist can *mimic the photojournalist* ... One of the basic ideas of my method was *simply following my nose*, going to great lengths to check stuff out and make sure there is a warrant for believing what I've been told. Here I was *simply doing what any competent reporter was doing*, but something which ethnographers have not taken as seriously in their work [?]. ... The genre of books based on sociological fieldwork can be distinguished from many firsthand works by journalists by the way each genre deals with anonymity... *I follow the practice of the journalists* rather than the sociologists" because it "holds me up to a higher standard of evidence. Scholars and journalists may speak with these people, visit the site I have studied, or replicate aspects of my study" (SW, pp. 340, 345, 348; emphasis added).

The personal "Afterword" to *Sidewalk* by vendor Hakim Hasan also contains gratuitous disparagement of a "sociological tradition which historically has found it all but impossible to write and theorize about blacks, especially poor blacks, as complex human beings" (SW, p. 321). One thinks here of the works of DuBois, Johnson, Frazier, Zora Neale Hurston, Drake and Cayton, Allison Davis, Gunnar Myrdal, Hortense Powdermaker, Kenneth Clark, Ulf Hannerz, Orlando Patterson, Douglas Massey, and William Julius Wilson, and wonders whether Duneier and Hasan deemed their writings worthy of being assigned to the class they taught together, or whether only "black books" offer "a [fairly accurate] history of [racial] navigation through the society" (SW, pp. 34–37, quote p. 34).

There is today a resurgence and blooming of ethnography in American academe, as attested by the notable increase in the number of practitioners and hires by top departments in sociology, the cautious return of anthropologists to the field after years of nihilistic rumination over the (im)possibility of ethnographic analysis, and its diffusion and rising popularity in new disciplines, such as geography, history, education, human development, gender studies, literature, the health sciences, media, law, and even management and design.[121] Even more so than policy-oriented research, ever more governed

---

[121] Read respectively, for starters, Judith Stacey, "Ethnography Confronts the Global Village: A New Home for a New Century?" (1999); George Marcus, *Ethnography through Thick and Thin* (1998); Sidney W. Mintz, "Sows' Ears and Silver Linings: A Backward Look at Ethnography" (2000, symposium with eight responses); Steve Herbert, "For Ethnography" (2000); Alan Mayne and Susan Lawrence, "Ethnographies of Place: A New Urban Research Agenda" (1999); Richard Jessor, Ann Colby, and Richard A. Shweder (eds.), *Ethnography and Human Development: Context and Meaning in Human Inquiry* (1996); Diane Wolf (ed.), *Feminist Dilemmas in Fieldwork* (1996); Simon Cottle, "New(s) Times: Towards a 'Second Wave' of News Ethnography" (2000); and Christina Wasson, "Ethnography in the Field of Design" (2000).

by criteria of direct political pertinence and technocratic utility, field-based studies couched in a narrative format are the public face of sociology.[122] This creates a unique opportunity for ethnography to contribute to the collective consciousness by bringing what Durkheim called the "special competencies" of sociology to bear on critical debates around civic issues. But this opportunity is fraught with the danger of *exoterism*, the desertion of these same competencies in favor of the facilities of "magazine sociology" (in wide currency in the contemporary French intellectual field, where the mixing of genres is prevalent), sociologically colored "human-interest" storytelling in which rationalism gives way to sentimentalism, reportage trumps analysis, and witnessing smothers theory. A century ago, Durkheim complained that, as it flowered, sociology was threatened by "too much worldly success."[123] The ethnographic tradition in American social science is facing the same dilemma today.

This danger is all the more pressing in light of the unwritten "code of writing about the (black) poor" in US sociology, which one can extract from these three books and the enthusiastic reception they have received. It comprises five cardinal rules. First you shall scrutinize their morality and separate the worthy from the unworthy (if under less openly judgmental terminology). Second, you shall spotlight the deeds of the worthy poor, exalt their striving, strength, and creativity, and emphasize success stories, even as these are marginal and nonreplicable. Third, you shall scrupulously eschew issues of power and domination, and therefore studiously repress the political roots and dimensions of the phenomenon—whence the ritualized exhortation to the "opening of opportunity." Fourth, you shall at once highlight empirically and euphemize analytically the intrusion and specificity of racial subjugation. Last but not least, you shall bring good news and leave the reader feeling reassured that individual- and local-level remedies are ready at hand to alleviate if not resolve a societal quandary.

These precepts of academic etiquette inscribe the century-old commonsense vision of poverty and racial division in the United States into its sociology, ensuring the smooth expurgation of everything that would so much as graze this bedrock of national self-understanding. In their queer coupling under the aegis of empiricism, moralism and depoliticization paradoxically transform social inquiry into an endlessly renewed exercise in *social*

---

[122] The new ASA journal *Contexts*, which seeks to create a bridge between academic sociology and the broader public, features a section called "Field Notes: Brief descriptions from an author's own ethnographic field work and the insights it generated." No comparable section exists for other methods of inquiry.

[123] Émile Durkheim, *Les Règles de la méthode sociologique* (1895, 1981), p. 144.

denegation and collective exorcism—of class bad faith, racial guilt, and liberal impotence. Together, they allow too many American social scientists to keep their heads buried deep in the soft sand of sentimentalism even as their own observations reveal the wretched state of the urban subproletariat teeming at the gates of their townhouses and campuses.

~ * ~

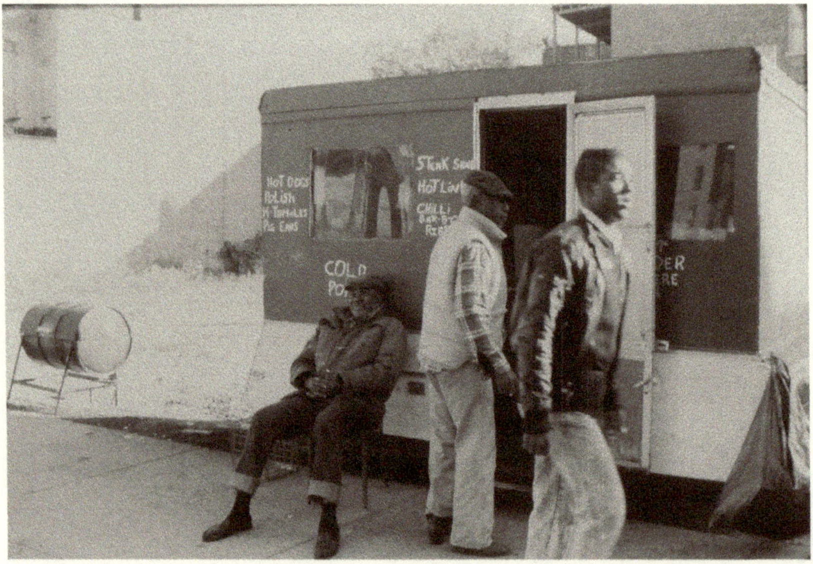
HOT DOGS
POLISH
PIG EARS
CHILLI
COLD

3
For a Political Epistemology of Fieldwork

> "A science that has no history, that is, a science in which there is no recusal of certain conditions of objectivity at a given moment and substitution of more objectively defined conditions of objectivity, a discipline so conceived is not a science."
>
> Georges Canguilhem, "Objectivité et historicité," 1970.

Needless to say, but it is better to say it, the target of "Scrutinizing the Street" was not the three authors discussed as "empirical individuals" (and even less as singular persons, whom I personally appreciate) but three "epistemic individuals,"[1] in this case the bearers of a way of practicing urban ethnography corresponding to a tradition and position then dominant in this American sociological subfield. What caught my attention were the operations of construction—or rather, in this case, destruction—of the ethnographic object. It is on this level, then, that I will respond to the rejoinders addressed to me by Anderson, Duneier, and Newman in the *American Journal of Sociology* (I had sent "Scrutinizing" to Anderson and Duneier well before its publication to benefit from their feedback, but they chose to remain silent). Similarly, it is clear, I hope, that the criticisms I address to my three interlocutors apply to my own work—but that their validity in no way depends on whether or not I meet the criteria I stipulate. Peer criticism is always in some way a self-criticism, for we are all part of the social, technical, and textual conglomerate that forms the field of the social sciences.

I invite readers of this book to take a closer look at these three responses to "Scrutinizing the Street" for themselves and to go beyond the necessarily selective account I am going to give here. I shall confine myself to three points, one for each author, which give some idea of the depth of the *epistemological*

---

[1] On this crucial distinction, essential for separating scientific polemics from personal quarrels, read Pierre Bourdieu, *Homo Academicus* (1984), pp. 13, 21, 36–40.

gulf that separates the historical rationalism that drives my questioning from the moral empiricism that guides their work and, hence, their responses.[2]

Anderson's reply raises the question of the relationship between theory and empiricism; Duneier's is a clear admission of the moralizing commitment of his work, and therefore of the strength of this tropism; and Newman depicts my critique (perverted by my nationality) as a political pamphlet and denies any autonomy to the scientist. The gangue of moralism that envelops their studies is so thick that they cannot help reaffirming their mission as *saviors of the stigmatized poor*, thus unwittingly adding grist to my mill. In the end, this leads to a dialogue of the deaf, from which I shall nevertheless try to draw some positive lessons liable to reinforcing scientific reflexivity in fieldwork. In particular, I will suggest how academic factors, linked to bureaucratic positions in a highly hierarchical and competitive sociological field, interfere with intellectual discussion.[3]

I will then propose a compact characterization of ethnography as an embodied and embedded modality of social inquiry. On the basis of this characterization, I will elaborate the notion of *ethnographism* and the *five fallacies* associated with it. It is these paralogisms that undermine from within the work of Duneier, Anderson, and Newman (and their *égérie* Alice Goffman in her infamous book, *On the Run*, as can be seen in the box, pp. 132–137) and limit the scope of ethnographies conducted in the vein of Chicago moral empiricism or in the wake of public policy debates. This leads me to contrast Geertz's *thick description* with Bourdieusian *thick construction*, which encompasses the ordinary construction of agents in the analytical construction of the scholar. Any sociological object, and not just the ethnographic one, is thus the product of a construction "squared" that requires a break with the immediate given and a remodeling of the primary perceptions that are the very stuff of field observation.

Reflexivity and the social conditions of intellectual debate

As an epigraph to his response to "Scrutinizing," Anderson quotes a Sherlock Holmes aphorism to the effect that "It is a capital mistake to theorise before

---

[2] For a compact presentation of historical epistemology, read Dominique Lecourt, *L'Épistémologie historique de Gaston Bachelard* (1969, 2002); Jean-François Braunstein, "Bachelard, Canguilhem, Foucault. Le style français en épistémologie" (2002); and Hans-Jörg Rheinberger, *Historicizing Ontology: An Essay* (2010), chapters 2 and 5. For a selection of texts, see Gaston Bachelard, *Épistémologie* (1980).

[3] On the two species of academic capital, bureaucratic and intellectual, see Bourdieu, *Homo Academicus*, chapter 3.

one has data. Insensibly one begins to twist facts to suit theories, instead of theories to suit facts," which speaks volumes about Anderson's radical empiricist proclivity, typical of Chicago-style ethnography.[4] For facts do not exist in and for themselves, already constituted as such in reality; they are "made," precisely, by the scientist armed with concepts, methods, and theory. The latter may be hard or soft, explicit or implicit, heuristic or not, but it is necessarily present as a rational principle of selection and organization of reality (I elaborate on this point in my discussion of the inductivist paralogism later in this chapter). But here, according to Anderson, my critique proceeds from a particular conception of theory that "demands that the ethnographer begin with a rigid commitment to a theory," since he or she "subordinates the cultural complexity he or she finds in the field to that theory," in this case "Marx à la Bourdieu" (p. 1534). But why should the articulation between concept and observation be "rigid" rather than flexible and dynamic, the one informing the other in a spiraling upward movement that leads to producing what Bachelard calls "an approximation of truth"?[5]

Following on from this, Anderson criticizes Bourdieu for having "no real conception of an autonomous, situational, microsociological level of analysis" and for "interpreting everything" as "part of an overall class structure" in which "'cultural capital' reproduces 'economic capital' and vice versa." As if that were not enough, he also criticizes me for "appl[ying] Bourdieu's ideas in dogmatic and ill-suited fashion" (p. 1535). But the idea of a multiplicity of social spaces nested like Russian dolls is precisely designed to enable a fluid multiscalar analysis that travels without difficulty from microcosm to macrocosm, from face-to-face encounters to larger structures such as those formed by a national society and even plurinational entities.[6] And the very purpose of the notions of plurality and convertibility of capital is to extricate us from an economic analysis that is blind to the specific effects and modes of reproduction of the different species of efficient resources in the social game—economic capital, cultural capital, social capital, and above all symbolic capital—as well as their derivatives in the different fields that make up a differentiated society.[7] On one point, I must plead guilty: the structural level of analysis logically and genetically takes precedence over the interactional

---

[4] Elijah Anderson, "The Ideologically Driven Critique" (2002), p. 1533; the pagination of the quotations that follow is cross-referenced in the body of the text.
[5] Gaston Bachelard, *Le rationalisme appliqué* (1949), p. 37.
[6] Pierre Bourdieu, *Microcosmes: Théorie des champs* (2022), pp. 83–99 (using the example of the religious field), and "Espace social et genèse des 'classes'" (1984). For two illustrations at both ends of the analysis scale: Wilfred Lignier and Julie Pagis *L'Enfance de l'ordre: Comment les enfants perçoivent le monde social* (2017), and Frédéric Lebaron, "Les élites européennes comme champ(s)" (2016).
[7] Pierre Bourdieu, "Les espèces de capital," in *Microcosmes*, pp. 613–639.

level (a point I emphasize below, pp. 141–143), even if, in scientific practice, it is by repeated to-and-fro that we discern and link these two levels of social reality.

Unable to escape the logic of the trial in which he believes I am engaged, Anderson then accuses me of taking up the cause of "street people" in the ghetto and "want[ing] to endorse the 'street' code as a political position" (p. 1535). He even argues that I "ignore" the "decent" vision and defend a "romantic" vision of "street people" as "rebels" (p. 1541). If I have given this impression, I regret it, for the sociologist does not, as such, have to take sides in the symbolic struggles that make and unmake the social world as a sensible world, in the double sense of sensory and signifying.[8] Her task is to produce a faithful account of them and to detect the historical possibilities that these struggles conceal and those that they exclude by the way they unfold. Anderson similarly suggests that my distorted reading of *Code of the Street* stems from "a top-down" imposition of the "structural theory of the 'field of power'" that I would take from Bourdieu, although he finds that my interpretation of Bourdieu is "more influenced by Marxist thought than by Lévi-Strauss." It is worth noting in passing that Marxism, even intellectually moribund, continues to function as anathema in the American academic field.

Anderson then criticizes me for "cavalierly dismissing as 'folk concepts'" the ordinary meanings in the ghetto, whereas what I am taking issue with is the use of common-sense categories as *analytical categories*. It is indeed the ethnographer's mission to discover and catalog the subjective conceptions of the social agents under study, and thus to bring to light the cognitive, emotional, and conative categories that move them in their ordinary world as well as during extraordinary episodes. But this does not imply that the sociologist adopt these categories as her own; they enter scientific analysis as *object and not tool*. In other words, it is not enough to write about the ghetto poor "in a way that is *faithful to their understanding of themselves*" (p. 1549, original italics) to have fulfilled her mission, any more than it is to contribute to changing the public's image of them.[9] This is a laudable intention, but it alone does not sum up ethnographic work. Here again, we diverge: this first stage of fieldwork must necessarily be accompanied by the construction of the system of material and symbolic relationships that give strength and sense to this understanding.

---

[8] This is in contrast to the position advocated by Howard Becker in his famous Sixties-style article "Whose Side are We On?" (1967).

[9] According to Anderson, "the ethnographer becomes in effect a kind of vessel, a virtual agent of the subjects themselves by interpreting their world and serving as a communication link to the uninformed" (p. 1538).

For this, the sociologist must deploy analytical concepts that break with ordinary concepts while at the same time encompassing them, so that she provides herself with the means to understand the agents' point of view as a "view taken from a point" in an objective social space[10] and, hence, fuse theory and observation, interpretation and explanation. It is precisely this indispensable stage in the construction of the object, ethnographic or otherwise, that Anderson scuttles when he asserts: "I did not start with a map [of social space] because there *is* no map and none is required" (p. 1543). This is a major disagreement between Bourdieu's *constructivist structuralism*, which aims to marry structure and interaction, positions and dispositions, field and habitus, and symbolic interactionism, which detaches and absolutizes the latter level of analysis and even goes so far as to deny the existence of historical structures transcending face-to-face encounters. Duly noted.

Duneier, for his part, accuses me of "failing to meet the minimum standards of scholarly criticism and debate," and complains of repeated misquotations or "selective quotations" that would caricature his argument and even make him say the opposite of what he writes.[11] However, the passages from his book that he points to in order to refute my arguments are the very ones that I quote and that I quote without distorting his text. Surfing on my reading, he suddenly discerns a complex, ambivalent reality in the street: "On the streets, I found a world filled with illegality, personal defect, and shame and also a world of mutual support, struggles for respectability, ingenuity, and resilience" (p. 1551). But, as evidence of these routine illegalisms he would have documented, he mentions this single sentence from *Sidewalk*: "*Only once did I see a man working with the vendors sell marijuana to a passerby*" (quoted p. 1559, original italics). He rewrites his book as drawing an ambiguous, multilayered portrait of magazine vendors that would avoid ordinary dualisms in the depiction of the city's marginalized: "There can be no sharp distinction between a 'worthy' and an 'unworthy' poor when we see the complexity of these men's lives" (SW, p. 1564). At the same time, however, he asserts that "these vendors will never be viewed as desirable members of the neighborhood. If *Sidewalk* convinces some readers that their presence—despite many 'indecencies'—is less harmful than those readers once believed, then it has served a useful function" (SW, p. 1562). And he cannot help but want to revalorize these vendors, acknowledging that *Sidewalk*

---

[10] Pierre Bourdieu, *Méditations pascaliennes* (1997), pp. 264–265.
[11] Mitchell Duneier, "What Kind of Combat Sport is Sociology?" (2002, p. 1573), a title that echoes Pierre Carles's film about Pierre Bourdieu, *La Sociologie est un sport de combat* (2001); the pagination of quotations is given in the course of the text. But why did he not point out these errors to me? I had sent him my *Sidewalk* text long before it was submitted for publication.

advocates "greater tolerance and respect for people working the sidewalks" (SW, p. 1564).

Indeed, in his effort to correct my supposedly erroneous interpretations, Duneier validates the gist of my critique: "The core issue of my agenda" is "understanding the ways in which moral behavior is and is not constructed within settings seemingly unfavorable to such behavior" (p. 1566). Or again: "To be sure, this is a 'personal interest,' but it is also a sociological problem, since the question of moral/norm-based behavior figures so strongly within many strands of sociological theory" (p. 1566)—but he does not flag any of them, and for good reason. It is one of the fundamentals of anthropology since its invention that all people, not matter how different and wretched, are endowed with morality.

Diverging from his book, Duneier now says that, "in fact, I *do* see an important epistemological divide between sociology and journalism. The former is committed to interrogating folk concepts, while the later generally employs them as a tool of analysis" (p. 1567). On this account, *Sidewalk* is a book of journalism, not sociology, for it does not produce a single analytical *construct* that can be detached from empirical description.[12] As proof of his commitment to theory, Duneier correctly points out that he "uses ethnographic data to modify the broken-window theory" (p. 1569). The problem is that said theory is not a social science theory but a police fable embellished by two criminal policy ideologues, George Kelling, a former Kansas City police chief, and James Q. Wilson, a neoconservative political scientist notorious for advocating hyperpunitive criminal policies, in an article published in the monthly magazine *The Atlantic Monthly* in 1982. What is more, as noted above (see *supra*, pp. 69, n.42), the notion has been logically dismantled and empirically refuted on multiple occasions.[13] Still on this point, Duneier is particularly unhappy that I have "accused" him of "endorsing the neoliberal state," but the policy of penalization of poverty and class-cleansing of the streets that he supports through his "zero tolerance" police amendment is at the heart of the

---

[12] Curiously, Duneier cites as evidence of his methodological rigor the fact that a *New York Times* reporter judged him to possess "far better fact-checking skills than most journalists" (p. 1554). No comment.

[13] George L. Kelling and James Q. Wilson, "Broken Windows" (1982). For an empirical refutation in the case of New York itself, see Bernard E. Harcourt and Jens Ludwig, "Broken Windows: New Evidence from New York City and a Five-City Social Experiment" (2006). The broken window theory served as a pseudoscholarly justification for the deployment of the police technique of "stop and frisk" (arrest, identity check, and body search on mere "reasonable suspicion" on the part of the police officer), leading to the aggressive identity checks of hundreds of thousands of young Blacks and Latinos every year, a policy that was declared unconstitutional by the courts in 2013. See Jeffrey Bellin, "The Inverse Relationship between the Constitutionality and Effectiveness of New York City Stop and Frisk" (2014); Aziz Z. Huq, "The Consequences of Disparate Policing: Evaluating Stop and Frisk as a Modality of Urban Policing" (2016).

construction of that state. It complements and supports the deregulation of the labor market and the disciplinary turn of welfare.[14]

Duneier cannot help but conclude his response by reaffirming the moral mission of field-based sociology: "The capacity of urban ethnography to humanize its subjects is one of its greatest strengths. (. . .) I do hope that through the complex portraits of the vendors, panhandlers, and scavengers in *Sidewalk*, readers will come to appreciate the basic humanity of these pariahs who are so often dehumanized" (p. 1575). Or: "A major thrust of my work has been to reveal the common elements of humanity. Most people have common bases of life, and many people who are presumed to be quite different have some salient 'moral' characteristics in common" with other citizens (p. 1574). A perfect definition of sociological moralism in action. *Quod erat demonstrandum.*

The title of Newman's response, "No Shame: The View from the Left Bank," is a clear indication of her mechanical reduction of an epistemological critique to a political argument. She portrays me as an uncontrollable French leftist who, fundamentally, understands nothing about America and its wholesome values[15]—in keeping with the popular adage, "If you want to kill your dog, accuse him of having rabies." But to do so, she has to disguise my positions and caveats about *No Shame in my Game*. Thus, Newman opens her reply by presenting me as an advocate of the notion of the "underclass," central to the work of my Chicago mentor William Julius Wilson,[16] against which her own work rises. This would be the hidden reason for my frontal opposition to her book. Problem: I am a precocious and ferocious critic of that true-false concept—which, to put it bluntly, singles out poor blacks for antisocial behavior and the accumulation of "social pathologies" in the inner city. In point of fact, I recently devoted a study in the historical sociology of the politics of knowledge on the topic, *The Invention of the "Underclass,"* from which it emerges that this categoreme, which pertains to social and racial fantasy, stood in the way of a rigorous sociology of the transformation of the black ghetto during the two decades of its undivided rule over research on race and poverty.[17] Newman could hardly have been unaware of this at the time since the only occasion we met in person, at a conference on the "underclass" in Berlin in June 1997—that is, five years before the *AJS* symposium—I

---

[14] Loïc Wacquant, "Crafting the Neoliberal State: Workfare, Prisonfare and Social Insecurity" (2010).
[15] Katherine S. Newman, "No Shame: The View from the Left Bank" (2002). I give the pagination of quotations throughout the text. On this point, Newman agrees with Anderson, who laments that I deliberately "inject ideology into social science to an extreme degree" that is "almost laughable" (p. 1545).
[16] William Julius Wilson, *The Truly Disadvantaged: The Inner City, the Underclass, and Public Policy* (1987, 2012).
[17] Loïc Wacquant, *The Invention of the "Underclass": A Study in the Politics of Knowledge* (2022).

had opened the proceedings, much to the chagrin of my German hosts infatuated with the notion, with a paper entitled, "The scholarly myth of the '*underclass*.'"[18]

Newman confuses my catalog of her book's shortcomings with my personal opinion on American ideology: "Wacquant may hate it, but that 'self-improvement' ideology is quite widespread among middle-class and upwardly mobile African-Americans and Latinos" (p. 1583). Problem: young Harlem fast-food employees are neither middle-class nor upwardly mobile, as *No Shame in my Game* abundantly demonstrates, and whether or not I believe in this ideology is logically irrelevant to the role that Newman gives it in her analysis. Similarly, Newman claims that I do not recognize the "real skills" of Burger Barn employees (p. 1585), but the problem is, rather, that their employers do not recognize them, and that the labor process in the fast-food sector is entirely based on the methodical deskilling of jobs in the active sense of the term. And, lending me her trademark moral reasoning, Newman thunders: "I do not see evil at every turn among inner-city employers" (p. 1586), as if the question were whether the bosses are good guys or bad guys.

This passage is its own commentary: "I plead guilty to admiring the fortitude of people like Jamal, who gets up at 5:00 a.m. to board a bus that crosses the city, to a job that pays him next to nothing. Maybe I should hold him in contempt, but I do not. I think the man deserves a medal. (. . .) Maybe Jamal would be better off on the barricades, but he does not think so. (. . .) I prefer to think Jamal understands something Wacquant does not, which is that until there are better possibilities in the offing, he is going to do his damned best to make a go of it" (NSMG, p. 1587). Here Newman offers not a reasoned analysis but a panegyric of the fast-food worker, the very thing I criticize her book for.

Newman also argues that I "ridicule [her] efforts to provide a nuanced, accurate, and complete portrait" of Burger Barn employees "because of [my] allegiance to the caricature of ghetto residents as lumpenproletariat" (NSMG, p. 1586) and that I "wish low-wage workers would embrace a radical agenda [. . .] but I have found no evidence of a revolutionary disposition" among them (p. 1589). Once again, this is to lend me a political reasoning that is not mine and to make me enter into a kind of arithmetic of the best and the worst that has nothing sociological about it. And, finally, we come to her major counter-objection: "The poor also have agency: moral impulsion (from values and aspirations) and material need are complementary, not incompatible,

---

[18] This paper was based on a text I had just published in French: Loïc Wacquant, "L'*underclass*' urbaine dans l'imaginaire social et scientifique de l'Amérique" (1996).

sources of action" (p. 1587).[19] But then, "Wacquant prefers a political position in which the poor have to be forced to take low-wage job" on the basis of "a structural quasi-Marxist argument" (p. 1590).

According to Newman, "Wacquant's perspective is distinctive mainly to the degree that he draws topdown, deterministic conclusions" whereas "sociologists and urban anthropologists have come some distance from theory that leaves no room for agency, for messy contradictions, for internal moral debates, or for self-determination" (p. 1598). In my critique of Anderson, I show how the concept of habitus as a system of durable and transposable dispositions, acquired over the course of social experience, and therefore of diachronic trajectory in social space,[20] makes it possible to differentiate the fine-tuned strategies of the two strata of the black working class, and thus to account for their respective practices and experiences, without falling into the national myth of "self-determination," which, incidentally, explains nothing: what determines "self-determination" since obviously not everyone has it?

As for the idea that "what bothers Wacquant most is that my book discusses reform rather than waiting for the revolution," it is truly bizarre. My reviews of *Sidewalk*, *Code of the Street*, and *No Shame in my Game* are not dependent on any political positioning—and, even less, political posturing. The fact that I stand "to the left" of their authors has nothing to do with my diagnosis of the shortcomings of their sociological argumentation and the flaws in their empirical data. This diagnosis would be exactly the same if I were a centrist or a hard-line Lepéniste. Why then were Duneier, Anderson, and Newman unable to perceive and therefore receive my criticism? I see two cumulative explanations.

The first is *epistemological*: it stems from the hiatus between the philosophy of social science that informs their books and that which guides my reading of them. The second is *social*: I have violated the practical rule of the American academic field according to which eminent researchers working in the same niche tacitly observe an intellectual "pact of non-aggression" with their peers, a pact that guarantees each and all of them full enjoyment of the material and symbolic advantages associated with a dominant position in the relevant subfield. And, to do so, I had to put aside the standards of *professional politeness* that envelop normal, because normalized, exchanges within the American sociological field, a highly hierarchical and competitive

---

[19] "Ghetto dwellers are not simply bearers of social relations or victims of social structure. Understanding life in the ghetto requires granting its residents far more agency than Wacquant allows and being prepared to accept an understanding of causation more varied and less deterministic than a single uniform logic of racial exclusion that sweeps all in its path" (p. 1595).
[20] Pierre Bourdieu, *Le Sens pratique* (1980), pp. 99–104.

field, where a favorable review in a top-ranked journal by a colleague from a top-ten department can be instantly monetized in a salary increase or earn the author of the book praised a job offer from a rival university.[21] Readers in France, Germany, Italy, Brazil, etc., will be able to judge the relevance of these two mechanisms to their national field by structural transposition. Social science is badly set out when considerations of honor and academic prebends take precedence over the veracity of facts and the logic of arguments.

The fact remains that it is primarily the gulf between the historical rationalism rooted in the French philosophical tradition and the moral empiricism that permeates the American sociological field that explains the impossibility of engaging in a dispassionate debate by rendering the epistemic reflexivity that drives "Scrutinizing the Street" utterly incomprehensible. And this, in turn, explains the virulence of the controversy: "Doxa, a belief that does not know itself as such, is harder to uproot than any dogma, and when it touches the bedrock of evidence and unconscious presuppositions that constitute it, academic struggles can assume extreme violence."[22]

Alice in the land of outlaws, or the ethnographic time bomb

The proof, if any were needed, that the flaws and deficits of American urban ethnography informed by moral empiricism that I identified twenty years ago are still with us, is Alice Goffman's best-selling, then scandal-ridden book, *On the Run: Fugitive Life in an American City* (2014), praised to the sociological and journalistic heavens before being discreetly shelved scientifically after the inconsistencies, exaggerations and other slips, controlled or otherwise, with which it abounds became apparent in the course of the public counterinvestigation of which it soon became the subject (1). This persistence is hardly surprising: *On the Run* is a dyed-in-the-wool product of the Chicago School, deriving as it does from a doctoral dissertation under the direction of Mitchell Duneier, based on an undergraduate thesis supervised by Elijah Anderson, and it tackles a burning political problem in the manner of Katherine Newman. The same epistemic causes produce the same scientific effects: penury of theory, uncontrolled adoption of folk concepts, disconnect between data and interpretations, submission to the doxic terms of public debate, obsessive moralism, and absence of reflexivity.

---

[21] In fact, this was the warning I received from an eminent ethnographer before the publication of "Scrutinizing": that I might interfere with the negotiations of one of the three criticized authors with several universities vying for his services following the success of his book.

[22] Pierre Bourdieu, "L'inconscient d'école" (2000), p. 3.

A veritable ethnographic time-bomb, *On the Run* was a runaway success from the moment it was published; its author was promoted within the discipline as never before by the leading lights of Chicago ethnography. She was invited to present her opus all over the country, and not just on university campuses: the *New York Times* devoted several long features to her and voted *On the Run* Book of the Year; newspapers, magazines and discussion sites flocked to interview her; she gave a *TED* talk seen by over two million Internet users. Her central thesis, that young men from the black ghetto are the target of a permanent hunt by a diligent, omnipresent, and omnipotent police force that turns them into "fugitives" in their own city and plunges them into social marginality, shook up its readers, electrified sociology, and shocked the citizenry at a time when the murders of black men by the police were making media-political headlines and the Black Lives Matter movement was about to surge.

But, from the outset, *On the Run* also had its detractors. Sociologists were divided. Some seasoned ethnographers were astonished by the enthusiasm that a book riddled with errors as crude as they were obvious (2) aroused among colleagues, but they were reluctant to take a public stand, since Goffman's tenure turned on this book: to criticize work based on her doctoral dissertation by a junior researcher would be seen as an unseemly attack on "smaller than you"—here again, we find the interference of academic factors with intellectual process. However, data abound that seem inaccurate, contradictory, false or, at the very least, embellished. A squad of journalists rushed to the field site of Goffman and located her respondents, who were easily identifiable given the lack of care she has taken to anonymize them, even though she embargoed her thesis and destroyed, she assures us, all her field notebooks to protect them. And journalists and legal experts were quick to dismantle her factual assertions and her most striking scenes—such as the claim, debunked by a counterinvestigation by public defenders in several East Coast cities, that police routinely dredged the waiting rooms of hospital emergency rooms to arrest young black men on the run as they came to get care.

An anonymous dossier of some sixty tightly packed pages pointing out the book's narrative inconsistencies, missing and conflicting information, and factual errors soon circulated on the internet, keeping the controversy alive. To which Alice Goffman stopped responding in 2015 on the advice of her attorney. *On the Run* would be her last publication of note; in 2019, the University of Wisconsin denied her tenure on the grounds that she had produced virtually nothing since the book, and she vanished from the academic world.

Alice Goffman thus found herself simultaneously in the eye of three cyclones. Empirical first: Are the facts she describes in the book verified, embellished or fabricated? Are the implausibilities that abound in the text the result of negligence, ignorance, or incompetence? But, besides, is the thesis it defends original? Victor Rios had already documented in the field, in his ethnography *Punished* (2010), how the police harass and penetrate the social circles of young blacks and Latinos; Jamie Fader had dissected in *Falling Back* (2013), a three-year ethnography following young offenders in Philadelphia, precisely how the experience of incarceration disrupts their life trajectories long after their release; criminologist Todd Clear had shown that hyperincarceration destabilizes dispossessed districts in *Imprisoning Communities* (2009)(3). Is this thesis even tenable in the extreme form given to it by Goffman, for whom the justice system is the one and only institution that shapes the lives of her subjects?

Then there is the methodological and ethical controversy: Is *On the Run* a model study in terms of its deep immersion and descriptive granularity, or a catalog of elementary errors to be avoided: failure to break with common sense, affective projection, presentist myopia, self-heroization (4)? Doesn't the author cross a deontological line in her dealings with her subjects when she acts as a faithful "chronicler of the group," subjecting her observations to their censorship (5), and when she participates in their criminal activities, even going so far as to volunteer for a manhunt to kill the presumed murderer of one of her informants?

Finally, to top it all, a political and identity debate, American-style to be sure, which was inflamed by gusts from the proponents of Critical Race Theory: What right does a rich, educated white woman have to write about the everyday lives of poor black men and, what is more, to make academic hay out of it? Doesn't the portrait she paints of them, which focuses on drugs, violence and crime, reinforce race and class prejudices? Doesn't her "privilege" invalidate *eo ipso* the knowledge she intends to produce? And doesn't the light she attracts by virtue of her family and academic pedigree overshadow the contributions of researchers of color?

A mystery remains that ruins the book's central thesis: why on earth would Philadelphia's chronically understaffed and budget-starved police force waste so many technical and human resources chasing after petty delinquents, when the courts are so clogged and the city's jail so overcrowded that judges release inmates by the thousands every year, dismissing all charges (6)? The resolution is that the "Sixth Street *boys*" are not innocent teenagers but unrepentant young adult criminals, guilty of a range of serious offenses well documented in the book, from drug dealing to assault with a deadly weapon to murder. Would it not be outrageous, then, if the police did *not* chase after them? For it is these outlaws, and not the police, who are primarily responsible for the street violence that plagues the local population. And it is these residents who, in the majority of cases, implore the police to intervene in the neighborhood by calling 911, despite the abuses they also suffer at the hands of law enforcement. The reality behind the caricatural vision of

On the Run is that the dispossessed neighborhoods of the American metropolis are *simultaneously* overpoliced and underpoliced; police intervention is both feared and demanded.

The book also creates the misleading impression that the penal state in America is a coherent, nimble institution capable of penetrating the social body in the manner of capillaries, to use Michel Foucault's image of the carceral (7). Nothing could be further from the truth: the justice system in a city like Philadelphia is not a "system" but a disjointed network of autonomous, uncoordinated organizations (city police, county court, prosecutors' and public defenders' offices, criminal bar and probation department), each in a permanent state of latent crisis due to lack of resources and personnel, and scandalously inefficient. As proof of the police's impotence, the number of unsolved warrants issued by the Philadelphia court exceeded 80,000 according to Goffman herself; in 2015, only four out of ten homicides resulted in an indictment; and the "clearance rate" for crimes involving the use of firearms was barely 27% (8). Finally, the propensity to stay away from official institutions due to contact with the criminal justice system is the same among white and black men with criminal records (9). This invalidates the thesis of a link between police harassment in the neighborhood and the social avoidance documented by Goffman, since such harassment is not observed in white neighborhoods. Going "on the run" is not the cause of their social withdrawal but the convenient excuse that Goffman's mates give themselves to avoid their responsibilities to school, family, and work.

There remains the fifty-page narcissistic logorrhea passed off as a methodological appendix, from which it emerges that, far from being a technique of systematic observation and analysis, ethnography is for the author of *On the Run* "a way of being" and a mysterious "tradition passed down from master to pupil"—and from father to daughter?—according to which the observer must magically disappear from the scene. This is how Goffman describes her efforts to become "like a good fly on the wall" by practicing what she calls "social shrinkrage—to become as small a presence as possible" (10). How credible is such a self-mystifying field technique? While it may be desirable for the ethnographer to minimize her interference with the practices she observes, this alone cannot assume the place of a methodological posture, and the researcher has much to learn from her subjects' reactions to her interference, which must be acknowledged and exploited rather than magically denied.

So how do we explain the book's success, despite its glaring defects? The first element of fascination, and not just among sociologists, is that the author is Erving Goffman's daughter, born just as he was dying of cancer at the height of his fame (he was then president of the American Sociological Association; he wrote his presidential address from his hospital bed and never delivered it). It is hard to exaggerate the *aura* that this filiation gave her—even her French publisher mentions it in the presentation of the book in translation. The author openly laid claim to this filiation: "The shadow of my late father may have pushed me to go further than was safe and expected" (11). Secondly, *On the Run is* a clash of opposites worthy of boulevard theater, the unlikely and titillating meeting of opposites, white woman/black man, educated rich and unschooled poor, damsel and rogue, urban olympus and inner-city underbelly. But, above all, the book describes a surprisingly binary world bathed in moral juice, divided by the binaries black/white, bad/good, guilty/victim, swinging with the gentle liberal breeze blowing across America during Obama's second presidential term (12). Finally, the book was the subject of a smart marketing plan designed to "bank" on these oppositions: it was agreed that the University of Chicago Press would have the rights to the book for only one year, in order to authenticate its academic value, before they reverted to the commercial house Picador for a speedy publication in paperback (which explains the lax writing in short two-sentence paragraphs and the absence of a bibliography and index).

On the Run is thus revealing of a *moment* in American sociological production; its reception illuminates the politics of ethnographic knowledge and an epistemic *constellation* of the *longue durée* in a straight line with Chicago's century-long moral empiricism. Goffman cannot help but write at the outset of her book that, despite the constant oppression to which they are subjected, "neighborhood residents are carving out a meaningful life for themselves betwixt and between police stops and probation meetings. The scope of punishment and surveillance does not prevent them from constructing a moral world in which they can find dignity and honor" (13). One grasps here the springs of the success of an exoticizing travel memoir that takes its coy readers into the city's "black zoo" (14), a veritable "jungle book" that deftly plays on the racial guilt complex of so-called liberal readers quick to confuse the TV series *The Wire* with the daily reality of the hyperghetto.

1. Alice Goffman, *On the Run: Fugitive Life in an American City* (2014).
2. For example, the first page of the preface begins with a string of five inaccurate statistics on incarceration; the count of police incidents observed *de visu* just does not make sense, and neither does the questionnaire survey in the neighborhood that is supposed to anchor the observation. Goffman confuses individuals wanted by the police (for crimes) with people who are the subject of a bench warrant (for failure to appear, usually to satisfy a simple bureaucratic procedure). She also confuses criminal court, civil court, and family court. Added to this is ignorance of the relevant literatures, starting with the voluminous criminological research on the police, which does not rate a single citation, nor is public data on crime and policing in Philadelphia used. As a result, there are no indicators of the intensity of police activity in relation to the incidence of crime, apart from the fleeting impressions of a naive, impressionable, and self-interested observer: during the "Author meets the critics" session on *On the Run* at the 2014 annual meetings of the

American Sociological Association, Goffman explained that "the purpose of the book is to make people really angry about injustice."
3. Victor M. Rios, *Punished: Policing the Lives of Black and Latino Boys* (2011); Jamie J. Fader, *Falling Back: Incarceration and Transitions to Adulthood among Urban Youth* (2013); Todd R. Clear, *Imprisoning Communities: How Mass Incarceration Makes Disadvantaged Neighborhoods Worse* (2009). Goffman cites neither Fader (even though her work had collected awards from scholarly associations) nor Clear, and generously gives one terse footnote to Rios.
4. Ana Portilla, "*On the Run*. L'ethnographie en cavale?" (2016).
5. Goffman's informants read her field notes over her shoulder as they were being written (on her smartphone), and when they told her "Don't write this down" or "I'm going to say some shit right now, and (. . .), I don't want that to go into your book," she "took careful heed and did as people requested" (*On the Run*, p. 239). Is this the work of an ethnographer or a publicist?
6. A resounding report by the Pew Charitable Foundation, *Philadelphia's Crowded, Costly Jails, 2010* (2011) shows this. It is not cited in *On the Run*, nor are any administrative sources relating to the local criminal justice chain available online.
7. Michel Foucault, *Surveiller et punir. Naissance de la prison* (1975).
8. Rebecca Rhynhart, *Data Release: Gun Violence Clearance Rates and Case Outcomes* (2022).
9. Brianna Remster and Rory Kramer, "Race, Space, and Surveillance: Understanding the Relationship between Criminal Justice Contact and Institutional Involvement" (2018).
10. Goffman, *On the Run*, pp. 207, 235–236. This appendix, embarrassing for its novelistic style and incriminating for its methodological inanity, which Goffman's academic mentors should have enjoined her to remove from the book, provides grist to the mill of ethnography's detractors and motivated legal scholar Steven Lubet to write an entire book on the supposed errant ways of participant observation: Steven Lubet, *Interrogating Ethnography: Why Evidence Matters* (2018). Read Michael Burawoy's scathing response to Lubet, "Empiricism and its Fallacies" (2019).
11. Goffman, *On the Run*, p. 229.
12. Obama was the first president in history to visit a federal prison and meet inmates there for a dialogue. In the same years, civil rights attorney Michelle Alexander's book *The New Jim Crow* (2010) became a bestseller and the bible of a growing movement for criminal justice reform aimed at "ending mass incarceration."
13. Goffman, *On the Run*, p. 8. This directly echoes her mentor Duneier, see *supra*, pp. 62–63, 66–67, 71–72.
14. Victor M. Rios, "Decolonizing the White Space in Urban Ethnography" (2015).

Ethnographism, paralogisms, and "thick construction"

With the benefit of two decades' hindsight, what more general lessons can we draw from this episode in the history of American urban ethnography for the practical conduct of fieldwork, its virtues, its shortcomings, and its generic difficulties? The *differentia specifica* of ethnography as a technique of social inquiry and analysis is twofold. In contrast to the statistical, historical, and hermeneutic approaches,[23] ethnography is research *that is embodied and embedded* in the very universe it studies. It is *embodied in* a double sense: (1) it deals with agents of flesh and blood who engage and suffer in the world, and not with automatons mechanically obeying norms or calculators maximizing their interest, the two models of action that dominate the social sciences and owe their plausibility only to the physical and social distance that commonly separates the investigator from the investigated;[24] (2) the researcher's main tool is his or her body proper, sentient, alert, intelligent and exposed, as far as possible, to the forces and contingencies of the microcosm under consideration. The living organism is treated here not as an obstacle to knowledge, but as a medium for the production of sociological knowledge, insofar as it is solicited with method and tact.

This is well expressed by Erving Goffman when he defines fieldwork as a technique "of getting data, it seems to me, by subjecting yourself, your own body and your own personality, and your own social situation, to the set of contingencies that play upon a set of individuals, so that you can physically and ecologically penetrate the circle of response to their their social situation, or their work situation, or their ethnic situation, or whatever. So that you are close to them while they are responding to what life does to them."[25] In other words, fieldwork is always an apprenticeship by body, more or less conscious and salient, even as it works through the mediation of language and text.

This *carnal dimension of ethnographic practice* is rarely thematized as such by the very people who engage in it.[26] It is a kind of methodological open secret; all fieldworkers know about it, but few talk about it (or they talk about it badly, in the heroic or narcissistic register, brought to its fusion point by Michel Leiris in *L'Afrique fantôme*),[27] because academic conventions push it into the background and epistemological propriety demands that one keep quiet about it on pain of being accused of free-falling into subjectivism. Added

---

[23] On the similarities and differences between these three modes of social inquiry, I recommend Robert Alford, *The Craft of Inquiry: Methods, Theories and Evidence* (1998).

[24] An in-depth critique of the "cardboard cutouts" of *homo economicus* and *homo culturalis* can be found in Loïc Wacquant, "For a Sociology of Flesh and Blood" (2015).

[25] Erving Goffman, "On Fieldwork" (1989), p. 125. Goffman continues: "That 'tunes your body up' and, with your 'tuned-up' body, and with the ecological right to be close to them (which you've obtained by one sneaky means or another), you are in a position to note their gestural, visual, bodily response to what's going on around them."

[26] A notable exception is Michael Herzfeld, "The Cultural Politics of Gesture: Reflections on the Embodiment of Ethnographic Practice" (2009). See also Sébastien Chauvin and Nicolas Jounin, "L'observation directe" (2010), pp. 154–156. Anthropologists, who generally conduct longer and more repeated fieldwork, are more likely to show this bodywork than sociologists, if by inadvertence.

[27] Michel Leiris, *L'Âge d'homme*, preceded by *L'Afrique fantôme* ([1934] 2014).

to this is the intellectualist bias constitutive of the academic condition—"we are all despisers of the body," Nietzsche famously wrote.[28] But, if ethnography is productive, it is first and foremost because the ethnographer is methodically *at one with* ("*fait corps avec*") the phenomenon under study, and methodically so, even if it is imperative that she *also* avails herself the technical and existential means to emerge from this body-to-body tussle (*corps-à-corps*) in order to objectivize the phenomenon.[29]

It is feminist ethnographers who have made the most progress towards full recognition of the "carnality" of participant observation, out of necessity, due to the recurrent sexual harassment they have to defend themselves against in the field;[30] in relation to the embedded study of bodily professions ordinarily reserved for women such as workers of intimacy (home medical assistant, prostitute, manicurist, housekeeper, etc.), fashion model, and bar hostess, which directly involve and stage corporeality;[31] and finally, by drawing on theories of gender and sexuality which, by definition, problematize the social and symbolic formation of the body, even if these theories all too often reduce the latter to a text to be read, rather than grasping it as the living seat of labor power, desire and knowledge of the world.[32] A particularly promising approach in this regard is the "gendering" of the phenomenology of the body proper as well as carnal sociology itself, which sets itself the task of producing not an ethnography *of* the body as a socially *constructed* object, but an ethnography *from* the body as the socially *constructing* subject of the world and seat of tacit and practical knowledge.[33]

Next, ethnography is an *embedded* mode of inquiry along three dimensions—social, symbolic, and temporal: (1) the researcher works to insert herself into

---

[28] Even Stéphane Beaud and Florence Weber's excellent *Guide de l'enquête de terrain* (2003) scotomizes this dimension. Ditto Anne-Marie Arborio and Pierre Fournier, *L'Enquête et ses méthodes. L'observation directe* (2015), and Martin Hammersley and Paul Atkinson, *Ethnography: Principles in Practice* (2019).

[29] This applies even to the ethnography of the most "mental" practices, such as the technological implementation of space missions, as demonstrated by Janet Vertesi in her magnificent book, *Seeing Like a Rover: How Robots, Teams, and Images Craft Knowledge of Mars* (2015).

[30] Rebecca Hanson and Patricia Richards, *Harassed: Gender, Bodies, and Ethnographic Research* (2019). See also the blog Badasses (Blog d'Autodéfense contre les Agressions Sexistes et Sexuelles dans l'Enquête en Science Sociales: https://badasses.hypotheses.org/).

[31] Eileen Boris and Rhacel Salazar Parreñas (eds.), *Intimate Labors: Cultures, Technologies, and the Politics of Care* (2010); Ashley Mears, *Pricing Beauty: The Making of a Fashion Model* (2011); Kimberly Kay Hoang, *Dealing in Desire: Asian Ascendancy, Western Decline, and the Hidden Currencies of Global Sex Work* (2015).

[32] See, for example, Janet Price and Margrit Shildrick (eds.), *Feminist Theory and the Body: A Reader* (1999); Iris Marion Young, *On Female Body Experience: "Throwing Like a Girl" and Other Essays* (2005); Judith Lorber and Lisa Jean Moore (eds.), *Gendered Bodies: Feminist Perspectives* (2010); Silvia Antosa (ed.), *Queer Crossings: Theories, Bodies, Texts* (2014).

[33] Wacquant, "For a Sociology of Flesh and Blood" and "Carnal Concepts in Action" (2023); Victoria Pitts-Taylor, "A Feminist Carnal Sociology? Embodiment in Sociology, Feminism, and Naturalized Philosophy" (2015); Kimberly Kay Hoang, "Gendering Carnal Ethnography: A Queer Reception" (2018).

the network of specific relationships so as to maximize her social embeddedness; (2) she pursues cultural learning to pierce the constellation of meanings proper to the universe studied in order to deepen her symbolic embeddedness; (3) it is temporal immersion that creates a positive synergy between social and symbolic embeddness, so that participation in social relationships provides the key to cultural constellations and conversely, in a mutually reinforcing movement stretching over weeks, months, and years. Hence the striking analytical difference between long-term ethnographies, which bring this synergy into full play, and field studies based on fleeting observation, which merely scratch the outer surface of their object.[34]

It follows from these two properties that the field sociologist faces specific "epistemological obstacles" (in Bachelard's sense), inasmuch as her imperative of social and symbolic embedding makes her liable to fall into what I shall call *ethnographism*—by analogy with "economism" as a mode of thinking that reduces everything to economic variables[35]—namely, the error of reasoning which consists in thinking that everything can be grasped and explained by the *hic et nunc* of the field and that the "totalization" of the object can be achieved without external elements of theorization, observation, and historical perspective.[36] Ethnographism can be broken down into five paralogisms or fallacies, some of which can be encoutered in other modalities of sociological inquiry and analysis (quantitative, historical, hermeneutic), but which particularly threaten field researchers: interactionism, inductivism, populism, presentism, and interpretativism. Moreover, these fallacies tend to implicate and reinforce each other so that it is difficult to escape one without giving in to the other.

To make my argumentation more concrete, I will try to indicate for each fallacy the practical operations the ethnographer can perform to avoid it, drawing on my recent fieldwork (whose analysis is in progress) on "The Social Life of the County Criminal Court" carried out in Northern California in the county of San Pedrito (a pseudonym). The criminal court, anchored by the prosecutor-public defender-judge triad, is a "strategic research site" à la Merton for grasping the state management of urban marginality in that it is the point of direct junction and friction between public authority and the city's dispossessed and dishonored populations. The overwhelming majority of defendants who pass through the court are indigent from the black and Hispanic working classes; they are both the first culprits and the first victims

---

[34] Alpa Shah, "Ethnography? Participant Observation, a Potentially Revolutionary Praxis" (2017).
[35] Richard K. Ashley, "Three Modes of Economism" (1983).
[36] For an enlightening discussion, see Nicolas Dodier and Isabelle Baszanger, "Totalisation et altérité dans l'enquête ethnographique" (1997).

of the criminality that erodes the social order at the bottom of the hierarchy of classes and places.[37]

1.-*The interactionist fallacy* consists in considering that the essential is given in the *encounter* in Goffman's sense, that is, the face-to-face interaction born of "physical co-presence" in a given place and institution, independently of the external structural forces that weigh on it.[38] It is the main virtue of fieldwork, the fact of being *in situ* and *in vivo*, that threatens here to turn against the ethnographer by creating the illusion of the transparency and completeness of the social immediately perceptible around us.

> "Interactions, which provide immediate satisfaction to empiricist dispositions—you can observe them, film them, in short, touch them with your finger—hide the structures that are realized in them. This is one of those cases where the visible, what is immediately given, hides the invisible that determines it. We thus forget that the truth of interaction is never entirely in the interaction as it is revealed to observation."
>
> Pierre Bourdieu, *Choses dites* (1986), p. 151.

The remedy to counter this slide is to mobilize the Bourdieusian concept of *social space* as an objective system of positions defined by the distribution of efficient resources in the universe under consideration. Bourdieu introduced the notion "to break with the tendency to think of the social world in a substantialist way" and promote "a *relational* apprehension of the social world."[39] But it is also the notion that makes it possible to establish a crucial analytical distinction between structure and interaction, the constructed and the given, the conceived and the perceived, and thus to grasp the forces at work within the observed environment unbeknownst to the agents. It is this invisible space which transcends the moment, elaborated by the sociologist (by means of biographical interviews, organizational analysis, prosopography, or multiple correspondence analysis), which governs interaction in the sense that it makes it possible and orients the practical strategies of agents in

---

[37] Criminal justice in the United States follows an "adversarial" logic in which prosecutors and public defenders (attorneys paid by the county to counsel indigent defendants) confront each other while the accused remains mute. The judge approves the negotiated "guilty plea" agreement and sets the sentence accordingly. Prosecutors and defenders are organized into two offices headed by the chief District Attorney and Public Defender, respectively. In San Pedrito County, each of these offices comprises around a hundred lawyers distributed into specialized teams dealing with specific types of crime.

[38] Erving Goffman, *Encounters: Two Studies in the Sociology of Interaction* (1961).

[39] Pierre Bourdieu, "Espace social et champ du pouvoir", in *Raisons pratiques* (1996), p. 53. For a reading of Bourdieu's theory as a "trialectic of symbolic space, social space and symbolic space," see Loïc Wacquant, *Bourdieu in the City: Challenging Urban Theory* (2023), pp. 6–11.

the relevant situation according to the position they occupy in it and the path by which they arrived there.

> To construct a social space [is] to construct the simple model that enables us to re-engender the space of differences, i.e. the structure of distributions, from a small number of mutually articulated variables...
>
> Having constructed the space in this way, we can situate each social agent in a region of this space and his position in the space gives a very strong predictability concerning... all sorts of practices. To cut up the regions in this space, I am going to draw a circle with a felt-tip pen, the hypothesis I have in mind being that the smaller my circle, the more properties, both actual and potential, the people inserted in that circle will have in common.[40]

This is to say that *all ethnography must be structural* or, better still, *topological*, even when it takes a narrative form. It cannot do without an objectivist moment of relational cartography, even as it seeks to capture the subjective point of view of the natives of the universe in question, and to capture the sensorial rhapsody of action. This space of positions imposes its own *specific gravity* and "refracts" forces external to the microcosm in question.[41] Now, it is precisely the notion of structure as a system of objective relationships exerting a "constraint" in Durkheim's sense that is lacking in Chicago-style ethnographies—and many others—rooted as they are in a superficial philosophy of action that can be described as moral individualism. This philosophy is disdainful of any abstract concept or objective relation of power, since everything is played out, for its followers, in face-to-face encounters guided by the "definition of the situation" negotiated locally by agents situated in a concrete *place*, instead of being the precipitate of a symbolic struggle rooted in a *space* understood as a distribution of capital.[42]

---

[40] Pierre Bourdieu, *Sociologie générale*, Volume 2: *Cours au Collège de France 1981–1983* (2016), p. 1127–1128. Constructing social space therefore involves an architectural set-up that goes beyond simply capturing interactional relationships "from both ends," as Matthew Desmond proposes in "Relational Ethnography" (2014).

[41] I use the term "structural" in a different sense from Burawoy, for whom structure is external, and not immanent, to interaction and manifests as constraints, and not possibilities: "The use of the term structural is intended to express the underlying limits of transactions, *limits that are set by forces beyond the site of the field* that can only be explored by theoretical frameworks and comparative logic" (Michael Burawoy, "On Desmond: The Limits of Spontaneous Sociology" [2017], p. 264, my italics). Structure is a methodological springboard to comparison for Burawoy, a topological tool for explicating interaction for Bourdieu.

[42] Robert S. Perinbanayagam, "The Definition of the Situation: An Analysis of the Ethnomethodological and Dramaturgical View" (1974). This position is taken to its zenith by Howard S. Becker in *Art Worlds* (1982), for whom everything is "collective action" in tangible and directly observable "collaborative networks"; his analysis can be compared to that of Pierre Bourdieu in *Les Règles de l'art. Genèse et structure du champ littéraire* (1992), which places the writer in the objective structure of the artistic microcosm and the latter in the field of power.

Here is a practical tip: Identify the forms of capital operating in the microcosm in question, that is, the efficient properties (attached to individuals, groups or institutions) and draw a diagram of the positions occupied by agents in their multidimensional distribution. These properties may be generic (age, gender, qualifications, income, etc.) or specific to the microcosm under study (seniority, organizational position, technical capital, etc.). Whether or not they become active or not depends on the position this universe itself occupies in the nested series of higher-scale social spaces.

Interactions between prosecutors and public defenders during a San Pedrito County criminal court hearing are overdetermined by the position each lawyer occupies in the division of legal work into teams that are themselves hierarchized; first by seniority and thus the embodied juridical capital in addition to the institutionalized juridical capital represented by the *Juris Doctor* diploma and the "bar card" (certificate of aptitude); then by symbolic capital, reputation for integrity ("straight shooter") or inflexibility ("true believer"); and finally by the structural power relations between the two offices, which are themselves the product of the history of the local bureaucratic and political fields.

The balance of power between prosecutors and defenders is, in a way, "arbitrated" by the judges, who, in every interaction during a hearing or private consultation in their chambers, tip the scales one way or the other according to the degree of autonomy and authority enjoyed by their collective body (bench) in the local bureaucratic-political space, but also according to their embodied juridical capital (technicality, experience, etc.). It is this *structural balance of power* that determines from above the form, contents, and results of the activities of the "courtroom workgroup," observable in the courtroom, which serves as both unit of observation and unit of analysis for the conventional sociology of the criminal court.[43]

Each office, the District Attorney and the Public Defender, is itself structured by the opposition between two poles, the one autonomous (defending a strict internalist reading of the penal code) and the other heteronomous (pushing for social factors to be taken into account in judicial decision making), so that they can be represented as two partially overlapping oblongs in which one can locate the relevant agents. Each office is in turn subject to external pressures from the media, political demand and popular *desiderata* through referendums, not to mention struggles within the local field of power (between the elected "commissioners" who run the county). The ethnographer can thus unearth the relevant properties and concretize the social space of the court by implementing the topological mode of thinking.

---

[43] James Eisenstein and Herbert Jacob, *Felony Justice: An Organizational Analysis of Criminal Courts* (1977); James Eisenstein et al., *The Contours of Justice: Communities and their Courts* (1988).

How did the idea of this Venn diagram representing the dual structure of the local juridical field that drives face-to-face interactions come to my mind? It did not "jump at me" on its own. I elaborated it bit by bit by consciously searching my observations and in my fieldnotes for dual oppositions homologous to those structuring the pairs prosecutor/public defender, victim/offender, right/left, masculine/feminine, sacred/profane, order/disorder, punishment/ protection, etc. (I had in mind Durkheim and Mauss's luminous essay on "Some Primitive Forms of Classification" and Bourdieu's diagrams of Kabyle rite and myth in *Le Sens pratique*).[44] It is this topological way of thinking that led me to notice the cantilevered position of the prosecutors who would sheepishly confess to me during interviews, under the seal of secrecy, that they could have become public defenders, and vice versa. This led me to realize that the staff of the two offices "overlapped" in terms of their dispositions and professional ethos, creating a space where the smooth negotiation of criminal cases can flourish.

2.-*The empiricist fallacy or the inductivist illusion* leads the ethnographer to abandon himself to the sensible world and to expect his preconstructed object to "speak" to him about itself. This is the posture advocated by Anselm Strauss and Barney Glazer in their fetish-book *The Discovery of Grounded Theory* (1967), according to which the researcher must present herself before the empirical world with her mind untouched by any conception, in total theoretical ignorance, and wait for the data to suggest concepts and hypotheses.[45] This is to forget that the social world only responds to the questions we put to it; noise only becomes a signal for those armed with a code, that is, a principle of selection and translation from the sensible into the intelligible. To carry out an induction, analytic or otherwise,[46] one cannot but start with an idea, however confused and shapeless, of the phenomenon to be observed, the properties attached to it, its proper perimeter, and the relationships it has with its milieu. This means resisting, rather than submitting to, the sensible on the basis of expectations born of past experience and social perceptions. It is a long way from the naive gaze to the sociological view of the world. Bachelard explains:

> Observation already needs a body of precautions that lead us to reflect before looking, that at least reform the first vision, so that it is never the first observation

---

[44] Émile Durkheim and Marcel Mauss, *De quelques formes primitives de classification* ([1903] 2017), and Pierre Bourdieu, "Le démon de l'analogie" in *Le sens pratique* (1980), pp. 333–439.

[45] "Generating a theory from data means that most hypotheses and concepts not only come from the data, but are systematically worked out in relation to the data during the course of the research." Barney G. Glaser and Anselm L. Strauss, *The Discovery of Grounded Theory: Strategies for Qualitative Research* (1967), p. 6.

[46] Jack Katz, "A Theory of Qualitative Methodology: The Social System of Analytical Fieldwork" (1983).

that is the right one. Scientific observation is always a polemical observation; it confirms or invalidates a previous thesis, a prior schema, an observation plan; it shows by demonstrating; it hierarchizes appearances; it transcends the immediate; it reconstructs reality after having reconstructed its schemas.[47]

The parable of Ireneo Funes (*Funes el memorioso*), the Jorge Luis Borges character who, following a fall from a horse, wakes up hypermnesic, endowed with an instantaneous and infallible memory and an infinite capacity for perception, and who is therefore drowning in the boundless ocean of facts, objects, and empirical properties that accumulate without respite or reason in his brain, speaks well of the impossibility of approaching the world in the manner of a photographic plate.[48] It totally invalidates Bruno Latour's hyperempiricist recommendation to "be content with describing" the social when he asserts: "If I were you, I would abstain from any [theoretical] framework altogether. Just describe the state of affairs at hand."[49] But how can we "record without filtering" and describe without categories, without sorting, without preliminary questions—in short, without theory? Every act of cognition implies a selection and organization of the sensible; better still, it is a form of action in the world. As recent developments in the cognitive sciences have shown, the relationship between the brain, the body, and the environment is one of mutual entanglement.[50]

In this sense, the very term "ethnography" is misleading: "graphy" suggests a purely descriptive form of writing (from the Greek verb *graphein*) that is content to *record* the culture of a people or tribe (*ethnos*), whereas all writing presupposes not only semantic and syntactic rules that must be learned, but also a literary creation and a world of texts into which it is inserted, and thus, once again, a horizon of expectations, social or scholarly. In other words, *there is no such thing as ethnography without theory*. To put it bluntly, what does exist are, on the one hand, ethnographers (rationalists) who have given themselves the reasoned means to think through their tools of thought, immersion, and observation, and, on the other, their colleagues (empiricists) who *are thought through by their social and methodological unconscious*, an unconscious that shapes their object unbeknownst to them. Notwithstanding its

---

[47] Gaston Bachelard, *Le Nouvel esprit scientifique* (1934), p. 26.
[48] Jorge Luis Borges, "Funes or Memory" ([1942] 1974). I borrow this short story from Javier Auyero, who uses it in his ethnography seminar in Austin to insist from the outset on the indispensable role of selection and abstraction in even the most deliberately positivist fieldwork.
[49] Bruno Latour, *Reassembling the Social: An Introduction to Actor-Network-Theory* (2007), p. 144.
[50] Andy Clark, *Mindware: An Introduction to the Philosophy of Cognitive Science* (2013).

extraordinary academic success, the radical inductivism of grounded theory is a paper fiction.[51]

Theory is therefore a *sine qua non* for fieldwork—as it is for statistical, historical and hermeneutic analysis. But how do we articulate theory and observation? Here we come upon three paths open to the ethnographer. The first is the "extended case method" invented by the Manchester School and codified in Berkeley by Michael Burawoy, which takes a theory as its starting point and seeks to generate data to revise and deepen it.[52] Backed by the epistemology of Imre Lakatos and his notion of "progressive research program," it sets out to embed everyday life in extralocal historical forces and to dissect processes by controlling the effects of power. Its main strength is to articulate a clear problematic linked to an ambitious agenda, which poses "big questions" at the macro-sociological level based on well-circumscribed fieldwork at the micro-sociological level (e.g., the contradictions that are bringing down state communism in Eastern Europe based on a comparative ethnography of the labor process in two industries in Hungary).[53] Its flaw is that it is *theoretico-centric*: it starts from theory and returns to it; the empirical object is no more than a convenient and incidental support; the criteria of granularity, affectivity, and carnality, three markers of quality ethnography, are foreign to it. The accounts it produces are typically flat and one-dimensional because the ethnographic site is merely a means of "framing" a macro-societal force.

The extended-case study is theoretically monotheistic: it is rooted in a principally theoretical or even dogmatic commitment—in Burawoy's case, a fierce attachment to a Gramscian-inflected Marxism. It prematurely closes the perimeter of observation by imposing an elaboration of the site before entering it. Another shortcoming is that its proponents do not practice what they preach: what ethnographer seeks data to refute his or her preferred theory?[54]

---

[51] Glaser and Strauss, *The Discovery of Grounded Theory*, and Kathy Charmaz, *Constructing Grounded Theory: A Practical Guide through Qualitative Analysis* (2006). Proof positive, over the past half century, grounded theory has hardly produced any of the new "formal theories, detachable from their object" that Glaser and Strauss called for. This raises the question of the reasons for its success. The most plausible is precisely that it allows its practitioners to merge with their object and dispense with the work of construction.

[52] Michael Burawoy, "The Extended Case Method" (1998), and Burawoy, *The Extended Case Method: Four Countries, Four Decades, Four Great Transformations, and One Theoretical Tradition* (2009).

[53] Michael Burawoy and János Lukács, *The Radiant Past: Ideology and Reality in Hungary's Road to Capitalism* (1992).

[54] "Our stance toward theory is kamikaze. In our fieldwork we do not look for confirmations but for theory's refutations. We need first the courage of our convictions, then the courage to challenge our convictions, and finally the imagination to sustain our courage with theoretical reconstruction. If these reconstructions come at too great a cost we may have to abandon our theory altogether and start afresh with a new, interesting theory for which our case is once more an anomaly" (Burawoy, "The Extended Case Method," p. 20).

Thus, for example, the two best orthodox monographs born of Burawoy-chaired doctoral theses —Jeffrey Sallaz, *The Labor of Luck*, on the economics of casinos in California and South Africa, and Z. Fareen Parvez, *Politicizing Islam*, on the relationship between politics and minority religion in India and France—neither seek to "disprove" or even revise a theory. Sallaz dismisses existing theories of neoliberal globalization to develop an original approach he calls "politico-performative."[55] Parvez draws on eclectic theories (Nancy Fraser, Hannah Arendt, various feminist authors) to highlight the variety of articulations between class, state, and religion, without reworking any of these theories.[56] Like grounded theory, the extended-case method is a scholastic meditation that does not quite correspond to the reality of ethnographic practice.

The second path for linking theory and observation is "abductive analysis" as developed by Iddo Tavory and Stefan Timmermans, based on the pragmatist philosophy of Charles Sanders Peirce.[57] It consists of "conjectural" reasoning that leads to the formulation of explanatory hypotheses based on observations that are surprising, either for their novelty or for their anomalous nature. In contrast to grounded theory, which requires the methodical ignorance of existing studies on its object of investigation, abductive analysis presupposes a mastery of the relevant theories, and proceeds by a "mutual and recursive adjustment of data and theories." The abductive ethnographer "must be neither theoretically atheistic nor avowed monotheists, but informed theoretical agnostics."[58] She constantly revisits her observations; aims for "defamiliarization" through textual engagement; and seeks to understand the same data from multiple perspectives.

The danger of abduction is that it confuses sociological reasoning with ordinary reasoning—according to Peirce, abductive thinking is what we all do in everyday life by recalibrating our expectations in response to surprising phenomena. In fact, according to Peircian philosophers themselves, the specificity of the notion of "abduction" is anything but clear.[59] Abductive reasoning seeks to account for surprises, anomalies, and enigmas, but an observation is

---

[55] Jeff Sallaz, *The Labor of Luck: Casino Capitalism in the United States and South Africa* (2009), pp. 235–249.

[56] Z. Fareen Parvez, *Politicizing Islam: The Islamic Revival in France and India* (2017), pp. 3–5, 11–27.

[57] Stefan Timmermans and Iddo Tavory, "Theory Construction in Qualitative Research: From Grounded Theory to Abductive Analysis" (2012), and Timmermans and Tavory, *Abductive Analysis: Theorizing Qualitative Research* (2014).

[58] Timmermans and Tavory, "Theory Construction in Qualitative Research," p. 169.

[59] Harry G. Frankfurt, "Peirce's Notion of Abduction" (1958). Philosophical debates on abduction are vigorous, plural, and highly technical. For an overview and defense of the notion, see Igor Douven, *The Art of Abduction* (2022).

only surprising in relation to a horizon of expectation—that is, a (proto-) theory. The same observation may be unexpected for several of the theories we get started with, but then which path to follow? Here again, abduction theorists do not always put their proclaimed principles into practice. In concrete terms, their recommendations result in a constant back-and-forth between deduction and induction, and not in a distinct mental operation as Tavory suggests.[60] Finally, the choice of the relevant theoretical palette (based on the question "of what is this a theoretical case?") presupposes having defined the object under consideration that the theory is precisely supposed to specify, turning into circular reasoning.[61]

The third path, advocated in this book, is what I call *"thick construction,"* in reference and in opposition to the *"thick description"* that Clifford Geertz borrows from the philosopher of mind Gilbert Ryle. The aim of thick description is to render, through writing, the complex fabric of meanings that people give to their actions; it pertains to social hermeneutics, leading to a pointillist account that "puts down on paper" the interpretative activity of agents evolving in the world under study, as if their conduct were a kind of theater play to be watched and appreciated.[62] Geertz explicitly states that "culture is public because meaning is public." He further asserts that "culture is not a power" that moves people, but "a context" that gives meaning to their conduct, so that "the object of ethnography [is] a stratified hierarchy of meaningful structures."[63]

Thick construction is the rationalist opposite of Geertzian empiricism. It is, fundamentally, a "construction squared": it operates the *scientific* (analytical) construction of an *ordinary* (folk) social construction. It fully recognizes that social agents jointly fabricate their lived world through cognitive elaboration and conative improvisation, and that the ethnographer must examine this fabrication, its tools, its secrets, and its products. At this level, the Bourdieusian approach is congruent with constructivist microsociologies, symbolic interactionism, Schutzian phenomenology, ethnomethodology, and the symbolic anthropology of which Geertz is the historical standard-bearer. But it also posits that the task of the sociologist—whether field-based or not—is to

---

[60] Iddo Tavory, *Summoned: Identification and Religious Life in a Jewish Neighborhood* (2016), pp. 162–163.
[61] Stefan Timmermans and Iddo Tavory, *Data Analysis in Qualitative Research: Theorizing with Abductive Analysis* (2022), pp. 155–156.
[62] Indeed, one of Clifford Geertz's most accomplished books is *Negara: The Theatre State in Nineteenth-Century Bali* (1980), and his most famous article also describes a quasi-theatrical scene: "Deep Play: Notes on the Balinese Cockfight" (1972).
[63] Clifford Geertz, "Thick Description: Toward an Interpretive Theory of Culture," p. 7.

produce her object through the controlled deployment of analytical categories capable of encompassing folk categories, establishing their genesis and uses, and grasping the objective forces that give the social world its specific gravity. Constructing the social space in which agents occupy points that inform their point of view requires theoretical tools, without which this space would remain invisible:

> Theory, it is a banality of the epistemological tradition, is what makes us see things that we would not have seen otherwise. The epistemological tradition has often multiplied examples of the effects of theory: when theory is constituted, phenomena that had remained unnoticed, realities that had been confounded, stand out and apart; in other words, we see only that for which we have the theory.[64]

Or again: "If it is certain that every scientific concept is constructed (in the sense that it is not inductively unearthed from reality), it is a constructive operation insofar as it is a general question that will receive its reality from the scientific work of empirical construction and confrontation with observations."[65]

Bourdieu liked to recall the Greek etymology of the word "theory," *theorein*, to observe or to contemplate, but he immediately distanced himself from it, emphasizing the pragmatic character of sociological theory as a program for the scientific fabrication of empirical objects.[66] This is how he defines it as "an instrument for seeing relationships," "a mode of thinking, a system of rigorously controlled schemata for perceiving the social world." Thus, for example, the concept of habitus sums up a dispositionalist philosophy of action, but also points to a series of practical operations aimed at reconstituting the trajectory of agents and the forms of body-based learning they have ensued, so as to pierce the combination of cognitive categories, conative skills, and emotive desires that characterizes them in their own right.[67] In his *Cours de sociologie générale*, Bourdieu gently mocks "theoretical jugglery" and firmly rejects the Althusserian notion of "theoretical work" detached from research practice and overhanging empirical investigation. Theory may birth data but it remains the servant of empirical research.

---

[64] Pierre Bourdieu, *Sociologie générale*, Volume 1: *Cours au Collège de France 1981–1983* (2015), p. 114.
[65] Pierre Bourdieu, *Sociologie générale*, Volume 2: *Cours au Collège de France 1981–1983* (2016), p. 26.
[66] On this conception of sociological theory as a system of intellectual and technical dispositions, read Rogers Brubaker's subtle article, "Social Theory as Habitus" (1993).
[67] Loïc Wacquant, "Habitus as Topic and Tool" (2011).

"Thick description" à la Geertz versus "thick construction" à la Bourdieu

For Geertz, leader and icon of the interpretive approach at the frontier between social science and the humanities, the social agent is an *animal symbolicum* "suspended in webs of significance he himself has spun." Culture is a "context," and the ethnographer's job is to interpret the agents' interpretations, and then use the density of the written word to convey the interweaving structures of meaning that give sense to their conduct. Everything is given on the surface, in the very moment of action, because "culture is public." Theory is resolved—or dissolved—in the multilayered account that delivers the intelligibility of the phenomenon. "Conducting an ethnography is like trying to read a manuscript (. . .) written, not in conventional graphics, but in transient examples of shaped behavior." The social world according to Geertz, like that of Chicago-style urban ethnographers, is an irenic universe, free of material inertia and power relationships, organized by communicative relations, and in which everything is visible and immediately accessible to the field observer.

"Believing, with Max Weber, that man is an animal suspended in webs of significance he himself has spun, I take culture to be those webs, and the analysis of it to be therefore not an experimental science in search of law but an interpretive one in search of meaning . . . The object of ethnography [is] a stratified hierarchy of meaningful" or "piled-up structures of inference and implication through which an ethnographer is continually trying to pick his way. . .

Ethnography is *thick* description. What the ethnographer is in fact faced with. . . is a multiplicity of complex conceptual structures, many of them superimposed upon or knotted into one another, which are at once strange, irregular, and inexplicit, and which he must contrive somehow first to grasp and then to render. . . . Culture is not a power, something to which social events, behaviors, institutions, or processes can be causally attributed; it is a context, something within which they can be intelligibly—that is, thickly—described. . . ."

"We begin with our own interpretations of what our informants are up to, or think they are up to, and then systematize those. It follows that the ethnographer's task is "to 'inscribe' social discourse. *He writes it down*."

Clifford Geertz, "Thick Description: Toward an Interpretive Theory of Culture," pp. 5, 7, 9–10, and 19.

For Bourdieu, the social agent is a historical being embedded in an objective structure of distribution of capital (in its various forms) resulting from the material and symbolic struggles that make history. The agent's subjective "point of view" is the view she takes from the point she occupies in social space. Symbolic structures are not only structured and structuring; they are also instruments of domination. Symbolic power, the epicenter of Bourdieusian sociology, arises from the very fact that the human being is a symbolic animal in Cassirer's sense, and that the social world is "multisided" (*vielseitig*) in Weber's sense, that is, liable to being constructed in different and rival ways.

The mission of the ethnographer, like that of any social scientist, is to produce a model that *works* the real by engaging concepts made for and by empirical investigation. This involves mapping the space of positions and outlining the flows of social trajectories; penetrating and specifying "the point of view of the natives" (to use Malinowski's famous expression, but *pluralized*) according to the position they occupy within it; and unraveling the struggles they wage to give form and sense to the world, starting with the symbolic struggles aimed at imposing this or that social principle of vision and division.

It is theory, as a system of practical schemata for scientific action, that brings phenomena into being by providing instruments for the reasoned questioning and organization of the sensory tumult of the world: "Certain relations can only be found if reality has been constructed in such a way as to find them," including the symbolic power relations that participate in the fabrication of the social world as an intrinsically double world, objectively objective and objectively subjective.

"What I want to point out is that this apparent coup de force implied by any adequate taxonomic construction is epistemologically justified. The entire epistemological tradition (Bachelard, etc.) establishes this. In the particular case of sociology, any adequate construction of the social world must be conquerred through a break with preconstructions, i.e., the classificatory preconditions produced by ordinary social usages . . . . There is no other way out, to practice social science, than these epistemological *coups de force* **which consist in imposing choices constructed from the outset. We can only find certain relationships if we have constructed reality in such a way as to find them"** (Volume 1, p. 81).

"I understand the word 'theory' much more in the sense of a method of thinking or even a method of perception than in the sense given to the word 'theory', unfortunately, in French discourse, where '*théorique*' is opposed to '*empirique*' and designates everything that is not empirical, everything that has nothing to do with anything. The word 'theory', if it does indeed designate, as I say, a system of schemata for constructing reality (or a scientific construction of reality), is a kind of scientific watchword" (Volume 1, p. 207).

> "Social science, in its objectivist or structuralist phase, records objective regularities, independent of individual consciousness and will, in which are expressed the effects of structural constraints that confer upon the social world its reality independent of thought. In so doing, it reduces to a state of appearance, of illusion, the representations that agents fashion of their world and the very experience they have of it. Being aware of the particularities of the position of the scholar, a person of *skholè*, inclined to what Austin called a 'scholastic view,' leads us to effect a second break with the vision born of the break with the common vision. Just as it was necessary to transcend the particular point of view associated with a particular position in the social world in order to access the panoramic vision that allows us to objectivize the primary point of view on the social world, so it is necessary to transcend the transcendent vision of the objectivist moment in order to reintroduce, as an integral part of the objective reality of the social world, the different, contrasting and even contradictory points of view that clash about this world. The objectivist construction that allows us to constitute the different perspectives on the social world as points of view taken from well-defined points in this world, is in no way contradicted by the analysis which, rising to a higher level, apprehends struggles about the world and its objectivity, and restores to them their proper efficacy in the very construction of the world.
>
> Overcoming the fictitious opposition between an objectivist structuralism and a subjectivist constructivism, we can thus set ourselves the goal of grasping both the objective structure of social universes (the social field as a whole or a particular specialized field) and the specifically political strategies that agents produce in order to make their point of view triumph. This is without forgetting that all the work of construction, practical or theoretical, individual or collective, by which agents contribute to producing social realities, in particular instituted groups (such as corporate bodies), and to inscribing them in the lasting objectivity of structures, is oriented by the perception they have of the social world and depends on their position in these structures, and on their dispositions, shaped by the structures" (Volume 2, pp. 1177–1178).
>
> Pierre Bourdieu, *Sociologie générale*, Volume 1 (2015), pp. 81 and 207; and *Sociologie générale*, Volume 2 (2016), pp. 1177–1178.

The aim of thick construction is not to "test" a theory by invalidating or confirming it, or to compare two theories for purposes of empirical adjudication. It is to *produce new objects* so as to shed new light on the social world. For, as Durkheim asserted over a century ago, "the object of all science is to make discoveries, and every discovery more or less disconcerts received opinions,"[68] including opinions theoretically established by preexisting research. Thus the

---

[68] Émile Durkheim, *Les Règles de la méthode sociologique* (1895, 1981), p. vi.

theory of school reproduction dismantles the vision of a "liberating" school erasing class inequalities; the theoretically postulated homology between economic structures and temporal structures elucidates the formation of the Algerian subproletariat; the joint study of ordinary consumption, artistic tastes, and political opinions reveals that they obey the same practical logic.[69]

So many facts that had to be methodically constructed by tearing away the screen of the taken for granted and of common perceptions that often run counter to reality, masking and disguising it. Hence this warning addressed to the ethnographer: "A good scientific theory—and this is one of the differences with the natural sciences—must encompass, integrate the theory of what is and the theory of the reasons why it is not perceived as it is; it must include a sociology of what things are and of the reasons why this is not seen."[70] Field-based sociology, whose ambition is to penetrate the practical logic of ordinary knowledge or cognition (*connaissance*), must also concern itself with the mechanisms of ordinary misrecognition (*méconnaissance*).[71]

Five scores for the theory-observation duet

For clarity's sake, we can diagram the relationship between theory and observation postulated by the five main approaches to ethnography available to the contemporary field worker as set out in Figure 3.1 (1).

Clifford Geertz's "thick description" presents itself as eschewing theory altogether in favor of local interpretation, where one observation sustains another in a revelatory sequence of potentially endless semantic regress from one layer of meaning to another. It is essentially *hermeneutic and celibate*, refusing as a matter of principle all intercourse with theory. Glaser and Strauss's "grounded theory" proposes to develop formal theory by discovering its concepts and their interconnections within observation conducted in deliberate ignorance of prior theories relevant to the question at hand. It is *inductive and chaste*, waiting for the right theory to reveal itself in the manner of Cinderella. Burawoy's "extended-case method" starts from a strong commitment to a favorite theory which guides the inquirer and then returns from the observations thus generated to that theory with the stated goal of falsifying or extending it. It is *deductive and monogamous*. The neo-Peircean approach codified by Iddo Tavory

---

[69] Pierre Bourdieu and Jean-Claude Passeron, *La Reproduction. Éléments pour une théorie du système d'enseignement* (1970); Pierre Bourdieu, *Algérie 60. Structures économiques et structures temporelles* (1977); Bourdieu, *La Distinction. Critique sociale du jugement* (1979).
[70] Pierre Bourdieu, *Sociologie générale*, Volume 1: *Cours au Collège de France 1981–1983* (2015), p. 105.
[71] See Javier Auyero and Débora Alejandra Swistun's magnificent demonstration in *Flammable: Environmental Suffering in an Argentine Shantytown* (2009).

and Stefan Timmermans deploys multiple theories, without being partial to any of them, to produce and respond to empirical surprises. It invites speculation about the possible mechanisms producing these surprises. It is *abductive and polygamous*.

Bourdieusian "thick construction" deploys self-aware theory to produce observations— that is, guided selections from the empirical manifold, answers to the questions formulated and brought into the field by the inquirer. These observations are then deliberately sifted and assembled to fabricate the sociological object as a textured model approximating the real (2). Thick construction entails both a rupture with, and the reintegration of, the primary grasp that agents have of the social world. It captures and subsumes folk notions under analytic notions. It meshes structure and meaning. It is *reflexive and polyamorous* (3). Above all, it strives to be heuristic by guiding inquiry into the double unfolding of history as embodied (habitus) and objectified (social space and field) and into their meeting at the point of practice.

Five ways of relating theory and observation

OBSERVATION ⇌ OBSERVATION

thick description

THEORY ⟵ OBSERVATION

grounded theory

THEORY ⟶ OBSERVATION
↑_____|

extended-case method

theory 1
theory 2 ⇌ OBSERVATION
theory 3

abductive analysis

THEORY ⟶ OBSERVATION ⟶ object 1
                                  ⟶ object 2
thick construction   ⟶ object 3

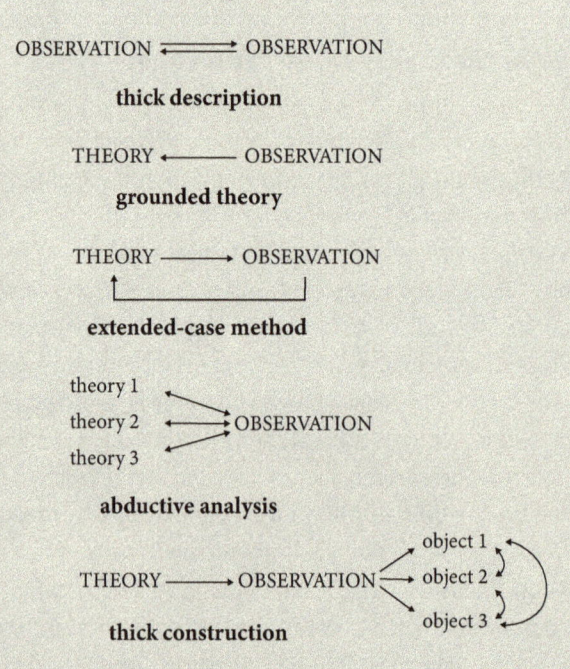

1. As any tool of visualization, these diagrams are necessarily simplifications. In practice, field workers can, and some do, combine different *substantive* theories to formulate or resolve their research questions. But they do so while following the *formal* core theory-observation schema of their self-proclaimed approach. On deploying graphical representations for the purpose of epistemological clarification, see Richard Swedberg, "Can You Visualize Theory?

> On the Use of Visual Thinking in Theory Pictures, Theorizing Diagrams, and Visual Sketches" (2016).
> 2. Gaston Bachelard, *Essai sur la connaissance approchée* (1928).
> 3. Bourdieu himself was theoretically polyamorous, maintaining affective intellectual relationships simultaneously with thinkers generally seen as incompatible if not antagonistic, Durkheim and Weber, the early Husserl and the late Wittgenstein, Mauss and Lévi-Strauss, Piaget and Austin, etc.

Bourdieusian thick construction thus aims first and foremost to generate parsimonious and efficient descriptions, interpretations, and explanations that the analyst would *not have been able to* elaborate without recourse to its concepts. It assembles the various relevant facets of the phenomenon into an *approximate image*. It then proceeds by *transposing* what has been learned from the construction of an object in one domain to work on the object in other domain, keeping in its line of sight this question: which properties are specific to object O1 and which are shared by objects O2, O3, etc.[72] What does such object, for instance the logic of consecration in the Church, tell us about another, such as the anointment effect of credentials awarded by elite schools? What do the strategies of honor among the Kabyle teach us about the strategies of distinction of the Parisian bourgeoisie or of firms on an industrial market? What do the revolutions effected by Heidegger in philosophy, Manet in the history of painting, and Beethoven in classical music reveal about the general logic of symbolic revolutions?[73] Homological reasoning is mobilized to specify at once the particularities of an object and its generic features.

Exhilarated by the atmosphere of the criminal court and by my success in penetrating its backstage areas and arcana (a seasoned prosecutor joked, "Forget about your book, you can 'deal' your own cases"), I got sucked into the field and, over a period of several months, I bobsleighed from one scene to another at full speed without any clear direction, carried along by the excitement of day-to-day interactions. The in-depth interviews then served as an anchor, providing me with a canvas of factors to identify in order to construct the *trajectories* of attorneys on both sides of the aisle. Thus I discovered that prosecutors from working-class and Catholic backgrounds were particularly punitive, which made me step back and reflect on the relationship to order and authority as a dimension of the relationship to the law, and prompted me to look for clues to the

---

[72] "The general theory of fields that I am trying to put forward has this merit that it makes it possible to pose general questions to all fields, which can only be answered by particular answers and by empirical studies of each field" (Bourdieu, *Sociologie générale*, Volume 2, p. 706). See also Pierre Bourdieu and Loïc Wacquant, *Invitation to Reflexive Sociology* (1992), pp. 118–162.

[73] Pierre Bourdieu, *Manet, une révolution symbolique: Cours au Collège de France (1998–2000)* (2013).

influence of religion on judicial practice (such as a crucifix or a biblical psalm posted on an office wall).

But the main technique for escaping inductivism was to draw a *diagram of the local judicial space* and to distribute my respondents within that space, the prosecutors in one oblong on the right, the defenders in a second oblong on the left. This Venn diagram helped me to identify the efficient properties of the different agents and to postulate that the two offices were themselves structured by an opposition between the *"true believers"* at the two extremes and the "hybrid" lawyers located in the zone of intersection between the two oblongs (they could have become either prosecutor or defender). This construction gave me a compass with which to reorient and discipline my day-to-day observations and gradually reconstruct my vision of the court as a system of positions and mechanisms for selecting protagonists and distributing strategies.

Far from the epistemological heroism of Burawoy and the epistemological prosaicism of Tavory and Timmermans, thick construction professes epistemological modesty and feeds on controlled analogy. *Theory according to Bourdieu is first and foremost a heuristic as well as an analytic,* that is, a toolbox for the construction of ethnographic objects that is achieved little by little, through the patient assembly of a series of conceptual and empirical displacements. Its value is therefore measured by its ability to produce accounts that satisfy the criteria of a good ethnography: triple embeddedness (social, symbolic, temporal), analytical acuity, depictive granularity, capture of affects and richness of poetics, mastery of ethical and political parameters, and, finally, reflexivity.

3.-*The populist fallacy*, which consists in glorifying the ways of thinking, feeling and acting of the agents studied, is a particular threat to the ethnographer who, by definition, invests her energy, emotions, and time in building and nurturing a personal connections with the people on the ground, and thus in managing fluctuating relationships of transference and counter-transference.[74] The researcher strives, as a matter of method, to get close to them and to *empathize* with them—a word derived from the Greek meaning to be attracted to, to have affinity with, and to share in the feelings of others, even when their actions, words and beliefs are criticizable, deplorable or even revolting.[75] Some even see this proclivity as the ethnographer's mission. For Stéphane Beaud and Florence Weber, "doing fieldwork means doing

---

[74] George Devereux, *From Anxiety to Method in the Behavioral Sciences* (1967).
[75] One thinks here of the Herculean hermeneutical effort required to take "in sympathy" the doctors of the Nazi camps: Robert Jay, *The Nazi Doctors: Medical Killing and the Psychology of Genocide* (1986). See also Kathleen M. Blee, "Evidence, Empathy, and Ethics: Lessons from Oral Histories of the Klan" (1993); Martina Avanza, "Comment faire de l'ethnographie quand on n'aime pas 'ses indigènes'? Une enquête au sein d'un mouvement xénophobe" (2008); Armèle Cloteau et al., "La banalisation du Front national au village" (2020).

justice to, or even rehabilitating, practices that have been ignored, misunderstood or despised."[76] This danger goes hand in hand with forgetting everything that the ways of being and doing of the dominated owe to domination, so that the sociologist may unwittingly contribute to the symbolic violence exerted upon the latter.[77] This is the risk incurred every time the ethnographer presents an unraveled, "dirty and nasty" world to an educated middle-class readership inclined to read accounts of urban savages from the inside with moral spectacles.

Note that this reasoning applies only to monographs on subaltern social categories, with which ethnography—especially urban ethnography—is too quickly identified. Indeed, field studies among the dominant do not encounter this dilemma. Worse still, the sociologists who conduct them are often suspected, in the eyes of their colleagues, of complacency or even social and scientific compromision, and they struggle to establish the legitimacy of their object, as if the empathetic gaze constitutive of the ethnographic posture should only be deployed from the top down.[78] Yet field studies of the rich and powerful have much to teach us about the social unconscious involved in the production and reception of the ethnographic enterprise. Thus we expect the researcher to reveal that people "down below" are not as "bad" as they may appear from afar and, *a contrario*, that people "up above" are not as "good" as they make themselves out to be. The ethnography of the dominated tends to elevate its subjects, that of the dominant to demean them.[79] In both cases, the sociologist takes on the beautiful role. We must strive to avoid this binary alternative and confine ourselves to *accounting for* the practices observed without seeking to invert the moral valence of the subjects of our investigation.

Epistemological populism, the counterpart to social populism, consists in granting primacy in principle to the ordinary or expert knowledge of the agents studied, and making their practical categories the categories of analysis. It finds expression in the "restitution"—or ritual of ethnographic absolution—which consists in having one's interpretations validated by those who are the subject of them, as if they were in a position to judge an

---

[76] Stéphane Beaud and Florence Weber, *Guide de l'enquête de terrain* (2003), p. 9.
[77] Jean-Claude Passeron and Claude Grignon, *Le Savant et le populaire. Misérabilisme et populisme en sociologie et en littérature* (1989).
[78] Monique Pinçon-Charlot and Michel Pinçon, *Voyage en grande bourgeoisie. Journal d'enquête* (2005), especially pp. 99–107, where the authors sift through their colleagues' reactions of discomfort, incompréhension, and even indignation at their studies of wealthy elites based on immersive fieldwork.
[79] Shamus Rahman Khan, *Privilege* (2010); Sylvie Tissot, *De bons voisins. Enquête dans un quartier de la bourgeoisie progressiste* (2011); Mikael Holmqvist, *Leader Communities: The Consecration of Elites in Djursholm* (2017); Ilan Wiesel, *Power, Glamour and Angst: Inside Australia's Elite Neighbourhoods* (2018); and Ashley Mears in *Very Important People: Status and Beauty in the Global Party Circuit* (2020).

analysis that purports to be sociological, and if the relationship of "information" between the observer and the observed were a horizontal relationship abstracted from any power gravity.[80]

Thus in the methodological appendix to *Sidewalk*, Mitchell Duneier reveals that, once the manuscript was completed, he "brought [it] to a hotel room and tried to read it to every person whose life was mentioned" (a dozen characters). He confesses: "It was not always easy to get people to sit and to listen to the larger argument of the book and to pay attention to all the places where they were discussed. Most people were more interested in how they looked in the photographs than in how they sounded or were depicted. I practically had to beg people to concentrate on what I was saying."[81] What is the function of such a ceremony other than to attest to the moral worth of the researcher? In addition to this, Duneier asked his main informant to write an afterword to the book, on the grounds that "it seemed fitting that [he] should have the last word."[82] Fitting by what scientific criterion? What is the significance of this ritual "sharing" of the concluding word other than to show that the author is "*a good guy*"?

Remedies: the ethnographer must work to give herself the means to *also* take an outside view and vary her distance to the respondents by periodically stepping away from his field physically and mentally; by compiling a field dictionary listing folk categories so as to objectivize them and, thence, better break with them; by formalizing the tangle of field social relations by means of graphic reasoning through figures and diagrams; by drawing up a table of the negative and positive properties commonly attributed to the protagonists so as to reexamine her own biases; by keeping a "secondary" field notebook, alongside one's "primary" notebook on the phenomenon, in which to record one's thoughts, emotions, doubts, anxieties, and joys from day to day, so as to control the relationship of seduction that the ethnographic object never fails to exert on the observer. The *exhilaration of ethnographic action*, which propels the investigator in the field, can easily turn into seduction and, thence, analytical myopia—as was my case in the investigation of the county criminal court. A final practical remedy to avoid this trouble is to write analytical memos at regular intervals during field immersion

---

[80] For a stimulating reflection on this return to the subjects of study, see Françoise Zonabend, "De l'objet et de sa restitution en anthropologie" (1994), who notes: "The ethnologist is no more a 'clerk' of the social than he is a 'public writer' of a society."

[81] Mitchell Duneier, *Sidewalk* (1999), p. 348. Duneier reproduces four pages in small print of an exchange with one of the book's characters, who reveals himself to be totally indifferent to the text being read to him (pp. 348–351).

[82] Duneier, *Sidewalk*, p. 352.

(e.g., every Saturday morning), which force the investigator to step out of her empathetic posture.[83]

The scholarly literature on prosecutors, written mainly by left-leaning law professors who have never set foot in a county criminal court, is struck with a systematic bias *against* them. A frequently cited article published in a legal ethics journal poses the question, without laughing in the least, "Can you be a good person and a good prosecutor"?[84] This *inverted populism*, which demonizes prosecutors and, by ricochet, worships public defenders, is an obstacle to the production and interpretation of field data, as it tends to skew the gaze. Realizing this led me to admit and reexamine my own anti-prosecutor bias—echoed by a local defense attorney who joked to an audience of his peers, "You're writing an exposé on the crooked prosecutors?" We must then be wary of falling into the opposite prejudice and embrace the vision that prosecutors have of their own work as that of the real "public defenders of the people" (i.e., the citizens who are the victims of crime). To maintain a balance, I conducted my in-depth interviews by alternating prosecutors and public defenders in my schedule, rather than interviewing them sequentially. This forced me to perform mental gymnastics that helped me to take on and then objectivize each side's point of view.

4.-*The presentist fallacy* locks the ethnographer into the immediate moment and makes him forget the *double history* that has shaped both the agent and the institution, a history that is always unfolding through their encounter, which describes a continuum running from perfect agreement, the principle of pre-reflexive reproduction and social happiness, to total discordance, which feeds perplexity, bewilderment, and strategic innovation, driven by social suffering or the disharmony between the person and the world.[85] This is where the life story, too infrequently used, finds its value. But for that it has to be a *structural life story*, one that aims to reconstruct not only the string of key events in a person's life and the "turning points" that interactionist symbolists are so fond of, with their notion of "moral career,"[86] but also and above all the sequence of positions occupied in the social spaces traversed over time by the agents under consideration.[87]

---

[83] On this point, see Catherine Turco's excellent methodological appendix in *The Conversational Firm: Rethinking Bureaucracy in the Age of Social Media* (2016), pp. 183–212.
[84] Abbe Smith, "Can You Be a Good Person and a Good Prosecutor?" (2000).
[85] Pierre Bourdieu, "Le mort saisit le vif. Les relations entre l'histoire réifiée et l'histoire incorporée" (1980). The second case is typical of the urban environment: Wacquant, *Bourdieu in the City*, pp. 175–176.
[86] Erving Goffman, "The Moral Career of the Mental Patient" (1959). For an exemplary deployment of ethnographic lifestories embedded in proximate social ties and broader political-economic structures, see Javier Auyero's luminous collective volume, *Portraits of Persistence: Inequality and Hope in Latin America* (2024).
[87] Pierre Bourdieu, "L'illusion biographique" (1986).

To historicize the agent is to acquire the means to characterize her *habitus* as an "acquired system of durable and transposable dispositions," deposited in the body by social experience, which at all times governs her ways of thinking, feeling, and acting, and thus her perception of possible courses of action. To historicize the world in which the agents in question evolve is to retrace, albeit in rough outline, the formative evolution of the social space in question. It is at the confluence of history as body and history as institution that interaction is born, as shown in the figure below.

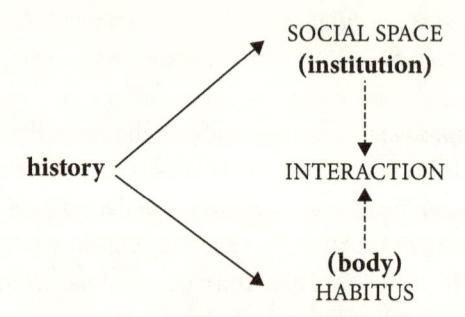

```
                    SOCIAL SPACE
                     (institution)
                          ↑
                          ↓
    history  <         INTERACTION
                          ↑
                          ↓
                       (body)
                      HABITUS
```

In this way, the cartography of positions, which allows us to nest interaction in the structure of social space (and avoid the interactionist fallacy), is articulated to a historical analysis of the evolution of this structure. The latter "is not immutable, and the topology that describes a state of social positions provides the basis for a dynamic analysis of the conservation and transformation of the distribution of active properties, and hence of social space" as "a field of struggles within which agents confront each other, with means and ends differentiated according to their position in the structure of the field of forces, thereby contributing to conserve or transform its structure."[88]

Ethnographers view themselves as "navigators of the contemporary," to borrow the title of David Westbrook's invitation to fieldwork,[89] and the vast majority of field-based articles and monographs are published contemporaneously with the phenomenon they study. But every field observation, no sooner recorded in a notebook or saved in a computer file, becomes *eo ipso* part of a historical record of a past action or cognition that can be erased without for that losing its scientific value.[90] A striking illustration: when Philippe Bourgois published his justly celebrated field study on the crack

---

[88] Pierre Bourdieu, "Espace social et champ du pouvoir," in *Raisons pratiques*, pp. 54–55; Bourdieu and Wacquant, *Invitation to Reflexive Sociology* (1992), pp. 139–162.

[89] David A. Westbrook, *Navigators of the Contemporary: Why Ethnography Matters* (2008).

[90] It may even be that the value of these field observations treated as a personal archive will increase over time when set against other archives, such as those of the spy services of a totalitarian country, in this case Ceaușescu's Romania, suspicious of the deeds, conduct and writings of a naive young anthropologist, as shown by Katherine Verdery's astonishing book, *My Life as a Spy: Investigations in a Secret Police File* (2018).

trade in East Harlem in 1995, a decade had passed since his observations and this economy had virtually collapsed.[91] This collapse in no way detracts from the validity of his account and its pertinence endures even as the social world it describes has disappeared.

Field notes are methodical, if idiosyncratic, archives. Ethnographers are *field historians* of a present in constant becoming. Practitioners of "microhistory" in the style of Carlo Ginzburg and *Alltagsgeschichte* in the wake of Alf Lüdtke, demonstrate this with their ethnographic reading of archives.[92] It is high time for ethnographers of a sociological bent to fully acknowledge *the historicity of their scriptural practices*, as their anthropological colleagues have been doing for some time now.[93] To put it another way: historical anthropologists like Ann Laura Stoler and cultural historians like Carlo Ginzburg invite us to read archives as field notes; it is time to perform the reverse operation, namely to read field notes as archives—which, incidentally, raises the thorny problem of their sharing and publicity in the digital age.[94]

The remedy to the presentist fallacy is therefore to implement a *doubly historicized structural ethnography*. To help achieve this, one recommended tool is the "revisit" the phenomenon, in the short or medium term, as a device for varying and controlling for the four factors that necessarily affect the construction of the ethnographic object according to Burawoy: the theory that the researcher brings with her to the field, the investigator–informant relationship, the processes internal to the milieu studied, and the forces external to the field site.[95] A final recommendation: search the historical record for a precursor or analogous phenomenon to the one studied in the field as a point of comparison and an instrument for "decentering" your investigation.

Thus, on the side of the agent, I conducted lengthy biographical interviews with one hundred prosecutors and one hundred public defenders in order to reconstruct the familial, educational, and professional genesis of their disposition toward the law and thus their vocation as court attorneys, and I paid particular attention to generational and seniority effects.[96] I also reconstructed the recent history of the District Attorney's office from interviews with veterans of the office.

---

[91] Philippe Bourgois, *In Search of Respect: Selling Crack in El Barrio* (1995, 2002). On the collapse of this booty economy, read Randol Contreras, *The Stickup Kids: Race, Drugs, Violence, and the American Dream* (2013).

[92] Carlo Ginzburg, *The Cheese and the Worms: The Cosmos of a Sixteenth-Century Miller* ([1976] 1980); Alf Lüdtke (ed.), *The History of Everyday Life: Reconstructing Historical Experiences and Ways of Life* (1995).

[93] Roger Sanjek (ed.), *Fieldnotes: The Makings of Anthropology* (1990).

[94] Alexandra K. Murphy *et al.*, "Ethnography, Data Transparency, and the Information Age" (2021).

[95] Michael Burawoy, "Revisits: An Outline of a Theory of Reflexive Ethnography" (2003).

[96] For a creative example of how to combine ethnography with historical prosopography, read Étienne Ollion, *Les Candidats. Novices et professionnels en politique* (2021), especially pp. 42–48. For a study that closely marries fieldwork and archival work, read Armando Lara-Millán, *Redistributing the Poor: Jails, Hospitals, and the Crisis of Law and Fiscal Austerity* (2021).

On the side of the structure, I sought out, and fortunately located, two historical studies of two neighboring counties with similar demographic profiles: one a study of crime and punishment in the late nineteenth century, the other a monograph conducted by a sociologist three decades earlier comparing San Pedrito with San Carlos. I also use the oral history of prosecutors' and public defenders' offices as well as judges, collected from strategic informants, to place the prosecutor-defender-judge triad in its medium-term evolution (the past quarter-century). Finally, I turned to works of social and judicial history on the institutionalization and role of the criminal court in the industrial city of the early twentieth century, the invention of "plea bargaining," as well as research on the use of this juridical procedure in other countries.[97]

5.-The interpretativist fallacy—the expression is not pretty but it is necessary—is paradoxical since it, too, is rooted in the distinctive virtue of ethnography, which is its ability to finely reconstitute the meanings that agents give to their actions, and to detect and capture the "constellations of meaning" (Weber), the "typifications" (Schutz), and the "common knowledge" (Garfinkel) that they deploy to construct their lived world. But this interpretive impulse can, when left unchecked and above all unframed, plunge the ethnographer—and her readers after her—into a bottomless hermeneutical abyss.

The uncontrolled swerve of the hermeneutist can take three directions. The first is to project the ethnographer's interpretative intent onto the subjects studied. This is at the heart of Bourdieu's critique of the Geertzian approach, which he labels the scholastic bias: "The seemingly humble and submissive forms of scientific work, such as 'thick description,' imply and impose on reality a preconstructed mode of construction that is none other than the scholastic vision of the world: it is clear indeed that, in his 'thick description' of a cockfight [in 'Deep Play: Notes on the Balinese Cockfight' (1972)], Geertz 'generously' lends the Balinese a hermeneutic and aesthetic gaze that is none other than his own."[98] Put another way: social reality is not a text to be read, what it is for the ethnographer, but a world of things to be done.

The second direction of the interpretativist fallacy consists in absolutizing the hermeneutic moment by detaching it from its anchorage in social structure, as if the signifying moment were somehow suspended in the

---

[97] Michael Willrich, *City of Courts: Socializing Justice in Progressive Era Chicago* (2003); Mary E. Vogel, *Coercion to Compromise: Plea Bargaining, the Courts, and the Making of Political Authority* (2007); and Stephen Thaman (ed.), *World Plea Bargaining: Consensual Procedures and the Avoidance of the Full Criminal Trial* (2010).
[98] Bourdieu, *Méditations pascaliennes*, p. 79, and "The Scholastic Point of View" (1990).

ether of representations. Now, since Durkheim and Mauss's fundamental essay on "Primitive Forms of Classification" (1903), we have known the benefits of linking the two and rooting collective representations in social morphology.[99] As for the third form of the hermeneutist's slippage, it proceeds from the second: it consists in reducing *diverse and rival points of view*, views taken from different points in social space, to a generic point of view attributed to a typical agent who is no more than a paper fiction.

What is "the native's point of view" that Malinowski canonized in *The Argonauts of the Western Pacific* (1922) and that Geertz invites us to revere as the ethnographer's point of honor?[100] Whose point of view and at what moment? Even in a small-scale society based on kinship, akin to Durkheim's "mechanical solidarity," such as the Trobriand Islands, there is social differentiation and hierarchy. Indeed, Malinowski emphasizes the distinctions in rank and power between districts, tribes, and totemic clans.[101] Clearly, the point of view of the village chief is not that of a commoner; the perspective and dispositions of an elderly widower from a high-ranking lineage are not those of an unmarried teenager from a lower totemic clan. Any system of action obeys a division of labor such that there coexists *points of view, plural*, as views taken from points within the objective structure of local social space. Moreover, there is a struggle, at every moment, to determine which properties and positions qualify as "native." Who is and who is not a full member? The answer to this question is always at stake in the social world itself and therefore cannot be resolved by fiat by the analyst.

The interpretativist bias finds its origin in a lack of embodiment—when the ethnographer remains on the sidelines rather than entering the field, as far as possible—or from the fact that the ethnographer pays insufficient attention to the practical "performance" of the phenomenon, that is, to the "techniques of the body" (in Marcel Mauss's sense) and sensibilities that shape the knowledge and conduct of the agents observed.[102] Ethnographies of bodily professions, which cannot avoid this carnal dimension of practice without missing their target entirely, have much to teach us on this chapter. I am thinking here in particular of Sorignet's books on dance,

---

[99] Émile Durkheim and Marcel Mauss, *De quelques formes primitives de classification* ([1903] 2017).
[100] Clifford Geertz, "'From the Native's Point of View': On the Nature of Anthropological Understanding" (1974).
[101] Bronislaw Malinowski, *Argonauts of the Western Pacific: An Account of Native Enterprise and Adventure in the Archipelagoes of Melanesian New Guinea* ([1922] 2013).
[102] For a model of how to take this into account, see Kathryn Geurts, *Culture and the Senses: Bodily Ways of Knowing in an African Community* (2003).

Schotté's on African long-distance runners, Desmond's on wildland firefighters, Jounin's on construction workers, Chauvin's on Chicago day laborers, and Mears's on fashion models.[103] For their arguments apply to all social practice: whatever their universe, social agents are always, first and foremost, "sentient, suffering, skilled, sedimented, and situated creature of flesh and blood."[104] Cognition itself is a socially and ecologically embedded activity, emerging from a dance in which body, mind, activity and world are intertwined.

The interpretativist temptation poses a particular threat to the ethnographer of the criminal court, since the latter is itself a *hermeneutic machine*, a human, technical, and discursive apparatus designed to interpret situations in terms of codes, and then to classify and tag the individuals involved; because, in the first instance, criminal law presents itself as a set of texts referring to other texts, and in the second, because the work of judges consists, very prosaically, in reading files, determining the meaning of the facts recounted and the intention that drives the protagonists, listening to arguments going in one direction and another, and finally placing the accused in a box corresponding to a sanction. On the surface, then, it is all a matter of interpretation.[105]

But, in reality, there is no perception and evaluation made by criminal law professionals that is not tinged by emotions, animated by feelings, and constrained by the materiality of bodies caught up in this apparatus. An experienced judge, in charge of sentencing for all felonies in the county, uses this move to explain the difference between the text and everyday penal action: "What counts is not this [he swivels in his chair to point to a large tome of the Penal Code on a shelf lined with thick volumes of legal texts] but this [he points to his stomach with a knowing smile]."

How do you capture the carnal dimension of penal action? By a constant effort aiming to spy and record in your field notebook the postures, gestures, moods, emotions, the tone of conversations and all the other outward signs of tension, fusion, and relaxation between the participants in the scene. Seemingly small nothings, the crumbs of the

---

[103] Pierre Emmanuel Sorignet, *Danser. Enquête dans les coulisses d'une vocation* (2010); Manuel Schotté, *La construction du "talent." Sociologie de la domination des coureurs marocains* (2012); Matthew Desmond, *On the Fireline: Living and Dying with Wildland Firefighters* (2007); Nicolas Jounin, *Chantier interdit au public. Enquête parmi les travailleurs du bâtiment* (2008); Sébastien Chauvin, *Les Agences de la précarité Journaliers à Chicago* (2010); Ashley Mears, *Pricing Beauty: The Making of a Fashion Model* (2011).

[104] For a discussion of each of these properties, see Wacquant, "For a Sociology of Flesh and Blood," especially pp. 243–244.

[105] A defense of the hermeneutic approach to law is Lawrence Rosen, *Law as Culture: An Invitation* (2006), especially chapter 4 on "Law as Cosmology."

interactional feast, but which, patiently amassed, will allow you to reconstitute the sensual dynamics of the conduct of lawyers and judges. Furthermore, in my interviews, I asked attorneys and judges to tell me about their thoughts and emotions—in the morning on the way to work, during court hearings, in their dealings with the opposing party, with the defendant, etc.—and how they felt about the way they conducted themselves.

The other reality that you must constantly interrogate and capture in your notes is the raw constraint of which the court is the vector and site, and which periodically erupts, as when a defendant appearing in custody refuses to cooperate with the bureaucratic ritual of arraignment (a hearing during which a judge notifies the accused of the charges) and must be subdued and carried off *manu militari*. The challenge is to invest yourself fully in the hermeneutical work without losing sight of the fact that it is only one dimension of the social life of the court, so as to hold together the two moments of penal law as a machine for exercising two forms of violence, physical and symbolic, which support and conceal one another.

Here are a few final tips on how to make your ethnographic monograph vibrate and not lose by default the rich insights gained through hard work in the field: apply yourself to capturing the grain of the action in a finely reconstituted setting that allows the reader to find herself on the scene, to get to know the key characters, to understand their idiom, to share their sensibility; do not hesitate to vary or even mix different forms of writing, narrative, vignettes, analysis, intervention;[106] give intelligibility to the points of view of relevant agents by integrating them into structurally anchored portraits; render the emotional climate and sensual dynamics of moments; deliver, in an apparently raw but in fact elaborated form, accounts of crucial scenes in the functioning of the universe under consideration from extracts of field notes; incorporate field documents (photos, sketches, maps, poster facsimiles, flyers, reproductions from archives, etc.) into the text, not as decorative elements but as analytical adjuvants that "speak" with the text; integrate the observer's presence and personality into the text, rather than hypocritically making it disappear (it is there in any case so it might as well be visible and assumed); and finally, clarify the parameters of fieldwork at the beginning of the book, not in an appendix at its end, since these parameters of production must be known in order to parametrize reception in turn.

---

[106] Franck Poupeau provides the model in *Altiplano. Fragments d'une révolution (Bolivia, 1999–2019)* (2021).

Bourdieu at *Mema's House*: **The five missions of ethnography**

Let us take this opportunity to *dedramatize and demystify the notion of "construction of the object."* First point: this approach is rooted in an uncompromising rejection of the pre-constructed, that is, of the common perception of the phenomenon, which is always to some degree misleading, and of the idea that the latter would be self-evident to grasp in its contours and articulations.[107] For, by force of social circumstances, the ethnographer always formulates her initial problem in terms contaminated by ordinary and scholarly preconceptions. On this front, Bachelard reminds us that "we know *against* prior knowledge, by destroying poorly made knowledge, by overcoming that which, in the mind itself, stands in the way of spiritualization."[108] In other words, there is no such thing as an object in itself, only objects either pre-constructed or scientifically constructed, well or not.

Secondly, the construction of the sociological object is not effected by a singular act at a pivotal moment when everything is decided like a throw of the dice. On the contrary, the expression refers to the *entire chain of operations* carried out by the ethnographer throughout the entire thickness and duration of the scientific process[109]—from the formulation of questions and the elaboration of concepts to the delimitation of the field site, the choice of scenes to observe and informants to cultivate, the taking of notes and their coding and condensation, to writing and laying out the final text.

In the third place, you must, at each of these stages, exercise *unfailing vigilance* by periodically taking a step back and objectivizing the tools and operations of the research itself; for example, by periodically reflecting on a questionnaire as it is being administered, and regularly asking yourself what it adds to or subtracts from observation; by trying out various codes on your fieldnotes to see how they color and transform the raw materials; and by wondering about the facets of the phenomenon left in the dark by the author's positioning and writing.

Lastly, scientific construction implies never losing sight of the fact that what we effect is *always a selection and an abstraction*—Bachelard speaks

---

[107] *"The pre-constructed is everywhere.* Like everyone else, the sociologist is literally besieged by it. He has to know an object, the social world, of which he is the product, so that the problems he poses himself about it, the concepts he uses, have every chance of being the product of this very object" (Pierre Bourdieu in Bourdieu et Wacquant, *Invitation à la sociologie réflexive*, p. 295). See also Pierre Bourdieu et al., *Le Métier de sociologue. Préalables épistémologiques* (1973), pp. 51–54 and 58–75.

[108] Gaston Bachelard, *La Formation de l'esprit scientifique. Contribution à une psychanalyse de la connaissance* (1938), pp. 15–16.

[109] For a reconstruction of this process in the case of the academic field, see Pierre Bourdieu, *Homo Academicus* (1984), chapter 1, especially pp. 16–43, and the sources used pp. 253–266.

of "a task of geometrization" of reality.[110] The work of the ethnographer is not aimed at *restituting* the empirical world in its infinite fugacity and diversity, *pace* Geertz, but at *resolving* it into a reasoned model, even when this model ultimately assumes a narrative form apparently stripped of concepts.[111] So much to say that the construction of the object guides and encompasses the description of the phenomenon—or, rather, its methodical and selective re-description through the hierarchization of its properties according to the epistemic point of view adopted.

Another reminder is in order here, concerning the *triple economy of power* into which all fieldwork is necessarily inserted. One of the hallmarks of ethnography, as we saw earlier, is that the researcher immerses herself as deeply as possible in the web of social and cultural ties that make up the universe, institution, or practice under study. Now, these links are, first and foremost, power relations, a series of snapshots of which the ethnographer captures on the fly in her observations: "What the scholar constructs is a state of the struggles about the social world, that is, struggles for the construction of the social world."[112] Unlike the distant observer, as in a quantitative survey, who can only grasp outcomes, the field sociologist is in a position to capture this dynamic in action, provided she is alerted to it.

It follows from this embeddedness—and this is the second circuit of power—that the ethnographer's relationship with his subjects is always one of *material and symbolic power*, even when it takes the form of indifference, curiosity (mutual or not), esteem, affection, or even friendship. The researcher may be globally dominated, when she studies social categories situated at the top or holders of esoteric knowledge,[113] or, in the most frequent case, dominant, when she explores a subaltern world, but she is always caught up in these relationships that Max Weber calls "*herrschaftliche*." Even when he is a "native" of the microcosm under study, like Randol Contreras returning to his childhood pals to study the drug economy in which they are immersed, the fact that he adopts an analytical posture irremediably distances him from his subjects and creates a vertical symbolic relationship, no matter what he does.[114] And all relationships between researcher and subject take on

---

[110] Bachelard, *La formation de l'esprit scientifique*, p. 7. Bachelard continues: "Abstraction must be posited as the normal and fruitful approach of the scientific mind" (p. 8).
[111] Loïc Wacquant, *Body and Soul: Notebooks of an Apprentice Boxer* (expanded anniversary edition, 2022), especially pp. 268–288.
[112] Pierre Bourdieu, *Sociologie générale*, volume 2: *Cours au Collège de France 1984–1987* (2016), p. 1135.
[113] Monique Pinçon-Charlot and Michel Pinçon, *Voyage en grande bourgeoisie. Journal d'enquête* (2005); Alizée Delpierre, *Servir les riches. Les domestiques chez les grandes fortunes* (2022); Diane Vaughan, *The Challenger Launch Decision: Risky Technology, Culture, and Deviance at NASA* (1996); Hugh Gusterson, *Nuclear Rites: A Weapons Laboratory at the End of the Cold War* (1996).
[114] Contreras, *The Stickup Kids* (2013).

a strategic dimension of manipulation and instrumentalization that operates *in both directions*, albeit in a typically asymmetrical way.

Finally, a third economy of power concerns the reception, valorization, censorship, and ramifying effects of the *ethnographic text* in the various microcosms in which it circulates, from the scientific field (and its various sectors) to the journalistic and bureaucratic field, where appropriate, not to mention the institutions and populations studied—what Didier Fassin calls the "afterlives" of fieldwork.[115] To manage these three dimensions of power, there is no magic formula, but a constant duty of reflexivity, vigilance, and honesty. Do not nourish any illusions, do not close your eyes to reality, clear the field from mines by anticipating problems and, above all, integrate reactions and resistances to ethnographic work into the work itself.

Provided it avoids the pitfalls of interactionism, inductivism, populism, presentism, and hermeneuticism, ethnography is positioned to play several key roles in the implementation of a research program which, ideally, will combine fieldwork with one or more other methods—statistical, historical, clinical, experimental, game theoretical, or hermeneutic—and roll out over the long term.[116] In addition to bringing the reader into a distinctive microcosm, immersive observation can serve five functions.

1.-Instrument of *rupture* with common sense, both ordinary and scholarly, in that it brings the researcher into direct contact with the raw phenomenon, which is bound to shake the preconceived ideas on which she sketched her problematic and provisionally delimited her field site.

Nothing, absolutely nothing, in the day-to-day workings of the criminal court corresponds to its image in the social and scholarly imaginary of the judicial system generated by TV series and legal scholars. From the very outset, I am taken aback by the abyss between the scholarly works I have read on the subject and the reality I observe. The complexity of the division of labor within the prosecutor's office; the speed and fluidity of the "deals" struck between prosecution and defense in a few whispered words; the clear professional superiority of public defenders over private lawyers; the glaring variations in procedures depending on the time of year (with Christmas discounts on sentences); the impact of the personality of judges on sentencing; the open assertion of a class bias

---

[115] Didier Fassin, "The Public Afterlife of Ethnography" (2015). For a poignant example of the ethnographer's return to the field to gauge the social and emotional shock caused by her work twenty years later, read Nancy Scheper-Hughes, "Ire in Ireland" (2000).

[116] On the importance of temporal unfolding in fieldwork, see again Poupeau, *Altiplano*, especially pp. 115–130, 471–482, 591–599, and Timothy Black, *When a Heart Turns Rock Solid: The Lives of Three Puerto Rican Brothers on and off the Streets* (2009), and his contribution to the volume edited by Anita Garey and her colleagues, *Open to Disruption: Time and Craft in the Practice of Slow Sociology* (2014).

("His job is his saving grace," intones one judge about a defendant to whom he grants a lenient sanction on this ground)—so many unexpected facets of court work, and I could multiply the examples.

So, when I start my investigation, in line with the activist vision, I am convinced that criminal injustice stems from the profusion of cases that are "false positives" (innocent people who are wrongly convicted). I soon discover to my amazement that the court produces far more "false negatives," implicating people about whom all indications point to guilt but who are released and their case dismissed for a whole range of technical, social, and organizational factors, such as the refusal to cooperate of witnesses to a homicide due to the culture of distrust of justice and the fear of reprisals in the hyperghetto, which explains that less than one-third of murders in the county's main city lead to an arrest or indictment, including cases where everyone in the neighborhood knows full well who the killer is.

Another example is on time management: like everyone else, I thought that delays in legal proceedings were the result of a failure on the part of the court, which could only be to the detriment of the accused, especially in serious felonies. Well, not exactly: in many configurations, "to age the case" (as the court lingo goes) proves to be a judicious strategy and seasoned defenders advise their clients to "sit down" in jail (rather than post bail to get out) and thus possibly obtain from the judge a more favorable sentence, sometimes equal to the time served in pretrial detention. A final example: far from seeking to maximize sentences, prosecutors and judges alike aim above all to "move stuff" to avoid being overwhelmed by the ever-mounting stream of cases: "We're not Pavlovian dogs, well, the goals isn't to notch as many years as possible."

2.-Springboard for the formulation of *hypotheses* which, on the basis of confirmation or surprise, can punctuate the phases and alter the directions of observation, before being methodically explored and revised in real time. The specific advantage of ethnography here is to buttress these hypotheses with observation, and to be able to test and adapt them *in vivo*, in the very flow of research.

While we must firmly resist *empiricist regression*, we must nonetheless remain *open to surprises* and not hesitate to explore new avenues that open up. This openness plays out in the formulation of hypotheses. On the basis of conversations between lawyers captured on the fly and in-depth interviews with veteran prosecutors, at the start of my research, I developed a paradoxical hypothesis: public defenders from working-class backgrounds are more likely to become "constitutionalists," who focus on formal respect for the rights of the accused (they defend the principles of the country's constitution), while their colleagues from bourgeois backgrounds become "populists," who defend the accused by any means necessary (including illegal ones) out of sense of class guilt and fantasized identification with society's underdogs (the so-called "white knight on the hill" syndrome). But soon the opposite hypothesis emerged, based on systematic observation of plea bargaining sessions: public defenders from working-class black and Hispanic families were the fiercest in protecting their clients out of ethnic and class solidarity. The study will produce field data supporting one or the other of these expectations.

A further source of inspiration can be found in monographs studying other mass public "people-processing institutions" in the tradition of Michael Lipsky's classic book *Street-Level Bureaucracies*, such as schools, hospitals, prisons, and welfare offices.[117] Comparing monographs on these institutions with fieldwork on the court immediately generates fresh hypotheses to be elaborated through systematic observation.

3.-Technique for the suggestion or detection of *mechanisms*, since it enables us to dismantle and identify the recurring processes that produce the social forms considered in action and at ground level.[118] Ethnography's *forte* is to open up what, for other methods, remain "black boxes."

The scholarly literature is nearly unanimous on one point: prosecutors are endowed with *absolute* discretion which, by definition, they abuse.[119] The reality is that they enjoy *bounded discretion*, by analogy with the "bounded rationality" of Herbert Simon's behaviorial economics. Five mechanisms combine to draw this boundary: the cognitive mechanism is anchored in the categories of perception of the prosecutor involved (e.g., his personal intolerance for crimes against children and his relative indifference to drug-related crimes); the social mechanism lies in belonging to a close-knit "team," headed by a supervisor and inserted into the office's division of labor, which effects a de facto regulation of individual decisions; the legal mechanism resides in the sentencing floors and ceilings set by the judge, who must imperatively endorse pleas agreements (he may, for example, reject a deal struck by a prosecutor and a public defender on the grounds that the penalty negotiated is too low in his eyes); the bureaucratic mechanism resides in the policy prescriptions of the District Attorney's office (e.g., the imposition of an automatic sentence of 180 days of jail time for illegal possession of a firearm, regardless of

---

[117] Michael Lipsky, *Street-Level Bureaucracy: Dilemmas of the Individual in Public Service* (1980), and Yeheskel Hasenfeld, "People Processing Organizations: An Exchange Approach" (1972). Two ethnographies of welfare counter staff in France and America explore this issue in great depth: Vincent Dubois, *La Vie au guichet. Relation administrative et traitement de la misère* (1999), and Zachary W. Oberfield, *Becoming Bureaucrats: Socialization at the Front Lines of Government Service* (2014).

[118] I am well aware that the *constructum* of "mechanism" is a contested notion in social science, as Peter Hedström and Peter Bearman's attempt at clarification in *The Oxford Handbook of Analytical Sociology* (2009), pp. 4–8, shows. For an application to fieldwork, see Diane Vaughan, "Analytic Ethnography" (2009), who compares the approaches of Jack Katz, Michael Burawoy, and Pierre Bourdieu with her own approach.

[119] See the book, paradigmatic to the point of caricature, by the legal scholar (and former public defender) Angela Davis, *Arbitrary Justice: The Power of the American Prosecutor* (2007).

the circumstances); and the cultural mechanism refers to the personal reputation of the prosecutor and the juridical tradition of the county, or even of a particular courthouse, which sets the "going rate" of cases close to which the prosecutor must pin his offer or risk triggering multilevel feedback.

4.-Instrument for the *construction* of the object by providing the data needed to characterize the distinctive facets of the phenomenon at stake and to articulate them analytically, including the "point of view" of the agents and the position they occupy in the social space under consideration.

The variable that quickly emerges as decisive following observation of plea bargaining is not the race, class, age, or gender of attorneys and defendants, but the seniority in employment of the court professionals involved. This is an efficient property that no quantitative survey could have detected inductively, and that the interview could only have alluded to.[120] It manifests itself in an authority recognized by peers and opponents alike, a juridical capital of specific experience (in a given position, for example, supervisor of the "sexual assault" team in charge of the heaviest and most sensitive cases), and a history of relationships with peers on both sides of the aisle. Immersive close-up observation allows us to detect the influence of this variable on daily interactions in court.

The same applies to the geographical variable: the "price of crime" i.e., the average sentence around which plea bargaining offers for a given offence are pegged, fluctuates from one locality to another in the same county in a range of 15 miles. The other facet of the court to be integrated into the model: the role of rumor in the production of the symbolic capital of judges, attorneys in the two offices, and the bar, which again can only be grasped by an assiduous and penetrating presence at the very scene of the action and by detailed knowledge of the individuals concerned.

5.-Instrument for the *depiction* of the phenomenon: "Thick description" proves useful here, provided it is driven by the intention to produce a *model* (in the sense of rational selection and articulation) *and not an image* of reality (more or less faithful). In particular, ethnography is well placed to capture the *carnality of acting-in-the-world*: its visceral anchoring, multisensory impulse, and emotional flow—everything stemming from the fact that the human is "a suffering creature," as Marx put it in his *1844 Manuscripts*.[121]

---

[120] It is this same capital of acquired experience that pushes prosecutors to become "centrists" open to compromise over time whereas their younger colleagues tend to be aggressive and inflexible, as they are anxious to prove their professional worth, as shown by Ronald F. Wright and Kay L. Levine, "The Cure for Young Prosecutors' Syndrome" (2014).

[121] For a selection of key texts on this theme, see David Howes (ed.), *Empire of the Senses: The Sensual Culture Reader* (2005).

Participant observation of day-to-day courtwork enables us to capture and render the embodied experience of judicial action, including the alternation between boredom and excitement, the temporal compression, cognitive overload, emotional costs, the physical consequences for lawyers (sweating, hair loss, weight loss or gain, ulcers, depression, etc.) and the psychic trauma it causes for court actors (especially lawyers handling sexual violence and homicide cases) as well as the emotional concussion of coming face-to-face with victims of violent crime.

You must feel it in your gut, be in the articifial and temporary role of the immersed observer, to grasp the *magnetism* that the court exerts on its members as a sensual and moral world in which "something different happens every day." One public defender remarks, "there's something macho about this office [yet headed by a woman], the bell rings and you're on, *it's showtime*, you can become an adrenaline *junkie*." An experienced prosecutor liked to confront me with the more visceral aspects of judicial practice "in the trenches," and never lost an opportunity to castigate the moral and sensory isolation of researchers ("You're a little too comfortable in your ivory tower").

A specifically American variant of ethnographic depiction is what its practitioners call *bearing witness* to the suffering of the dominated and the existential damage inflicted on them by the prevalent arrangement of institutions. This mission is rooted in a religious or spiritualist vision of social science that makes the researcher a kind of missionary who will lighten the burden of misery by making it public, in the hope of provoking shame or lucidity among the dominant or the mobilization of the dominated and, thence, spurring public policies aimed at reducing inequality and marginality.[122] This mission of "moral lookout" is not exercised for the dominant categories which, by definition, enjoy privileges and control their image. In their case, the unveiling takes the form of what Americans call an *exposé*, the revelation of a social scandal.[123]

In European countries, this testimonial function is rightfully the preserve of investigative journalism or militant documentary (I am thinking of Günter Wallraff's *Ganz Unten* and Luc Bronner's *La Loi du ghetto*),[124] and

---

[122] My thanks to Matt Desmond for pointing out this social mission of sociological ethnography focusing on the city in America in a personal communication. His book *Evicted: Poverty and Profit in the Inner City*, which won the Pulitzer Prize in the nonfiction category in 2017, is a successful example of this testimonial vocation: It brought the critical issue of housing evictions into the public arena and had a direct impact on federal policies to protect against eviction, during and after the Covid-19 pandemic. But books with such practical impact are the exception, not the rule, and Desmond was only able to take on this task because he was already academically consecrated and endowed with a rare literary pen.

[123] That is how we can explain the public stir caused by Alizée Delpierre's excellent book, *Servir les riches. Les domestiques chez les grandes fortunes* (2022).

[124] Günter Wallraff's *Ganz Unten* (1985) tackles the (mis)treatment of Turkish immigrants in German society based on immersive underground observation while disguised as a Turk. Luc Bronner's *La Loi du ghetto. Enquête sur les banlieues françaises* (2009) presents itself as "a fascinating and implacable document" on youth in "sensitive neighborhoods" (back cover).

the sociologist who insists on writing in this vein will be devalorized or even ridiculed by his peers. In Latin America, the sociological field recognizes this function of bearing witness to the condition of the dominated, but as part of a collective—as a member of a social movement, an indigenous group or an ethnic community—and not as an individual.[125] This is another illustration of how the social and scientific unconscious of each country shapes ethnographic practice.

Breaking with ordinary and scholarly common sense, formulating hypotheses, detecting mechanisms, constructing the object, depicting the phenomenon: by fulfilling these five functions, ethnography can also be a *powerful adjuvant to other methods* of social investigation, but particularly to quantitative questionnaire surveys. It helps indeed to gauge the pertinence of the categories and the appropriateness of the terms used in the questionnaire, to avoid the imposition of a problematic, to reveal new themes to be explored, and to establish the practical feasibility of the study. In its absence, a good deal of quantitative research on dispossessed and dishonored categories misses its target: the outcasts of the city are, by experience, suspicious of the intrusion of official institutions, and they are quick to equate sociological investigation with the surveillance of state agencies for the management of poverty.

Conventional survey research also suffers from the common use of bureaucratic categories that mask, rather than reveal, the properties of the social structure and cultural texture at the bottom of the social and physical space of the city. Three examples: the rigid definition of "household," which presupposes a clear boundary between members and non-members that does not apply to the fluid, open regime of precariat households; questions about criminal record, for which respondents and analysts alike will commonly confuse jail and prison, remand detention and confinement after a conviction; and questions about occupational status, which presuppose a clear delimitation between work and nonwork that is not operative at the margins of the labor market and in the street economy.

I have argued in this book that the historical philosophy of science of Bachelard, Canguilhem, and Koyré and the genetic structuralism of Bourdieu provide us with flexible and powerful tools for building and implementing research designs that fully exploit the virtues of ethnography and limit as far as possible the risk of falling into the epistemological pitfalls that are especially associated with it (of the kind that derailed Mitchell Duneier, Elijah Anderson and Katherine Newman, as I showed in the previous chapter, and Alice Goffman in their wake).

---

[125] According to Javier Auyero and Franck Poupeau, personal communication, November 2022.

A seasoned practitioner of the "extended-case method," Jeffrey Sallaz nevertheless raises the question of "whether a Bourdieusian ethnography is possible," given the caveats expressed here and there by the author of *Méditations pascaliennes* about this method.[126] He detects three problematic properties of the knowledge generated by fieldwork in Bourdieu's eyes: it is partial, as with any method; it is incapable of grasping the dynamics that pertain to the logic of fields when studying differentiated societies; and it is risky in the sense that it is particularly exposed to the "scholastic bias" that consists in imputing to the agent the model that the scholar constructs of her conduct. This is precisely Bourdieu's criticism of Geertz's "thick description."[127]

It is true that Bourdieu's position on the virtues and vices of ethnography has evolved over time. His early work on social upheavals in colonial Algeria and the crisis of peasant society in Béarn (which must be read together to fully gauge their intent and cross-cutting implications)[128] is firmly rooted in fieldwork, conducted alone or as part of a team with Abdelmalek Sayad. In *Travail et travailleurs en Algérie* (1963), Bourdieu stresses that "there is no method that may be considered more exact and rigorous in itself," and he calls for—and, above all, puts into practice—a close collaboration between ethnography, which grasps the sense of action, and statistics, which measures its frequency and variations.[129] Similarly, in *Le Métier de sociologue* (1968, 1973), Bourdieu and his coauthors assert that "we must restore to methodical and systematic observation its epistemological primacy," against the "undisputed privilege" unduly accorded to quantitative surveys.[130] But a decade later, *Le sens pratique* (1980) warned against the illusions of "participation" in these uncompromising terms:

> The undue projection of the subject into the object is never more evident than in the case of the *primitivist participation of the bewitched or mystical ethnologist* who, as in populist immersion, still plays on the objective distance from the object to play the game as a game, waiting to get out and tell the tale. This means that participant observation is, in a way, a contradiction in terms (as anyone who has tried it has

---

[126] Jeffrey J. Sallaz, "Is a Bourdieusian Ethnography Possible?" (2018).

[127] For Bourdieu, Geertz attributes to the Javanese participants in the famous cockfight the "hermeneutic and aesthetic" perspective which is his own as an analyst and which constitutes the scene as a spectacle (*Méditations pascaliennes* [1997], p. 79). See the discussion of the interpretativist slippage, *supra*, pp. 163–166.

[128] Loïc Wacquant, "Following Pierre Bourdieu into the Field" (2004).

[129] Pierre Bourdieu, *Travail et travailleurs en Algérie* (1963), p. 20. "Thus, statistical regularities have sociological value only when they can be understood. Conversely, subjectively comprehensible relationships constitute sociological models of real processes only when they can be empirically observed with a significant degree of confidence" (pp. 23–24).

[130] Pierre Bourdieu, Jean-Claude Chamboredon, and Jean-Claude Passeron, *Le Métier de sociologue. Préalables épistémologiques* (1968, 1973, 2022), p. 65.

been able to verify practically); and that the critique of objectivism and its inability to apprehend practice as such in no way implies the rehabilitation of immersion in practice.[131]

Swinging back in the other direction is Bourdieu's collective exercise in socioanalysis leading to *La Misère du monde* (*The Weight of the World*, 1993), in which he praises the "active, methodical listening" of what might be characterized as *structural interviewing*, i.e., interviewing informed by the positional and dispositional properties of the respondent and the methodical control of her distance from the interviewer. When he praises this variant of interviewing as "a form of spiritual exercise, aimed at achieving, through *self-forgetfulness*, a genuine *conversion of the gaze* upon others in the ordinary circumstances of their life" and even "a kind of *intellectual love*,"[132] is he not describing the comprehension generated by ethnographic immersion that he otherwise decries? Finally there is a further warning in the "Huxley Medal Lecture" given at the Royal Anthropological Institute in London in December 2000, which elaborates the distinction between "participant observation," which Bourdieu rejects, and "participant objectivation," that is, the objectivation of the point of view and the very act of objectivation, which he advocates.[133]

Two points emerge from these apparent changes in position. Firstly, Bourdieu draws a strong, even rigid, distinction between *direct* observation, such as he learned it in the field in Algeria drawing from Marcel Maget's *Guide d'étude directe des comportements culturels* (1953),[134] which is that of a researcher present but outside of the social relations being elucidated, a perspective he approves of, and *participant* observation, which he deems self-mystifying. But Bourdieu is not Bourdieusian enough here: he invokes a clear-cut dichotomy between participant/observer, native/researcher, instead of problematizing the very notion of native and recognizing that there are

---

[131] Pierre Bourdieu, *Le Sens pratique* (1980), p. 57.
[132] Pierre Bourdieu, "Comprendre," in *La Misère du monde* (1993, original italics), pp. 912, 914. This approach is very close to the "ethnographic interview" as codified by Stéphane Beaud: "L'usage de l'entretien en sciences sociales. Plaidoyer pour l'entretien ethnographique'" (1996).
[133] Pierre Bourdieu, "Participant Objectivation" (2003), pp. 281–282. Bourdieu insists on "the difficulty of such a posture [of participant observation], which presupposes a kind of splitting of consciousness that is difficult to maintain. How can we be both subject and object, the one who acts and the one who, in a way, watches himself act? What is certain is that we are right to doubt the possibility of truly participating in foreign practices, inscribed in the tradition of another society, and presupposing, as such, another apprenticeship, different from that of which the observer and his dispositions are the product, and therefore a completely different way of being and living the experiences in which he intends to take part."
[134] Among the "tried and tested, codified methods" of ethnographic research, Bourdieu lists "morphological description, technology, cartography, lexicology, biography, genealogy, etc.," that is, fundamentally objectivist techniques that by definition exclude hermeneutic apprehension (Bourdieu et al., *Le Métier de sociologue*, p. 65).

always different ways of being such, but also that the relationship between the student and the studied describes a continuum running from native familiarity to complete exteriority.[135]

Next, we must break with the author of *La Distinction* here: deep immersion as advocated by *enactive ethnography*, based on the performance of the phenomenon and the acquisition, as far as possible, of the practical schemas of "perception, appreciation and action" that inform conduct in the world under study, has its own virtues; it can perfectly well be inserted into a rigorous construction of the object, as long as it constitutes a methodological stage and not terminus. The ethnographer can thus alternate between the enactive and analytical modes, *without ever falling into the illusion that she is a "native."* What is more, she can vary the form and depth of her participation in the phenomenon over the course of the investigation so as to detect what each degree and form of involvement brings to light or disappears.

The ethnography of the endotic in the wake of Bourdieu

Pierre Bourdieu's reservations about participant observation—as distinct from direct observation—did not prevent him from influencing and even shepherding the fieldwork of many researchers in his immediate circle. So much so, in fact, that one can speak of a Bourdieusian ethnographic strand characterized by deep understanding, a long-term commitment, an enveloping vision, a sustained attention to the "little nothings" of everyday existence and, above all, the infusion of the theory of practice into the empirical material it gives rise to. A striking feature of this generation is the paradoxical choice of familiar field sites and objects close to the investigator's own heart—in other words, the quest for the *endotic* rather than the *exotic*, which extends ethnography into a genuine socioanalysis (1).

A number of members of the Centre de Sociologie Européenne have devoted themselves to the study of the lower classes and their transformations from the inside out. The reshaping of the peasant world from above is dissected by Sylvain Maresca in *Les Dirigeants paysans* (1983) and from below by Patrick Champagne in *L'Héritage refusé* (2002)(2). The crisis of the industrial working world at the end of Fordism is elucidated by Stéphane Beaud and Michel Pialoux in *Retour sur la classe ouvrière* (1995) and in Pialoux's articles collected under the revealing title, *Le Temps d'écouter* (*A Time for Listening*, 2019)(3). The ordinary culture of the private world of this same working class is explored by Yvette Delsaut using documents as banal as they are intimate—class photos, house plans, wedding ceremony records—in *Carnets de socioanalyse* (2020)(4); Abelmalek Sayad's work on the social experience

---

[135] For an example of hybrid positioning, native by family socialization and foreign by gender, see Christel Coton, *Officiers. Des classes en lutte sous l'uniforme* (2017).

of immigration among Algerians in France, which spans three decades, from *Un Nanterre algérien, terre de bidonvilles* (1995), to the three volumes of *L'Immigration ou les paradoxes de l'altérité* (2006, 2006, 2014); and Gérard Mauger's studies *Les Bandes, le milieu et la bohème populaire* (5). In the higher regions, we find the mapping of *L'Espace de la noblesse* by Monique de Saint-Martin, as well as studies of the strategies of distinction and reconversion of the other fractions of the dominant class by Béatrix Le Witta and by Monique and Michel Pinçon (6).

These investigations, monomaniacal for most of them, which typically overspill beyond the framework of a monograph closed unto itself as is customary for the genre, have the shared characteristic of taking place within the sociologist's own "tribe." As a result, foiling the "scholastic bias," they make ethnography not only a technique for investigating a social microcosm, but also an instrument for the *reappropriation of self by the analyst*, which, according to Bourdieu, is an indispensable step in the production of sociological knowledge, as well as the possible path to wisdom in the world. They also contain a warning: *the ethnographer must imperatively and continually work to control her relationship with the object*, particularly when the latter is remote, mysterious, or socially sulphurous.

1. This was the motivation behind Bourdieu's youthful fieldwork in his native Béarn (*Le Bal des célibataires. Crise de la société paysanne en Béarn* [2002]), but also the methodological gamble launched by the sociologist and his collaborators three decades later in *La Misère du monde* (1993).
2. Sylvain Maresca, *Les Dirigeants paysans* (1983); Patrick Champagne, *L'Héritage refusé. Crise de la reproduction sociale de la paysannerie française* (2002). See also Charles Suaud, *La Vocation. Conversion et reconversion des prêtres ruraux* (1978).
3. Stéphane Beaud and Michel Pialoux, *Retour sur la condition ouvrière. Enquête aux usines Peugeot de Sochaux-Montbéliard* (1999); Michel Pialoux, *Le Temps d'écouter. Enquêtes sur les métamorphoses de classe ouvrière* (2019).
4. Yvette Delsaut, *Carnets de socioanalyse. Écrire les pratiques ordinaires* (2020).
5. Abdelmalek Sayad *Un Nanterre algérien, terre de bidonvilles* (1995); *L'Immigration ou les paradoxes de l'altérité*. Vol. 1, *L'Illusion du provisoire* (2006); Vol. 2, *Les Enfants illégitimes* (2006); Vol. 3, *La Fabrication des identités culturelles* (2014); and Gérard Mauger, *Les Bandes, le milieu et la bohème populaire. Études de sociologie de la déviance des jeunes des classes populaires (1975–2005)* (2006).
6. Monique de Saint Martin, *L'Espace de la noblesse* (1993); Béatrix Le Wita, *Ni vue, ni connue. Approche ethnographique de la culture bourgeoise* (1988); Michel Pinçon and Monique Pinçon-Charlot, *Grandes Fortunes. Dynasties familiales et formes de richesse en France* (1996). Michel Villette's work on the corporate world, such as *L'Homme qui croyait au management* (1988), is in the same vein: Villette was a manager by day and a sociologist by night.

A privileged instrument of carnal sociology, enactive ethnography—in the sense of the cognitive sciences—[136] is based on the principle of "performing the phenomenon" as a means of approximative knowledge. Inverting the duality of participant observation into *observant participation* means revoking the spectatorial posture to strive to grasp "action-in-the-act" and, in so doing, unearth those implicit constituents of practice that are not articulated, symbolized, and objectified as such: the doxic categories, phronetic capacities, and ordinary modes of being, feeling, and acting of the agents studied.[137] The first commandment of embodied inquiry is therefore to enter the theater of action in an ordinary capacity and, as far as possible, through durable immersion, to apprentice oneself in the habits and customs of these agents—whether pugilists, politicians, professors, or prosecutors—so as to acquire a visceral apprehension of their universe as material and springboard for its analytical reconstruction. It enjoins us to position ourselves not *above or alongside the action, but at its point of production*, treating habitus as both object and method.[138]

Of course, it is not always possible, easy, or obvious to get in and play on the social stage you envisage studying: becoming an active and recognized member usually takes time and requires specific qualities or yet the acquisition of titles and certificates. You may well lack the necessary poise to be a policeman or the minimum flexibility to be a ballerina; you cannot expect to become a probation officer in short order, and it is fortunate that you are not allowed to perform brain surgery in an elite hospital for the sole purpose of sociological understanding. But you could well become a machinist for the ballet, sign up as a volunteer trainee in a probation service, or work as an operating room orderly. There are always several doors and corridors leading to "*where the action is*," to evoke Goffman's classic text—[139] and so many opportunities to experience and experiment with the components of the phenomenon by learning to play a role, however minor, and assume the position of one or other of the protagonists of the social drama under consideration. So much to say that *"enactivity" is a matter of degree*, rather than a binary all-or-nothing terms, and we can benefit greatly from a research design constructed to exploit these variations.

This is well demonstrated by Josh Seim's two-step study of the emergency ambulance profession, *Bandage, Sort, and Hustle* (2020).[140] First, Seim carries out classic *participant*

---

[136] Francisco Varela, Evan Thompson, and Eleanor Rosch, *The Embodied Mind: Cognitive Science and Human Experience* (1991); Lawrence Shapiro, *Embodied Cognition* (2019).
[137] Loïc Wacquant, "Carnal Concepts in Action" (2023).
[138] Loïc Wacquant, "Habitus as Topic and Tool: Reflections on Becoming a Prizefighter" (2011), and Wacquant, *Body and Soul: Notebooks of an Apprentice Boxer* (2022), especially the afterword to the anniversary edition, pp. 256–289.
[139] Erving Goffman, "Where the Action Is" (1967).
[140] Josh Seim, *Bandage, Sort, and Hustle: Ambulance Crews on the Front Lines of Urban Suffering* (2020).

observation as an ambulance attendant, sitting next to the emergency medical technicians in their vehicle, backed up by an analysis of the organization of this work in the private firm that employs them, as any field sociologist would. Then, having undergone the necessary training and obtained the required diploma, he engages in *observant participation* in that same company, taking on the job of ambulance driver and subjecting himself in the first person to the stressors, risks, and responsibilities of the professional in action. Finally, in a third step, he theorizes the differences, advantages, and disadvantages of these two methodological positionings, demonstrating in concrete terms how enactivity transforms and enriches both the process and the result of sociological production.[141] This is without ever pretending to erase the existential and epistemic caesura that inevitably separates the ambulance driver by trade, who does it for a living, from the ambulance driver by opportunity, who indulges in it for a limited time as in a game for the sake of knowledge production.

Embodied inquiry requires a zest of audacity and a great deal of tenacity. A major reason why most ethnographies fall back into the textual or hermeneutic vision nurtured by a *contemplative posture* towards the social world (forbidden by definition to those who practice "observant participation") is that their authors do not persevere in their efforts to gain access and deepen their embeddedness. They stall and promptly retreat, instead of forging ahead and trying every possible route to penetrate the arena of action. Yet tenacity often pays off in the end: Joan Cassell was refused entry into the masculine world of the operating theatre and invited to study female orderlies instead.[142] But, by dint of obstinacy, she ended up observing surgeons at work in some fifteen hospitals during some two hundred operations. Cassell had planned to conduct her investigation in eighteen months; she would spend a total of thirty-three months in the field, at the end of which she was invited to step onto the surgical stage and handle the retractors as the interns do.

Likewise, it is obvious that I could not magically transform myself into a prosecutor, a defense attorney, or a judge for purposes of my investigation into the San Pedrito county criminal court. But this in no way implied that I was condemned to the role of passive, distant spectator—and even less to the mission of inert, silent watchdog of the courtroom's bureaucratic ceremonial as in the "courtwatch" programs rolled out by criminal justice activists.[143] Thus, I was able to start from the inside, by volunteering as an "intern" in the

---

[141] Josh Seim, "Participant Observation, Observant Participation, and Hybrid Ethnography" (2021).
[142] Joan Cassell, *Expected Miracles: Surgeons at Work* (1991).
[143] Nick Gill and Jo Hynes, "Courtwatching: Visibility, Publicness, Witnessing, and Embodiment in Legal Activism" (2021).

department responsible for preparing the bail requisition of defendants, after having followed the workings of the "homeless court" for several months. From this vantage point of observation in action (I was handling cases in a constant state of hurry like the other interns, pre-law students, and rubbing shoulders with the attorneys in the courtroom's corridors), I managed to seduce the judge supervising this courthouse's daily "calendar" and get stationed in his office during the morning to observe the haggling over the allocation of cases, prosecutors, defenders, judges, and courtrooms. This enabled me to learn a host of technical procedures, to sniff the judicial air, to grasp on the fly the categories of penal understanding guiding the protagonists, but also to get to know them and pin down their professional personalities.

Building on this familiarity (now signified by my field nickname, "The Professor"), I insinuated myself into the bosom of the court, namely the judges "chambers," where all cases are decided in furtive exchanges "off the record," several of whom took me under their wing to teach me the judicial ropes. One particularly thoughtful veteran prosecutor took it upon himself to teach me the art of "dealing" cases, so I found myself at his side during his plea negotiations, able to dissect their legal, social, and emotional parameters in real time.[144] All this while knowledgeable colleagues at the Berkeley Law School and professionals in the field had assured me that I would never gain access to the backstages of the court. One sardonic lawyer even warned me: "You're French—and the American middle class hates the French. You have a Ph.D, you're overeducated. You're not macho enough, you wear tight pants."

But I must stress that there is nothing heroic about that: it was by dint of patience, endurance, and diplomacy that I was able to get as close as possible to the judicial fire. And because I had the firm intention of doing so, guided by the intuition that it was imperative to forsake the spectatorial vision which, by reproducing the semiological logic of the court's public ceremonial, constitutes here the first obstacle to the construction of the object. Another essential point is that enactive ethnography is not self-sufficient and self-centred: it must be combined with a structural and historicized approach, or risk falling into the bottomless pit of subjectivist or even narcissistic storytelling.

We need to apply to Bourdieusian theory the test that its epistemology commands: Is the ethnography that draws on it *heuristic*, in the sense that it enables us to see facets of a phenomenon that would otherwise remain invisible to us, produce innovative interpretations and elaborate convincing explanations? The best way to answer this question is to dissect a

---

[144] On the mechanics of these negotiations, through which 97 percent of local criminal court cases in the United States are resolved, see Milton Heumann, *Plea Bargaining: The Experiences of Prosecutors, Judges, and Defense Attorneys* (1977).

monograph that passes this "test" and brilliantly illustrates the conceptual flexibility, theoretical productivity, and empirical richness of Bourdieusian ethnography: Annick Prieur's book *Mema's House, Mexico City* is a perfect example of "thick construction" in action, and proof positive that, despite all the obstacles pertaining to the methodology and the object, it is possible to produce a rich ethnography of poverty. But first let me be clear: there is no such thing as a perfect ethnography—although some monographs come close in certain ways.[145] There is always a *trade-off* and a *compromise* to be found, for example, between analytical acuity and poetic richness, between historical depth and contemporary granularity, or between attention to structures and focus on agents. A deep social and symbolic anchorage makes the interactionist temptation stronger; attention to the carnal logic of action makes the fall into populism more likely, and so on.

Drop a lanky, blond-haired, blue-eyed young Norwegian ethnosociologist into a sanctuary home for young homosexual men threatened by AIDS in a poor Mexico City neighborhood and equip her with a keen sense of social diplomacy, a lush sense of humor, a sharp eye for practical detail and an ear for subtle meanings, the full range of gender theories and Pierre Bourdieu's conceptual framework, and you have got an ethnographic gem.

In *Mema's House, Mexico City: On Transvestites, Queens, and Machos* (1998), Annick Prieur demonstrates concretely what the "construction" in the social construction of the body and gender entails. In this house, some fifteen *jotas* (homosexuals) and *vestidas* (transvestites) "gather to chat, flirt, listen to music, smoke marijuana and maybe also have sex."[146] But the house has rules and "Mema is the boss," who unquestionably deserves a place in the academic pantheon of key informants. Prieur deciphers these rules and shows how the regulars of the place play with them to engender a fragile

---

[145] I am thinking in particular—to stick to ethnographies "from below," and the list is not exhaustive—of Paul Willis, *Learning to Labour* (1977), on social reproduction within the working class; Judith Rollins, *Between Women* (1985), on housekeepers and their women employers; Douglas Harper, *Working Knowledge* (1987), on a mechanic in an isolated rural town; Olivier Schwartz, *Le Monde privé des ouvriers* (1990), about intimate family life in a northern French mining town; George Lipsitz, *A Life in the Struggle* (1995), about the oppositional culture of black American activists in the second twentieth century; Nancy Scheper-Huges, *Death Without Weeping* (1992), about motherhood and social suffering in a village in Brazil's Nordeste region; Philippe Bourgois and Jeffrey Schoenberg, *Righteous Dopefiend* (2009), on San Francisco's heroin-addicted homeless; Timothy Pachirat, *Every Twelve Seconds* (2011), on the organization of labor in Nebraska's slaughterhouses; Sébastien Chauvin, *Les Agences de la précarité* (2013), on day labor in postindustrial Chicago; Javier Auyero and Maria Fernanda Berti, *In Harm's Way* (2015), on multifaceted violences in an Argentinian *villa miseria*; Fabien Truong, *Loyautés radicales* (2017), on religious temptation among marginalized youth at the intersection of immigration and delinquency; Stéphane Beaud, *La France des Belhoumi* (2020), on long-term life trajectories in an immigrant family. I also recommend the practitioners of Italian "micro-history" (Carlo Ginzburg, Giovanni Levi, Alessandro Portelli) and German *Alltagsgeschichte* (Alf Lüdtke, Hans Medick, David Sabean).

[146] Annick Prieur, *Mema's House, Mexico City: On Transvestites, Queens, and Machos* (1998), p. 7.

community and build a frail sense of self, against a backdrop of violence and abuse from their families, tolerance from their neighbors and exclusion from school and work. She demonstrates how the binary opposition between the sexes is paradoxically reproduced by the very agents who disrupt it in their thoughts, feelings, and behaviors such as the stylization of the body, and "why widespread homophobia, machismo, and widespread male bisexuality can go so well together."[147] Arguably the best Bourdieu-inspired field study to date, *Mema's House* also reminds us that there is a reason to live a life that sociologists too often overlook: the sheer pursuit of pleasure and joy.

Prieur met Mema at a conference on AIDS and accepted his invitation to visit him in the informal shelter house he ran in Neza, a poor town in the Mexico City conurbation. Mema, who had worked as a prostitute, hairdresser, cook, clerk, and street vendor before becoming a health educator, proved to be a first-rate "lay ethnographer."[148] He took Prieur under his wing, introduced her to the regulars, protected her and helped her to understand the behaviors she observed, the words she heard, the emotions she felt. The Norwegian sociologist thus carried out four intense periods of complete immersion, for a total of six months, during which she spent her days and nights in Mema's lair, becoming its "mascot," and then following her subjects for eight years. She became deeply embedded in the relationships between the house's residents: "They were leading very self-destructive and dangerous lives, with hard drug use and exposure to violence and sexually transmitted diseases. I tried to influence them in the same direction as Mema did: I scolded them when they had sniffed glue, I counseled them in love affairs, I corrected their makeup and put condoms in their pockets when they went to a party. But I did not try to get them to stop stealing or selling sex."[149]

Prieur claims to have adopted an approach that is "somewhat more inductive than deductive," and strives "[to] write in a positioned manner, to make my presence in the field and my standpoint clear, and not to veil my subjectivity."[150] But she foils the *inductivist trap* insofar as her inductions are ensconced in a strong theoretical framework that combines Bourdieu's genetic sociology, feminist anthropology, and sexuality studies to illuminate "the social construction of gender in the light of masculine domination." Likewise, she claims to be inspired by Geertzian "thick description," but insists at the same time that the researcher can by no means limit herself to interpreting significations:

---

[147] Prieur, *Mema's House, Mexico City*, p. 232.
[148] Prieur, *Mema's House, Mexico City*, p. 14.
[149] Prieur, *Mema's House, Mexico City*, pp. 18–19.
[150] Prieur, *Mema's House, Mexico City*, p. 37.

"must also have a vision of *the social space* in which they take place, of the underlying material, economic and social conditions."[151]

Prieur avoids the *interactionist trap* when she clearly positions Mema's residents within the social structure of their family, neighborhood, street, and peer group—and positions herself within the interlacing relationships inside the house.[152] The portraits she paints of the young *jotas* are always situated in the network of social relationships that transcend and determine the practices within Mema's house. Thus, the unstable mix of violence, respect and affection that permeates their family relationships contrasts with the amused indifference of people in the neighborhood, their joyful acceptance in nightlife entertainment venues and their brutal exclusion from school and employment—the only trades open to them without hostility are prostitution and hairdressing.

Prieur navigates nimbly between the reefs of *populism* and *miserabilism* as she unravels the threads of the *mala vida* of the *jotas*, made up of parties, binge drinking, drugs, theft, sex, quarrels, arrests, detention, and violence fueled by poverty but also by the paradoxical quest for masculine respect (which dictates never accepting humiliation in public). Through her immersion, she shares with the reader the strange mix of dullness and excitement that characterizes this life driven by the search for thrills, without passing moral judgment, positive or negative. A *jota* who works as an employee dressed as a man during the week and prostitutes herself on the week-ends explains: "I can take the monotony of the week, because I know I'll be different on the weekend. Then I can project myself the way I want to, and there will be a new adventure, something unknown—maybe my death, maybe an accident, maybe a quarrel, but there's always something different."[153] However, the pursuit of pleasure comes at a high price in illness, suffering, and early death.

The young homosexuals at Mema's House "make up a subculture but not a counter-culture"; they are viscerally attached to conventional society, starting with the patriarchal family, and the youngest among them "dream about a peaceful life with a regular lover and a hairdressing parlor or a shop."[154] In point of fact, far from constituting a cultural island, *jota* culture can be read as a variant of the art of living of the working classes: "The taste for immediate

---

[151] Prieur, *Mema's House, Mexico City*, p. 40, emphasis added. In her conclusion, Prieur reiterates: "*I have endeavoured to take the actors' point of view seriously, but also to understand the objective conditions of this point of view" (p. 273).
[152] Prieur, *Mema's House, Mexico City*, chapter 2 on "The daily life of a *jota*."
[153] Prieur, *Mema's House, Mexico City*, p. 73.
[154] Prieur, *Mema's House, Mexico City*, p. 62 and 96.

pleasures also expresses a popular ethic—of solidarity, enjoying the present moment and taking tomorrow as it comes."[155]

At the start of the book, Prieur draws up a refined catalog of folk terms for the various recognized sexual identities (*vestida, jota, tortilla, mayate, buga, internacional, futbalera*, etc.) and their uses. In the chapter entitled "Little boys in their mother's closet," she historicizes the social life of these categories and traces the process whereby the youth welcomed by Mema discovered, learned, and affirmed their sexual identity. She reviews theoretically and empirically the role of biological and psychological factors, homosexual practices in early childhood, labeling processes, and the influence of subcultures. In so doing, she partially avoids the trap of presentism and opens the door to a genetic apprehension of the agents studied—partially because a social history of sexual categorizations in relation to changes in ethnic and class structure is lacking.

Finally, *Mema's House* is a model of carnal ethnography in its attention to the embodied dimension of social existence, to emotions and the workings of the senses, and in particular to the practices of transformation, accoutrement, and sexualization of the body to communicate "fuckability": "What the *vestidas* want is precisely that: to be perceived as sexually available women (or almost-women)."[156] Wearing foam-rubber padding on the thighs, hips and buttocks, injecting oil into the posterior, ingesting hormones, undergoing cosmetic surgery: these are all techniques that "show a phenomenon that transcends the dialectic of the habitus concept" by participating in "an active and conscious fashioning of the body."[157] The *vestidas*, kitschy when fervent and *camp* when ironic, fabricate feminine bodies for themselves even as they deploy a masculine sociability among themselves at Mema's.[158] Their dream: to have the possibility of seducing men that women enjoy, but without the subordinate relationship that comes with it. One *vestida* puts it this way: "I have watched women. They are slaves, they are servants. That's the way it is in my country. Maids and other idiots. No, I would have preferred to be a woman, but not like that, no."[159]

In the end, the hypothesis on which the book was based is vividly verified: "I believed that these feminine, homosexual men would bring to light deeply embedded truths about gender, since they were both a provocation against the gender order and a logical result of it."[160] The *jotas* are indeed *homines*

---

[155] Prieur, *Mema's House, Mexico City*, p. 97.
[156] Prieur, *Mema's House, Mexico City*, pp. 146 and 149.
[157] Prieur, *Mema's House, Mexico City*, p. 160.
[158] Prieur, *Mema's House, Mexico City*, p. 171.
[159] Prieur, *Mema's Mema's House, Mexico City*, p. 177.
[160] Prieur, *Mema's House, Mexico City*, p. xiv.

in extremis who reveal the making of identity as an embodied, collective, symbolic, and historical process all at once. And they validate an iconoclastic thesis: "Desire cannot be reduced to its social aspects; it is not in itself socially produced, only socially channeled; and I believe it should be regarded as a force on its own, one that often runs counter to social forces."[161] Finally, on a methodological level, Prieur demonstrates, *contra* Bourdieu, the distinctive value of intensive immersion and active participation as vectors of sociological knowledge. Without this physical, sensual, and moral participation in the milieu studied, she would never have been able to grasp what Garfinkel calls "the demonic logics of action" among the regulars at Mema's house.

Before concluding, I must be clear on one point: my plea for an *enactive, structural, and historicized ethnography* in no way implies that there is only one right and fruitful way to conduct fieldwork, and that Bourdieu's genetic and reflexive sociology is the only one capable of theoretically guiding such research. Participant observation is an umbrella concept that embraces different intellectual styles and different modalities of scientific production, ranging from the rationalist positivism of a Martín Sánchez-Jankowski in *Cracks in the Pavement* to the intimist subjectivism of a Michael Jackson in *At Home in the World*; from the deep dive of Laurence Ralph in a local microcosm in *Renegade Dreams* to the tracing of networks spanning the globe by Kimberley Hoang in *Spiderweb Capitalism*; from the pointillist realism of Abdelmalek Sayad in *Un Nanterre algérien, terre de bidonvilles* to the narrative lyricism of Alpa Shah in *Nightmarch*.[162] These are all ways of practising the craft, each with its own objectives and distinctive criteria of excellence, and each more or less precisely adapted to the questions they seek to formulate and resolve.

Indeed, the opposition between art and science, the literary and the analytical, interpretation and explanation, the idiographic and the nomothetic, which structures the human sciences as a whole, is found in an *attenuated form and shifted toward the hermeneutic pole* within the very space of ethnographic practices, and this dispersion is a source of dynamism and creativity. So much to say that the ambition of the present book is not to establish any theoretical or methodological orthodoxy in field research and thus reduce the array of variants available to the ethnographer. The fact remains, however,

---

[161] Prieur, *Mema's House, Mexico City*, p. 40. She validates here Max Weber's thesis that sexual desire is fundamentally resistant to rationalization.

[162] Martín Sánchez-Jankowski, *Cracks in the Pavement: Social Change and Resilience in Poor Neighborhoods* (2008); Michael Jackson, *At Home in the World* (2000); Laurence Ralph, *Renegade Dreams: Living through Injury in Gangland Chicago* (2014); Kimberly Kay Hoang, *Spiderweb Capitalism: How Global Elites Exploit Frontier Markets* (2022); Abdelmalek Sayad (with Éliane Dupuy), *Un Nanterre algérien, terre de bidonvilles* (1995); Alpa Shah, *Nightmarch: Among India's Revolutionary Guerrillas* (2019).

that all practitioners of the genre, insofar as they aspire to produce accounts of the social world in the scientific register—that is, logically reasoned and empirically founded—must sooner or later, whether they like it or not, confront the fallacies of ethnographism and decide to privilege one or other of the missions of ethnography. They can then come together and commune within what attracts and retains them all in this vein of social science: the pure pleasure of ethnographic action in its various guises.

The world of science, a masculine place of collective ascesis and the sacralization of the true, values the austere, the "serious" and the "laborious" (hence the term "laboratory," the place of labor), and correlatively rejects the pleasure of research as on the side of profane entertainment, "frivolous" and feminine. Thus the ethnographer is always suspected by her positivist colleagues of "enjoying herself" (too much), of doing things to her "heart's content," and thus of taking unspeakable liberties with the criteria of methodological control and empirical adequacy that define the scholar as such.[163] In response to this scientistic and masculinist prejudice, we must forcefully affirm the immense achievements of ethnography, which, like all scientific methods, strives to marry reason and observation to produce *models approximating the real* that are no more and no less rigorous than those developed by practitioners of quantitative, historical, and hermeneutic methods. One can be a sociologist dedicated to science body and soul without for that renouncing one's *libido ethnographica*.

~ * ~

---

[163] This is the caricature that animates the book by legal scholar Steven Lubet, *Interrogating Ethnography: Why Evidence Matters* (2018), which, following the scandal caused by Alice Goffman's book *On the Run*, lectures sociologists and enjoins ethnography to adopt the criteria of veridicity of criminal court or journalism. As if the logic of legal proof, established for all eternity on strictly formal legal criteria of what counts as evidence, and guaranteed by the state, were the same as that of scientific inference, which is probabilistic in nature and forever open to challenge by the research community.

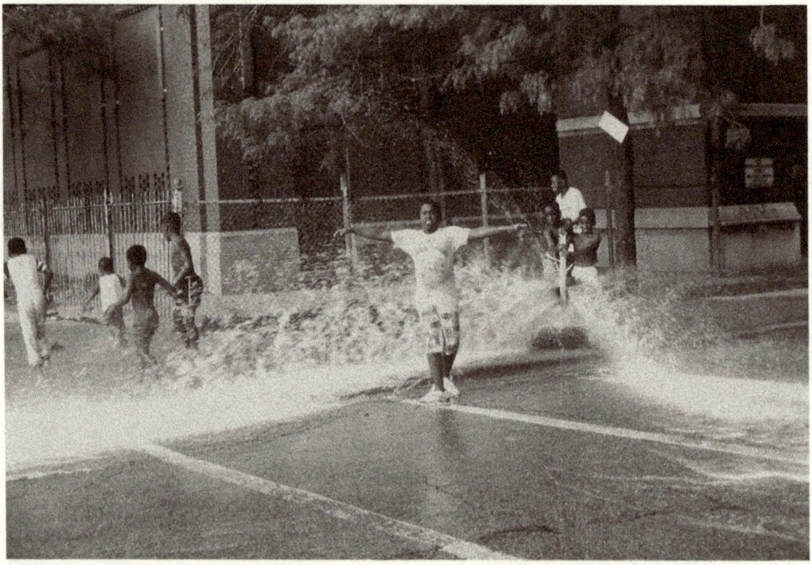

Epilogue

Bachelard in the Ghetto

"I believe that the sociology of sociology or, more precisely, the sociology of the social conditions of the production of sociological sciences is one of the fundamental conditions for the progress of sociological knowledge."

Pierre Bourdieu, "Epistémologie et sociologie
de la sociologie," 1967.

This book has endeavored to put in historical and analytical perspective a controversy over the ethnography of the relationship between race, class, and morality in and around the black American ghetto in the age of triumphant neoliberalism, with the aim of drawing positive lessons for the theory and practice of fieldwork. Thoughtless empiricism, blissful acceptance of problematics prefabricated by ordinary and political common sense, constant confusion between folk and scientific categories, blind confinement to the immediate perimeter of interaction, rampant moralism, and finally a deficit of reflexivity: these are the shortcomings I discerned in the course of a close reading of three canonized books on the subject.[1] These are the pitfalls, it seems to me, that every ethnographer, including the author of these lines, encounters sooner or later, and that can only be overcome by *collective vigilance*. Added to this is the fact that the object studied is socially low, symbolically tainted, and politically vulnerable, the bearer of a heavy and strident racial and class unconscious that never ceases to interfere with what Jürgen Habermas calls "knowledge interest."[2]

It was not the aim of this book to have "the last word" in the silent controversy generated by "Scrutinizing the Street," for, on closer inspection, such closure of debate is rare and generally illusory in the history of science. It

---

[1] I was guided, in the writing that followed, by the model of the long critical notes published by Émile Durkheim and his collaborators in *L'Année sociologique*, which are genuine instruments of analytical "expatriation" and "denationalization," and thus of progress in sociological thought.

[2] Jürgen Habermas, *Knowledge and Interest* ([1968] 1979).

would even be a pernicious fallacy, according to Robert Merton.[3] Rather, its aim has been to uncover the social and intellectual underpinnings of a distorted and eluded debate so as to advance knowledge, not only of the object under consideration, but also and above all of the conditions of its production and reception. If the errors in the construction of the object that "Scrutinizing" points out are real, then it is all of us—authors, critics and readers—who benefit from this clarification. Conversely, if I have erred in my criticism, and Anderson's, Duneier's, and Newman's defenses of their theses are valid—and that is for each reader to decide—it is still all of us together who benefit from their specification and their refutation. The subject of social science is not a *cogito* isolated in the world and alone in front of its blank sheet of paper, but, as Bachelard taught, a *cogitamus*, a collectivity of researchers who both *collaborate and battle at the same time* to produce knowledge that, collectively, they will judge to be "true" given the state of the instruments of scientific production and evaluation at that moment.

This epistemological return was also an opportunity to point out the danger of *ethnographism*, the tendency to want to describe, interpret, and explain a phenomenon based solely on the elements discerned through fieldwork, and to call for the correlative practice of an *enactive, structural, and historicized ethnography* that sets out to embed the observed microactions in the nested series of social spaces that shape them and give them sense—that is, direction and meaning. Such an ethnography, the product of a "thick construction," avoids falling into one or another of the five ethnographic fallacies I have characterized as interactionism, inductivism, populism, presentism, and the hermeneutic drift.

According to Alexandre Koyré, to study the history of scientific thought is to "grasp the progress of this thought in the very movement of its creative activity." It means "placing the works studied in their intellectual and spiritual milieu, [and] interpreting them in terms of the mental habits, preferences and aversions of their authors," and above all it means "studying errors and failures with as much care as successes."[4] This is what I set out to do by shedding light on the social and mental conditions of possibility of a failed sociology of the intersection of race and poverty in the turn-of-the-century American metropolis emblematic of an entire current of urban research. Identifying the

---

[3] On the three forms of the paralogism of the last word in the history of science, read Robert K. Merton's illuminating article, "The Fallacy of the Latest Word: The Case of 'Pietism and Science'" (1984).

[4] Alexandre Koyré, *Études d'histoire de la pensée scientifique* (1973), p. 14. Koyré continues: "The errors of a Descartes and a Galileo, the failures of a Boyle and a Hooke, are not only instructive; they reveal the difficulties that had to be vanquished, the obstacles that had to be overcome."

causes and reasons for the poverty of the ethnography of poverty in America is to give ourselves the means to reduce it and, in so doing, contribute to a better mastery of sociological reason in the making.

~ * ~

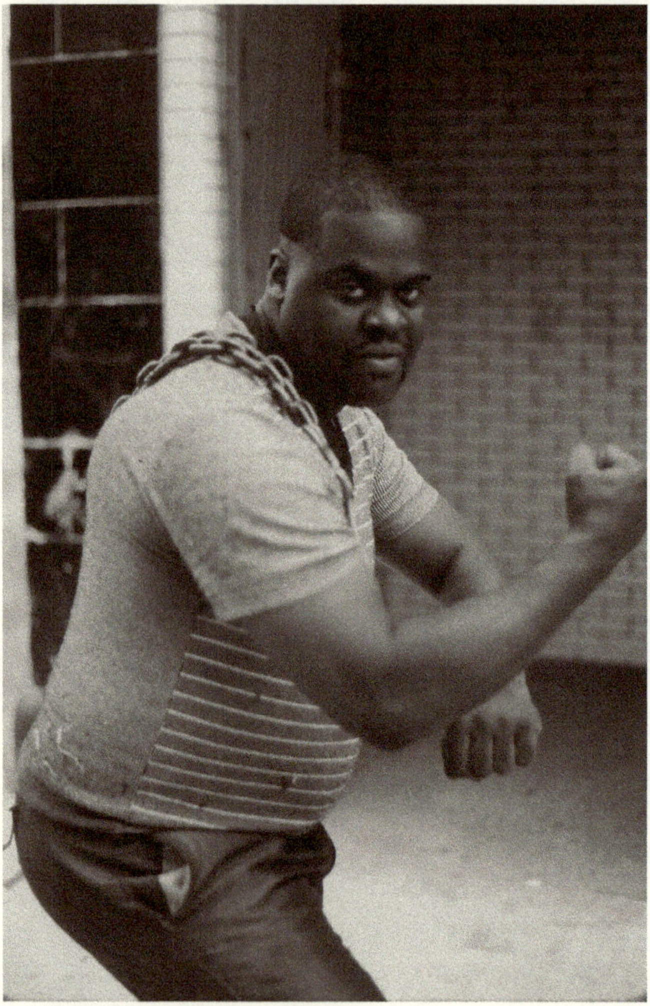

Acknowledgments

For reading and reacting to various chunk and successive versions of this text, my thanks go to Javier Auyero, Timothy Black, Jérôme Bourdieu, Philippe Bourgois, Sébastien Chauvin, Mark de Rond, Matt Desmond, Chris Herring, Kimberly Kay Hoang, Zach Levenson, Yan Long, Jordanna Matlon, Ékédi Mpondo-Dika, Chris Muller, Étienne Ollion, Mary Pattillo, Amín Perez, Virgílio Pereira, Ana Portilla, Annick Prieur, Franck Poupeau, Josh Seim, David Showalter, Martín Sánchez-Jankowski, Victor Shammas, and Ana Villareal—with apologies to those whom I am inadvertently omitting. Their criticism and suggestions have been invaluable, even when I have not followed them. The photographs that open each part of the book are extracted from my field archives in Chicago; they were taken in the neighborhood of Woodlawn, on the city's South Side, between 1989 and 1991.

References

Abbott, Andrew. 1999. *Department and Discipline: Chicago Sociology at One Hundred.* Chicago: University of Chicago Press.
Abrahams, Roger D. 1964. *Deep Down in the Jungle: Negro Narrative Folklore from the Streets of Philadelphia.* New Brunswick, NJ: Transaction.
Abu-Lughod, Janet L. 2007. *Race, Space, and Riots in Chicago, New York, and Los Angeles.* New York: Oxford University Press.
Adler, William M. 1991. *Land of Opportunity: One Family's Quest for the American Dream in the Age of Crack.* Ann Arbor: University of Michigan Press, reprint 2021.
Alford, Robert. 1998. *The Craft of Inquiry: Methods, Theories and Evidence.* New York: Oxford University Press.
Alexander, Michelle. 2010. *The New Jim Crow: Mass Incarceration in the Age of Colorblindness.* New York: New Press.
Alston, Lee J. and Joseph P. Ferrie. 1999. *Southern Paternalism and the American Welfare State.* New York: Cambridge University Press.
Anderson, Elijah. 1978. *A Place on the Corner.* Chicago: University of Chicago Press, expanded edition, 2008.
Anderson, Elijah. 1990. *Streetwise: Race, Class and Change in an Urban Community.* Chicago: University of Chicago Press.
Anderson, Elijah. 1999. *Code of the Street: Decency, Violence, and the Moral Life of the Inner City.* New York: W.W. Norton.
Anderson, Elijah. 2002. "The Ideologically Driven Critique." *American Journal of Sociology* 107, no. 6: 1533–1550.
Anderson, Elijah. 2022. *Black in White Space: The Enduring Impact of Color in Everyday Life.* Chicago: University of Chicago Press.
Anderson, Nels. 1923. *The Hobo: The Sociology of the Homeless Man.* Chicago: University of Chicago Press, reprint 2014.
Antosa, Silvia (ed.). 2014. *Queer Crossings: Theories, Bodies, Texts.* 2nd edition. London: Mimesis International.
Arborio, Anne-Marie and Pierre Fournier. 2015. *L'enquête et ses methods: L'observation directe.* Paris: Armand Colin.
Ashley, Richard K. 1983. "Three Modes of Economism." *International Studies Quarterly* 27, no. 4: 463–496.
Auyero, Javier. 2000. *Poor People's Politics: Peronist Survival Networks and the Legacy of Evita.* Durham, NC: Duke University Press.
Auyero, Javier. 2012. *Patients of the State: The Politics of Waiting in Argentina.* Durham, NC: Duke University Press.
Auyero, Javier (ed.). 2024. *Portraits of Persistence: Inequality and Hope in Latin America.* Austin: University of Texas Press.
Auyero, Javier and María Fernanda Berti. 2015. *In Harm's Way: The Dynamics of Urban Violence.* Princeton, NJ: Princeton University Press.
Auyero, Javier and Débora Alejandra Swistun. 2009. *Flammable: Environmental Suffering in an Argentine Shantytown.* New York: Oxford University Press.

Avanza, Martina. 2008. "Comment faire de l'ethnographie quand on n'aime pas 'ses indigènes'? Une enquête au sein d'un mouvement xénophobe." Pp. 41–58 in Didier Fassin and Alban Bensa (eds.), *Les politiques de l'enquête*. Paris: La Découverte.
Bachelard, Gaston. 1928. *Essai sur la connaissance approchée*. Paris: Vrin.
Bachelard, Gaston. 1934. *Le nouvel esprit scientifique*. Paris: PUF.
Bachelard, Gaston. 1938. *La formation de l'esprit scientifique: Contribution à une psychanalyse de la connaissance*. Paris: Vrin, new printing 2004.
Bachelard, Gaston. 1949. *Le rationalisme appliqué*. Paris: PUF, 2004.
Bachelard, Gaston. 1980. *Épistémologie*. Paris: PUF.
Baldwin, Davarian L. 2007. *Chicago's New Negroes: Modernity, the Great Migration, and Black Urban Life*. Chapel Hill: University of North Carolina Press.
Balto, Simon. 2019. *Occupied Territory: Policing Black Chicago from Red Summer to Black Power*. Chapel Hill: University of North Carolina Press.
Baltzell, E. Digby. 1964. *The Protestant Establishment: Aristocracy and Caste in America*. New Haven, CT: Yale University Press, reprint 1987.
Banfield, Edward C. 1970. *The Unheavenly City: The Nature and Future of Our Urban Crisis*. Boston: Little, Brown.
Bartram, Robin. 2022. *Stacked Decks: Building Inspectors and the Reproduction of Urban Inequality*. Chicago: University of Chicago Press.
Batista, Vera Malaguti. 1998. *Difíceis ganhos fáceis: Drogas e juventude pobre no Rio de Janeiro*. Rio de Janeiro: Editora Freitas Bastos.
Beaud, Stéphane. 1996. "L'usage de l'entretien en sciences sociales: Plaidoyer pour l'"entretien ethnographique."" *Politix: Revue des sciences sociales du politique* 35: 226–257.
Beaud, Stéphane. 2020. *La France des Belhoumi: Portraits de famille (1977–2017)*. Paris: La Découverte.
Beaud, Stéphane and Michel Pialoux. 1999. *Retour sur la condition ouvrière: Enquête aux usines Peugeot de Sochaux-Montbéliard*. Paris: La Découverte.
Beaud, Stéphane and Florence Weber. 2003. *Guide de l'enquête de terrain*. Paris: La Découverte.
Becker, Howard S. 1963. *Outsiders: Studies in the Sociology of Deviance*. New York: Free Press.
Becker, Howard S. (ed.). 1964. *The Other Side: Perspectives on Deviance*. New York: Free Press.
Becker, Howard S. 1967. "Whose Side are We On?". *Social Problems* 14, no. 3: 239–247.
Becker, Howard S. 1983. *Art Worlds*. Berkeley: University of California Press, expanded edition, 2008.
Bellin, Jeffrey. 2014. "The Inverse Relationship between the Constitutionality and Effectiveness of New York City Stop and Frisk." *Boston University Law Review* 94: 1495–1550.
Bittner, Egon. 1967. "Police Discretion in Emergency Apprehension of Mentally Ill Persons." *Social Problems* 14, no. 3: 278–292.
Black, Timothy. 2009. *When a Heart Turns Rock Solid: The Lives of Three Puerto Rican Brothers on and off the Streets*. New York: Pantheon.
Blee, Kathleen M. 1993. "Evidence, Empathy, and Ethics: Lessons from Oral Histories of the Klan." *The Journal of American History* 80, no. 2: 596–606.
Blumer, Herbert. 1966. *Symbolic Interactionism: Perspective and Method*. Berkeley: University of California Press.
Bogue, Donald J. 1955. "Urbanism in the United States, 1950." *American Journal of Sociology* 60, no. 5: 471–486.
Bonnell, Victoria E. and Lynn Hunt (eds.). 1999. *Beyond the Cultural Turn: New Directions in the Study of Society and Culture*. Berkeley: University of California Press.
Borges, Jorge Luis. [1942] 1974. "Funes ou la mémoire," in *Fictions*. Paris: Gallimard.

Boris, Eileen and Rhacel Salazar Parreñas (eds.). 2010. *Intimate Labors: Cultures, Technologies, and the Politics of Care*. Stanford, CA: Stanford University Press.

Boswell, John and Jack Corbett. 2015. "Who Are We Trying to Impress? Reflections on Navigating Political Science, Ethnography and Interpretation." *Journal of Organizational Ethnography* 4, no. 2: 223–235.

Bourdieu, Pierre. [1963] 2021. *Travail et travailleurs en Algérie*, expanded and updated edition. Paris: Raisons d'Agir Éditions.

Bourdieu, Pierre. 1972. *Esquisse d'une théorie de la pratique, précédé de trois études d'ethnologie kabyle*. Geneva: Droz. Reprint, Seuil, 2000.

Bourdieu, Pierre. 1977. *Algérie 60: Structures économiques et structures temporelles*. Paris: Minuit.

Bourdieu, Pierre. 1979. *La Distinction: Critique sociale du jugement*. Paris: Minuit.

Bourdieu, Pierre. 1980. *Le Sens pratique*. Paris: Minuit.

Bourdieu, Pierre. 1980. "Le mort saisit le vif: Les relations entre l'histoire réifiée et l'histoire incorporée." *Actes de la recherche en sciences sociales* 32: 3–14.

Bourdieu, Pierre. 1984. *Homo Academicus*. Paris: Minuit.

Bourdieu, Pierre. 1984. "Espace social et genèse des 'classes.'" *Actes de la recherche en sciences sociales* 52: 3–14.

Bourdieu, Pierre. 1986. *Choses dites*. Paris: Minuit.

Bourdieu, Pierre. 1986. "L'illusion biographique." *Actes de la recherche en sciences sociales* 62: 69–72.

Bourdieu, Pierre. 1990. "The Scholastic Point of View." *Cultural Anthropology* 5, no. 4: 380–391.

Bourdieu, Pierre. 1992. *Les Règles de l'art. Genèse et structure du champ littéraire*. Paris: Seuil.

Bourdieu, Pierre, et al. 1993. *La Misère du monde*. Paris: Seuil.

Bourdieu, Pierre. 1994. *The Field of Cultural Production*. New York: Columbia University Press.

Bourdieu, Pierre. 1997. *Méditations pascaliennes*. Paris: Seuil.

Bourdieu, Pierre. 2000. "L'inconscient d'école." *Actes de la recherche en sciences sociales* 135: 3–5.

Bourdieu, Pierre. [1982] 2000. *Langage et pouvoir symbolique*. Paris: Seuil.

Bourdieu, Pierre. 2001. *Science de la science et réflexivité*. Paris: Raisons d'Agir Éditions.

Bourdieu, Pierre. 2002. *Le Bal des célibataires. Crise de la société paysanne en Béarn*. Paris: Seuil.

Bourdieu, Pierre. 2003. "Participant Objectivation." *Journal of the Royal Anthropological Institute* 9, no. 2: 281–294.

Bourdieu, Pierre. 2013. *Manet, une révolution symbolique. Cours au Collège de France (1998–2000) suivis d'un manuscrit inachevé de Pierre et Marie-Claire Bourdieu*. Paris: Seuil and Raisons d'Agir Édition.

Bourdieu, Pierre. 2015. *Sociologie générale*, Vol. 1, *Cours au Collège de France 1981–1983*. Paris: Seuil and Raisons d'Agir Éditions.

Bourdieu, Pierre. 2016. *Sociologie générale*, Vol. 2, *Cours au Collège de France 1984–1987*. Paris: Seuil and Raisons d'Agir Éditions.

Bourdieu, Pierre. 2022. *Microcosmes. Théorie des champs*. Paris: Seuil and Raisons d'Agir Éditions.

Bourdieu, Pierre. 2022. *Retour sur la réflexivité*. Paris: Éditions de l'EHESS.

Bourdieu, Pierre and Jean-Claude Passeron. 1970. *La Reproduction. Éléments pour une théorie du système d'enseignement*. Paris: Minuit.

Bourdieu, Pierre and Loïc Wacquant. 2014. *Invitation à la sociologie réflexive*. Paris: Seuil, revised and expanded edition.

Bourdieu, Pierre, Jean-Claude Chamboredon, and Jean-Claude Passeron. [1968] 1973, 2022. *Le Métier de sociologue. Préalables épistémologiques.* Paris: Éditions de l'EHESS.
Bourgois, Philippe. [1995] 2003. *In Search of Respect: Selling Crack in El Barrio.* Cambridge, MA: Cambridge University Press.
Bourgois, Philippe. 2001. "Culture of Poverty." Pp. 11904–11907 in Neil J. Smelser and Paul B. Baltes (eds.), *International Encyclopedia of the Social and Behavioral Sciences.* Oxford: Elsevier.
Bourgois, Philippe and Jeffrey Schonberg. 2009. *Righteous Dopefiend.* Berkeley: University of California Press.
Bowling, Benjamin. 1999. "The Rise and Fall of New York Murder: Zero Tolerance or Crack's Decline?" *British Journal of Criminology* 39, no. 4: 531–554.
Boyer, Paul S. 1978. *Urban Masses and Moral Order in America, 1820–1920.* Cambridge, MA: Harvard University Press.
Braunstein, Jean-François. 2002 "Bachelard, Canguilhem, Foucault: Le 'style français' en épistémologie." Pp. 920–963 in Pierre Wagner (ed.), *Les philosophes et la science.* Paris: Gallimard.
Brint, Steven G., and Jerome Karabel. 1989. *The Diverted Dream: Community Colleges and the Promise of Educational Opportunity in America, 1900–1985.* New York: Oxford University Press.
Bronner, Luc. 2009. *La loi du ghetto: Enquête sur les banlieues françaises.* Paris: Calmann-Lévy.
Brown, Claude. 1965. *Manchild in the Promised Land.* New York: Bantam, new ed. 2011.
Brown, Michael. 1999. *Race, Money, and the American Welfare State.* Ithaca, NY: Cornell University Press.
Brubaker, Rogers. 1993. "Social Theory as Habitus." Pp. 212–234 in Craig Calhoun, Edward LiPuma, and Moishe Postone (eds.). *Bourdieu: Critical Perspectives.* Chicago: University of Chicago Press.
Bryant, Christopher G.A. 1985. *Positivism in Social Theory and Research.* London: Macmillan.
Burawoy, Michael. 1979. "The Anthropology of Industrial Work." *Annual Review of Anthropology* 8: 231–266.
Burawoy, Michael. 1998. "The Extended Case Method." *Sociological Theory* 16, no. 1: 4–33.
Burawoy, Michael. 2003. "Revisits: An Outline of a Theory of Reflexive Ethnography." *American Sociological Review* 68, no. 5: 645–679.
Burawoy, Michael. 2009. *The Extended Case Method: Four Countries, Four Decades, Four Great Transformations, and One Theoretical Tradition.* Berkeley: University of California Press.
Burawoy, Michael. 2017. "On Desmond: The Limits of Spontaneous Sociology." *Theory & Society* 46, no. 4: 261-284.
Burawoy, Michael. 2019. "Empiricism and its Fallacies." *Contexts* 18, no. 1: 47–53.
Burawoy, Michael and János Lukács. 1992. *The Radiant Past: Ideology and Reality in Hungary's Road to Capitalism.* Chicago: University of Chicago Press.
Butterfield, Fox. 1995. *All God's Children: The Bosket Family and the American Tradition of Violence.* New York: Avon.
Calhoun, Craig. 1996. *Critical Social Theory: Culture, History, and the Challenge of Difference* Cambridge, MA: Basil Blackwell.
Caplow, Theodore, et al. 1982. *Middletown Families: Fifty Years of Change and Continuity.* New York: Bantam.
Caplow, Theodore et al. 2001. *The First Measured Century: An Illustrated Guide to Trends in America, 1900–2000.* Washington: The AEI Press.
Carles, Pierre. 2001. *La sociologie est un sport de combat.* Available on DVD, C-P Productions.
Cassell, Joan. 1991. *Expected Miracles: Surgeons at Work.* Philadelphia: Temple University Press.

Castells, Manuel. 1996. *The Rise of the Network Society*. Vol. 1, *The Information Age: Economy, Society and Culture*. Cambridge, MA: Wiley-Blackwell.
Cefaï, Daniel (ed.). 2003. *L'enquête de terrain*. Paris: La Découverte.
Champagne, Patrick. 2002. *L'héritage refuse: Crise de la reproduction sociale de la paysannerie française*. Paris: Seuil/Points.
Chapoulie, Jean-Michel. 2001. *La tradition sociologique de Chicago, 1892–1961*. Paris: Seuil.
Charmaz, Kathy. 2006. *Constructing Grounded Theory: A Practical Guide through Qualitative Analysis*. Newbury Park, CA: Sage.
Chicago Tribune. 1986. *The American Millstone: An Examination of the Nation's Permanent Underclass*. Chicago: Review Press.
Chauvin, Sébastien. 2010. *Les agences de la précarité: Journaliers à Chicago*. Paris: Seuil.
Chauvin, Sébastien and Nicolas Jounin. 2010. "L'observation directe." Pp. 1143–1165 in Serge Paugam (ed.), *L'enquête sociologique*. Paris: PUF.
Clair, Matthew. 2020. *Privilege and Punishment: How Race and Class Matter in Criminal Court*. Princeton, NJ: Princeton University Press.
Clark, Andy. 2013. *Mindware: An Introduction to the Philosophy of Cognitive Science*. Oxford: Oxford University Press.
Clark, Darlene and Kathleen Thompson. 1998. *A Shining Thread of Hope: The History of Black Women in America*. New York: Broadway Books.
Clark, Kenneth B. 1965. *Dark Ghetto: Dilemmas of Social Power*. New York: Harper & Row.
Clear, Todd R. 2009. *Imprisoning Communities: How Mass Incarceration Makes Disadvantaged Neighborhoods Worse*. New York: Oxford University Press.
Cloteau, Armèle, Guillaume Letourneur, Pierre Rouxel, and Julien Bourdais. 2020. "La banalisation du Front national au village." *Actes de la recherche en sciences sociales* 232/233: 70–85.
Colyer, Corey J. 2015. "W.I. Thomas and the Forgotten Four Wishes: A Case Study in the Sociology of Ideas." *The American Sociologist* 46, no. 2: 248–268.
Conn, Steven. 2014. *Americans Against the City: Anti-Urbanism in the Twentieth Century*. New York: Oxford University Press.
Contreras, Randol. 2013. *The Stickup Kids: Race, Drugs, Violence, and the American Dream*. Berkeley: University of California Press.
Coton, Christel. 2017. *Officiers. Des classes en lutte sous l'uniforme*. Marseilles, France: Agone.
Cottle, Simon. 2000. "New(s) Times: Towards a 'Second Wave' of News Ethnography." *Communications* 25, no. 1: 19–41.
Cressey, Paul. 1932. *The Taxi-Dance Hall: A Sociological Study in Commercialized Recreation and City Life*. Chicago: University of Chicago Press, reprint 1969.
Da Col, Giovanni and David Graeber. 2011. "Foreword: The Return of Ethnographic Theory." *HAU: Journal of Ethnographic Theory* 1, no. 1: vi–xxxv.
Damer, Séan. 1989. *From Moorepark to "Wine Alley": The Rise and Fall of a Glasgow Housing Scheme*. Edinburgh: Edinburgh University Press.
Daniel, E. Valentine and Jeffrey M. Peck (eds.). 1996. *Culture/Contexture: Explorations in Anthropology and Literary Studies*. Berkeley: University of California Press.
Dash, Leon. 1996. *Rosa Lee: A Mother and her Family in Urban America*. New York: Plume.
Davis, Angela J. 2007. *Arbitrary Justice: The Power of the American Prosecutor*. New York: Oxford University Press.
Davis, Kathy. 2008. "Intersectionality as Buzzword: A Sociology of Science Perspective on What Makes a Feminist Theory Successful." *Feminist Theory* 9, no. 1: 67–85.
Deckard, Faith M. and Javier Auyero. 2022. "Poor People's Survival Strategies: Two Decades of Research in the Americas." *Annual Review of Sociology* 48: 373–395.

Delpierre, Alizée. 2022. *Servir les riches: Les domestiques chez les grandes fortunes*. Paris: La Découverte.
Delsaut, Yvette. 2020. *Carnets de socioanalyse. Écrire les pratiques ordinaires*. Paris: Raisons d'Agir Éditions.
Desmond, Matthew. 2007. *On the Fireline: Living and Dying with Wildland Firefighters*. Chicago: University of Chicago Press.
Desmond, Matthew. 2014. "Relational Ethnography." *Theory & Society* 43, no. 5: 547–579.
Desmond, Matthew. 2016. *Evicted: Poverty and Profit in the American City*. New York: Crown.
Devereux, Georges. 1967. *From Anxiety to Method in the Behavioral Sciences*. La Hague: Mouton.
Dewey, John 1916. *Democracy and Education: An Introduction to the Philosophy of Education*. New York: Create Space.
Dirks, Nicholas B. (ed.). 1997. *Near Ruins: Cultural Theory at the End of the Century*. Minneapolis: University of Minnesota Press.
Dodier, Nicolas and Isabelle Baszanger. 1997. "Totalisation et altérité dans l'enquête ethnographique." *Revue française de sociologie* 38, no 1: 37–66.
Dordick, Gwendolyn. 1997. *Something Left to Lose: Personal Relations and Survival among New York's Homeless*. Philadelphia: Temple University Press.
Douven, Igor. 2022. *The Art of Abduction*. Cambridge, MA: MIT Press.
Drake, St. Clair and Horace Cayton. [1945] 1993. *Black Metropolis: A Study of Negro Life in a Northern City*. Chicago: University of Chicago Press.
Du Bois, W.E.B. 1899. *The Philadelphia Negro: A Social Study*. Philadelphia: University of Pennsylvania Press, new edition, 1995.
Du Bois, W.E.B. 1903. *The Souls of Black Folk*. Washington: American Library, 1982.
Du Bois, W.E.B. 1974. *On Sociology and the Black Community*. Edited by Dan S. Green and Edwin D. Driver. Chicago: University of Chicago Press.
Dubois, Vincent. 1999. *La vie au guichet: Relation administrative et traitement de la misère*. Paris: Économica.
Dubois, Vincent. 2021. *Contrôler les assistés: Genèses et usages d'un mot d'ordre*. Paris: Raisons d'Agir Éditions.
Dum, Christopher P. 2016. *Exiled in America: Life on the Margins in a Residential Motel*. New York: Columbia University Press.
Duneier, Mitchell. 1992. *Slim's Table: Race, Respectability, and Masculinity*. Chicago: University of Chicago Press.
Duneier, Mitchell. 1999. *Sidewalk*. New York: Farrar, Straus and Giroux.
Duneier, Mitchell. 2002. "What Kind of Combat Sport is Sociology?" *American Journal of Sociology* 107, no. 6: 1551–1576.
Duneier, Mitchell. 2016. *Ghetto: The Invention of a Place, the History of an Idea*. New York: Farrar, Strauss and Giroux.
Duneier, Mitchell, Philip Kasinitz, and Alexandra Murphy (eds.). 2014. *The Urban Ethnography Reader*. New York: Oxford University Press.
Durkheim, Emile. 1895. *Les règles de la méthode sociologique*. Paris: PUF, 1981.
Durkheim, Emile. 1925. *L'éducation morale*. Paris: PUF, 2018.
Durkheim, Émile and Marcel Mauss. [1903] 2017. *De quelques formes primitives de classification*. Paris: PUF.
Edin, Kathryn and Laura Lein. 1997. *Making Ends Meet: How Single Mothers Survive Welfare and Low-Wage Jobs*. New York: Russell Sage Foundation.
Edsall, Thomas Byrne and Mary D. Edsall. 1992. *Chain Reaction: The Impact of Race, Rights, and Taxes on American Politics*. New York: W.W. Norton.

Eisenstein, James and Herbert Jacob. 1977. *Felony Justice: An Organizational Analysis of Criminal Courts*. Boston: Little, Brown.
Eisenstein, James, Roy B. Flemming, and Peter F. Nardulli. 1988. *The Contours of Justice: Communities and their Courts*. Boston: Little, Brown.
Elias, Norbert. [1968] 1993. *Qu'est-ce que la sociologie ?* Paris: Pocket, Collection "Agora."
Engels, Friedrich. [1845] 2009. *The Condition of the Working Class in England*. London: Penguin.
Erdmans, Mary Patrice and Timothy Black. 2015. *On Becoming a Teen Mom: Life Before Pregnancy*. Berkeley: University of California Press.
Esping-Andersen, Gösta. 1999. *Social Foundations of Postindustrial Economies*. Oxford: Oxford University Press.
Fader, Jamie J. 2013. *Falling Back: Incarceration and Transitions to Adulthood among Urban Youth*. New Brunswick, NJ: Rutgers University Press.
Fagan, Jeffrey and Deanna L. Wilkinson. 1998. "Guns, Youth Violence, and Social Identity in Inner Cities." Pp. 105–188 in Michael Tonry et Mark H. Moore (eds.), *Youth Violence*. Chicago: University of Chicago Press.
Fagan, Jeffrey, Franklin Zimring, and June Kim. 1998. "Declining Homicide in New York City: A Tale of Two Trends." *Journal of Criminal Law and Criminology* 88, no. 4: 1277–1324.
Fantasia, Rick. 1995. "Fast Food in France." *Theory & Society* 24, no. 2: 201–243.
Fassin, Didier. 2015. "The Public Afterlife of Ethnography." *American Ethnologist* 42, no. 4: 592–609.
Feeley, Malcolm M. 1979. *The Process is the Punishment: Handling Cases in a Lower Criminal Court*. New York: Russell Sage Foundation.
Fernández-Kelly, Patricia M. 1994. "Towanda's Triumph: Social and Cultural Capital in the Transition to Adulthood in the Urban Ghetto." *International Journal of Urban and Regional Research* 18, no. 1(March): 88–111.
Fernández-Kelly, Patricia. 2014. *The Hero's Fight: African Americans in West Baltimore and the Shadow of the State*. Princeton, NJ: Princeton University Press.
Flamm, Michael W. 2005. *Law and Order: Street Crime, Civil Unrest, and the Crisis of Liberalism in the 1960s*. New York: Columbia University Press.
Form, William. 1987. "On The Degradation Of Skills." *Annual Review of Sociology* 13: 29–47.
Forman, Robert E. 1971. *Black Ghettos, White Ghettos, and Slums*. Englewood Cliffs, NJ: Prentice-Hall.
Foucault, Michel. 1975. *Surveiller et punir. Naissance de la prison*. Paris: Gallimard.
Frankfurt, Harry G. 1958. "Peirce's Notion of Abduction." *The Journal of Philosophy* 55, no. 14: 593–597.
Freeman, Richard. 1995. "The Labor Market." Pp. 171–192 in James Q. Wilson and Joan Petersilia (eds.). *Crime*. San Francisco: ICS Press.
Freeman, Richard. 1999. *The New Inequality: Creating Solutions for Poor America*. Boston: Beacon Press.
Freidenberg, John (ed.). 1995. "The Anthropology of Lower Income Urban Enclaves: The Case of East Harlem." *Annals of the New York Academy of Sciences* 749.
Friedman, Milton and Rose D. Friedman. 1980. *Free to Choose: A Personal Statement*. New York: Mariner Books.
Gaber, John. 1994. "Manhattan's 14th Street Vendors' Market: Informal Street Peddlers' Complementary Relationship with New York City's Economy." *Urban Anthropology* 23, no. 4: 373–408.
Gallie, Duncan and Serge Paugam (eds.). 2000. *Welfare Regimes and the Experience of Unemployment in Europe*. Oxford: Oxford University Press.

Gans, Herbert J. 1965. *The Urban Villagers: Group and Class in the Life of Italian-Americans*. New York: Free Press, New edition, 1982.

Gans, Herbert J. 1967. *The Levittowners: How People Live and Politics in Suburbia*. New York: Columbia University Press.

Gans, Herbert J. 1995. *The War against the Poor. The Underclass and Antipoverty Policy*. New York: Basic Books.

Gardner, Carol Brooks. 1995. *Passing By: Gender and Public Harassment*. Berkeley: University of California Press.

Garey, Anita, Rosanna Hertz, and Margaret K. Nelson (eds.). 2014. *Open to Disruption: Time and Craft in the Practice of Slow Sociology*. Nashville: Vanderbilt University Press.

Garfinkel, Harold. 1967. *Studies in Ethnomethodology*. Englewood Cliffs, NJ: Prentice-Hall. Traduction: *Recherches en ethnométhodologie*, PUF, 2020.

Garson, Barbara. 1988. *The Electronic Sweatshop: How Computers are Transforming the Office of the Future into the Factory of the Past*. New York: Simon & Schuster.

Geertz, Clifford. 1972. "Deep Play: Notes on the Balinese Cockfight." *Daedalus* 101, no. 1: 1–37.

Geertz, Clifford. 1973. "Thick Description: Toward an Interpretive Theory of Culture." Pp. 3–30 in *The Interpretation of Cultures*. New York: Basic Books.

Geertz, Clifford. 1974. "'From the Native's Point Of View': On The Nature of Anthropological Understanding." *Bulletin of the American Academy of Arts and Sciences* 28, no. 1: 26–45.

Geertz, Clifford. 1980. *Negara: The Theatre State in Nineteenth-Century Bali*. Princeton, NJ: Princeton University Press.

Geurts, Kathryn. 2003. *Culture and the Senses: Bodily Ways of Knowing in an African Community*. Berkeley: University of California Press.

Gilbert, Alan. 2007. "The Return of the Slum: Does Language Matter?" *International Journal of Urban and Regional Research* 31, no. 4: 697–713.

Gilens, Martin. 1999. *Why Americans Hate Welfare: Race, Media, and the Politics of Anti-Poverty Policy*. Chicago: University of Chicago Press.

Gill, Nick and Jo Hynes. 2021. "Courtwatching: Visibility, Publicness, Witnessing, and Embodiment in Legal Activism." *Area* 53, no. 4: 569–576.

Ginzburg, Carlo. [1976] 1980. *The Cheese and the Worms: The Cosmos of a Sixteenth-Century Miller*. Baltimore: Johns Hopkins University Press.

Glaeser, Andreas. 2000. *Divided in Unity: Identity, Germany, and the Berlin Police*. Chicago: University of Chicago Press.

Glaser, Barney G. and Anselm L. Strauss. 1967. *The Discovery of Grounded Theory: Strategies for Qualitative Research*. Chicago: Aldine.

Goffman, Erving. 1959. *The Presentation of Self in Everyday Life*. New York: Anchor.

Goffman, Erving. 1959. "The Moral Career of the Mental Patient." *Psychiatry* 22, no. 2: 123–142. Reprinted in *Asylums: Essays on the Social Condition of Mental Patients and Other Inmates* (1961).

Goffman, Erving. 1961. *Encounters: Two Studies in the Sociology of Interaction*. Indianapolis: Bobs-Merrill.

Goffman, Erving. 1967. "Where the Action Is." Pp. 149–270 in *Interaction Rituals: Essays on Face-to-Face Behavior*. New York: Pantheon.

Goffman, Erving. 1989. "On Fieldwork." *Journal of Contemporary Ethnography* 18, no. 2: 123–132.

Goffman, Alice. 2014. *On the Run: Fugitive Life in an American City*. Chicago: University of Chicago Press; New York: Picador, 2015.

González de la Rocha, Mercedes. 1994. *The Resources of Poverty: Women and Survival in a Mexican City*. Cambridge, MA: Blackwell.

Gordon, Linda. 1994. *Pitied But Not Entitled: Single Mothers and the History of Welfare 1890–1935*. New York: Free Press.
Gottlieb, Peter. 1997. *Making Their Own Way: Southern Blacks' Migration to Pittsburgh, 1916–30*. Urbana: University of Illinois Press.
Gouldner, Alvin. 1973. "The Sociologist as Partisan: Sociology and the Welfare State." Pp. 27–68 in *For Sociology*. New York: Basic Books.
Gowan, Teresa. 2009. "New Hobos or Neo-Romantic Fantasy? Urban Ethnography beyond the Neoliberal Disconnect." *Qualitative Sociology* 32, no. 3: 231–257.
Gowan, Teresa. 2010. *Hobos, Hustlers, and Backsliders: Homeless in San Francisco*. Minneapolis: University of Minnesota Press.
Greek, Cecil E. 1992. *The Religious Roots of American Sociology*. New York: Garland.
Greenberg, Cheryl Lynn. 1991. *Or Does It Explode? Black Harlem During the Great Depression*. New York: Oxford University Press.
Greenberger, Ellen and Laurence Steinberg. 1986. *When Teenagers Work: The Psychological and Social Costs of Adolescent Employment*. New York: Basic Books.
Greene, Judith A. 1999. "Zero Tolerance: A Case Study of Police Policies and Practices in New York City." *Crime and Delinquency* 45, no. 2: 171–187.
Gregory, Steven. 1999. *Black Corona: Race and the Politics of Place in an Urban Community*. Princeton, NJ: Princeton University Press, 1999.
Guillory, Monique and Richard C. Green (eds.). 1998. *Soul: Black Power, Politics, and Pleasure*. New York: NYU Press.
Gusterson, Hugh. 1996. *Nuclear Rites: A Weapons Laboratory at the End of the Cold War*. Berkeley: University of California Press.
Gwaltney, John Langston. 1980. *Drylongso: A Self-Portrait of Black America*. New York: Vintage.
Habermas, Jürgen. [1968] 1979. *Connaissance et intérêt*. Paris: Gallimard.
Hagan, John and Bill McCarthy. 1999. *Mean Streets: Youth Crime and Homelessness*. New York: Cambridge University Press.
Hagedorn, John M. 1998. "Gang Violence in the Postindustrial Era." Pp. 365–419 in Michael Tonry and Mark H. Moore (eds.), *Youth Violence*. Chicago: University of Chicago Press.
Hammersley, Martin and Paul Atkinson. 2019. *Ethnography: Principles in Practice*. London: Routledge.
Handler, Joel F., and Yeheskel Hasenfeld. 1997. *We the Poor: Work, Poverty and Welfare*. New Haven, CT: Yale University Press.
Hannerz, Ulf. 1969. *Soulside: Inquiries into Ghetto Culture and Community*. New York: Columbia University Press.
Hannerz, Ulf. 1974. "Research in the Black Ghetto: A Review of the Sixties." *Journal of Asian and African Studies* 9, no. 3/4: 139–159.
Hannerz, Ulf. 1980. *Exploring the City*. New York: Columbia University Press.
Hannerz, Ulf. 2004. *Foreign News: Exploring the World of Foreign Correspondents*. Chicago: University of Chicago Press.
Hanson, Rebecca and Patricia Richards. 2019. *Harassed: Gender, Bodies, and Ethnographic Research*. Berkeley: University of California Press.
Harcourt, Bernard. 1998. "Reflecting on the Subject: A Critique of the Social Influence Conception of Deterrence, the Broken Windows Theory, and Order-Maintenance Policing NewYork–Style." *Michigan Law Review* 97, no. 2 (November): 291–389.
Harcourt, Bernard E. 2001. *Illusions of Order: The False Promise of Broken Windows Policing*. Cambridge, MA: Harvard University Press.

Harcourt, Bernard E. and Jens Ludwig. 2006. "Broken Windows: New Evidence from New York City and a Five-City Social Experiment." *University of Chicago Law Review* 73: 271–320.
Harper, Douglas. 1982. *Good Company: A Tramp Life.* Chicago: University of Chicago Press.
Harper, Douglas. 1987. *Working Knowledge: Skill and Community in a Small Shop.* Chicago: University of Chicago Press.
Hasenfeld, Yeheskel. 1972. "People Processing Organizations: An Exchange Approach." *American Sociological Review* 37, no. 3: 256–263.
Hays, Sharon. 2003. *Flat Broke with Children: Women in the Age of Welfare Reform.* New York: Oxford University Press.
Hedström, Peter and Peter S. Bearman (eds.). 2009. *The Oxford Handbook of Analytical Sociology.* Oxford: Oxford University Press.
Herbert, Steve. 2000. "For Ethnography." *Progress in Human Geography* 24, no. 4: 550–568.
Herzfeld, Michael. 2009. "The Cultural Politics of Gesture: Reflections on the Embodiment of Ethnographic Practice." *Ethnography* 10, no. 2: 131–152.
Heumann, Milton. 1977. *Plea Bargaining: The Experiences of Prosecutors, Judges, and Defense Attorneys.* Chicago: University of Chicago Press.
Higginbotham, Evelyn Brooks. 1992. "African-American Women's History and the Metalanguage of Race." *Signs: Journal of Women in Culture and Society* 17, no. 2: 251–274.
Higginbotham, Evelyn Brooks. 1994. *Righteous Discontent: The Women's Movement in the Black Baptist Church, 1880–1920.* Cambridge: Harvard University Press, 1994.
Hirsch, Arnold R. 1983. *Making the Second Ghetto: Race and Housing in Chicago 1940–1960.* 2nd edition. New York: Cambridge University Press, 2009.
Hoang, Kimberly Kay. 2015. *Dealing in Desire. Asian Ascendancy, Western Decline, and the Hidden Currencies of Global Sex Work.* Berkeley: University of California Press.
Hoang, Kimberly Kay. 2018. "Gendering Carnal Ethnography: A Queer Reception." Pp. 230–246 in D'Lane Compton, Tey Meadow, and Kristen Schilt (eds.), *Other, Please Specify: Queer Methods in Sociology.* Berkeley: University of California Press.
Hoang, Kimberly Kay. 2022. *Spiderweb Capitalism: How Global Elites Exploit Frontier Markets.* Princeton, NJ: Princeton University Press.
Hochschild, Arlie Russell. 1973. *The Unexpected Community: Portrait of an Old-Age Culture.* Englewood Cliffs, NJ: Prentice-Hall.
Hochschild, Arlie with Anne Machung. 1989. *The Second Shift: Working Families and the Revolution at Home.* New York: Penguin.
Holmqvist, Mikael. 2017. *Leader Communities: The Consecration of Elites in Djursholm.* New York: Columbia University Press.
Holzer, Harry. 1996. *What Employers Want.* New York: Russell Sage Foundation.
Howes, David (ed.). 2005. *Empire of the Senses: The Sensual Culture Reader.* New York: Routledge.
Hughes, Everett C. 1971. *The Sociological Eye: Selected Papers.* Edited by David Riesman and Howard S. Becker. New Brunswick, NJ: Transaction; reprint Routledge, 2017.
Hughes, Everett C. 1971. "Principle and Rationalization in Race Relations." Pp. 212–219 in *The Sociological Eye.* New Brunswick, NJ: Transaction Press.
Humphreys, Laud. 1970. *Tearoom Trade: Impersonal Sex in Public Places.* New Brunswick, NJ: Transaction Publishers.
Hunt, Alan. 2003. "From Moral Science to Moral Regulation: Social Theory's Encounter with the Moral Domain." Pp. 364–382 in Gerard Delanty and Engin F. Isin (eds.), *Handbook of Historical Sociology.* London: SAGE.
Huq, Aziz Z. 2016. "The Consequences of Disparate Policing: Evaluating Stop and Frisk as a Modality of Urban Policing." *Minnesota Law Review* 101: 2397–2481.

Hyra, Derek S. 2012. "Conceptualizing the New Urban Renewal: Comparing the Past to the Present." *Urban Affairs Review* 48, no. 4: 498–527.
Irwin, John. 1973. "Surfing: The Natural History of an Urban Scene." *Urban Life and Culture* 2, no. 2: 131–160.
Irwin, John. 1980. *The Jail: Managing the Underclass*. Berkeley: University of California Press.
Itzigsohn, José and Karida L. Brown. 2020. *The Sociology of W.E.B. Du Bois: Racialized Modernity and the Global Color Line*. New York: NYU Press.
Jackson, John L. 2001. *Harlemworld: Doing Race and Class in Contemporary Black America*. Chicago: University of Chicago Press.
Jackson, Michael. 2000. *At Home in the World*. Durham, NC: Duke University Press.
Jacobs, Jane. 1961. *The Death and Life of Great American Cities*. New York: Vintage, 1992.
Jahoda, Marie, Paul F. Lazarsfeld, and Hans Zeisel. [1933] 2017 *Marienthal: The Sociography of an Unemployed Community*. London: Routledge.
Jay, Robert. 1986. *The Nazi Doctors: Medical Killing and the Psychology of Genocide*. New York: Basic Books.
Jeffers, Camille. 1967. *Living Poor: A Participant Observer Study of Priorities and Choices*. Ann Arbor: Ann Arbor Publishers.
Joanes, Ana. 1999. "Does the New York City Police Department Deserve Credit for the Decline in New York City's Homicide Rates? A Cross-City Comparison of Policing Strategies and Homicide Rates." *Columbia Journal of Law and Social Problems* 33: 265–318.
Jencks, Christopher and Paul Peterson (eds.). 1991. *The Urban Underclass*. Washington: The Brookings Institution.
Jessor, Richard, Ann Colby, and Richard A. Shweder (eds.). 1996. *Ethnography and Human Development: Context and Meaning in Human Inquiry*. Chicago: University of Chicago Press.
Joas, Hans. 1996. *The Creativity of Action*. Chicago: University of Chicago Press.
Jones, Jacqueline. 1998. *American Work: Four Centuries of Black and White Labor*. New York: W.W. Norton.
Jones, Yvonne V. 1988. "Street Peddlers as Entrepreneurs: Economic Adaptation to an Urban Area." *Urban Anthropology* 17, nos. 2/3: 143–170.
Jounin, Nicolas. 2008. *Chantier interdit au public: Enquête parmi les travailleurs du bâtiment*. Paris: La Découverte.
Kaplan, Elaine Bell. 1997. *Not Our Kind of Girl: Unraveling the Myths of Black Teenage Motherhood*. Berkeley: University of California Press.
Katz, Jack. 1983. "A Theory of Qualitative Methodology: The Social System of Analytical Fieldwork." Pp. 127–148 in Robert Emerson (ed.), *Contemporary Field Research*. Prospect Heights, IL: Waveland Press.
Katz, Jack. 1989. *Seductions of Crime: On the Moral and Sensual Attractions of Doing Evil*. New York: Basic Books.
Katz, Jack. 1997. "Ethnography's Warrants." *Sociological Methods and Research* 25, no. 4: 391–423.
Katz, Jack. 2001. "Analytic Induction." Pp. 480–484 in Neil J. Smelser and Paul B. Baltes (eds.), *International Encyclopedia of the Social and Behavioral Sciences*. Oxford: Elsevier.
Katz, Michael B. (ed.). 1993. *The "Underclass" Debate: Views from History*. Princeton, NJ: Princeton University Press.
Katz, Michael B. [1986] 1996. *In the Shadow of the Poorhouse: A Social History of Welfare in America*. New York: Basic Books.
Katz, Michael B. 2013. *The Undeserving Poor: America's Enduring Confrontation with Poverty*. New York: Oxford University Press.

Keil, Charles. 1966. *Urban Blues*. Chicago: University of Chicago Press, 1991.
Kelling, George L. and James Q. Wilson. 1982. "Broken windows." *Atlantic Monthly* 249, no. 3: 29–38.
Kerner Commission. [1968]. 1989. *The Kerner Report: The 1968 Report of the National Advisory Commission on Civil Disorders*. New York: Pantheon.
Khan, Shamus Rahman. 2010. *Privilege*. Princeton, NJ: Princeton University Press, 2010.
Kochman, Thomas (ed.). 1972. *Rappin' and Stylin' Out: Communication in Urban Black America*. Urbana: University of Illinois Press.
Kohler-Hausmann, Issa. 2018. *Misdemeanorland: Criminal Courts and Social Control in an Age of Broken Windows Policing*. Princeton, NJ: Princeton University Press.
Kotlowitz, Alex. 1991. *There Are No Children Here*. Garden City, NJ: Doubleday.
Koyré Alexandre. 1973. *Études d'histoire de la pensée scientifique*. Paris: Gallimard.
Ladner, Joyce. 1971. *Tomorrow's Tomorrow: The Black Woman*. Lincoln: University of Nebraska Press, 1995.
Ladner, Joyce A. (ed.). 1973. *The Death of White Sociology: Essays on Race and Culture*. Baltimore: Black Classic Press, 1998.
Laé, Jean-François and Numa Murard. 1985. *L'Argent des pauvres: La vie quotidienne en cité de transit*. Paris: Editions du Seuil.
Lamont, Michèle. 2000. *The Dignity of Working Men: Morality and the Boundaries of Race, Class and Immigration*. Cambridge, MA: Harvard University Press.
Lanzarini, Catherine. 2000. *Survivre dans le monde sous-prolétaire*. Paris: PUF.
Lara-Millán, Armando. 2021. *Redistributing the Poor: Jails, Hospitals, and the Crisis of Law and Fiscal Austerity*. New York: Oxford University Press.
Latour, Bruno. 2007. *Reassembling the Social: An Introduction to Actor-Network-Theory*. New York: Oxford University Press.
Lebaron, Frédéric. 2016. "Les élites européennes comme champ(s)." *Cultures & conflits* 102: 121–147.
Lecourt, Dominique. [1969] 2002. *L'épistémologie historique de Gaston Bachelard*. Paris: Vrin.
Leidner, Robin. 1993. *Fast Food, Fast Talk: Service Work and the Routinization of Everyday Life*. Berkeley: University of California Press.
Leiris, Michel. [1934] 2014. *L'âge d'homme, précédé de L'Afrique fantôme*. Paris: Gallimard.
Lemann, Nicolas. 1986. *The Promised Land: The Great Black Migration and How it Changed America*. New York: Knopf.
Lentacker, Antoine. 2010. *La Science des institutions impures. Bourdieu critique de Lévi-Strauss*. Paris: Raisons d'Agir Éditions.
Lepoutre, David. 1997. *Cœur de banlieue. Codes, rites et langages*. Paris: Flammarion.
Levy, Peter B. 2018. *The Great Uprising: Race Riots in Urban America during the 1960s*. New York: Cambridge University Press.
Lewis, David Levering. 1981. *When Harlem was in Vogue*. New York: Penguin Books.
Lewis, Oscar. [1961] 2011. *The Children of Sanchez: Autobiography of a Mexican Family*. New York: Vintage.
Lewis, Oscar. 1966. *La Vida: A Puerto Rican Family in the Culture of Poverty*. New York: Random House.
Lewis, Oscar. 1966. "The Culture of Poverty." *Scientific American* 215, no. 4: 19–25.
Le Wita, Béatrix. 1988. *Ni vue, ni connue: Approche ethnographique de la culture bourgeoise*. Paris: Éditions de la MSH.
Liebow, Elliott. 1967. *Tally's Corner: A Study of Negro Streetcorner Men*. Boston, MA: Little, Brown. Expanded edition, Rowman & Littlefield, 2003.
Liebow, Elliot. 1993. *Tell Them Who I Am: The Lives of Homeless Women*. New York: Simon and Schuster.

Light, Ivan. 1977. "Numbers Gambling among Blacks: A Financial Institution." *American Sociological Review* 42, no. 6: 892–904.
Lignier, Wilfried and Julie Pagis. 2017. *L'enfance de l'ordre. Comment les enfants perçoivent le monde social*. Paris: Seuil.
Lindner, Rolf. 1996. *The Reportage of Urban Culture: Robert Park and the Chicago School*. Cambridge, UK: Cambridge University Press.
Lipsitz, George. 1995. *A Life in the Struggle. Ivory Perry and the Culture of Opposition*. Philadelphia: Temple University Press.
Lipsky, Michael. 1980. *Street-Level Bureaucracy: Dilemmas of the Individual in Public Service*. New York: Russell Sage Foundation.
Longo, Matthew and Bernardo Zacka. 2019. "Political Theory in an Ethnographic Key." *American Political Science Review* 113, no. 4: 1066–1070.
Lopez-Aguado, Patrick. 2018. *Stick Together and Come Back Home: Racial Sorting and the Spillover of Carceral Identity*. Berkeley: University of California Press.
Lorber, Judith and Lisa Jean Moore (eds.). 2010. *Gendered Bodies: Feminist Perspectives*. New York: Oxford University Press.
Lubet, Steven. 2018. *Interrogating Ethnography: Why Evidence Matters*. New York: Oxford University Press.
Lüdtke, Alf (ed.). 1995. *The History of Everyday Life: Reconstructing Historical Experiences and Ways of Life*. Princeton, NJ: Princeton University Press.
Lynd, Robert S. and Helen Merrell Lynd. 1929. *Middletown: A Study in Contemporary American Culture*. New York: Harcourt, Brace.
Lynd, Robert S. and Helen Merrell Lynd. 1937. *Middletown in Transition: A Study in Cultural Conflicts*. New York: Harcourt, Brace and Company.
MacLeod, Jay. 1987, 1995, 2011, 2018. *Ain't No Makin' It: Aspirations and Attainment in a Low-Income Neighborhood*. New York: Routledge.
Maget, Marcel. 1953. *Guide d'étude directe des comportements culturels*. Paris: Civilisations du Sud, CNRS.
Maines, David R. 1977. "Social Organization and Social Structure in Symbolic Interactionist Thought." *Annual Review of Sociology* 3: 235–259.
Majors, Richard and Janet Billson. 1992. *Cool Pose: The Dilemmas of Black Manhood in America*. Lanham, MD: Lexington Books.
Malinowski, Bronislaw. [1922] 2013. *Argonauts of the Western Pacific: An Account of Native Enterprise and Adventure in the Archipelagoes of Melanesian New Guinea*. New York: Routledge.
Maple, Jack and Chris Mitchell. 1999. *The Crime Fighter: How You Can Make Your Community Crime-Free*. New York: Broadway Books.
Marcus, George. 1998. *Ethnography through Thick and Thin*. Princeton, NJ: Princeton University Press.
Maresca, Sylvain. 1983. *Les dirigeants paysans*. Paris: Minuit.
Marquez, Patrícia. 2000. *The Street is my Home: Youth and Violence in Caracas*. New Haven, CT: Yale University Press.
Mauger, Gérard. 2006. *Les bandes, le milieu et la bohème populaire: Études de sociologie de la déviance des jeunes des classes populaires (1975–2005)*. Paris: Belin.
Mauss, Marcel, and Henri Beuchat. [1904] 1950 "Essai sur les variations saisonnières des sociétés Eskimos: Étude de morphologie sociale." Pp. 389–397 in Marcel Mauss, *Sociologie et Anthropologie*. Paris: PUF.
Maynard, Douglas W. and Steven E. Clayman. 1991. "The Diversity of Ethnomethodology." *Annual Review of Sociology* 17: 385–418.

Mayne, Alan and Susan Lawrence. 1999. "Ethnographies of Place: A New Urban Research Agenda." *Urban History* 26, no. 3: 325–348.
McCord, William. 1969. *Life Styles in the Black Ghetto*. New York: W.W. Norton.
McKee, James B. 1993. *Sociology and the Race Problem: The Failure of a Perspective*. Urbana: University of Illinois Press, 1993.
McRoberts, Omar M. 2005. *Streets of Glory: Church and Community in a Black Urban Neighborhood*. Chicago: University of Chicago Press.
Mears, Ashley. 2011. *Pricing Beauty: The Making of a Fashion Model*. Berkeley: University of California Press.
Mears, Ashley. 2020. *Very Important People: Status and Beauty in the Global Party Circuit*. Princeton, NJ: Princeton University Press.
Merton, Robert K. 1968. *Social Theory and Social Structure*. Enlarged Edition. New York: Free Press.
Merton, Robert K. 1984. "The Fallacy of the Latest Word: The Case of 'Pietism and Science.'" *American Journal of Sociology* 89, no. 5: 1091–1121.
Miller, Eleanor M. 1987. *Street Woman*. Philadelphia: Temple University Press.
Miller, Reuben Jonathan. 2021. *Halfway Home: Race, Punishment, and the Afterlife of Mass Incarceration*. Boston, MA: Little, Brown.
Mintz, Sidney W. 2000. "Sows' Ears and Silver Linings: A Backward Look at Ethnography." *Current Anthropology* 41, no. 2 (April): 169–189.
Moffatt, Michael. 1992. "Ethnographic Writing about American Culture." *Annual Review of Anthropology* 21: 205–229.
Monroe, Sylvester and Peter Goldman. 1988. *Brothers: Black and Poor—A True Story of Courage and Survival*. New York: William Morrow.
Moore, William Jr. 1969. *The Vertical Ghetto: Everyday Life in an Urban Project*. New York: Random House.
Morales, Alfonso. 1997. "Uncertainty and the Organization of Street Vending Businesses." *The International Journal of Sociology and Social Policy* 17, nos. 3/4: 191–212.
Murphy, Alexandra K., Colin Jerolmack, and DeAnna Smith. 2021. "Ethnography, Data Transparency, and the Information Age." *Annual Review of Sociology* 47: 41–61.
Morris, Aldon. 2015. *The Scholar Denied: W.E.B. Du Bois and the Birth of Modern Sociology*. Berkeley: University of California Press.
Newman, Katherine S. 1983. *Law and Economic Organization: A Comparative Study of Preindustrial Societies*. New York: Cambridge University Press.
Newman, Katherine S. 1988. *Falling from Grace: Downward Mobility in the Age of Affluence*. New York: Free Press. Republication, University of California Press, 1999.
Newman, Katherine S. 1993. *Declining Fortunes: The Withering of the American Dream*. New York: Basic.
Newman, Katherine. 1999. *No Shame in my Game: The Working Poor in the Inner City*. New York: Russell Sage Foundation and Knopf.
Newman, Katherine. 2002. "No Shame: The View from the Left Bank." *American Journal of Sociology* 107, no. 6: 1577–1599.
Newport, Frank. 2018. "Americans Big on Living in the Country." Gallup poll, December 7 (www.news.gallup.com).
Oberfield, Zachary W. 2014. *Becoming Bureaucrats: Socialization at the Front Lines of Government Service*. Philadelphia: University of Pennsylvania Press.
O'Connor, Alice. 2001. *Poverty Knowledge: Social Science, Social Policy, and the Poor in Twentieth-Century U.S. History*. Princeton, NJ: Princeton University Press.
Ollion, Étienne. 2021. *Les candidats: Novices et professionnels en politique*. Paris: PUF.

Ortner, Sherry (ed.). 1999. *After Culture: Geertz and Beyond*. Berkeley: University of California Press.
Pachirat, Timothy. 2011. *Every Twelve Seconds: Industrialized Slaughter and the Politics of Sight*. New Haven, CT: Yale University Press.
Pachirat, Timothy. 2017. *Among Wolves: Ethnography and the Immersive Study of Power*. New York: Routledge.
Padilla, Felix M. 1992. *The Gang as an American Enterprise*. New Brunswick, NJ: Rutgers University Press.
Paik, Leslie. 2022. *Trapped in a Maze: How Social Control Institutions Drive Family Poverty and Inequality*. Berkeley: University of California Press.
Park, Robert E. 1921. "Sociology and the Social Sciences: The Social Organism and the Collective Mind." *American Journal of Sociology* 27, no. 1: 1–21.
Park, Robert E. and Ernest Burgess. 1925. *The City*. Chicago: University of Chicago Press.
Parvez, Z. Fareen. 2017. *Politicizing Islam: The Islamic Revival in France and India*. New York: Oxford University Press.
Passeron, Jean-Claude and Claude Grignon. 1989. *Le savant et le populaire: Misérabilisme et populisme en sociologie et en littérature*. Paris: Seuil.
Patterson, James T. 2000. *America's Struggle against Poverty in the Twentieth Century*. Cambridge, MA: Harvard University Press.
Patterson, James T. 2010. *Freedom Is Not Enough: The Moynihan Report and America's Struggle over Black Family Life—From LBJ to Obama*. New York: Basic Books.
Patterson, Orlando. 1998. "Broken Bloodlines." Pp. 1–167 in *Rituals of Blood: Consequences of Slavery in Two American Centuries*. New York: Basic/Civitas Books.
Pattillo, Mary. 1999. *Black Picket Fences: Privilege and Peril among the Black Middle Class*. Chicago: University of Chicago Press, 2013.
Pattillo, Mary. 2010. *Black on the Block: The Politics of Race and Class in the City*. Chicago: University of Chicago Press.
Peck, Jamie and Nik Theodore. 2001. "Contingent Chicago: Restructuring the Spaces of Temporary Labor." *International Journal of Urban and Regional Research* 25, no. 3: 471–496.
Peirano, Mariza G.S. 1998. "When Anthropology is at Home: The Different Contexts of a Single Discipline." *Annual Review of Anthropology* 27: 105–128.
Peretz, Henri. 2004. "The Making of *Black Metropolis*." *The Annals of the American Academy of Political and Social Science* 595, no. 1: 168–175.
Perinbanayagam, Robert S. 1974. "The Definition of the Situation: An Analysis of the Ethnomethodological and Dramaturgical View." *Sociological Quarterly* 15, no. 4: 521–541.
Perlstein, Rick. 2008. *Nixonland: The Rise of a President and the Fracturing of America*. New York: Simon & Schuster.
Phillips, Kimberley Louise. 1999. *AlabamaNorth: African-American Migrants, Community, and Working-Class Activism in Cleveland, 1915–45*. Urbana: University of Illinois Press.
Pialoux, Michel. 2019. *Le Temps d'écouter. Enquêtes sur les métamorphoses de la classe ouvrière*. Paris: Raisons d'Agir Éditions.
Pinçon, Michel and Monique Pinçon-Charlot. 1996. *Grandes Fortunes. Dynasties familiales et formes de richesse en France*. Paris: Payot.
Pinçon-Charlot, Monique and Michel Pinçon. 2005. *Voyage en grande bourgeoisie: Journal d'enquête*. Paris: PUF.
Pitts-Taylor, Victoria. 2015. "A Feminist Carnal Sociology? Embodiment in Sociology, Feminism, and Naturalized Philosophy." *Qualitative Sociology* 38, no. 1: 19–25.
Portes, Alejandro and Alex Stepick. 1993. *City on the Edge: The Transformation of Miami*. Berkeley: University of California Press.

Portilla, Ana. 2016. "On the Run. *L'ethnographie en cavale?*" *Genèses* 102: 123–139.

Poupeau, Franck. 2021. *Altiplano: Fragments d'une révolution (Bolivie, 1999–2019)*. Paris: Raisons d'Agir Éditions.

Price, Janet and Margrit Shildrick (eds.). 1999. *Feminist Theory and the Body: A Reader*. New York: Routledge.

Prieur, Annick. 1998. *Mema's House, Mexico City: On Transvestites, Queens, and Machos*. Chicago: University of Chicago Press.

Quadagno, Jill. 1994. *The Color of Welfare: How Racism Undermined the War on Poverty*. New York: Oxford University Press.

Rainwater, Lee. 1970. *Behind Ghetto Walls: Black Families in a Federal Slum*. New York: Aldine.

Rainwater, Lee (ed.). 1970. *Soul: Black Experience*. New Brunswick, NJ: Transaction.

Rainwater, Lee. 1974. *What Money Buys: Inequality and the Social Meanings of Income*. New York: Basic Books.

Rainwater, Lee and Timothy M. Smeeding. 2003. *Poor Kids in a Rich Country: America's Children in Comparative Perspective*. New York: Russell Sage Foundation.

Ralph, Laurence. 2014. *Renegade Dreams: Living through Injury in Gangland Chicago*. Chicago: University of Chicago Press, 2014.

Reed, Christopher Robert. 2011. *The Rise of Chicago's Black Metropolis, 1920–1929*. Urbana: University of Illinois Press.

Reissman, Leonard. 1964. *The Urban Process: Cities in Industrial Societies*. Glencoe, IL: Free Press.

Remster, Brianna and Rory Kramer. 2018. "Race, Space, and Surveillance: Understanding the Relationship Between Criminal Justice Contact and Institutional Involvement." *Socius* 4: 1–6.

Rheinberger, Hans-Jörg. 2010. *Historicizing Ontology: An Essay*. Stanford, CA: Stanford University Press.

Rhynhart, Rebecca. 2022. *Data Release: Gun Violence Clearance Rates and Case Outcomes*. Philadelphia: Office of the Comptroller.

Rios, Victor M. 2011. *Punished: Policing the Lives of Black and Latino Boys*. New York: NYU Press.

Rios, Victor M. 2011. *Street Life: Poverty, Gangs, and a Ph. D*. Berkeley: Five Rivers Press.

Rios, Victor M. 2015. "Decolonizing the White Space in Urban Ethnography." *City & Community* 14, no. 3: 258–261.

Rios, Victor M., Nikita Carney, and Jasmine Kelekay. 2017. "Ethnographies of Race, Crime, and Justice: Toward a Sociological Double-Consciousness." *Annual Review of Sociology* 43: 493–513.

Rodman, Hyman. 1977. "Culture of Poverty: The Rise and Fall of a Concept." *The Sociological Review* 25, no. 4: 867–876.

Rojas, Fabio. 2010. *From Black Power to Black Studies: How a Radical Social Movement Became an Academic Discipline*. Baltimore: Johns Hopkins University Press.

Rollins, Judith. 1985. *Between Women: Domestics and their Employers*. Philadelphia: Temple University Press.

Rosette, Jason. 2000. *The Book Wars*. New York: Camerado (film available on VHS, 78 minutes).

Rosen, Eva. 2020. *The Voucher Promise: "Section 8" and the Fate of an American Neighborhood*. Princeton, NJ: Princeton University Press.

Rosen, Lawrence. 2006. *Law as Culture: An Invitation*. Princeton, NJ: Princeton University Press.

Ross, Dorothy. 1992. *The Origins of American Social Science*. New York: Cambridge University Press.

Rossi, Peter H. (ed.). 1970. *Ghetto Revolts*. New York: Routledge, 2019.
Royle, Tony and Brian Towers (eds.). 2002. *Labour Relations in the Global Fast Food Industry*. London: Routledge.
Sallaz, Jeff. 2009. *The Labor of Luck: Casino Capitalism in the United States and South Africa*. Berkeley: University of California Press.
Sallaz, Jeffrey J. 2018. "Is a Bourdieusian Ethnography Possible?" Pp. 481–502 in Tom Medvetz and Jeffrey J. Sallaz (eds.), *The Oxford Handbook of Pierre Bourdieu*. New York: Oxford University Press.
Saint Martin, Monique de. 1993. *L'espace de la noblesse*. Paris, Éditions Métailié.
Sampson, Robert J. and Stephen W. Raudenbush. 1998. "Systematic Social Observation of Public Spaces: A New Look at Disorder in Urban Neighborhoods." *American Journal of Sociology* 105-3 (November): 603–651.
Sánchez-Jankowski, Martín. 1991. *Islands in the Street: Gangs in Urban American Society*. Berkeley: University of California Press.
Sánchez-Jankowski, Martín. 2008. *Cracks in the Pavement: Social Change and Resilience in Poor Neighborhoods*. Berkeley: University of California Press.
Sanjek, Roger (ed.). 1990. *Fieldnotes: The Makings of Anthropology*. Ithaca, NY: Cornell University Press, 2019.
Sanjek, Roger. 2000. *The Future of Us All: Race and Neighborhood Politics in New York City*. Ithaca, NY: Cornell University Press.
Sayad, Abdelmalek with the collaboration of Éliane Dupuy. 1995. *Un Nanterre algérien, terre de bidonvilles*. Paris: Autrement.
Sayad, Abdelmalek. 2006. *L'Immigration ou les paradoxes de l'altérité*. Vol. 1, *L'illusion du provisoire, Les enfants illégitimes*. Paris: Raisons d'Agir Éditions.
Sayad, Abdelmalek. 2006. *L'Immigration ou les paradoxes de l'altérité*. Vol. 2: *Les enfants illégitimes*. Paris: Raisons d'Agir Éditions.
Sayad, Abdelmalek. 2014. *L'Immigration ou les paradoxes de l'altérité*. Vol. 3: *La fabrication des identités culturelle*. Paris: Raisons d'Agir Éditions.
Sayer, Andrew. 2005. *The Moral Significance of Class*. New York: Cambridge University Press.
Schatz, Edward (ed.). 2013. *Political Ethnography: What Immersion Contributes to the Study of Power*. Chicago: University of Chicago Press.
Scheper-Hughes, Nancy. 1992. *Death without Weeping: The Violence of Everyday Life in Brazil*. Berkeley: University of California Press.
Scheper-Hughes, Nancy. 2000. "Ire in Ireland." *Ethnography* 1, no. 1: 117–140.
Schiffrin, André. 2000. *The Business of Books: How the International Conglomerates Took Over Publishing and Changed the Way We Read*. London: Verso.
Schulz, David. 1969. *Coming Up Black: Patterns of Ghetto Socialization*. Englewood-Cliffs, NJ: Prentice-Hall.
Schwartz, Olivier. 1990. *Le monde privé des ouvriers: Hommes et femmes du Nord*. Paris: PUF.
Scott, Daryl Michael. 1997. *Contempt and Pity: Social Policy and the Image of the Damaged Black Psyche, 1880–1996*. Chapel Hill: University of Carolina Press.
Seim, Josh. 2020. *Bandage, Sort, and Hustle: Ambulance Crews on the Front Lines of Urban Suffering*. Berkeley: University of California Press.
Seim, Josh. 2021. "Participant Observation, Observant Participation, and Hybrid Ethnography." *Sociological Methods & Research* 50121-152.
Sexton, Patricia Cayo. 1965. *Spanish Harlem: An Anatomy of Poverty*. New York: Harper & Row.
Shah, Alpa. 2017. "Ethnography? Participant Observation, a Potentially Revolutionary Praxis." *HAU Journal of Ethnograhic Theory* 7, no. 1: 45–59.

References

Shah, Alpa. 2019. *Nightmarch: Among India's Revolutionary Guerrillas*. Chicago: University of Chicago Press.

Shapiro, Lawrence. 2019. *Embodied Cognition*. 2nd edition. New York: Routledge.

Sharff, Jagna Wojcicka. 1998. *King Kong on 4th Street: Families and the Violence of Poverty on the Lower East Side*. Boulder, CO: Westview Press.

Shaw, Clifford R and Henry D. McKay. 1942. *Juvenile Delinquency and Urban Areas*. Chicago: University of Chicago Press.

Shils, Edward. 1965. ""Charisma, Order, and Status." *American Sociological Review* 30, no. 2: 199–213.

Schotté, Manuel. 2012. *La Construction du "talent". Sociologie de la domination des coureurs marocains*. Paris: Raisons d'Agir Éditions.

Simmons, Erica S. and Nicholas Rush Smith. 2019. "The Case for Comparative Ethnography." *Comparative Politics* 51, no. 3: 341–359.

Skogan, Wesley. 1990. *Disorder and Decline: Crime and the Spiral of Decay in American Neighborhoods*. Berkeley: University of California Press.

Small, Mario Luis. 2004. *Villa Victoria: The Transformation of Social Capital in a Boston Barrio*. Chicago: University of Chicago Press.

Small, Mario Luis and Jessica McCrory Calarco. 2002. *Qualitative Literacy: A Guide to Evaluating Ethnographic and Interview Research*. Berkeley: University of California Press.

Smith, Abbe. 2000. "Can You Be a Good Person and a Good Prosecutor?" *Georgetown Journal of Legal Ethics* 14: 355–401.

Snow, David A. and Leon Anderson. 1993. *Down on Their Luck: A Study of Homeless Street People*. Berkeley: University of California Press.

Sorignet, Pierre-Emmanuel. 2010. *Danser: Enquête dans les coulisses d'une vocation*. Paris: La Découverte.

Spradley, James P. 1970. *You Owe Yourself a Drunk: An Ethnography of Urban Nomads*. Boston: Little, Brown.

Stacey, Judith. 1999. "Ethnography Confronts the Global Village: A New Home for a New Century?" *Journal of Contemporary Ethnography* 28, no. 6: 687–697.

Stack, Carol B. 1974. *All Our Kin: Strategies for Survival in a Black Community*. New York: Harper & Row.

Stave, Bruce M. 1998. "A Conversation with Charles Tilly: Urban History And Urban Sociology." *Journal of Urban History* 24, no. 2: 184–225.

Stoller, Paul. 1996. "Spaces, Places, and Fields: The Politics of West African Trading in New York City's Informal Economy." *American Anthropologist* 98, no. 4: 776–788.

Strauss, Anselm L. 1978. "A Social World Perspective." *Studies in Symbolic Interaction* 1: 119–128.

Stuart, Forrest. 2016. *Down, Out, and Under Arrest: Policing and Everyday Life in Skid Row*. Chicago: University of Chicago Press.

Stuart, Forrest. 2020. *Ballad of the Bullet: Gangs, Drill Music, and the Power of Online Infamy*. Princeton, NJ: Princeton University Press.

Suaud, Charles. 1978. *La vocation: Conversion et reconversion des prêtres ruraux*. Paris: Minuit.

Sugrue, Thomas J. 1996. *The Origins of the Urban Crisis: Race and Inequality in Postwar Detroit*. Princeton, NJ: Princeton University Press, expanded edition, 2014.

Sullivan, Esther. 2018. *Manufactured Insecurity: Mobile Home Parks and Americans' Tenuous Right to Place*. Berkeley: University of California Press.

Sullivan, Teresa A., Elizabeth Warren, and Jay Lawrence Westbrook. 2000. *The Fragile Middle Class: Americans in Debt*. New Haven, CT: Yale University Press.

Sudnow, David. 1978. *Ways of the Hand: The Organization of Improvised Conduct*. Cambridge, MA: MIT Press, 1991.
Suttles, Gerald D. 1968. *The Social Order of the Slum: Ethnicity and Territory in the Inner City*. Chicago: The University of Chicago Press.
Suttles, Gerald D. 1972. *The Social Construction of Communities*. Chicago: University of Chicago Press.
Swedberg, Richard. 2016. "Can You Visualize Theory? On the Use of Visual Thinking in Theory Pictures, Theorizing Diagrams, and Visual Sketches." *Sociological Theory* 34, no. 3: 250–275.
Tannock, Stuart. 2001. *Youth at Work: The Unionized Fast-Food and Grocery Workplace*. Philadelphia: Temple University Press.
Tavory, Iddo. 2016. *Summoned: Identification and Religious Life in a Jewish Neighborhood*. Chicago: University of Chicago Press.
Tavory, Iddo and Stefan Timmermans. 2014. *Abductive Analysis: Theorizing Qualitative Research*. Chicago: University of Chicago Press.
Taylor, Keeanga-Yamahtta. 2021. *From #BlackLivesMatter to Black Liberation*. Preface by Angela Y. Davis. 2nd edition. Chicago: Haymarket Books.
Taylor, Ralph B. 2001. *Breaking Away from Broken Windows: Baltimore Neighborhoods and the Nationwide Fight Against Crime, Grime, Fear, and Decline*. Boulder, CO: Westview.
Thaman, Stephen (ed.). 2010. *World Plea Bargaining: Consensual Procedures and the Avoidance of the Full Criminal Trial*. Durham, NC: Carolina Academic Press.
Tilly, Chris. 1996. *Half a Job: Bad and Good Part-Time Jobs in a Changing Labor Market*. Philadelphia: Temple University Press.
Timmermans, Stefan and Iddo Tavory. 2012. "Theory Construction in Qualitative Research: From Grounded Theory to Abductive Analysis." *Sociological Theory* 30, no. 3: 167–186.
Timmermans, Stefan and Iddo Tavory. 2022. *Data Analysis in Qualitative Research: Theorizing with Abductive Analysis*. Chicago: University of Chicago Press.
Tissot, Sylvie. 2011. *De bons voisins. Enquête dans un quartier de la bourgeoisie progressiste*. Paris: Raisons d'Agir Éditions.
Thomas, Piri. [1967] 1991. *Down These Mean Streets*. New York: Vintage.
Thrasher, Frederic M. 1927. *The Gang: A Study of 1,313 Gangs in Chicago*. Chicago: University of Chicago Press, 2013.
Tolnay, Stewart E. 2003. "The African American 'Great Migration' and Beyond." *Annual Review of Sociology* 29: 209–232.
Topalov, Christian. 2008. "Sociologie d'un étiquetage scientifique: *Urban sociology*". *L'Année sociologique* 58: 203–234.
Topalov, Christian. 2015. *Histoires d'enquêtes: Londres, Paris, Chicago (1880–1930)*. Paris: Garnier.
Trotter, Joe William. 1985. *Black Milwaukee: The Making of an Industrial Proletariat, 1915–45*. Urbana: University of Illinois Press.
Trotter, Joe W. 1995. "African Americans in the City: The Industrial Era, 1900–1950." *Journal of Urban History* 21, no. 4: 438–457.
Truong, Fabien. 2017. *Loyautés radicales: L'islam et les "mauvais garçons" de la nation*. Paris: La Découverte.
Turco, Catherine. 2016. *The Conversational Firm: Rethinking Bureaucracy in the Age of Social Media*. New York: Columbia University Press.
Valentine, Bettylou. 1978. *Hustling and other Hard Work: Life Styles in the Ghetto*. New York: Free Press.
Varela, Francisco, Evan Thompson, and Eleanor Rosch. 1991. *The Embodied Mind: Cognitive Science and Human Experience*. Cambridge, MA: MIT Press.

Vaughan, Diane. 1996. *The Challenger Launch Decision: Risky Technology, Culture, and Deviance at NASA*. Chicago: University of Chicago Press.

Vaughan, Diane. 2009. "Analytic Ethnography." Pp. 688–711 in Peter Hedström and Peter Bearman (eds.), *The Oxford Handbook of Analytical Sociology*. Oxford: Oxford University Press.

Verdery, Katherine. 2018. *My Life as a Spy: Investigations in a Secret Police File*. Durham, NC: Duke University Press.

Vertesi, Janet. 2015. *Seeing like a Rover: How Robots, Teams, and Images Craft Knowledge of Mars*. Chicago: University of Chicago Press.

Vickerman, Milton. 1999. *Crosscurrents: West Indian Immigrants and Race*. New York: Oxford University Press.

Vidich, Arthur J. and Joseph Bensman. 1958. *Small Town in Mass Society: Class, Power, and Religion in a Rural Community*. Garden City, NY: Doubleday.

Villette, Michel. 1988. *L'homme qui croyait au management: Récit, suivi d'une brève mise en perspective historique*. Paris: Seuil.

Vitale, Alex S. 2008. *City of Disorder: How the Quality of Life Campaign Transformed New York Politics*. New York: NYU Press.

Vogel, Mary E. 2007. *Coercion to Compromise: Plea Bargaining, the Courts, and the Making of Political Authority*. New York: Oxford University Press.

Wacquant, Loïc. 1992. *Invitation to Reflexive Sociology*. Chicago: University of Chicago Press.

Wacquant, Loïc. 1993. "De la 'terre promise' au ghetto: La 'Grande Migration' noire américaine, 1916-1930." *Actes de la recherche en sciences sociales* 99: 43–51.

Wacquant, Loïc. 1993. "Désordre dans la ville." *Actes de la recherche en sciences sociales* 99: 79–91.

Wacquant, Loïc. 1996. "L'*underclass*' urbaine dans l'imaginaire social et scientifique américain." Pp. 248–262 in Serge Paugam (ed.), *L'exclusion: L'état des savoirs*. Paris: La Découverte.

Wacquant, Loïc. 2001. "Deadly Symbiosis: When Ghetto and Prison Meet and Mesh." *Punishment & Society* 3, no. 1: 95–134.

Wacquant, Loïc. 2002. *Corps et âme. Carnets ethnographiques d'un apprenti boxeur*. 2nd enlarged edition. Marseilles: Agone (English: *Body and Soul: Notebooks of an Apprentice Boxer*. Expanded anniversary edition, New York, Oxford University Press, 2022).

Wacquant, Loïc. 2002. "Scrutinizing the Street: Poverty, Morality, and the Pitfalls of Urban Ethnography." *American Journal of Sociology* 107, no. 6: 1468–1532.

Wacquant, Loïc. 2003. «"Lettre à propos de 'Scrutinizing the Street.'"» *Liens sociaux* 4 (April): 1–3.

Wacquant, Loïc. 2004. «Following Pierre Bourdieu into the Field.» *Ethnography* 5, no. 4: 387–414.

Wacquant, Loïc. 2005. «Les deux visages du ghetto.» *Actes de la recherche en sciences sociales* 160: 4–21.

Wacquant, Loïc. 2005. "Shadowboxing with Ethnographic Ghosts: A Rejoinder." *Symbolic Interaction* 28, no. 3: 441–447.

Wacquant, Loïc. 2006. *Parias urbains: Ghetto, banlieue, État*. Paris: La Découverte.

Wacquant, Loïc. 2008. *Urban Outcasts: A Comparative Sociology of Advanced Marginality*. Cambridge, UK: Polity Press.

Wacquant, Loïc. 2009. *Prisons of Poverty*. Minneapolis: University of Minnesota Press.

Wacquant, Loïc. 2009. *Punishing the Poor: The Neoliberal Government of Social Insecurity*. Durham, NC: Duke University Press.

Wacquant, Loïc. 2010. "Crafting the Neoliberal State: Workfare, Prisonfare, and Social Insecurity." *Sociological Forum* 25, no. 2: 197–220.

Wacquant, Loïc. 2010. "Designing Urban Seclusion in the 21st Century: The 2009 Roth-Symonds Lecture." *Perspecta* 43: 165–175.
Wacquant, Loïc. 2011. "Habitus as Topic and Tool: Reflections on Becoming a Prizefighter." *Qualitative Research in Psychology* 8, no. 1: 81–92.
Wacquant, Loïc. 2012. "A Janus-Faced Institution of Ethnoracial Closure: A Sociological Specification of the Ghetto." Pp. 1–31 in Ray Hutchison and Bruce Haynes (eds.), *The Ghetto: Contemporary Global Issues and Controversies*. Boulder, CO: Westview Press.
Wacquant, Loïc. 2014. "Marginality, Ethnicity and Penality in the Neo-Liberal City: An Analytic Cartography." *Ethnic and Racial Studies* 37, no. 10: 1687–1711.
Wacquant, Loïc. 2015. "For a Sociology of Flesh and Blood." *Qualitative Sociology* 38: 1–11.
Wacquant, Loïc. 2016. "Revisiting Territories of Relegation: Class, Ethnicity and State in the Making of Advanced Marginality." *Urban Studies* 53, no. 6: 1077–1088.
Wacquant, Loïc. 2022. *The Invention of the "Underclass": A Study in the Politics of Knowledge*. Cambridge, UK: Polity Press.
Wacquant, Loïc. 2022. *Body and Soul: Notebooks of an Apprentice Boxer*. New York: Oxford University Press, expanded anniversary edition.
Wacquant, Loïc. 2022. "Resolving the Trouble With 'Race.'" *New Left Review* 133: 67–88.
Wacquant, Loïc. 2023. *Bourdieu in the City: Challenging Urban Theory*. Cambridge, UK: Polity Press.
Wacquant, Loïc. 2023. "Carnal Concepts in Action." *Thesis Eleven* 181, no. 1: 111–144.
Wacquant, Loïc. 2024. *Racial Domination*. Cambridge: Polity Press.
Wacquant, Loïc. forthcoming. *The Two Faces of the Ghetto*. Cambridge: Polity Press.
Waldinger, Roger. 1996. *Still the Promised City? African-Americans and New Immigrants in Postindustrial New York*. Cambridge, MA: Harvard University Press.
Walker, Michael L. 2022. *Indefinite: Doing Time in Jail*. New York: Oxford University Press.
Wallraff, Günther. [1985] 1986. *Tête de Turc*. Paris: La Découverte, préface de Gilles Perrault.
Warner, W. Lloyd. 1963. *Yankee City, the One-Volume Abridged Edition*. New Haven, CT: Yale University Press.
Wasson, Christina. 2000. "Ethnography in the Field of Design." *Human Organization* 59, no. 4: 377–388.
Waters, Mary C. 1999. *Black Identities: West Indian Immigrant Dreams and American Realities*. Cambridge and New York: Harvard University Press and Russell Sage Foundation.
Waterston, Alisse. 1993. *Street Addicts in the Political Economy*. Philadelphia: Temple University Press.
Watkins-Hayes, Celeste. 2009. *The New Welfare Bureaucrats: Entanglements of Race, Class, and Policy Reform*. Chicago: University of Chicago Press.
Weaver, R. Kent. 2000. *Ending Welfare as we Know It*. Washington, DC: Brookings Institution Press.
Weber, Max. 1948. *From Max Weber: Essays in Sociology*. Edited by Hans Gerth and C.-Wright Mills. New York: Oxford University Press.
Weber, Max. [1904] 1949. "Objectivity in Social Science and Social Policy." in *The Methodology of the Social Sciences*, ed. 50–112. New York: Free Press.
Weber, Max. [1918–1920] 1978. *Economy and Society: Outline of Interpretive Sociology*. Berkeley: University of California Press.
Weber, Max. [1920] 2014. *La Domination*. Paris: La Découverte.
Wedeen, Lisa. 2010. "Reflections on Ethnographic Work in Political Science". *Annual Review of Political Science* 13, no. 1: 255–272.
Westbrook, David A. 2008. *Navigators of the Contemporary: Why Ethnography Matters*. Chicago: University of Chicago Press.

White, Deborah Gray. 1998. *Too Heavy a Load: Black Women in Defense of Themselves, 1894–1994*. New York: Oxford University Press.

Whitten, Norman E. Jr. and John F. Szwed (eds). *Afro-American Anthropology: Contemporary Perspectives*. New York: Free Press.

Whyte, William Foote. 1943. "Social Organization in the Slums." *American Sociological Review* 8, no. 1: 34–39.

Whyte, William Foote. 1948, 1955, 1992. *Street-Corner Society: The Social Structure of an Italian Slum*. Chicago: University of Chicago Press. Traduction: *Street Corner Society. La structure sociale d'un quartier italo-américain*. Paris: La Découverte, 2007.

Wiesel, Ilan. 2018. *Power, Glamour and Angst: Inside Australia's Elite Neighbourhoods*. London: Palgrave Macmillan.

Williams, Terry. 1992. *Crackhouse: Notes from the End of the Line*. Reading, MA: Addison-Wesley.

Willis, Paul. 1977. *Learning to Labour: How Working Class Kids get Working Class Jobs*. New York: Columbia University Press.

Willrich, Michael. 2003. *City of Courts: Socializing Justice in Progressive Era Chicago*. New York: Cambridge University Press.

Wilson, William Julius. 1987. *The Truly Disadvantaged: The Inner City, the Underclass, and Public Policy*. Chicago: University of Chicago Press, expanded edition 2012.

Wilson, William Julius. 1996. *When Work Disappears: The World of the New Urban Poor*. New York: Knopf.

Wilson, William Julius. 2009. *More Than Just Race: Being Black and Poor in the Inner City*. New York: W.W. Norton.

Wilson, William Julius. 2010. "Why Both Social Structure and Culture Matter in a Holistic Analysis of Inner-City Poverty." *The Annals of the American Academy of Political and Social Science* 629, no. 1: 200–219.

Wilson, William Julius and Anmol Chaddha. 2009. "The Role of Theory in Ethnographic Research." *Ethnography* 10, no. 4: 549–564.

Wolf, Diane (ed.). 1996. *Feminist Dilemmas in Fieldwork*. Boulder, CO: Westview Press.

Ronald F. Wright and Kay L. Levine. 2014. "The Cure for Young Prosecutors' Syndrome." *Arizona Law Review* 56: 1065–1126.

Wright, Richard T. and Scott H. Decker. 1997. *Armed Robbers in Action: Stickups and Street Culture*. Boston: Northeastern University Press.

Young, Alford A. 2004. *The Minds of Marginalized Black Men: Making Sense of Mobility, Opportunity, and Future Life Chances*. Princeton, NJ: Princeton University Press.

Young, Iris Marion. 2005. *On Female Body Experience: "Throwing Like a Girl" and Other Essays*. New York: Oxford University Press.

Zipp, Samuel. 2013. "The Roots and Routes of Urban Renewal." *Journal of Urban History* 39, no. 3: 366–391.

Zonabend, Françoise. 1994. "De l'objet et de sa restitution en anthropologie." *Gradhiva: Revue d'histoire et d'archives de l'anthropologie* 16, no. 1: 3–14.

Zorbaugh, Harvey W. 1929. *The Gold Coast and the Slum: A Sociological Study of Chicago's Near North Side*. Chicago: University of Chicago Press, reprint 1983.

Zuberi, Tukufu and Eduardo Bonilla-Silva (eds.). 2008. *White Logic, White Methods: Racism And Methodology*. Lanham, MD: Rowman & Littlefield.

Zwed, John (ed.). 1970. *Black American*. New York: Basic Books.

Index

For the benefit of digital users, indexed terms that span two pages (e.g., 52–53) may, on occasion, appear on only one of those pages.

abduction, 149–150
abductive analysis, 149–150
abstraction. *See* construction of the object; model; selection
academic
  field, 14, 34, 128, 133–134
  capital, 126
  debate, 6–12
  consecration, 157
academic controversy, genesis of, 6–7
  protagonists, 10
  setting up scene, 7–9
Academy of Management Journal, 47
addiction, 30, 44, 59–60, 64, 84–85. *See also* drugs
Administrative Science Quarterly, 47
African Americans. *See various entries*
Ain't No Makin' It (McLeod), 34–35
All God's Children (Butterfield), 78–79
All Our Kin (Stack), 34–35
American ideology, Newman opinion in, 132
American Journal of Sociology, 6–8, 125
American Sociological Association, 8–10
analytic, 2, 53, 58–59, 119, 146, 158
Anderson, Elijah, 7–10, 105, 125
  and perennial pitfalls of urban ethnography, 60–61, 112–113
  poverty, race, and moralism in urban ethnography, 51–54
  as protagonist, 11
  and social conditions of intellectual debate, 126–129
Anderson, Nels, 14
anthropology, 1–2, 12, 21–24, 80–81, 119, 130, 150–151, 184–185
anti-urbanism, 13
approximation (of the real), 126–127
Arensberg, Conrad, 21–22

Argonauts of the Western Pacific, The (Malinowski), 165
Atlantic Monthly, The, 130–131
autonomy, 33–34, 46–47, 53–54, 90, 104, 126, 145. *See also* heteronomy, intellectual

Bachelard, Gaston, 146, 168–169
Baltimore, hyperghetto in, 46–47
Beaud, Stéphane, 178–179
Becker, Howard, 12–14, 18–19
Behind Ghetto Walls: Black Family Life in a Federal Slum (Rainwater), 27–30
BIDs. *See* Business Improvement Districts
Billson, Janet, 77–78
Black, Timothy, 39–40
Black Metropolis (Cayton), 17
Black on the Block (Pattillo), 39–40
black sociology, 34
Blumer, Herbert, 37–38
Book Wars, The (Rosette), 64
bootleggers. *See Soulside: Inquiries into Ghetto Culture and Community* (Hannerz)
booty capitalism, 98
Bougois, Philippe, 39–40
Bourdieu, Pierre, 2–3, 8, 39, 75n51, 80–81, 126–129, 143–145, 150–153, 156, 158, 164, 168n107, 175
  ethnography of endotic in wake of, 178
  testing theory of, 182–188
bourgeoisie (upper class, middle class), 14, 17, 22, 26–27, 30–32, 39–40, 157
Bourgois, Philippe, 34–35, 162–163
broken windows theory, 68–71
Brooks, Carol, 36
Brown, Claude, 22
Burawoy, Michael, 8, 148–149

Business Improvement Districts
  (BIDs), 54–55
Butterfield, Fox, 78–79

capital
  accumulation of, 30–31
  conversion of, 63
  cultural, 127–128
  distribution of, 144, 152–153
  economic, 127–128
  social, 30–31, 127–128
  symbolic, 127–128, 145, 173
carnal ethnography, model of, 186
Carter, Ovie, 54–55
Cassell, Joan, 181
Cayton, Horace, 17
Champagne, Patrick, 178–179
Chapple, Eliot, 21–22
Chicago, Illinois, urban ethnography
  in, 18–22, 59–60, 126–127, 135
Chicago School, 1–2, 11, 17–19, 35, 39,
  53–54, 64, 134
city. *See* anti-urbanism, inner city
Clark, Kenneth, 22, 30
class
  black middle class, 22, 31
  lower class, 17, 23–24, 28–29, 78–79,
    178–179
  upper class, 12, 58–59, 98
  white middle class, 11, 38
  working class, 10–11, 17, 19–20, 30–31,
    99–102, 125, 142–143, 178–179,
    185–186
Clear, Todd, 135–136
"code of the street," 73, 77–81, 87–88,
  105–106
Code of the Street (Anderson), 7–10
  battle between "street" and "decent"
    orientations in ghetto, 89–90
  characterization of "street family," 76
  "code of the street" *vs.* "code of civility" as
    labels, 74–76
  demonstrating wholesome "role
    models," 81–85
  fieldwork in black Philadelphia, 72–74
  final two chapters of, 85–89
  and perennial pitfalls of urban
    ethnography, 60–61, 112–113
  poverty, race, and moralism in urban
    ethnography, 51–54

problematic relationship between theory
  and observation in, 116–118
tracing genesis of the "code of the
  street," 79–81
and transformation of politics of
  publishing, 60–61, 118
workings of the "code of the street," 77–79
cognition, 13–14, 53, 147, 155, 162–163,
  165–166
common sense, 13–14, 35, 37–38
communal ghetto, 27–30
community
  policing, 68–69, 109
  problematic construct, 5–6, 52–53
  studies, 17
  vagueness of, 22, 30
concepts
  analytical, 1–2, 129
  distorted engagement, 46
  double consciousness, 25
  folk, 1–2, 75, 76, 125, 128, 134
  habitus, 133, 151
  social space, 125–126
construction of the object, 129, 168–169,
  173, 178, B1P2
constructivism, 129, 150–151, 153. *See also*
  objectivism, structure
Contreras, Randol, 39–40
Cooley, Charles Horton, 35
cool pose, "code of the street" and, 77–78.
  See also Code of the Street (Anderson)
Cracks in the Pavement
  (Sánchez-Jankowski), 39–40
Cressey, Paul, 14
crime
  incidence of, 68, 138
  as paradoxical vehicle, 44
  price of, 173
  urban crime, 55
  violent crime, 173
Critical Race Theory, 136
critique. *See* intellectual debate, social
  conditions of
cultural capital, 127–128
culture
  being public, 150, 152
  and folk concepts of residents, 73
  instantaneous precipitate of, 93
  oppositional culture of masculine
    defiance, 73

of poverty, 22, 24, 27, 33–34
subculture, 20, 27, 28, 113–114, 185–186
of work, 96–98, 105, 106, 110–111

Dark Ghetto: Dilemmas of Social Power (Clark), 22, 30
Davis, Fred, 18–19
Death and Life of Great American Cities, The (Jacobs), 55
Death of White Sociology, The (Ladner), 34
decent daddy, role model, 81–85
deduction, 149–150
description. *See* explanation, interpretation; thick description
deserving/undeserving, categories, 13–14, 38, 46–47, 96–97
Desmond, Matthew, 41–42
deviance, cultural, 110
Dewey, John, 2, 18–19
diagnostic ethnography, 66–67
dignity, 5–6, 23–24, 30, 44–45, 95–96, 104, 115, 138
direct observation research, 14, 59–60, 177–178
Discovery of Grounded Theory, The (Strauss), 146
dispositions, 46–47, 64, 87–89, 129, 133, 143, 151, 162, 165. *See also* habitus
domination
  ethnoracial, 32
  masculine, 184–185
  racial, 78, 87
  white, 14, 28–32
Dordick, Gwendolyn, 61
double history, establishing, 161–163
Down These Mean Streets (Thomas), 22
Doxa, 134
Drake, St. Clair, 17
drugs, 42, 61, 63, 66, 73, 83, 85–86, 98, 136, 184
Du Bois, W.E.B., 14
Dum, Christopher, 42–43
Duneier, Mitchell, 7–10, 125
  completing manuscript, 160
  and journalism, 119–120, 130–131n12
  and perennial pitfalls of urban ethnography, 60–61, 112–113
  poverty, race, and moralism in urban ethnography, 51–54
  as protagonist, 10

and social conditions of intellectual debate, 129–131
Durkheim, Émile, 38, 144, 154–155, 164–165

economy
  apartheid, 112
  as cause of behavior, 39–40, 67–68
  changes in, 64–66, 90, 93–94
  drug, 169–170
  hyperghetto, 88–89
  illegal, 61
  informal, 61, 87
  numbers game in, 26–27
  service, 51–52, 93, 97, 104
  sidewalk, 57
  street, 34–35, 94, 103–104, 109, 175
Elias, 75
Embeddedness, 87, 141–142, 158, 169–170, 181
Embodiment, 117, 139–141, 156, 165–166, 173, 180–181, 186
emotions, 158–161, 165–166
empiricism, 146–161
  as epistemological position, 1–2
  as fallacy, 146–158
  moral empiricism, 1–2, 40, 125–126, 134–138
empiricist fallacy, 146–158
enactive ethnography, 178–181
endotic, 178
epistemology, political. *See* fieldwork, political epistemology of
esoterism, 169–170
ethnicity, 5, 20. *See also* race
ethnographic unconscious, dissecting
  discovery of state of misery, 39–48
  genesis of academic controversy, 6–12
  overview, 5–6
  postindustrial hyperghetto, 30–32
  three ages of American "urban ethnography," 13–48
ethnographers, 8–9, 27–28, 32, 47, 117, 120, 135, 147–148, 162–163
Ethnographic Café, 48
ethnographic time bomb, 134
ethnographism, 141–143
  carnal dimension of ethnographic practice, 140–141
  danger, 192

ethnographism (*Continued*)
  differentia specifica of
    ethnography, 139–140
  empiricist (or inductivist)
    fallacy, 146–158
  ethnography as embedded mode of
    inquiry, 141–143. See also embodiment
  interactionist fallacy, 143–145
  interpretativist fallacy, 164–167
  populist fallacy, 158–161
  presentist fallacy, 161–163
ethnography
  bearing witness, 174–175
  Bourdieu positions, 176–180
  and embodied inquiry, 181
  of endotic in wake of Bourdieu, 178
  five missions of, 168–188
  as instrument for construction of
    object, 173
  as instrument for depiction of
    phenomenon, 173
  as instrument of rupture with common
    sense, 170
  as springboard for formulation of
    hypotheses, 171
  as technique for suggestion/detection for
    mechanisms, 172
  term, 147–148
  as thick description, 152
ethnomethodology, 150–151
Etnografia e ricerca qualitativa, 47–48
Evicted (Desmond), 41–42
exaltation (of agents, moral values), 107, 121
exhilaration of ethnographic
  action, 160–161
Exiled in America (Dum), 42–43
exoterism, 1, 120–121
exoticism, 22, 38–39, 138, 178
explanation, 63, 86–89, 129, 133, 157,
  182–183, 187–188. See also description;
  interpretation
exposé, 160–161, 174
extended case method, 148–149, 176

Fader, Jamie, 135–136
fallacies
  empiricist (or inductivist)
    fallacy, 146–158
  interactionist fallacy, 143–145
  interpretativist fallacy, 164–167

populist fallacy, 158–161
presentist fallacy, 161–163
Falling Back (Fader), 135–136
Falling From Grace (Newman), 12
fast food, establishment/work
  benign portrait of fast-food
    industry, 106–108
  desecrating value of
    independence, 104–106
  discipline in ghetto youngsters, 97–99
  moral tales of family hardship and
    individual courage, 95–97
  problems with employees reorganizing
    lives, 102–104
  sermonizing about hidden virtues
    of, 99–102
  wedding to business-first and "small
    government" vision, 108–112
feminism, 119, 140–141, 148–149, 184–185
Fernández-Kelly, Patricia, 46
field historians. See ethnographers
fieldwork, political epistemology of
  carnal dimension of ethnographic
    practice, 140–141
  differentia specifica of
    ethnography, 139–140
  ethnographic time bomb, 134
  ethnography as embedded mode of
    inquiry, 141–143
  ethnography as embodied mode of
    inquiry, 141–143
  fallacies, 143–167
  five missions of ethnography, 168–173
  overview, 125–126
  social conditions of intellectual
    debate, 126–134
first age of urban ethnography, 14–17
Flat Broke with Children (Hays), 40
Frazier, E. Franklin, 39–40
Friedson, Elliot, 18–19
functionalism, 14, 17
Funes, Ireneo (character), 147

Gang, The (Thrasher), 14
Gans, Herbert, 20–22
Gardner, Burleigh, 27–28
Garfinkel, Harold, 164, 186–187
Geertz, Clifford, 2–3, 150–151

gender/sex. 14, 40–41, 58–59,78–79, 82, 82–83n63, 140–141, 183, 184–185. *See also* masculinity
homosexuals in *Mema's House, Mexico City*, 182–188
ghetto, 37
 battle between "street" and "decent" orientations in, 89–90
 black ghetto, 6–7, 11, 17, 19, 22, 29–30, 33–34, 131–132
 collecting life stories from, 91–94
 communal ghetto, 27–30
 employment problems of urban ghettos, 112
 field monographs on, 22–29
 ghettoization, 29–30, 32
 hyperghetto, 27–30, 40, 42, 46, 78–79, 138
 male orientations in, 25–27
 riots, 29
 transformation of, 30
Glaser, Barney, 146
Goffman, Alice, 48, 134–138
Goffman, Erving, 11, 18–19, 18–19n50, 27–28, 140, 143, 180
Gold Coast and the Slum, The (Zorbaugh), 14
Great Depression, 17
Greenwich Village, saints of. *See Sidewalk* (Duneier)
grounded theory, 66–67, 147–149, 155–156
Gusfield, Joseph, 18–19

habitus, 80, 87–89, 129, 133, 151, 156, 162, 180, 186
Hannerz, Ulf, 22, 25–27, 29, 37
hard case, "code of the street" and, 79–80. *See also Code of the Street* (Anderson)
HAU: Journal of Ethnographic Theory, 47–48
Hays, Sharon, 40
hermeneutic drift (as fallacy), 192
hermeneuticism, 170
Hero's Fight, The (Fernández-Kelly), 46
heteronomy, intellectual, 119
heuristics, 47–48, 126–127, 156, 158, 182–183
historical epistemology, 125–126, 175
historical rationalism. *See* historical epistemology

historicization, historical method/archives, 115–116
history. *See also* habitus; structure
 incarnate, 11
 objectified, 180
Hobo, The (Anderson), 14
honor, 30, 71, 78–80, 82, 97, 103–104
Hughes, Everett C., 18–19
hyper-criminalization, 44
hyperghetto, 27–30, 40, 42, 46, 78–79, 138. *See also* ghetto, inner city
hypermasculinity, 44. *See also* masculinity
hypothesis, 143–144, 171, 186–187

illusion
 of being a native, 144, 153, 169–170
 of ethnography without theory, 147–148
 of participation, 176
 of transparency of social world, 143
Imprisoning Communities (Clear), 135–136
Indefinite (Walker), 45
independence, desecration of value of, 104–106
inductivist illusion, empiricist fallacy of, 146–158
inner city, 13. *See* ghetto, hyperghetto
 as euphemism, 35–36
 fast-food workers in, 91–112
 monographs of urban ethnography, 36
 moral life of, 72–91
 role models in, 81–85
inner-city grandmother, role model, 81–85
In Search of Respect (Bourgois), 34–35
Insecurity
 social, 41–42
 economic, 110–111
 criminal, 110–111
 housing, 43
 work, 112
instrumental positivism, 14
intellectual debate, social conditions of
 Anderson criticisms, 126–129
 Duneier criticisms, 129–131
 explanations for rejecting criticism, 133–134
 Newman criticisms, 131–133
interactionist bias, 37
interactionist fallacy, 143–145

224 Index

interpretation, 21–22, 52, 61, 63, 85, 113, 128, 130, 134, 155–156, 159–161, 165–166, 182–183, 187–188
interpretativist fallacy, 164–167. *See also* hermeneuticism
intersectionality, 5–6
Invention of the "Underclass," The (Wacquant), 10, 33–34n96, 110n99, 131–132

jail, 44, 85–86. *See also* prison
   as alternative to working McDonald's, 46
   drug addicts in, 56–57
   Duneier and, 69
   organic ethnography of, 45
   time management, 170
James, William, 18–19
Johnson, Lyndon B., 13
journalism
   difference with ethnography, 119–120, 130–131
   investigative, 12, 119
   standards, 119, 174–175
Journal of Contemporary Ethnography, 18–19
journals, publication of, 47
jungle (of black ghetto), 6–7, 14, 138

Katz, Jack, 12
Kelling, George, 69–70, 130–131
kinship servitude, 84–85
Kohler-Hausmann, Issa, 45

Labor of Luck, The (Sallaz), 148–149
Ladner, Joyce, 34
language, 20–21, 53, 94, 103, 107, 110
Latour, Bruno, 147
Lemann, Nicolas, 78–79
Lewis, Oscar, 33–34
liberal(ism), 53–54, 89–90, 109, 110–111, 113–115, 138
Liebow, Elliott, 13–14, 22–25, 29
Lynd, Robert and Helen, 17

"mainstream," category/value, 27, 75–76, 92, 94, 105
mainstreamers, 25–26. *See also Soulside: Inquiries into Ghetto Culture and Community* (Hannerz)
Majors, Richard, 77–78
Malinowski, Bronislaw, 165

Manchild in the Promised Land (Brown), 22
Manufactured Insecurity (Sullivan), 43
Maresca, Sylvian, 178–179
marginality
   economic, 24, 28–29, 32, 88–89
   social, 72, 135, 142–143
   urban, 40, 42, 52, 88–89, 113–115, 142–143
masculinity. *See also* gender
   and denigration of work, 23–25
   ghetto-specific masculinity, 25–27
   and hyperghetto, 27–30
   and workings of "code of the street," 77–81
Mauss, Marcel, 65, 164–165
McJobs. *See* fast food, establishment/work
McLeod, Jay, 34–35
Mead, George Herbert, 2, 17, 37–38
mechanism, 2, 30, 60, 79–80, 172
Mema's House, Mexico City (Prieur), 182–188
methodology, multi-method, 182–183
Métier de sociologue, Le (Bourdieu), 176
Middletown (Lynd), 17
Middletown in Transition (Lynd), 17
Mills, C.-Wright, 39–40
Misdemeanorland (Kohler-Hausmann), 45
miserabilism, 185
model
   adjunctive model, 45
   as inescapable, 88–89
   role models, 60, 87, 89–90
   as selection, 146
   five models relating theory and observation, 155–156
moral empiricism, 1–2
moral individualism, 12, 144
moralism, 7–8, 38–39. *See also* urban ethnography
Moynihan, Daniel Patrick, 33–34
Moynihan Report, 33

Nader, Laura, 12
National Youth Apprenticeship Program, 108–109. *See also* fast food, establishment/work
networks, 20, 28, 34–35, 37, 65–66, 102
Newman, Katherine, 7–10, 125
   banal street scene inspiring, 91–94

benign portrait of fast-food industry in, 106–108
discipline in ghetto youngsters, 97–99
moral tales of family hardship and individual courage, 95–97
neoliberal policies of, 110–112
and perennial pitfalls of urban ethnography, 60–61, 112–113
poverty, race, and moralism in urban ethnography, 51–54
problems with employees reorganizing lives, 102–104
as protagonist, 11–12
sermonizing about hidden virtues of fast-food work, 99–102
and social conditions of intellectual debate, 131–133
on value of independence, 104–106
wedding to business-first and "small government" vision, 108–112
New Welfare Bureaucrats, The (Watkins-Hayes), 40–41
New York City, zero tolerance in. *See Sidewalk* (Duneier)
No Shame in My Game (Newman), 7–12
banal street scene inspiring, 91–94
benign portrait of fast-food industry in, 106–108
desecrating value of independence, 104–106
discipline in ghetto youngsters, 97–99
moral tales of family hardship and individual courage, 95–97
and perennial pitfalls of urban ethnography, 60–61, 112–113
poverty, race, and moralism in urban ethnography, 51–54
problematic relationship between theory and observation in, 116–118
problems with employees reorganizing lives, 102–104
sermonizing about hidden virtues of fast-food work, 99–102
and transformation of politics of publishing, 60–61, 118
wedding to business-first and "small government" vision, 108–112
"No Shame: The View from the Left Bank" (Newman), 131–132

numbers game. *See Soulside: Inquiries into Ghetto Culture and Community* (Hannerz)

object (scientific), 116–118, 129, 142, 149–155, 157, 168–169, 173, 176, 178, 179, 181, 191–192
objectivation, 177
objectivism, 144, 176, 177–178n134. *See also* subjectivism
observation
  as guided by theory, 156
  modalities, 126, 142, 187
  as selection, 66–67
  as vehicle for constructing a model, 44
On the Run: Fugitive Life in an American City (Goffman), 134
Organization Studies, 47
Outline of a Theory Practice (Bourdieu), 80–81

Paik, Leslie, 41
panhandling, 61, 66, 68–69
paralogisms
  carnal dimension of ethnographic practice, 140–141
  danger, 192
  differentia specifica of ethnography, 139–140
  empiricist fallacy, 146–158
  ethnography as embedded mode of inquiry, 141–143
  interactionist fallacy, 143–145
  interpretativist fallacy, 164–167
  populist fallacy, 158–161
  presentist fallacy, 161–163
Park, Robert, 14
Parvez, Z. Fareen, 148–149
penal state, 44–46, 114, 137
perception, 38, 53–54, 126, 146–147, 153, 155, 162, 168, 172
phenomenology, 46, 140–141
Philadelphia, 24
  "code of the street" *vs.* "code of civility" as labels, 74–76
  demonstrating wholesome "role models," 81–85
  ethnographic time bomb in, 134
  fieldwork in black Philadelphia, 72–74
  final two chapters of, 85–89

Philadelphia (*Continued*)
  and perennial pitfalls of urban ethnography, 60–61, 112–113
  poverty, race, and moralism in urban ethnography, 51–54
  problematic relationship between theory and observation in, 116–118
  sociologist in, 72–91
  tracing genesis of the "code of the street," 79–81
  and transformation of politics of publishing, 60–61, 118
  workings of the "code of the street," 77–79
Philadelphia Negro, The (Du Bois), 14
Pialoux, Michel, 178–179
pleasure
  of ethnography, 188
  of subject, 185–186
point of view
  adopting, 41, 116, 168–169
  canonizing "native point of view," 165
  constructing social space for, 150–151
  depiction of phenomenon, 177
  and interpretativist fallacy, 164–165
  object construction and, 173
  parroting, 116–117
  reconstructing, 14
  and structured ethnography, 144
  subjectiveness of, 152–153
  understanding as "view taken from a point," 129
  vindicating, 76
police/policing
  crises of respect of, 62–63
  Duneier and, 68
  and ethnographic time bomb, 134
  and hyper-criminalization, 44
  "quality-of-life" policing, 67–70
  and sidewalk, 114
  "therapeutic" policing, 44
  thesis about crime and, 67–70
  zero-tolerance policing, 45, 55, 71, 130–131
policy
  disciplinary social policy, 40
  poverty, 35, 91
  public, 11–12, 33, 43, 47, 52, 67–68, 90, 126
  workfare policy, 40–41
Politicizing Islam (Parvez), 148–149
politics, 5–6, 17, 47, 53–54, 114, 115–116, 118, 138
politics of knowledge, 6–12
poor, new division of labor of domestication of, 114
populism, 142, 159–160, 170, 185, 192
populist fallacy, 158–161
positions
  space of, 144, 153
  structure of, 162
  system of, 143–144, 157
positivism, 14, 187
postindustrial era, hyperghetto of, 31–32
poverty, poverty of ethnography of, 1–2
  conclusions, 191–193
  dissecting ethnographic unconscious, 5–48
  moralism in urban ethnography, 51–61
  political epistemology of fieldwork, 125–188
power
  symbolic, 105–106, 152–153, 169–170
  triple economy of, 169–170
  white, 29
precarity, 32, 39–41, 175
presentism, 29–30, 142, 170, 186, B1P3
presentist fallacy, 161–163
Prieur, Annick, 182–188
"Primitive Forms of Classification" (Durkheim and Mauss), 164–165
prison, 39–40, 44, 45–46, 68, *See also* jail
problematic
  articulated, 66–67
  failure of constructing, 113–114
  prefabricated, 52–53
problematics, historization of, 115–116
profession
  academic, 14, 34, 128, 133–134
  competence, 8, 135–136
  ethics, 8–9, 59
  reputation, 14, 172
  standard, 78–79, 119, 129–130, 133–134
  versus intellectual, 8–9
Promised Land, The (Lemann), 78–79
public policy, 11–12, 33, 43, 47, 52, 67–68, 90, 126
publishers, pressure on, 118
Punished (Rios), 44, 135–136
punishment, 138, 145, 163

qualitative studies, 2–3, 18–19, 147, 147–148n51. *See also* grounded theory

race, relationship between class and, 5, 35–36, 44, 64
Rainwater, Lee, 22, 27–30. *See also Behind Ghetto Walls: Black Family Life in a Federal Slum* (Rainwater)
Rationalism, 120–121, 125–126, 134, 147–148. *See also* historical epistemology
  empiricism and, 134, 150–151
  historical, 125–126
reflexivity, 1, 5–8, 115–116, 126, 134, 170, 191
  egological, 5–6
  textual, 5–6
  epistemic, 5–6
rehabilitation (of subject), 41
relational ethnography, 42. *See also* social space
respect. *See also* honor
  crises of, 62
  earning, 56–57
  masculinity and, 26
  mutual, 57–58
  self-respect, 57, 71–72, 96–98
Righteous Dopefiend (Mills), 39–40
Rios, Victor, 44, 135–136
role enactment, static theory of, 88–89
Rosette, Jason, 64
Ross, Edward, 35
Rupture (as moment in construction of object), 126, 129, 136, 143–144, 153, 156, 160–161, 170
Ryle, Gilbert, 150–151

Sallaz, Jeffrey, 148–149, 176
Sánchez-Jankowski, Martín, 39–40
Sayad, Abelmalek, 178–179
scholastic bias, 148–149, 153, 164, 179
Schonberg, Jeffrey, 39–40
Schutz, Alfred, 150–151, 164
"Scrutinizing the Street" (Wacquant), 6–9, 125, B1P2
second age of urban ethnography
  analytical overview of trajectories, 35–39
  author contributions, 22
  "discovery" of poverty, 19–22
  ethnography drought, 33–35

  field monographs on black ghetto, 22–29
  ghetto-specific masculinity, 25–27
  hyperghetto, 27–30
  men's denigration of work, 23–25
  Second Chicago School, 18–19
Second Chicago School, 18–19, 53–54, 64
Selection, 126–127, 146, 147, 156
self-determination, myth of, 133
senses, 186. *See also* embodiment
settlement movement, 14, 35
Shils, Edward, 10
Sidewalk (Duneier), 7–10
  aim of, 54–55
  appendix, 160
  as book of journalism, 130–131
  censoring unflattering/deviant behavior, 61–62
  disconnecting legal from illegal economy, 61
  findings, 55–60
  hierarchized roles of sidewalk commerce, 56–60
  and perennial pitfalls of urban ethnography, 60–61, 112–113
  poverty, race, and moralism in urban ethnography, 51–54
  problematic relationship between theory and observation in, 116–118
  reducing crimes on streets on Greenwich Village, 67–70
  serious gaps in, 64–66
  skewing display/data, 63
  symbolism of vendor's table, 60
  theoretical flaw of, 66–67
  and transformation of politics of publishing, 60–61, 118
Slim's Table (Shils), 10
Social Order of the Slum, The (Suttles), 20–21
Social Organization in the Slums" (Whyte), 21–22
social space, 28, 75, 112, 116, 127–129, 143–144, 156, 162
social world, 1–2, 117, 165, 187–188
  according to Geertz, 152
  being "multisided," 152–153
  of black homeless magazine vendors, 10
  constructing struggles about, 169
  construction of, 153
  contemplative posture toward, 181

social world (*Continued*)
  Duneier conception of, 66
  ethnographers, 162–163
  and first age of urban ethnography, 14
  relational apprehension of, 143–144
  responding to questions, 146
  shedding new light on, 154–155
  and social science, 153
  specific gravity of, 150–151
  studying, 64
  theory and, 151
  thick construction, 156
  unmaking, 128
socioanalysis, 177
sociologist, moralism of, 38–39
Soulside: Inquiries into Ghetto Culture and Community (Hannerz), 25–27
Stack, Carol B., 34–35
state of misery, discovery of. *See* third age of urban ethnography
Stickup Kids, The (Contreras), 39–40
stigma, 31–32, 42–43, 59–60, 73–74, 77–78, 93, 97, 112–113
Strauss, Anselm, 1n2 18–19, 146
streetcorner men. *See Soulside: Inquiries into Ghetto Culture and Community* (Hannerz)
Street-Corner Society (Whyte), 21
street families. *See Soulside: Inquiries into Ghetto Culture and Community* (Hannerz)
Streetwise: Race, Class, and Change in an Urban Community (Anderson), 11
Streit, 6–7
structural locations, 75
structure (social, of social space), 27, 32, 37–38, 87–90, 96, 112, 127–128, 143–145, 150, 152–153, 162, 163–165, 182–183
  and social interaction, 77–78, 129, 143–144, 156, 185
subjectivism, 140–141, 181, 184–185, 187. *See also* objectivism
Sullivan, Esther, 43
survey research, 89, 103, 175
Suttles, Gerald, 20–22
swingers. *See Soulside: Inquiries into Ghetto Culture and Community* (Hannerz)
symbolic dimension of social life, 90

symbolic power, 105–106, 152–153, 169–170
symbolic violence. *See* violence

Tally's Corner: A Study of Negro Streetcorner Men (Liebow), 23–25
Tavory, Iddo, 155–156
Taxi-Dance Hall, The (Cressey), 14
theoretical mooring, weakness of, 37
theory, term, 151
theory and observation, linking
  abductive analysis, 149–150
  empiricist fallacy, 146–148
  extended case method, 148–149
  five scores for theory-observation duet, 155
  thick construction, 150–158
thick construction, 2–3
  aim of, 154–155
  and empiricist fallacy, 150–158
  five scores for theory-observation duet, 155
  Mema's House, Mexico City as perfect example of, 182–188
  thick description *versus*, 150–152
thick description, 126
  as construction squared, 2–3
  five scores for theory-observation duet, 155
  thick construction *versus*, 152
third age of urban ethnography
  disciplinary social policy, 40–41
  Ethnographic Café, 48
  European fieldwork, 47–48
  fieldwork in sociology, 48
  life trajectories in Baltimore hyperghetto, 46–47
  precarious housing, 41–43
  race, class, and the penal state, 44–46
  studies of, 39–40
  triple development, 47
Thomas, Piri, 22
Thomas, William Isaac, 37
Thrasher, Frederick M., 14
Timmermans, Stefan, 155–156
traditional grandmother, role model. *See* inner-city grandmother, role model
transference, 158–159
Trapped in a Maze (Paik), 41

Travail et travailleurs en Algérie (Bourdieu), 176
Trondman, Mats, 47–48
Truly Disadvantaged, The (Wilson), 72–73
Turner, John, 85–89

unconscious
 epistemological, 37–38
 racial, 8
 social, 5–6, 159
United States, F2P3, 11, 52, 112, 114
 academic etiquette in, 60–61
 debating "Scrutinizng" outside, 8–9
 "doing" theory in, 37–38
 fast-food franchises in, 106
 historicization of problematics in, 115–116
 leading journal in, 6
 low-wage work, 110–111
 social and academic history of, 13
 sociology in, 14
 studies of white working-class neighborhoods in, 22
 study of city in, 13–14
 urban ethnography in, 40, 47, 53–54
urban ethnography, 12
 factors for understanding, 13–14
 first age of, 14–17
 moralism in, 51–61
 perennial pitfalls of, 60–61, 112–113
 second age of, 18–39
 third age of, 39–48
 three ages of American, 13–48
Urban Ethnography Reader, The, 36
urban sociology, 14
Urban Villagers: Group and Class in the Life of Italian-Americans (Gans and Suttles), 20

vendors, studying. See *Sidewalk* (Duneier)
vigilance, 168, 170, B1P1. *See also* reflexivity
violence
 domestic, 44, 95
 implements and purposes of, 80
 rampant, 78–79, 84–85
 symbolic, 67, 158–159
 urban, 115

Walker, Michael, 45
Warner, W. Lloyd, 17, 27–28
War on Poverty, 13, 33
Waterson, Alisse, 61
Watkins-Hayes, Celeste, 40–41
Weber, Max, 39–40, 164
Weight of the World, The (Bourdieu), 177
Westbrook, David, 162–163
When a Heart Turns Rock Solid (Black), 39–40
white man, 29, 82–83
white sociology, 34
white working-class neighborhoods, studying, 19–22
Whyte, William Foote, 21
Willis, Paul, 47–48
Wilson, James Q., 69–70, 130–131
Wilson, William Julius, 8–9, 39–40, 72–73, 131–132
work
 benign portrait of fast-food industry, 106–108
 desecrating value of independence, 104–106
 deserving/undeserving (categories), 13–14, 38, 46–47, 96–97
 discipline in ghetto youngsters, 97–99
 ethic of, 13–14, 52–53, 81–82, 91–94, 96, 97, 104, 105–106, 113–114
 men's denigration of, 23–25
 moral tales of family hardship and individual courage, 95–97
 problems with employees reorganizing lives, 102–104
 sermonizing about hidden virtues of, 99–102
 wage work, 39–40, 52, 99–100, 103, 105–106, 110–111, 115
 wedding to business-first and "small government" vision, 108–112
 working family, stereotype, 92–94

Yankee City Series, The (Mead), 17

zero tolerance policing, 45, 55, 68–71, 130–131
Zorbaugh, Harvey, 14
Zustandreduktion, 75